John Gillies

Aristotle's Ethics and Politics

Comprising his practical philosophy. Vol. 1

John Gillies

Aristotle's Ethics and Politics
Comprising his practical philosophy. Vol. 1

ISBN/EAN: 9783337020095

Printed in Europe, USA, Canada, Australia, Japan

Cover: Foto ©Thomas Meinert / pixelio.de

More available books at **www.hansebooks.com**

ARISTOTLE's

ETHICS AND POLITICS.

VOL. I.

ARISTOTLE's
ETHICS AND POLITICS,

COMPRISING HIS

PRACTICAL PHILOSOPHY,

TRANSLATED FROM THE GREEK.

ILLUSTRATED BY INTRODUCTIONS AND NOTES;

THE CRITICAL HISTORY OF HIS LIFE;

AND A NEW ANALYSIS OF HIS SPECULATIVE WORKS;

By JOHN GILLIES, LL.D.

F. R. S. and S. A. LONDON; F. R. S. EDINBURGH; and
Historiographer to his Majesty for SCOTLAND.

Magna animi contentio adhibenda est in explicando Aristotele.
CICERO FRAGMENT. PHILOSOPH.

IN TWO VOLUMES.

VOL. I.

LONDON:
Printed for A. STRAHAN; and T. CADELL Jun. and W. DAVIES, in the Strand.
1797.

PREFACE.

ARISTOTLE is the most voluminous, and generally deemed the most obscure, of all the Greek writers of classic antiquity. His imperfect yet copious remains, which are now rather admired than read [a], and which were formerly much read and little understood, still naturally arrange themselves in the minds of those capable of digesting them, under their original form of an encyclopedy of science; in many parts of which, the author's labours are, doubtless, excelled by those of modern philosophers; while in other parts, and those of the most important nature, his intellectual exertions remain hitherto unrivalled. It seemed high time, therefore, to draw the line between those writings of the Stagirite which

[a] I except the small but incomparable Treatise on Poetry, excellently translated and commented in two recent publications in English; the books on Rhetoric and the History of Animals, to which Mr. Cassandre and Mr. Camus have respectively done justice in French; and the Organum, or Logic, still studied in some Universities.

PREFACE.

which still merit the most serious attention of the modern reader, and those of which the perusal is superseded by more accurate and more complete information. This line I have presumed to draw in the present work, by endeavouring to the best of my abilities to translate the former perspicuously and impressively, while I contented myself with giving a distinct and comprehensive analysis of the latter.

The " Ethics to Nicomachus and the Politics" ought never to have been disjoined, since they are considered by Aristotle himself as forming essential parts of one and the same work[b]; which, as it was the last[c] and principal object of his studies, is of all his performances the longest, the best connected, and incomparably the most interesting. The two treatises combined, constitute what he calls his *practical philosophy*[d]; an epithet to which, in comparison with other works of the same kind, they will be found peculiarly entitled. In the Ethics, the reader will see a full and satisfactory delineation of the moral

---

[b] See vol. i. p. 150, and p. 408, & seq.

[c] Compare vol. i. p. 408, & seqq. and vol. ii. pp. 338, 369. The Magna Moralia and Ethics to Eudemus are chiefly to be considered as the first imperfect sketch of this great work.

[d] See vol. i. p. 176. He elsewhere calls it " His Philosophy concerning Human Affairs." Ibid. p. 408.

moral nature of man, and of the discipline and exercise best adapted to its improvement. The Philosopher speaks with commanding authority to the heart and affections, through the irresistible conviction of the understanding. His morality is neither on the one hand too indulgent, nor on the other impracticable. His lessons are not cramped by the narrow, nor perverted by the wild, spirit of system; they are clear inductions, flowing naturally and spontaneously from a copious and pure source of well-digested experience.

According to the Stagirite, men are and always have been not only moral and social, but also *political* animals; in a great measure dependent for their happiness and perfection on the public institutions of their respective countries. The grand inquiry, therefore, is, what are the different arrangements that have been found under given circumstances, practically most conducive to these main and ultimate purposes? This question the Author endeavoured to answer in his " Politics," by a careful examination of two hundred systems of legislation, many of which are not any where else described; and by proving how uniformly, even in political matters, the results of observation and experiment

PREFACE.

periment confpire with and confirm the deductions of an accurate and full theory. In this incomparable work, the reader will perceive "the genuine fpirit of laws" deduced from the fpecific and unalterable diftinctions of governments; and with a fmall effort of attention, may difcern not only thofe difcoveries in fcience, unjuftly claimed by the vanity of modern writers[e], but many of thofe improvements in practice[f], erroneoufly afcribed to the fortunate events of time and chance in thefe latter and more enlightened ages. The fame invaluable treatife difclofes the pure and perennial fpring of all legitimate authority; for in Ariftotle's "Politics," and HIS *only*, government is placed on fuch a natural and folid foundation,

[e] Compare, for example, the works of the modern œconomifts, not excepting thofe of Hume and Smith, with the Fifth Book of the Ethics, p. 270, and the Firft Book of the Politics, p. 38, & feq. Compare Montefquieu's Spirit of Laws with Books iii, vi, and viii, of the Politics throughout: and judge whether the admirable French work be, as the Author's motto boafts, "Proles fine matre creata." Compare likewife Machiavel's "Prince," with the laft chapters of Book vii. of the Politics, p. 374, & feqq. from which the Italian treatife is entirely copied. Yet none of all thofe Authors acknowledge their obligations to Ariftotle.

[f] For the doctrine of reprefentative government, (with which the ancients are faid to have been totally unacquainted,) fee the following tranflation, vol. ii. pp. 64, & feqq. 304, & feqq. and 408, & feqq. For that of governments of reciprocal controul, fee p. 293, & feqq.

PREFACE.

tion, as leaves neither its origin incomprehensible, nor its stability precarious: and his conclusions, had they been well weighed, must have surmounted or suppressed those erroneous and absurd doctrines which long upheld despotism on the one hand, and those equally erroneous and still wilder suppositions of conventions and compacts, which have more recently armed popular fury on the other.

But our Author's principles and doctrines will speak convincingly for themselves. The intention of this Preface is merely to explain the plan and object of the present performance; which, besides giving a translation of Aristotle's practical philosophy, contains a new analysis of his speculative works. This addition appeared the more necessary, because the Stagirite's intellectual system is so compactly built, and so solidly united, that its separate parts cannot be completely understood, unless the whole be clearly comprehended. The writings indeed here translated, stand more detached and more independent than almost any other; yet, without the aid of the prefixed " Analysis," even the Ethics and Politics would require frequent, almost perpetual elucidation. The reader, I feared, would be soon tired with the

PREFACE.

unconnected prolixity of notes[f]; he will, I hope, be entertained by the Analyſis even of thoſe treatiſes to which, independently of any ſubſtantial utility, his attention may be ſtill allured by a liberal and commendable curioſity.

In my work throughout, I am ambitious of exhibiting fully, yet within a narrow compaſs, the diſcoveries and attainments of a man deemed the wiſeſt of antiquity; and to whom, even in modern times, it will be eaſier to name many ſuperiors in particular branches of knowledge, than to find any one rival in univerſal ſcience. Conſidered under this general aſpect, my " Engliſh Ariſtotle" is the natural companion and fit counterpart to my "Hiſtory of Ancient Greece;" ſince the learning of that country properly terminates in the Stagirite, by whom it was finally embodied into one great work; a work rather impaired than improved by the labours of ſucceeding ages. My time, I acknowledge, was miſerably miſ-
ſpent

---

[f] I have alſo avoided to ſwell my work with hiſtorical notes; a thing as eaſy as it is uſeleſs. Ariſtotle relates with the utmoſt preciſion, the particulars neceſſary for juſtifying his concluſions; and to introduce other events and circumſtances, altogether unconnected with the ſubject, appears to me to be better calculated for diſplaying an author's erudition, than for informing the mind of his reader.

PREFACE.

spent in examining his numerous commentators [b]; Greek, Arabic, and Latin; but the attention with which I have many times perused the whole of his invaluable remains, with a view of rendering him a perpetual commentary on himself, and thereby expressing his genuine sense clearly and forcibly, will not, I hope, prove useless to those who study Greek literature on an enlarged and liberal plan; not merely as grammarians and philologists, but as philosophers, moralists, and statesmen. To this class of readers, many pages of the present work are peculiarly addressed; but the far greater part of it, bearing an immediate reference to the people at large, will not, it is hoped, by the public, be either unregarded or unapplied; especially in an age when, through the ardent activity of the press, salutary information, whatever be its *original* form, speedily circulates to all classes of the community in *new* and fit channels.

PORTMAN-STREET,   J. G.
September 1797.

[b] I am dispensed from the necessity of speaking of former translations of the Ethics and Politics, because I have not borrowed a single sentence, nor derived the smallest assistance, from any of them. The Ethics, which is incomparably the more difficult work of the two, has never, as far as I know, been translated into any modern language.

CONTENTS.

CHAP. I.
LIFE OF ARISTOTLE.

Ariſtotle's Birth-place.—His Education at Atarneus—at Athens.—His reſidence with Hermeias—Singular fortune of that Prince.—Ariſtotle's reſidence in Leſbos—in Macedon.—Plan purſued in the education of Alexander.—Ariſtotle's reſidence in Athens—Employment there.—Calumnies againſt him.—His retreat to Chalcis, and death.—His teſtament.—Sayings.—Extraordinary fate of his Works—Publiſhed at Rome by Andronicus of Rhodes.—Their number and magnitude. *Page* 1

CHAP. II.
A NEW ANALYSIS OF ARISTOTLE's SPECULATIVE WORKS.

Senſation—Its nature explained.—Imagination and memory.—Aſſociation of perceptions.—Reminiſcence.—Intellect.—Its power and dignity.—Ariſtotle's organon.—Origin of general terms.—Categories.—Diviſion and Definition.—Propoſitions.—Syllogiſms—Their nature and uſe.—Second analytics.—Topics.—Ariſtotle's organon perverted and miſapplied.—Demonſtration.—Ariſtotle's metaphyſics—Proper arrangement thereof.—Truth vindicated.—Introduction to the firſt philoſophy—Its hiſtory.—Refutation of the doctrine of ideas.—Elements—Analyſis of the bodies ſo called.—Their perpetual tranſmutations.—Doctrine of atoms refuted.—Motion or change—Its different kinds.—Works of Nature.—How her operations are performed.—Matter.—Form.—Privation.—The ſpecific form or ſight.—State of capacity and energy.—Ariſtotle's aſtronomy.—The earth and its productions.—Hiſtory of animals.—Philoſophy of natural hiſtory.—His book on energy.—The firſt energy, eternally and ſubſtantially active.—His attributes.—Antiquity of the doctrine that Deity is the ſource of being—Inculcated in Ariſtotle's exoteric works.—Objections to Ariſtotle's philoſophy—Anſwers thereto. 39

CONTENTS.

ARISTOTLE's ETHICS.

BOOK I.

INTRODUCTION. - - - - - *Page* 143
Human action.—Operations and productions.—Happiness—Opinions concerning it—Consists in virtuous energies—Proved by induction—Solon's saying concerning it explained.—Analysis of our moral powers. - - - 149

BOOK II.

INTRODUCTION. - - - - - - 173
Moral virtues acquired by exercise and custom—Consist in holding the mean between blameable extremes.—Test of virtue.—The virtues, habits.—The nature of these habits ascertained.—Why vices mistaken for virtues, and conversely.—Practical rules for the attainment of virtue. - - - 175

BOOK III.

INTRODUCTION. - - - - - - 193
Moral election and preference.—Our habits voluntary.—Courage—Its different kinds distinguished.—Temperance.—Natural and adventitious wants.—Comparison of intemperance and cowardice. - - - - - 195

BOOK IV.

INTRODUCTION. - - - - - - 225
Liberality—Vices opposite thereto.—Magnificence; its contraries.—Magnanimity.—Meekness; its contraries.—Courtesy; its contraries.—Plain-dealing; its contraries.—Facetiousness; its contraries.—Shame. - - 227

BOOK V.

INTRODUCTION. - - - - - - 255
Difference between intellectual and moral habits.—Different acceptations of the word injustice.—Justice strictly so called.—Distributive justice.—Corrective justice.—Retaliation.—Natural justice, independent of positive institution.—Misfortunes.—Errors.—Crimes.—Equity. - - - - 257

CONTENTS.

BOOK VI.

INTRODUCTION. - - - - - *Page* 285
Senfation, intellect, and appetite.—Their different offices.—The five intellectual habits—Science—Art—Prudence—Common fenfe—Wifdom—Quicknefs of apprehenfion.—Juftnefs of fentiment.—Importance of the intellectual habits.—Virtue, natural and acquired.—Their difference. - - - 287

BOOK VII.

INTRODUCTION. - - - - - - - 305
Vice.—Weaknefs.—Ferocity.—Self-command, and its contrary.—Unnatural depravities, different from vices.—Voluptuoufnefs more deteftable than irafcibility—Reafons of this.—Intemperance and incontinency.—Their difference. - - - - - - - - - 307

BOOK VIII.

INTRODUCTION TO BOOKS VIII AND IX. - - 327
Utility and beauty of friendfhip.—Qualities by which it is generated.—Three kinds of friendfhip.—Thefe kinds compared.—Characters moft fufceptible of friendfhip.—Unequal friendfhips.—Their limits.—Friendfhips founded on propinquity. - - - - - - - - 329

BOOK IX.

Friendfhip does not admit of precife rules.—Diffolution of friendfhip when juftifiable.—Analogy between our duties to ourfelves, and thofe to our friends.—Happinefs of virtue.—Wretchednefs of vice.—Good-will.—Concord.—Exquifite delight of virtuous friendfhip. - - - - 355

BOOK X.

INTRODUCTION. - - - - - - - 379
Pleafure—Its ambiguous nature—Defined.—Happinefs—Intellectual—Moral—Compared.—Education.—Laws.—Tranfition to the fubject of Politics. 381

ERRATA in VOL. I.

Page 98. line 18. *for* acceſſaries *read* acceſſories
108. — 7 of the note, *for* εναντωσις *read* εναντιωσις
109. — 4 of the note, *for* ιυατοι *read* ιαυτοι
127. — 20. *for* a microſcope *read* the microſcope
129. — 15 of the note, *for* gems *read* germs
216. — *antepenult. for* Scyonians *read* Sicyonians

THE WORKS OF ARISTOTLE.

CHAP. I.
LIFE OF ARISTOTLE.

ARGUMENT.

Aristotle's birth-place—His education at Atarneus—at Athens—His residence with Hermeias—Singular fortune of that Prince—Aristotle's residence in Lesbos—in Macedon—Plan pursued in the education of Alexander—Aristotle's residence in Athens—Employment there—Calumnies against him—His retreat to Chalcis, and death—His testament—Sayings—Extraordinary fate of his Works—Published at Rome by Andronicus of Rhodes—Their number and magnitude.

IT is my design in the present work to give a more distinct, and, I flatter myself, a juster view, than has yet been exhibited, of the learning of an age, the most illustrious in history for great events and extraordinary revolutions, yet still more pre-eminent in speculation than it is renowned in action. A century before the reign of Alexander the Great, there sprang up

CHAP.
I.

up and flourished in Greece a species of learning, or science, totally unlike to any thing before known in the world. This science was carried to its highest perfection by Aristotle: it decayed with the loss of his writings, and revived with their recovery. But the imperfect and corrupt state of those writings rendered them peculiarly liable to be misinterpreted by ignorance, and misrepresented by envy; his philosophy, therefore, has been less frequently inculcated or explained, than disguised, perverted, and calumniated. It has not certainly, since his own time, received any material improvement. To the philosophical works of Cicero, though that illustrious Roman professes to follow other guides, the world at large is more indebted for a familiar notion of several of Aristotle's most important doctrines, than to the labours of all his commentators [a] collectively. But how loose and feeble (and often how

---

[a] All these commentators lived many centuries after Aristotle. They are Greek, Arabic, and Latin. The first began in the age of the Antonines, in Alexander Aphrodisienfis at Rome, and Ammonius Sacchus in Alexandria; they continued to flourish through the whole succession of Roman emperors, under the once revered names of Aspasius, Plotinus, Porphyry, Proclus, the second Ammonius, Simplicius, and Philoponus. Aristotle was ardently studied, or rather superstitiously adored, by the Saracens, during upwards of four centuries of their proud domination, till the taking of Bagdat by the Tartars in 1258. The names of the Arabian commentators, Alfarabius, Avicenna, and Averroes, long resounded even in the schools of Europe. But the Aristotelian philosophy, or rather logic, had early assumed a Latin dress in the translation of Boethius Severinus, the last illustrious consul of Rome, in the beginning of the sixth century. After a long interval of more than six hundred years, Latin translations and commentaries began to abound, through the industry of Albertus Magnus, Thomas Aquinas, and the succeeding scholastics; and multiplied to such a pitch that, towards the close of the sixteenth century, Patricius reckons twelve thousand commentators on different works of the Stagirite. (Discuss. Peripatet.) This vast and cold mass of Gothic and Saracenic dulness is now consigned to just oblivion. But even to the best of Aristotle's commentators there are two unanswerable objections:

how erroneous?) is the Roman transcript, when compared with the energetic precision of the Greek original! Yet the works of Cicero are known universally to the whole literary world, while those of Aristotle (with the exception of a few short and popular treatises) are allowed to moulder away in the dust of our libraries, and condemned to a treatment little less ignominious than that which, as we shall have occasion to relate, befel them soon after their composition, when they were immured in a dungeon, and remained for near two centuries a prey to dampness and to worms. It is time once more to release them from their *second* unmerited captivity; to revive, and, if possible, to brighten, the well-earned fame of an author, sometimes as preposterously admired, as at others unaccountably neglected; and whose fate with posterity is most singular in this, not that his authority should have been most respected in the ages least qualified to appreciate his merit, but that philosophers should have despised his name almost exactly in proportion as they adopted his opinions. The multiplied proofs of this assertion, which I shall have occasion to produce in examining his works, will not, it is presumed, appear uninteresting to men of letters. Those who know something of Aristotle, must naturally be desirous of knowing all that can be told; and of seeing, comprised within a narrow compass, the life and writings of a man, whose intellectual magnitude ought to have preserved and shewn him in his proper shape to the impartial eye

tions: first, they universally confound his solid sense with the fanciful visions of Plato, thus endeavouring to reconcile things totally incongruous: secondly, they ascribe to their great master innumerable opinions which he did not hold, by making him continually dogmatise, where he only means to discuss. To the same objections those more modern writers are liable, who have drawn their knowledge of Aristotle's philosophy from any other than the original fountain.

CHAP. I.

Aristotle's birth place, Stagira.

eye of history, but whose picture, beyond that of all other great characters, has been most miserably mangled.

Aristotle, who flourished in Athens when Athens was the ornament of Greece, and Greece, under Alexander, the first country on earth, was born at Stagira towards the beginning of the ninety-ninth olympiad, eighty-five years after the birth of Socrates [b], and three hundred and eighty-four before the birth of Christ. The city of Stagira [c] stood on the coast of Thrace, in a district called the Chalcidic region, and near to the innermost recess of the Strymonic gulf [d]. It was originally built by the Andrians [e], afterwards enlarged by a colony from Euboean Chalcis [f], and long numbered among the Greek cities of Thrace, until the conquests of Philip of Macedon extended the name of his country far beyond the river Strymon, to the

Its history,

confines of mount Rhodope [g]. Stagira, as well as the neighbouring

---

[b] Socrates drank the hemlock, according to most authors, the first year of the ninety-fifth olympiad; and, according to Diodorus Siculus, the first year of the ninety-seventh. Socrates therefore died at least eight years before Aristotle was born. The latter was one year older than Philip, and three years older than Demosthenes. Vid. Dionyf. Halicarn. Epist. ad Ammæum. This chronology is clearly ascertained by various critics. See Bayle's Dictionary, article "Aristotle." I know not therefore why Lord Monboddo and the late Mr. Harris (two modern writers who have paid great attention to Aristotle's works) should say, and frequently repeat, on no better authority than that of the *Life of Aristotle* ascribed to Ammonius, or Johannes Philoponus, that the Stagirite was three years a scholar of Socrates.

[c] Strabo Excerpt. ex lib. vii. p. 331. He calls the place Stageirus.

[d] Ptolemei Geograph. According to his division, Stagira was in the Amphaxetide district of Macedon.

[e] Herodot. l. vii. c. 115.; & Thucydid. l. iv. p. 311. [f] Justin. l. viii. c. 13.

[g] Thence the frivolous dispute among modern biographers, whether Aristotle, who was really a Greek, ought to be deemed a Macedonian or a Thracian. See Stanley and Brucker's Lives of Aristotle.

LIFE OF ARISTOTLE.

bouring Greek cities, enjoyed the precarious dignity of independent government: it was the ally of Athens in the Peloponnesian war, and, like other nominal allies, experienced the stern dominion of that tyrannical republic. It afterwards became subject to the city and commonwealth of Olynthus; which, having subdued Stagira and the whole region of Chalcidicé, was itself besieged by Philip of Macedon; and, with all its dependencies, reduced by the arms or arts of that politic prince, in the first year of the 108th olympiad, and 348 years before the Christian æra [h]. That the resistance of Stagira was obstinate, may be inferred from the severity of its punishment; the conqueror rased it to the ground [i]. Aristotle, who was then in his thirty-seventh year, had been removed from Stagira almost in his childhood; and he appears not, in that long interval, to have ever resided in, and even rarely to have visited, it [k]. But the misfortunes which fell on that city gave him an opportunity of shewing such ardent affection for his birth-place, as is the indubitable proof of a feeling heart. Through his influence with Alexander the Great, Stagira was rebuilt [l]; both its useful defences and its ornamental edifices were restored; its wandering citizens were collected, and reinstated in their possessions; Aristotle himself regulated their government by wise laws;

CHAP.
I.

---

[h] History of Ancient Greece, vol. iv. c. xxxv.

[i] Plutarch. adversus Colot. p. 1126.; & de Exil. p. 605.

[k] Dionys. Halicarn. Epist. ad Ammæum. Ammonius & Diogen. Laert. in Aristot.

[l] Plin. Nat. Hist. l. vii. c. 29.; & Valer. Maxim. l. v. c. 6. Plutarch prefers to all the pleasures of the Epicurean, the delights which Aristotle must have felt when he rebuilt his native city, and placed in their hereditary seats his expatriated countrymen. Plutarch. adverf. Epicur. p. 1097. He ascribes the rebuilding of Stagira to Aristotle's influence with Philip.

CHAP. I.

connected with that of Aristotle and his family.

laws; and the Stagirites instituted a festival, to commemorate the generosity of Alexander, their admired sovereign, and the patriotism of Aristotle, their illustrious townsman [m].

The city of Stagira indeed owes its celebrity wholly to Aristotle and his family; and, if its name is still familiar to modern ears, this proceeds merely from its having communicated to our philosopher the appellation of Stagirite [n]. His father Nicomachus, who was the physician and friend [o] of Amyntas, king of Macedon, derived his descent, through a long line of medical ancestors, from Æsculapius, the companion of the Argonauts, whose skill in the healing art had raised him to a seat among the gods [p]. Nicomachus improved a branch of knowledge, which was the inheritance of his family, by writing six books on natural philosophy and medicine [q]. To the same illustrious origin which distinguished Nicomachus, the testimony of one ancient biographer [r] (but his only) traces up the blood of Phestis, Aristotle's mother; who, whatever was her parentage, certainly acknowledged for her country [s] the middle district of Eubœa, which lies within twelve miles of the Attic coast. Aristotle was deprived of his parents in early youth [t]; yet it is an agreeable, and not altogether an unwarranted conjecture, that by his father Nicomachus he was inspired with that ardent love for the study of nature, which made him long be regarded as her best

---

[m] Plutarch. advers. Colot. p. 1126.; & Ammonius in Vit. Aristot.
[n] Strabo Excerp. ex lib. vii. p. 331.
[o] He was held by Amyntas, ἐν φίλου χώρα. Diogen. Laert. in Aristot.
[p] Lucian. Jupiter Tragædus; & Suidas in Nicomach.   [q] Idem ibid.
[r] Ammon. Vit. Aristot.   [s] Dionys. Halic. Epist. ad Ammæum.
[t] Diogen. Laert. in Aristot.

LIFE OF ARISTOTLE.

best and chosen interpreter "; while from his mother Phestis he first imbibed that pure and sweet Atticism which every where pervades his writings.

Aristotle also inherited from his parents a large fortune; and their early loss was supplied and compensated by the kind attentions of Proxenus, a citizen of Atarneus in Mysia, who received the young Stagirite into his family, and skilfully directed his education *. These important obligations our philosopher, in whose character gratitude appears to have been a prominent feature, amply repaid to Nicanor the son of Proxenus, whom he adopted, educated, and enriched *. At the age of seventeen *, the young Stagirite was attracted by the love of learning to Athens, and particularly by the desire of hearing Plato in the Academy, the best school of science as well as of morals then existing in the world; and where the most assiduous student might find competitors worthy of exciting his emulation and sharpening his diligence. Plato early observed of him, that he required the rein rather than the spur *. His industry in perusing and copying manuscripts was unexampled, and almost incredible; he was named, by way of excellence, "the student or reader *." Plato often called him the "soul of his school *;" and, when Aristotle happened to be absent from his prelections, often complained that he spoke to a *deaf audience* *. As the student

CHAP. I.

Aristotle's education at Atarneus,

and at Athens.

His literary industry.

" Αριστοτλης της φυσεως γραμματευς τε. Anonym. apud Suid. in Aristot. Literally, "Nature's secretary."

* Diogen. Laert. in Aristot.   y Idem ibid.
z Dionys. Epist. ad Ammæum. Diogen. Laert. ibid.   a Idem ibid.
b Diogen. Laert. ibid.
c Or rather the mind or intellect, ως της διατριβης. Idem ibid.
d Philoponus de Eternit. Mund. adverf. Proclum, vi. 27.

LIFE OF ARISTOTLE.

CHAP. I.

student advanced in years, his acuteness was as extraordinary in canvassing opinions, as his industry had been unrivalled in collecting them [e]: his capacious mind embraced the whole circle of science; and, notwithstanding his pertinacity in rejecting every principle or tenet which he could not on reflection approve, his very singular merit failed not to recommend him to the discerning admiration of Plato, with whom he continued to reside twenty years, even to his master's death; alike careless of the honours of a court, to which the rank and connections of his family might have opened to him the road in Macedon; and indifferent to the glory of a name, which his great abilities might early have attained, by establishing a separate school, and founding a new sect in philosophy [f].

His person, and supposed foibles.

At the same time that Aristotle applied so assiduously to the embellishment of his mind, he was not neglectful, we are told, of whatever might adorn his person. His figure was not advantageous; he was of a short stature, his eyes were remarkably small, his limbs were disproportionably slender, and he lisped or stammered in his speech [g]. For his ungracious person Aristotle is said to have been anxious to compensate by the finery and elegance of his dress: his mantle was splendid; he wore rings of great value; and he was foppish enough (such is the language of antiquity) to shave both his head and his face, while the other scholars of Plato kept their long hair and beards.

Reflections thereon.

To some learned men, the omission of such particulars might appear

---

[e] Diogen. Laert. ubi supra.

[f] ὅτι σχολὴν ἡγούμενος, ὅτι ἰδίαν πεπονηκὼς ἀίρεσιν. Dionys. Epist. ad Ammæum.

[g] Diogen. Laert. in Aristot. Plutarch. de Discrim. Adulat. & Amic. p. 53. says, "that many imitated Aristotle's stuttering, as they did Alexander's wry neck."

appear unpardonable; yet, in a life of Ariſtotle, ſuch particulars are totally unworthy of being told, ſince his love for oſtentatious finery (probably much exaggerated by his enemies) was in him merely an acceſſory, which neither altered his character, nor weakened that ardent paſſion for knowledge which reigned ſole miſtreſs of his ſoul. In men born for great intellectual atchievements, this paſſion muſt, at ſome period of their lives, ſuppreſs and ſtifle every other; and, while it continues to do ſo, their real happineſs is probably at its higheſt pitch. The purſuit of ſcience indeed, not having any natural limitations, might be ſuppoſed to invigorate with manhood, to confirm itſelf through cuſtom, and to operate through life with unceaſing or increaſing energy. But this delightful progreſs is liable to be interrupted by other cauſes than the decline of health and the decay of curioſity; for great exertions are not more certainly rewarded by celebrity, than celebrity is puniſhed with envy, which will ſometimes rankle in ſecret malice, and ſometimes vent itſelf in open reproach: wrongs will provoke reſentment; injuries will be offered and retorted; and, a ſtate of hoſtility commencing, the philoſopher, in defending his opinions and his fame, becomes a prey to the wretched anxieties incident to the vulgar ſcrambles of ſordid intereſt and ſenſeleſs ambition. Of this melancholy remark, both the life and the death of Ariſtotle will afford, as we ſhall ſee hereafter, very forcible illuſtrations.

Plato died in the firſt year of the 108th olympiad, and 338 years before the Chriſtian æra. He was ſucceeded in the academy by Speuſippus, the ſon of his ſiſter Potona; a man far inferior to the Stagirite in abilities; and however well he might be acquainted with the theory, not ſtrongly confirmed in

Ariſtotle's gratitude to Plato.

the practice, of moral virtue, since he was too often and too easily vanquished both by anger and pleasure [h]. Aristotle appears not to have taken offence that, in the succession to his admired master, the strong claim of merit should have been sacrificed to the partialities of blood. In some of the latest of his writings, he speaks of Plato with a degree of respect approaching to reverence. Soon after that philosopher's decease, Aristotle wrote verses in his praise, and erected altars to his honour [i]: and the connections which he himself had already formed with some of the most illustrious as well as the most extraordinary personages of his own or any age, might naturally inspire him with the design of leaving Athens, after he had lost the philosopher and friend whose fame had first drawn him thither, and whose instructive society had so long retained him in that celebrated city.

His residence with Hermeias. The singular history of that prince.

One of the memorable characters with whom Aristotle maintained a close and uninterrupted correspondence was Hermeias, stiled, in the language of those days, tyrant of Assus and Atarneus; a man whose life forcibly illustrates the strange vicissitudes of fortune. Hermeias is called a slave and a eunuch [k]; but he was a slave whose spirit was not to be broken, and a eunuch whose mind was not to be emasculated. Through the bounty of a wealthy patron, he had been enabled early to gratify his natural taste for philosophy; and having become a fellow-student with Aristotle at Athens, soon united with him in the bands of affectionate esteem, which finally cemented into firm

---

[h] Diogen. Laert. in Speusipp.   [i] Idem; & Ammonius in Aristot.

[k] Ευνχος ων και δυλος ηρχεν Ερμειας. His master's name was Eubulus, a prince and philosopher of Bithynia. Suidas.

firm and unalterable friendship. Aristotle through life pursued the calm and secure paths of science, but Hermeias ventured to climb the dangerous heights of ambition. His enterprising spirit, seconded by good fortune, raised him to the sovereignty of Assus and Atarneus, Greek cities of Mysia, the former situate in the district of Troas, the latter in that of Æolis, and both of them, like most Grecian colonies on the Asiatic coast, but loosely dependant on the Persian empire. Hermeias availed himself of the weakness or distance of the armies of Artaxerxes, and of the resources with which his own ambition was supplied by a wealthy banker, to gain possession of those strong-holds, with all their dependencies; and endeavoured to justify this bold usurpation of the sceptre, by the manly firmness with which he held it [l]. Upon the invitation of his royal friend, Aristotle, almost immediately after Plato's death, revisited Atarneus [m], the same city in which he had spent the happy years of his youth under the kind protection of Proxenus; and might we indulge the conjecture that this worthy Atarnean still lived, our philosopher's voyage to Æolis must have been strongly recommended by his desire of repaying the favours of a man whom his gratitude always regarded as a second father, and of thus propping, by his friendly aid, the declining age of his early guardian.

CHAP. I.

Aristotle found at Atarneus the wish of Plato realised; he beheld, in his friend Hermeias, philosophy seated on a throne. In that city he resided near three years, enjoying the inexpressible happiness of seeing his enlightened political maxims illustrated in the virtuous reign of his fellow-student and sovereign.

Destroyed by Mentor the Rhodian.

[l] Diodor. Sicul. l. xvi. sect. 122.   [m] Dionys. Epist. ad Ammæum.

CHAP.
I.
reign. But, to render his condition enviable, an essential requisite was wanting, namely, that of security. Artaxerxes, whose success against the rebels in Egypt had exceeded his most sanguine hopes, could no longer brook the dismemberment of the fair coast of Mysia, through the usurpation of a slave and a eunuch. Mentor [n], a Greek, and kinsman of Memnon the Rhodian, a general so famous in the Persian annals, had signalised his zeal and valour in the Egyptian war. He was one of those crafty and unprincipled Greeks, whom the ambitious hopes of raising a splendid fortune often drew to a standard naturally hostile to their country; and his recent merit with Artaxerxes recommended him as the fittest instrument to be employed in chastising the Mysian usurper. This employment he did not decline, although the man whom he was commissioned to destroy had formerly been numbered among his friends [o]. Mentor marched with a powerful army to the western coast. He might have effected his purpose by open force; but to accomplish it by stratagem, was both more easy in itself, and more suitable to his character. He had been connected with Hermeias by the sacred ties of hospitality; the sanctity of this connection was revered by the greatest profligates of antiquity; but the impious Mentor knew no religion but obedience to his master's commands. He employed his former intimacy with Hermeias as the means of decoying that unwary prince to an interview:

[n] Aristotle himself brands with infamy this successful knave, by contrasting his profligate dexterity with the real virtue of prudence. Ἀλλὰ δή, ὥς φησι καὶ ὁ Φαῦλος λέγεται, &c. "A scoundrel may be clever; for example, Mentor, who seemed to be very clever, but surely was not prudent; for it belongs to prudence to desire and prefer only the best ends, and to carry such only into execution: but cleverness implies barely that fertility in resource, and dexterity in execution, by which any purposes, whether good or bad, may be fitly and speedily accomplished." *Magn. Moral.* l. i. c. 25. p. 171.

[o] Diodor. Sicul. l. xvi. sect. 122.

LIFE OF ARISTOTLE.

view: Mentor seized his person, and sent him privately to Upper Asia, where, by order of Artaxerxes, he was hanged as a traitor [p]. The cruel artifices of Mentor ended not with this tragedy. Having possessed himself of the ring which the unfortunate Hermeias usually employed as his signet, he sealed with it his own dispatches, and immediately sent them to the cities that acknowledged the sovereignty of a man, whose mild exercise of power tended, in the minds of his subjects, to justify the irregular means by which he had acquired it. In these dispatches Mentor signified that, through his own intercession, Hermeias had obtained peace and pardon from the great king. The magistrates of the revolted cities easily gave credit to intelligence most agreeable to their wishes; they opened their gates without suspicion to Mentor's soldiers, who instantly made themselves masters both of those Mysian strong-holds, which might have made a long and vigorous resistance to the Persian arms, and of the powerful garrisons by which they were defended [q]. One further deception crowned the successful perfidy of Mentor. He affected to treat the conquered places with unexampled moderation. He was particularly careful to keep in their offices the same collectors of revenues and intendants who had been employed by Hermeias. Those officers, when they were first apprised of the danger which threatened their master, concealed their treasures under ground, or deposited them with their friends; but when they found themselves treated with so much unexpected generosity by the invader, they resumed their wonted confidence, and conveyed back into their own coffers their long-accumulated wealth; of which circumstance Mentor was no-

CHAP.
I.

His singular and cruel artifices.

---

[p] Diodor. ubi supra. Helladius apud Phot. Biblioth. p. 866. Polyaen. Stratag. vi. 48.
[q] Diodor. ubi supra.

CHAP. I.

Aristotle escapes to Lesbos.

no sooner informed by his emissaries, than he seized both the effects and the persons of those too credulous collectors'.

The veil of moderation which Mentor's policy had assumed in his first transactions at Atarneus, enabled Aristotle to avoid the punishment which too naturally fell on the ambition of his friend. By a seasonable flight he escaped to Mitylene in the isle of Lesbos, in company with Pythias, the kinswoman and adopted heiress of the king of Assus and Atarneus, but now miserably fallen from the lofty expectations in which her youth had been educated. But this sad reverse of fortune only endeared her the more to Aristotle, who married the fair companion of his flight in his thirty-seventh year'; which is precisely that age pointed out by himself as the fittest, on the male side, for entering into wedlock '. Pythias died shortly afterwards, leaving an infant daughter, whom Aristotle named after a wife tenderly beloved, and who repaid his affection with the most tender sensibility. It was her last request that, when Aristotle (which might the Fates long avert!) should die, her own bones might be disinterred, and carefully inclosed within the monument of her admired husband ".

His marriage with Pythias.

Is invited to Macedon.

The Stagirite passed but a short time in the soft island of Lesbos, in the tender indulgence either of love or of melancholy. During his residence in Athens, he had strengthened his hereditary friendship with Philip of Macedon, a prince one year younger than himself, who, having lived from the age of fifteen

---

' We learn this particular, which is necessary to explain what follows in the text, from Aristotle himself, in his curious treatise De Cura Rei familiaris, p. 508.

° Comp. Dionys. Epist. ad Ammæum ; & Diogen. Laert. in Aristot.

' Politic. l. vii. sect. 16. " Diogen. Laert. ubi supra.

fifteen to that of two-and-twenty in Thebes and the neighbouring cities, ascended the throne of his ancestors in the twenty-third year of his age. The busy scenes of war and negociation in which Philip was immediately after his accession engaged by necessity, and in which he continued to be involved during his whole reign by ambition, seem never to have interrupted his correspondence with the friends of his youth; with those who either possessed his affection, or who merited his admiration [u]. In the fifth year of his reign his son Alexander was born; an event which he notified to Aristotle in terms implying much previous communication between them: "Know that a son is born to us. We thank the gods for their gift, but especially for bestowing it at the time when Aristotle lives; assuring ourselves that, educated by you, he will be worthy of us, and worthy of inheriting our kingdom [x]." If this letter was written at the æra of Alexander's birth, it must have found Aristotle at Athens in his twenty-ninth year, still a diligent student in the school of Plato. But it is certain that the Stagirite did not assume the office of preceptor to the son of Philip till fourteen years afterwards, when the opening character of this young prince seemed as greatly to merit, as peculiarly to require, the assistance of so able an instructor [y]. In the second year of the 109th

CHAP. I.

Philip's letter to him.

---

[u] History of ancient Greece, vol. iv. c. 33.   [x] Aulus Gellius, l. ix. c. 3.

[y] The chronology is clearly ascertained by Dionysius of Halicarnassus's letter to Ammæus; yet the accurate Quintilian, because it served to enforce his argument, says, "An Philippus, Macedonum rex," &c. "Would Philip, king of the Macedonians, have thought fit that Aristotle, the greatest philosopher of the age, should have been employed in teaching his son Alexander the first rudiments of learning, or would Aristotle himself have accepted of such an office, had he not believed it of the utmost importance to the success of our future studies, that their first foundation should be laid by a teacher of consummate skill?" QUINTIL. *Instit.* l. i. c. 1.

LIFE OF ARISTOTLE.

CHAP. I.

109th olympiad, Aristotle, probably in consequence of a new invitation from Philip, sailed from the isle of Lesbos, in which he had resided near two years, escaped the dangers of the Athenian fleet, which then carried on war against Macedon, and arrived at the court of Pella [a], to undertake one of the few employments not unworthy of an author qualified to instruct and benefit the latest ages of the world.

His merit and success in the education of Alexander.

In the education of Alexander, the Stagirite spent near eight years; during which long period, in an office of much delicacy, he enjoyed the rare advantage of giving the highest satisfaction to his employers, while he excited the warmest gratitude in his pupil [b]. The temper of Alexander, prone to every generous affection, loved and esteemed many; but Aristotle is the only one of his friends whose superior genius he appears unceasingly to have viewed with undiminished admiration, and whom he seems to have treated through life with uniform and unalterable respect.

Honours bestowed on him by Philip.

By Philip and his proud queen Olympias, our philosopher was honoured with every mark of distinction which greatness can bestow on illustrious merit. Philip placed his statue near to his own: he was admitted to the councils of his sovereign, where his advice was often useful, always honourable; and where his kind intercession benefited many individuals, and many communities [c]. On one occasion the Athenians rewarded his good services, by erecting his statue in the citadel [d]: and his letters, both to Philip and to Alexander, attested his unremitting exertions in the cause of his friends and of the publick, as well as his manly freedom in admonishing kings of their

---

[a] Dionys. Halicarn. ubi supra.
[b] Plutarch. in Alexand. tom. i. p. 668.; & advers. Colot. t. ii. p. 1126.
[c] Ammonius Vit. Aristot.
[d] Pausanias Eliac.

LIFE OF ARISTOTLE.

their duty [d]. But the ruling paſſions of Philip and Alexander, the intereſted policy of the one, and the lofty ambition of the other, were too ſtrong and too ungovernable to be reſtrained by the power of reaſon, ſpeaking through the voice of their admired philoſopher. The ambition of Alexander had early taken root; and the peculiarities of his character had diſplayed themſelves, in a very public and very important tranſaction, which happened ſeveral months before the Stagirite arrived at the court of Pella. During Philip's Illyrian expedition, Macedon was honoured with an embaſſy from the Great King. In the abſence of his father, Alexander, ſcarcely fourteen years old, received the ambaſſadors; and his converſation with thoſe illuſtrious ſtrangers, at a period in hiſtory when the public conferences of great perſonages conſiſted not merely in words of ceremony, afforded a juſt ſubject of praiſe and wonder. Inſtead of admiring their external appearance, or aſking them ſuch ſuperficial queſtions as correſponded with the unripeneſs of his years, he inquired into the nature of the Perſian government; the character of Ochus, who then reigned; the ſtrength and compoſition of his armies; the diſtance of his place of reſidence from the weſtern coaſt; the ſtate of the intermediate country, and particularly of the high roads leading to the great capitals of Suſa and Babylon [e]. To his premature love of aggrandizement, Alexander already added ſingular dexterity and unexampled boldneſs in his exerciſes, particularly in horſemanſhip; the moſt fervid affections, invincible courage, and unbending dignity [f].

CHAP. I.

Peculiarities of Alexander's character.

In

---

[d] Ammonius, ibid. See alſo the fragments ſtill remaining in Du Valle's edition, p. 1102. & ſeq.   [e] Plutarch. in Alexand.   [f] Idem ibid.

CHAP. I.

The plan followed by Aristotle in his education.

In training such a youth, the Stagirite had a rich field to cultivate; but he could only hope to give a new direction to passions, which it was too late to moderate or control. In his treatise on Politics, he has carefully delineated the plan of education best adapted to persons of the highest rank in society; and, in performing the task assigned to him by Philip, this plan was to be skilfully modified, by adjusting it to the peculiar circumstances and extraordinary character of his pupil. Alexander's loftiness could not be conquered, but it might be made to combat on the side of virtue: if he was angry, it was proved to him that anger was the effect of insult, and the mark of inferiority[g]. His love for military glory, which, while it is the idol of the multitude, will always be the passion of the great, could neither be restrained nor moderated; but, to rival this tyrant of his breast, still more exalted affections were inspired, which rendered Alexander as much superior to conquerors, as conquerors deem themselves superior to the lowest of the vulgar. Agreeably to a maxim inculcated in that book of Aristotle's Politics which relates to education, the two years immediately following puberty constitute that important period of life, which is peculiarly adapted for improving and strengthening the bodily frame, and for acquiring that corporeal vigour which is one main spring of mental energy. During this interesting period of youth, with the proper management of which the future happiness of the whole of life is so intimately connected, Aristotle observes that the intellectual powers ought indeed to be kept in play, but not too strenuously exercised, since powerful exertions of the mind and body cannot be made at once,

nor

---

[g] Ælian. Var. Hist. l. xii. c. 54.

LIFE OF ARISTOTLE.

nor the habits of making them be simultaneously acquired. In conformity with this principle, Alexander was encouraged to proceed with alacrity in his exercises, till he acquired in them unrivalled proficiency; after which, the whole bent of his mind was directed to the most profound principles of science.

It is the opinion of many, that a slight tincture of learning is sufficient for accomplishing a prince. Both Philip and Aristotle thought otherwise; and the ardent curiosity of Alexander himself was not to be satisfied with such superficial and meagre instructions as have been sometimes triumphantly published for the use of persons destined to reign. The young Macedonian's mind was therefore to be sharpened by whatever is most nice in distinction, and to be exalted by whatever is most lofty in speculation [h]; that his faculties, by expanding and invigorating amidst objects of the highest intellection, might thereby be rendered capable of comprehending ordinary matters the more readily and the more perfectly [i]. This recondite philosophy, which was delivered by the Stagirite, first to his royal pupil, and afterwards to his hearers in the Lyceum, received the epithet of *acroatic* [k], to distinguish those parts of his lectures which

Aristotle's acroatic philosophy.

---

[h] Plutarch. in Alexand.

[i] Aristot. de Anima, l. iii. c. 5 & 6. & Ethic. Nicom. l. x. c. 7 & 8.

[k] This division of Aristotle's works into *acroatic* and *exoteric*, has given rise to a variety of opinions and disputes; which all have their source in the different accounts given by Plutarch and Aulus Gellius, on one hand; and by Strabo, Cicero, and Ammonius, on the other. The former writers (Plutarch. in Alexand.; & Aulus Gellius, l. xx. c. 4.) maintain that the acroatic, or, as they call them, the acroamatic works, differed from the exoteric in the nature of their subjects, which consisted in natural philosophy and logic; whereas the subjects of the exoteric were rhetoric, ethics, and politics.

CHAP. I.

Highly prized by Alexander.

which were confined to a select audience, from other parts called exoteric, because delivered to the public at large. It has been supposed that, in those two kinds of lectures, the Stagirite maintained contradictory doctrines on the subjects of religion and morality. But the fact is far otherwise: his practical tenets were uniformly the same in both; but his exoteric or popular treatises nearly resembled the philosophical dialogues of Plato or Cicero; whereas his acroatic writings (which will be explained in the following chapter) contained, in a concise energetic style peculiar to himself, those deep and broad principles on which all solid science is built, and, independently of which, the most operose reasonings, and the most intricate combinations, are but matters of coarse mechanical practice[1]. The sublimity of this abstract and recondite philosophy admirably accorded with the loftiness of Alexander's mind; and how highly he continued to prize it, amidst the tumultuary occupations of war and government,

---

politics. But the opinions of both Plutarch and Gellius (for they do not entirely coincide) are refuted by Aristotle's references, as we shall see hereafter, from his *Ethic* to his exoteric works. The latter class of writers (Strabo, l. xiii. p. 608.; Cicero ad Attic. xiii. 19.; & Ammonius Herm. ad Catægor. Aristot.) maintain, that the acroatic works were distinguished from the exoteric, not by the difference of the subjects, but by the different manner of treating them; the former being discourses, the latter dialogues.

[1] Simplicius and Philoponus allow other writings besides the dialogues to have been exoteric, as historical disquisitions, and whatever else did not require for understanding them intense thought in the reader. Simplicius says that Aristotle was purposely obscure in his acroatic writings: "ut segniores ab eorum studio repelleret & dehortaretur." Simplic. ad Auscult. Physic. fol. ii. This would have been a very unworthy motive in the Stagirite: but the truth is, that the obscurity of Aristotle's works proceeds from a corrupt text. When the text is pure, his writings are as easily intelligible, as a mere syllabus of lectures on most abstruse subjects can well be rendered.

vernment, appears from the following letter, written soon after the battle of Gaugamela, and while he was yet in pursuit of Darius: "Alexander wishing all happiness to Aristotle. You have not done right in publishing your acroatic works. Wherein shall we be distinguished above others, if the learning, in which we were instructed, be communicated to the public. I would rather surpass other men in knowledge than in power. Farewell ᵐ." Aristotle, not considering this letter as merely complimental, answered it as follows: "You wrote to me concerning my acroatic works, that they ought not to have been published. Know that in one sense this still is the case, since they can be fully understood by those only who have heard my lectures ⁿ." Of those much-valued writings, the theological part, if at all published, was probably most involved in a sublime obscurity. To have maintained, in plain and popular language, the unity and perfections of the Deity, must have excited against the Stagirite an earlier religious persecution than that which really overtook him. Yet in this pure theology Alexander was carefully instructed; as his preceptor reminded him in the midst of his unexampled victories and unbounded conquests, concluding a letter with this memorable admonition; that "those who entertain just notions of the Deity are better entitled to be high-minded, than those who subdue kingdoms°."

Aristotle's love of philosophy did not, like that of Plato, set him at variance with poetry. He frequently cites the poets, particularly

Aristotle's genius for poetry.

ᵐ Aulus Gellius, l. xx. c. 5.

ⁿ Idem ibid. If these letters be ascribed to their right authors, they prove in what light Aristotle regarded his acroatic works; he considered them merely as text-books.

° Plutarch. in Alexand.

LIFE OF ARISTOTLE.

CHAP. I.

particularly Homer; and he prepared for his pupil a correct copy of the Iliad, which that admirer of kindred heroes always carried with him in a casket, whence this transcript was called "the Iliad of the Casket [p]." The Stagirite was not only the best critic in poetry, but himself a poet of the first eminence. Few of his verses indeed have reached modern times; but the few which remain prove him worthy of founding the lyre of Pindar [q]; and it is not the least singularity attending this extraordinary man, that with the nicest and most subtile powers of discrimination and analysis, he united a vigorous and rich vein of poetic fancy.

The nature of his instructions to Alexander in ethics and politics.

Aristotle carefully instructed his pupil in ethics and politics. He wrote to him, long afterwards, a treatise on government; and exhorted him to adjust the measure of his authority to the various character of his subjects; agreeably to a doctrine which he frequently maintains in his political works, that different nations require different modes of government, respectively adapted to their various turns of mind, and different habits of thinking [r]. From the ethic writings of Aristotle which still remain, and which are the most practically useful of any that pagan antiquity can boast, it is easy to detect that wicked calumny of his enemies, "that, for sordid and selfish purposes, he accommodated the tenets of his philosophy to the base morals of courts [s]." It may be safely affirmed that, if Alexander

is

---

[p] Plutarch. in Alexand. vol. i. p. 688.

[q] Menag. Observat. in Diogen. Laert. l. v. p. 189.   [r] Plutarch. in Alexand.

[s] This absurdity is brought forward and insisted on by Brucker, Histor. Philosoph. vol. i. p. 797. Nothing can be more erroneous or more unintelligible than Brucker's account of Aristotle's philosophy. I have heard it said in his own country, that this laborious German did not understand Greek!

is distinguished above other princes for the love of knowledge [t] and virtue, he was chiefly indebted for this advantage to his preceptor: the seeds of his haughtiness and ambition were sown before Aristotle was called to direct his education; his excellencies therefore may be ascribed to our philosopher [u]; his imperfections to himself, to Philip, above all to the intoxicating effects of unbounded prosperity. This is the language of antiquity, and even of those writers who are the least partial to the fame of the Stagirite.

After the most intimate communication during the space of eight years [x], the pupil and the preceptor separated for ever, to pursue, in a career of almost equal length, the most opposite paths to the same immortal renown; the one by arms, the other by philosophy; the one by gratifying the most immoderate lust of power, the other by teaching to despise this and all similar gratifications. During his eastern triumphs, terminated in the course of ten years by his premature death, Alexander (as we shall have occasion to relate) gave many illustrious proofs of gratitude to the virtuous director of his youth. One incident, and one only, seems to have occasioned some disgust between them. At leaving the Court of Pella, Aristotle recommended, as worthy of accompanying Alexander in his Persian expedition, his own kinsman Callisthenes, an Olynthian; a learned

CHAP.
I.

Aristotle recommends Callisthenes to Alexander. His character and behaviour.

[t] See the proofs of this in Plutarch, p. 668. Alexander spared the house of Pindar, in the sack of Thebes; and the town of Eressus in Lesbos, in his war with the Persians, because it was the birth-place of Theophrastus and Phanias, Aristotle's disciples. In the midst of his expedition, he wrote to Athens for the works of the tragic poets, with the dithyrambics of Telestus and Philoxenus, and the history of Philistus.

[u] Αριστοτελης τα διοντα συμβουλευει Αλεξανδρῳ πολλοις εφιλμος τι. Ælian. Var. Hist. l. xii. c. 54.   [x] Dionys. Halicarn.; & Diogen. Laert. ubi supra.

LIFE OF ARISTOTLE.

CHAP. I.

learned and certainly an honest man, but of a morose unaccommodating temper, pertinaciously attached to the old system of republicanism, which the father of Alexander had overturned in Greece; equally daring and inflexible in his purposes, and unseasonably bold in his speech [y]. Aristotle himself perceived and lamented his faults, and admonished him in a line of Homer, " that his unbridled tongue might occasion his early death [z]." The prophecy was fulfilled. Callisthenes, not reflecting that " he who has once condescended" (in the words of Arrian) " to be the attendant of a king, ought never to be wanting in due deference to his will," rudely and outrageously opposed Alexander's resolution of exacting the same marks of homage from the Greeks which were cheerfully paid to him by the Persians [a]. The manner of Callisthenes's punishment and death is related more variously [b] than almost any historical event of such public notoriety; but most writers concur in opinion, that he met with the just reward of his rashness and arrogance. This transaction, it is asserted, much estranged Alexander from his ancient preceptor. The assertion however is not accompanied with any solid proof [c]; and the absurd calumny, that Aristotle not only regarded this pretended displeasure

Supposed rupture between Aristotle and Alexander.

---

[y] Arrian. Exped. Alexand. l. iv. c. 8.

[z] Ωκυμορος δη μοι τεκος εσσεαι οι' αγορευεις. Il. xviii. 95.

[a] Arrian. ubi supra.

[b] By Arrian, Curtius, Justin, Diogenes Laertius, Philostratus, and Suidas.

[c] Alexander's resentment is inferred from a vague and hasty expression in a letter to Antipater; " Τον δε σοφιστην εγω κολασω, και τους εκπεμψαντας αυτον—I will punish the Sophist (meaning Callisthenes) and those who sent him." Plutarch. in Alexand. p. 696. Alexander, it is true, sent presents to Xenocrates; but so did Antipater, who always remained Aristotle's sincere and confidential friend.

pleasure as an injury, but even proceeded to the wickedness of joining in a conspiracy against Alexander's life, is warranted by nothing in history, but a hearsay preserved in Plutarch [d], and the affected credit given to the monstrous report by the monster Caracalla, for the unworthy purpose of justifying his own violence in destroying the schools of the Aristotelian philosophers in Alexandria, the burning their books, and depriving them of all those privileges and revenues which they enjoyed through the munificence of the Ptolemies, Alexander's Egyptian successors [e].

Plan of Aristotle's life in Athens.

Having taken leave of the Macedonian capital, Aristotle returned to his beloved Athens; where he spent thirteen [f] years, almost the whole remainder of his life, instructing his disciples, and improving the various branches of his philosophy. His *acroatic* lectures were given in the morning to those who were his regular pupils [g]. A considerable part of them is still preserved in his works, which form an abstract or syllabus of treatises on the most important branches of philosophy. His *exoteric* discourses were held after supper with occasional visitors, and formed the amusement of his evening walks [h]; for he thought " exercise peculiarly useful after table for animating and invigorating the natural heat and strength, which the too rapid succession of sleep to food seemed fitted to relax and encumber [i]." Before his arrival at Athens, Sheusippus was dead; and

---

[d] " Those who say that Aristotle advised Antipater to destroy Alexander by poison, cite for their authority a certain Agnothemis, who heard it from king Antigonus." Plut. in Alexand. p. 707.

[e] Dion in Caracall. [f] Dionys. Epist. ad Ammæum.
[g] Aulus Gellius, l. xx. c. 5. [h] Idem ibid.
[i] Plutarch, Conjug. Præcept. p. 133.

CHAP. I.

and Xenocrates, whose dull gravity and rigid austerity a man of Aristotle's character could not much admire, had taken possession of the academy[k]. The Stagirite, therefore, settled in a *gymnasium* in the suburbs, well shaded with trees, near to which the soldiers used to exercise, and adorned by the temple of Lycian Apollo, from whose *peripaton*, or walk, Aristotle and his followers were called Peripatetics[l]. It is reported that he opened his school, observing, "That it would be shameful for himself to be silent while Xenocrates publicly taught[m]." Aristotle is not likely to have uttered such a presumptuous boast; but if it was really made, even this arrogant speech was certainly very fully justified by the fame which the Lyceum speedily acquired, which the Stagirite himself maintained unimpaired through life, and which was ably supported by his disciple and successor Theophrastus.

Such is the genuine history of Aristotle's life, in the most important passages of which all the ancient writers[n], who have expressly treated his biography, unitedly concur. By arranging the subject, therefore, according to our present method, both

my

[k] Diogen. Laert. in Xenocrat.

[l] Menagius ad Diogen. Laert. l. v. sect. 2.

[m] Diogen. Laert. in Aristot. But Cicero, Quintilian, and Dionysius Halicarn. read "Isocrates" instead of "Xenocrates." The reading in the text is the more probable, for Isocrates and Aristotle, following very different pursuits, were not naturally rivals; besides, the former is said to have died soon after the battle of Chæronæa in extreme old age, and Aristotle did not return to Athens till three years after that decisive engagement. Compare my Life of Isocrates, and the History of Ancient Greece, vol. iv. c. 33.

[n] Dionysius of Halicarnassus, Diogenes Laertius, and Ammonius: the ancient Latin translation of this last, first published by Nunnesius (Helmestadij 1767), contains some additional circumstances, but those of little value, and of doubtful authority.

my own labour will be abridged, and the reader's time will be saved; for the calumnies against Aristotle will be no sooner mentioned than they will refute themselves, and they could not pass unnoticed, because they are perpetuated in the sarcasms of Lucian°, and the lying whispers of Athenæus ᵖ, which have been too often mistaken, even by the learned, for true history.

CHAP. I.

The absurd reports that Aristotle first served in the army, that he there dissipated his fortune by low profligacy, and then followed for bread the trade of an apothecary ᵠ, may be confidently rejected by those who know, on unquestionable authority, that he became, at the early age of seventeen, a diligent student in the academy at Athens, where he remained during the long period of twenty years. The reader who has seen the testimonies of his gratitude to Plato, will not easily be persuaded that he could treat this revered master with the grossest brutality ʳ; and let him who reads the Ethics to Nicomachus ask his own heart, whether it is likely that the author of such a treatise should, instead of restraining and correcting, have flattered

Calumnies against Aristotle.

° Lucian treats both Aristotle and his pupil with equal injustice. Vid. Dialog. Diogen. & Alexand. et Alexand. & Philip.

ᵖ Athenæus Deipnos. l. viii. p. 354.

ᵠ Athenæus ubi supra, and Aristocles apud Eusebium. Their report rests on a suppositious letter of Epicurus on Study, and the assertion of Timæus of Tauromenon in Sicily; an author nicknamed Epitimæus, the Detractor. Diodorus Siculus, l. v. c. 1. Athenæus, l. vi. p. 272.

ʳ Αριστοτελης ημας απιλακτισε.—" Aristotle has kicked at us;" a strong metaphor. Diogenes Laert. l. v. sect. 2. Ælian Var. Histor. l. iii. c. 19. ascribes both to Plato and to Aristotle a behaviour totally inconsistent with every thing that we know of their characters. Comp. Ælian, Var. Hist. l. iv. c. 19. Photius, Biblioth. c. 279. Augustin. de Civitate Dei, l. viii. c. 12. Such contradictory reports mutually destroy each other.

LIFE OF ARISTOTLE.

CHAP. I.

flattered[e] and fomented the vices of Alexander. Instead of farther examining these wild fictions, which stand in direct contradiction to the matters of fact above related, it is of more importance to inquire whence such improbable tales could have originated; especially as this inquiry will bring us to the events which immediately preceded our philosopher's death.

Wherein they originated.

From innumerable passages in the moral and political works of which we have presumed to offer the translation to the public, it will appear that Aristotle regarded with equal contempt vain pretenders to real science, and real professors of sciences which he deemed vain and frivolous. His theological opinions, also, were far too refined for the grossness of paganism. He sought only for truth, and was careless of the obstacles which stood in his way to attaining it, whether they were found in the errors of philosophers, or in the prejudices of the vulgar. Such a man, in such a city as Athens, where, since the days of Socrates, the learned taught publicly and conversed freely with all descriptions of persons, could not fail to have many rivals and many enemies. Sophists and sciolists, soothsayers and satirists, and that worst of banes, satirical historians[f], heaped obloquy on a character, the ornament of his own age, and destined to be the instructor of posterity. But the name of Alexander, which then filled the world, was duly respected, even in the turbulent democracy of Athens; and it was not till the year following the

---

[e] Lucian, Dial. Diogen. & Alexand.

[f] Aristocles (apud Eusebium) says, that Aristotle was attacked by a host of writers, "whose books and memories have perished more completely than their bodies." Even his fellow student, Aristoxenus, who had treated him most respectfully while he lived, heaped the most illiberal reproaches on his memory, because he preferred to himself Theophrastus for his successor. Suidas in Aristoxen. & Aristocles apud Eusebium.

the death of that incomparable prince, that the rancorous malignity, which had been long suppressed, burst forth against Aristotle with irresistible violence. He was accused of irreligion before the Areopagus by the hierophant Eurymedon, abetted by Demophilus, a man of weight in the republic; and both of them instigated to this cruel prosecution by our philosopher's declared enemies ". The heads of the accusation were, " that Aristotle had commemorated the virtues both of his wife Pythias and of his friend Hermeias, with such ceremonies and honours as the piety of Athens justly reserved for the majesty of the gods." To Hermeias, indeed, he erected a statue at Delphi; he also wrote an ode in his praise. Both the inscription and the ode have come down to modern times; the former simply relating " the unworthy and treacherous death of Hermeias;" and the latter " extolling virtue above all earthly possessions; and especially that generous patriotism, for the sake of which the native of Atarneus, rivalling the merit of Hercules and Achilles, had willingly relinquished the light of the sun; whose fame therefore would never be forgotten by the Muses, daughters of memory; and as often as it was sung would redound to the glory of *Hospitable Jove*ˣ, and the honour of firm friendship ʸ."
From the frivolousness of the accusation respecting Hermeias, which was considered as the chief article of the impeachment, we may warrantably conjecture that the reproach of worshipping Pythias with honours due to Eleusinian Ceres, was altogether groundless: but in a philosopher, whose intellectual rather than his moral virtues have been the object of panegyric, we may remark with pleasure both the strength of his friendship,

His accusation at Athens.

ᵘ Diogen. Laert. l. v. sect. 4 & 5.
ˣ See above, p. 11. ʸ Laertius in Aristot. Athenæus, xv. p. 697.

LIFE OF ARISTOTLE.

CHAP. I.

ship, and the sincere tenderness of his love, since both affections must have been expressed with an amiable enthusiasm, to enable even the malice of his enemies to interpret them into the crime of idolatry.

His tenets ignorantly calumniated.

It must not be dissembled that the accusation, and consequent condemnation of Aristotle by the Areopagus, has been ascribed to a different cause from that above assigned, and referred merely to the impiety of his tenets. He is said by those who have carelessly examined his works, to have denied a Providence, and thence to have inferred the inefficacy of prayers and sacrifices: doctrines, it is observed, which could not but enrage the priesthood, as totally subversive of its functions, establishments, and revenues [y]. But never was any accusation urged more falsely or more ignorantly. Aristotle, as it will be shewn hereafter, enumerates the priesthood among the functions or offices essentially requisite to the existence of every community. In writing to Alexander he says, that those are not entitled to be high-minded who conquer kingdoms, but rather those who have learned to form just notions of the gods [z]; and in his life, as well as in his works, he uniformly shewed his veneration for religion in general, by treating, with great tenderness [a], even that distorted image of it reflected from the puerile superstitions of his country [b].

He

---

[y] Origines contra Celsum & Bruckeri, Histor. Critic. vol. i. p. 790.

[z] Plutarch in Alexand.

[a] This tenderness, however, did not, probably, satisfy the Athenian priests; who, as it will appear from the following analysis of his works, had more to apprehend from his real piety, than to fear from his pretended irreligion.

[b] Diogen. Laert. l. v. sect. 16. But the best proof of this will appear hereafter, when we come to examine Aristotle's works.

LIFE OF ARISTOTLE.

He is said to have written his own defence, and to have inveighed, in a strong metaphor, against the increasing degeneracy of the Athenians [c]. His discourse, of which the boldness would only have inflamed the blind zeal of his weak or wicked judges, was not delivered in court; since he escaped his trial by seasonably quitting Athens for Chalcis in Euboea, saying, in allusion to the death of Socrates, that he was unwilling to afford to the Athenians a second opportunity of sinning against philosophy [d]. He survived his retreat to the shores of the Euripus, scarcely a twelvemonth; persecution and banishment having probably shortened his days [e].

His testament, preserved in Diogenes Laertius, accords with the circumstances related concerning his life, and practically illustrates the liberal maxims of his philosophy. Antipater, the confidential minister of Philip, regent of Macedon both under Alexander and after his demise, is appointed the executor of this testament, with an authority paramount, as it should seem, to

CHAP. I.

His retreat to Chalcis, and death.

His testament.

---

[c] Laert. l. v. sect. 16. Ὀχνη ἐπ ὄχνη γηράσκει. Homer's description of the gardens of Alcinous. "The fig rotting on the fig," alludes to the Athenian sycophants, so called originally from informing against the exporters of figs.

[d] Ælian, iii. 36.

[e] St. Justin (in admon. ad gentes) and Gregory of Naxianzen (contra Julian.) say that he died through the uneasiness of discontent at not being able to explain the cause of the tides of the Euripus; upon which authority the puerile story is engrafted of his throwing himself into that arm of the sea, saying, "You shall contain me, since I cannot comprehend you." Others say that he ended his life by poison to escape the vengeance of the Athenians (Rapin's Comparaison de Platon & d'Aristote). Such unwarranted reports would not be worthy of mention, did they not afford an opportunity of observing the extreme improbability that Aristotle should have been guilty of suicide, since he always speaks of it as of a shameful and cowardly crime.

to that of the other persons who are afterwards conjoined with him in the same trust. To his wife Herpylis, (for he had married a second time,) Aristotle, besides other property in money and slaves, leaves the choice of two houses, the one in Chalcis, the other his paternal mansion at Stagira; and desires, that whichever of them she might prefer, should be properly furnished for her reception. He commends her domestic virtues; and requests his friends that, mindful of her behaviour towards him, they would distinguish her by the kindest attention; and should she again think of a husband, that they would be careful to provide for her a suitable marriage. To Nicomachus, the son of this Herpylis, and to Pythias, the daughter of his first wife, he bequeathed the remainder of his fortune, with the exception of his library and writings, which he left to his favourite scholar Theophrastus[1]. He desires that his daughter, when she attained a marriageable age, should be given to Nicanor, the son of his ancient benefactor Proxenus; and failing Nicanor, that his esteemed disciple Theophrastus should accept her hand and fortune. The bones of his first wife Pythias, he ordered to be disinterred, and again buried with his own, as she herself had requested. None of his slaves are to be sold; they are all of them either emancipated by his will, or ordered to be manumitted by his heirs, whenever they seem worthy of liberty; an injunction conformable to the maxims inculcated in his "Politics," that slaves of all descriptions ought to be set free, whenever they merited freedom, and are qualified for enjoying it. He concludes with a testimony of external deference at least for the religion of his country, by ordering that the dedications which he had vowed for the safety of

---

[1] Strabo, xiii. 413.

LIFE OF ARISTOTLE.

of Nicanor, should be presented at Stagira to Jupiter and Minerva, the saviours.

Thus lived and thus died, in his 63d year, Aristotle the Stagirite. His enlightened humanity was often seasoned by pleasantry. Many strokes of genuine humour, little suspected by his commentators, will be found in his political writings. His smart sayings and quick repartees were long remembered and admired by those incapable of appreciating his weightier merits. Some of these sayings, though apparently not the most memorable, are preserved in Diogenes Laertius; of which the following may serve for a specimen. Being asked, What, of all things, soonest grows old?—Gratitude. What advantage have you reaped from study?—That of doing through choice what others do through fear. What is friendship?—One soul in two bodies. Why do we never tire of the company of the beautiful?—The question of a blind man! Such apophthegms would be unworthy of mention, had they not, by their perpetual recurrence in our philosopher's conversation, shewn a mind free and unincumbered amidst the abstrusest studies; and, together with the most intense thought, a readiness of wit, which never failed to repel sneerers, and to abash arrogance [g]. He exhibited a character as a man, worthy of his pre-eminence as a philosopher; inhabiting courts, without meanness and without selfishness; living in schools, without pride and without austerity [h]; cultivating with ardent affection every domestic and every social virtue, while with indefatigable industry he reared that wonderful edifice of science, the plan of which we are still enabled to delineate from his imperfect and mutilated writings.

The

[g] Diogen. Laert. in Aristot. & Diogen.
[h] Plutarch. de Virtut. Moral. p. 448.

CHAP. I.

The extraordinary fate of his writings.

The extraordinary and unmerited fate of these writings, while it excites the curiosity, must provoke the indignation of every friend to science. Few of them were published in his lifetime; the greater part nearly perished through neglect; and the remainder has been so grosly misapplied, that doubts have arisen whether its preservation ought to be regarded as a benefit. Aristotle's manuscripts and library were bequeathed to Theophrastus, the most illustrious of his pupils. Theophrastus again bequeathed them to his own scholar Neleus, who carrying them to Scepsis, a city of the ancient Troas, left them to his heirs in the undistinguished mass of his property. The heirs of Neleus, men ignorant of literature and careless of books [h], totally neglected the intellectual treasure that had most unworthily devolved to them, until they heard that the king of Pergamus, under whose dominion they lived, was employing much attention and much research in collecting a large library [i]. With the caution incident to the subjects of a despot, who often have recourse to concealment in order to avoid robbery, they hid their books under ground; and the writings of Aristotle, as well as the vast collection of materials from which they had been composed, thus remained in a subterranean mansion for many generations, a prey to dampness and to worms [k]. At

[h] Strabo, lib. xiii. p. 608 & 609. Bayle gives too strong a meaning to ιδιωταις ανθρωποις, when he calls them "gens idiots:" ιδιωτης means one who confines his attention to the private affairs of life, in opposition to philosophers and statesmen.

[i] Strabo, lib. xiii. p. 608.

[k] Athenæus, l. i. p. 3. says, that Neleus sold Aristotle's books to Ptolemy Philadelphus; and Bayle (article Tyrannion) endeavours with Patricius (Discuss. Peripatet. t. i. p. 29.) to reconcile this account with that of Strabo, by supposing that Neleus indeed sold Aristotle's library and works to king Ptolemy, but not before he had taken the precaution of having the whole carefully copied. According to those writers, the

books

At length they were released from their prison, or rather raised from the grave, and sold for a large sum, together with the works of Theophrastus, to Apellicon of Athens, a lover of books rather than a scholar [1]; through whose labour and expence the work of restoring Aristotle's manuscripts, though performed in the same city in which they had been originally written, was very imperfectly executed. To this, not only the ignorance of the editors, but both the condition and the nature of the writings themselves did not a little contribute. The most considerable part of his acroatic works, which are almost the whole of those now remaining, consist of little better than text books, containing the detached heads of his discourses; and, through want of connexion in the matter, peculiarly liable to corruption from transcribers, and highly unsusceptible of conjectural emendation.

What became of Aristotle's original manuscript, we are not informed; but the copy made for Apellicon was, together with his whole library, seized by Sylla, the Roman conqueror of Athens, and by him transmitted to Rome [m]. Aristotle's works excited

Published at Rome by Andronycus of Rhodes.

---

books thus copied, and not the originals, suffered the unworthy treatment mentioned in the text. This supposition seems highly improbable; for not to mention the difficulty of copying, in a short time, many thousand volumes, it cannot be believed that Ptolemy, had he been in possession of the genuine works of Aristotle, would have purchased at a high price those counterfeits, which had no other connection with that philosopher than bearing his forged name on their title-page. (Ammonius ad Categor sub init.) Had a correct copy of the Stagirite's works adorned the library of Alexandria under the first Ptolemies, his genuine philosophy would have struck deeper root, and made farther progress than it ever did, in that Egyptian capital. Vossius (de Sect. Philosoph. c. xvi. p. 89.) endeavours to prove that Athenæus's words (which are certainly incorrect) imply that Neleus retained Aristotle's works when he sold all the rest.

[1] Strabo says, "rather than a philosopher."   [m] Plutarch in Sylla.

LIFE OF ARISTOTLE.

CHAP. I.

excited the attention of Tyrannion, a native of Amyſus in Pontus, who had been taken priſoner by Lucullus in the Mithridatic war, and inſolently manumitted [a], as Plutarch ſays, by Muraena, Lucullus's lieutenant. Tyrannion procured the manuſcript by paying court to Sylla's librarian; and communicated the uſe of it to Andronycus of Rhodes, who flouriſhed as a philoſopher at Rome, in the time of Cicero and Pompey; and who, having undertaken the taſk of arranging and correcting thoſe long injured writings, finally performed the duty of a ſkilful editor [b].

Their number and magnitude.

Though the works which formed the object of Andronycus's labours had ſuffered ſuch injuries as the utmoſt diligence and ſagacity could not completely repair [c], yet in conſequence of thoſe labours the Peripatetic philoſophy began to reſume the luſtre of which it had been deprived ſince the days of Theophraſtus; and the later adherents to that ſect, as they became acquainted with the real tenets of their maſter, far ſurpaſſed the

---

[a] Plutarch ſpeaks with the dignity becoming a man of letters, who feels himſelf ſuperior to the prejudices of his times: "That to give liberty by manumiſſion to a man of Tyrannion's education and merit, was to rob him of that liberty which he naturally and eſſentially poſſeſſed." Plutarch in Lucull. p. 504. I have melted into one ſentence ὃν γαρ ιξιον (read αξιον) Λουκουλλος ανδρα δια παιδιιαι ισπουδασμενον—and αφαιρεσις γαρ τι της υπαρχουστς η της δοκουστς ελευθεριας δοσις.

[b] Plutarch in Syll. Porphyr. in Vitâ Plotini. Boetius in Procemio libri de interpret. Strabo only ſays that Tyrannion, in the manner mentioned in the text, got poſſeſſion of the manuſcript; which was copied for the Roman bookſellers by careleſs tranſcribers, who did not even take the pains of comparing their copies with the original: a negligence, he obſerves, too common among the tranſcribers both in Rome and Alexandria.

[c] Even after this publication, Ariſtotle's followers were obliged τα πολλα εικοτως λεγειν δια το πληθος των αμαρτιων, "often to gueſs at his meaning, through the faultineſs of his text." Strabo, in the place above cited.

LIFE OF ARISTOTLE.

the fame and merit of their ignorant and obscure predecessors [a]. From the æra of Andronycus's publication to that of the invention of printing, a succession of respectable writers on civil and sacred subjects (not excepting the venerable fathers of the Christian church) confirm, by their citations and criticisms, the authenticity of most of the treatises still bearing Aristotle's name; and of more than ten thousand [b] commentators, who have endeavoured to illustrate different parts of his works, there are incomparably fewer than might have been expected, whose vanity has courted the praise of superior discernment by rejecting any considerable portion of them as spurious [c]. According to the most credible accounts, therefore, he composed above four-hundred [d] different treatises, of which only forty-

---

[a] Strabo, l. xiii. p. 609. He observes, " that the Peripatetic philosophers succeeding Theophrastus had, till this time, but few of their master's works, and those few chiefly of the exoteric kind; so that they were more conversant about words than things; and instead of reasoning accurately and profoundly, were contented with displaying their skill in dialectic and rhetoric." I have thus paraphrased the obscurity of the original φιλοσοφειν πραγματικως; and θεσεις ληκοθιζιν, because Strabo, who had himself diligently studied Aristotle's philosophy (Strabo, l. xvi. p. 757.), uses the word πραγματικως, most probably, in the same sense in which it occurs in Aristotle, as synonymous with ακριβως, κατα αληθειαν; and in opposition to διαλεκτικως and το διαλογιοθαι λογικως.

[b] Patricius Discuss. Peripatet.

[c] Compare Diogenes Laertius in Vit. Aristot. Patric. Discuss. Peripatetic. Fabricius Bibliothec. Græc. & Bruckerus Histor. Philos. artic. Aristot.

[d] Diogenes Laertius (in Vit. Aristot.) makes Aristotle's volumes amount to four hundred; Patricius Venetus, a learned professor of Padua in the sixteenth century, endeavours to prove that they amounted to nearly double that number. (Patric. Discuss. Peripat.) The laborious Fabricius employs one hundred pages of his second volume in enumerating and ascertaining Aristotle's remains; which still exceed four times the collective bulk of the Iliad and Odyssey. The whole works of Aristotle, therefore, must have contained a quantity of prose, equal to sixteen times 29,088 verses; a fact

CHAP. I.

forty-eight * have been tranfmitted to the prefent age. But many of thefe laft confift of feveral books, and the whole of his remains together ftill form a golden chain of Greek erudition, exceeding four times the collective bulk of the Iliad and Odyffey.

a fact the more extraordinary, fince the greater part of his writings are merely elegant and comprehenfive text books, containing the heads of his lectures; laborious, but clear reafonings; and often original difcoveries in the moft difficult branches of fcience. The following paffage concerning him in the French Encyclopedie, article Ariftotelifme, muft excite a fmile of fomething more than furprife. "Le nombre de fes ouvrages eft prodigieux; on en peut voir les titres en Diogene Laerce... encore ne fommes nous pas fûrs de les avoir tous: il eft même probable que nous en avons perdu plufieurs," &c.

* The treatifes de Plantis & de Mundo are rejected by moft writers. The former is, indeed, of little value; the latter, of the greateft; but I do not cite it as an authority, becaufe it is my ambition to place my account of his philofophy beyond the reach of cavil.

CHAP. II.

A NEW ANALYSIS OF ARISTOTLE'S SPECULATIVE WORKS.

ARGUMENT.

Sensation—Its nature explained—Imagination and memory—Association of perceptions—Reminiscence—Intellect—Its power and dignity—Aristotle's organon—Origin of general terms—Categories—Division and Definition—Propositions—Syllogisms—Their nature and use—Second analytics—Topics—Aristotle's organon perverted and misapplied—Demonstration—Aristotle's metaphysics—Proper arrangement thereof—Truth vindicated—Introduction to the first philosophy—Its history—Refutation of the doctrine of ideas—Elements—Analysis of the bodies so called—Their perpetual transmutations—Doctrine of atoms refuted—Motion or change—Its different kinds—Works of nature—How her operations are performed—Matter—Form—Privation—The specific form or sight—State of capacity and energy—Aristotle's astronomy—The earth and its productions—History of animals—Philosophy of natural history—His book on energy—The first energy eternally and substantially active—His attributes—Antiquity of the doctrine that Deity is the source of being—Inculcated in Aristotle's exoteric works—Objections to Aristotle's philosophy—Answers thereto.

THE Works of Aristotle derive their importance and splendour, neither from their number nor their magnitude, but from their variety and their aim. Disdaining the conquest of particular provinces, he daringly invaded the whole empire of

CHAP. II.
The different branches into which it is divided.

CHAP. II.

of philosophy; and his persevering and generally successful exertions in this bold enterprise excites the justest admiration of his genius and industry. The heavens and the earth; things human and divine; God, man, and nature; under these comprehensive divisions of whatever is the object of human thought, the Stagirite distributes the different articles of his truly philosophical Encyclopædia; of which time has yet spared to us the distinct outline, with many groups imperfectly sketched, and others totally defaced, yet filled up in some of its most essential parts with exquisite skill, and delineated throughout with unexampled boldness and inimitable precision.

In endeavouring to communicate to the reader, in few words, a clear and correct notion of the condition in which Aristotle found, and in which he left philosophy, it will be impossible strictly to adhere to the capricious order in which his Works have been arranged by his editors. Agreeably to his own maxim, I shall begin, not with what is absolutely first either in time or in dignity, but with what is first in relation to man; that is, with what is first in the order of his thoughts or conceptions; endeavouring, in my discourse throughout, to preserve the modesty and impartiality of an historian, and to be as faithful in explaining my author's opinions, as cautious in interposing my own judgment.

The sources of human knowledge.

It is the doctrine of Aristotle, a doctrine long and obstinately disputed, but now very generally admitted, that all our direct knowledge originates in perceptions of sense [a]. Of the five senses,

---

[a] De Anima, l. iii. c. ix. p. 656. ο τοις ειδεσι τοις αισθητοις τα νοητα εςι... και δια τουτο ετι αισθωμενος μηδεν μην αν μαθοι, ηδε συνιη. τα δε πρωτα νοηματα, τι διοισει τω μη φαντασματα ειναι; η ηδε ταυτα φαντασματα, αλλ' ηκ ανυ φαντασματων; but I no where find in Aristotle the words universally ascribed to him, "Nihil est in intellectu, quid non prius fuerit in sensu."

senses, that of touch, he observes, is generally diffused through the whole animal frame, and cannot therefore be destroyed without destroying the animal [b]. The sense of taste Aristotle regards as a particular kind of touch, requisite for the purpose of nutrition, and therefore essential to life [c]. But the three other senses, always residing in particular organs, are in some animals altogether wanting, in others extremely imperfect; and even in those animals in whom they are most vigorous, are often, without destruction to the animal itself, overwhelmed, weakened, or totally destroyed, by the too powerful operation of their respective objects [d].

Sensation.

Colours and sounds are perceived respectively by the eye and the ear, and by them only; motions and figures are conveyed to the mind through the instrumentality of more senses than one; and a third class of perceptions are communicated and impressed through the united energy of all the senses [e]. Those of touch and of taste seem to be nearly a-kin, because external objects seem to operate on them by direct and immediate application. This, however, is not probably the case; because, were it true, the analogy of nature would here be violated, since it is found by experiment, that external objects, directly and immediately applied to the organs of the three other senses, totally obstruct the motions on which their power of sensation depends, and

---

[b] Compar. Aristot. de Anima, l. ii. c. iii. p. 633. and c. xi. p. 624. & seq.

[c] ὁ δὲ χυμός, ἐν τι τῶν ἁπτῶν ἐστι. Comp. l. ii. de Anima, c. iii. p. 633, and c. 10, p. 643. & seq.

[d] De Anima, l. ii. c. 6, 7, 8, 9.
ἡ τε αἰσθητοῦ ἐνέργεια ἐν τῷ αἰσθητικῷ; and again, ἡ δὲ τοῦ αἰσθητοῦ ἐνέργεια καὶ τῆς αἰσθήσεως ἡ αὐτὴ μέν ἐστι καὶ μία. De Anima, l. iii. c. i. p. 648.

[e] De Anima, l. ii. c. vi. p. 638.

NEW ANALYSIS OF

CHAP. II.

and render their respective objects, sounds, colours, and odours, altogether imperceptible[f]. By a rapid and continuous agitation of the air, sonorous bodies affect the ear; through the intervention of light, colours are distinguished by the eye; and odours are communicated in a subtile vapour, which must in some animals, before perception can have place, be accompanied with the act of inspiring by the nostrils[g]. Agreeably to this analogy, it is probable that the fleshy and tender part of our external frame, which seems to us to be endowed with such a delicate sense of touch, is nothing more than the medium through which the perceptions of hardness, softness, and other qualities of that kind, are conveyed and communicated[h].

Its nature explained.

The real qualities of external objects are supposed to be made known to us by our senses; but in fact those qualities, such as they are by us conceived and denominated, have not any actual existence until they are perceived[i]. Previously to this, they exist only in power or capacity; which, in the language of Aristotle, here means that they exist only in their causes[k];

causes

---

[f] εαν γαρ τις θη το ιχων χρωμα επ' αυτην την οψιν, ουκ οψεται ... ὁ δε αυτος λογος και περι ψοφου και οσμης εςι, &c. De Anima, l. ii. c. vii. p. 639.

[g] De Anima, l. ii. c. ix. p. 643.

[h] De Anima, c. xi. p. 641. How far is this conjecture connected with the discovery of the nerves and their functions? And to how many discoveries might the shrewd guesses of Aristotle, attentively examined, still give birth?

[i] ἡ δε του αισθητου ενεργεια και της αισθησεως ἡ αυτη μεν εςι και μια. De Anima, l. iii. c. i. p. 638. And again, αναγκη αμα φθειρεσθαι και σωζεσθαι την ὁτω λεγομενην ακοην και ψοφον, χυμην και γευσιν, και τα αλλα ὁμοιως. De Anima, l. iii. c. i. p. 649.

[k] Compare διχως γαρ λεγομενης της αισθησεως και του αισθητου, των μεν κατα δυναμιν, των δε κατ' ενεργειαν, &c. De Anima, l. iii. c. i. p. 649. And το μεν ουν μητι τα αισθητα ιναι, μητε τα αισθηματα, ισως αληθες. το γαρ αισθανομενον παθος τουτο εςι· το δε τα υποκειμενα μη ιναι ἁ ποιει την αισθησιν, και ανευ αισθησεως, αδυνατον. Metaphys. l. iv. c. v. p. 879.

causes which, though themselves imperceptible, have the power of moving and agitating our organs¹, and thereby of producing in them that variety of sensations, which relieves man from solitude, and connects him with the external world. To beings differently constituted, or to man himself, enjoying a direct and immediate intimacy with the causes of his perceptions, this world would probably assume an appearance altogether different from that which it now wears; for all sensation directly and immediately depends, not merely on the nature of its external causes, but on that also of the motions and changes produced in the organs of sense. Aristotle, therefore, justly reproves Democritus for saying, that if no medium were interposed, a pismire would be visible in the heavens[m]; asserting, on the contrary, that if vacuity alone intervened, nothing possibly could be seen, because all vision is performed by changes or motions in the organ of sight; and all such changes or motions imply an interposed medium[n].

Between the perceptions of the eye and of the ear there is a striking analogy. Bodies are only visible by their colour; and colour is only perceptible in light; and unless different motions were excited by light in the eye, colour and the distinctions of colour would no more be visible, than, independently of different vibrations communicated to the ear, sound, and the distinctions of

---

[l] ἡ δὲ λεγομένη αἴσθησις ὡς ἐνέργεια, κίνησίς τις διὰ τοῦ σώματος τῆς ψυχῆς ἐστι. De Somn. & Vigilia, c. i. p. 685. ἡ δὲ αἴσθησις ἐν τῷ κινεῖσθαί τε καὶ πάσχειν συμβαίνει. De Anima, l. ii. c. 5. p. 636.

[m] De Anima, l. ii. c. viii. p. 639.

[n] De Sensu & Sensili, c. ii. p. 665.

CHAP. II.

of sound, would be audible[o]. When the vibrations in a given time are many, the sensation of sharpness or shrillness follows; when the vibrations are, in the same time, comparatively few, the sensation of flatness is the result: but the first sound does not excite many vibrations because it is shrill or sharp, but it is sharp because it excites many vibrations; and the second sound does not excite few vibrations because it is flat or grave, but it is grave because it excites few vibrations[p].

Imagination and memory.

The powers of imagination and memory owe their origin to the senses, and are common to man with many other animals. As sensation is carried on by means of certain motions excited in our organs, so imagination and memory, which are the copies of sensation, exert their energy by means of similar but fainter motions, representatives of the former[q]. That independently of external causes such motions are produced, is demonstrable from what happens in sleep[r]. In some kinds of madness too, the phantoms of the brain are mistaken for realities[s]; and, in other kinds, realities are mistaken for phantoms[t]. But when

our

---

[o] De Anima, l. ii. c. viii. p. 641. See also l. ii. c. vii. p. 638. The intrepid ignorance of Voltaire might maintain, that Aristotle considered light as a quality merely; and that luminous and coloured bodies had qualities exactly such as they excited the ideas of in us. (Voltaire's Newtonian Philosophy.) But how could the learned Warburton assent to this erroneous account of the Peripatetic philosophy? See Divine Legation of Moses, &c. b. iv. sect. 6.

[p] De Anima, l. ii. c. viii. p. 641.

[q] ἡ δε φαντασια εστι αισθησις τις αισθησης. Rhetor. l. i. c. xi. p. 536. The same doctrine is maintained De Anima, l. iii. c. 4. p. 652. and De Memor. & Reminiscent. c. i. p. 680. c. ii. 682 & 683.

[r] De Anima, l. iii. c. iv. p. 651.

[s] Of this see an extraordinary example in Mirabil. Auscult. p. 1152.

[t] De Anima, l. iii. c. iv. p. 652. and De Mem. & Reminisc. c. i. p. 680.

our senses are found and awake, we can easily distinguish between perceptions arising from external causes, and those called into being by the mere agency of our internal constitution; and in many cases we can discover and explain the laws by which the energy of this constitution operates [u]. For the perceptions of imagination and memory, though not rigidly governed, like those of sense, by the power and presence of external objects, do not, however, float at random, but are subjected to a certain order and progression, conformably to established laws of association, which Aristotle was the first philosopher that attempted to investigate, to enumerate, and to explain [w]. He investigated them in analising the complex act of reminiscence or recollection, in which the principles of association operate under the immediate direction of the human will. He enumerated them, as far as seemed requisite to the subject which he was then treating, by saying that they might be reduced to the four following heads: proximity in time; contiguity in place; resemblance or similarity; contrariety or contrast [x]: And he explains them by shewing, that in every

CHAP. II.

Association of ideas or perceptions.

---

[u] De Memor. & Reminiscent. c. i. p. 680.   [w] Ibid. c. 2. p. 681.

[x] Mr. Hume says, "I do not find that any philosopher has attempted to enumerate or class all the principles of association; a subject, however, that seems very worthy of curiosity. To me there appears to be only three principles of connexion among ideas; resemblance, contiguity in time or place, and cause or effect." Essays, sect. iii. of the Association of Ideas, vol. ii. p. 24. Mr. Hume might be ignorant that Aristotle had attempted to enumerate the principles of association; but it is an unpardonable error in logic, to assign cause and effect as one of those principles, since cause and effect, as far as association is concerned, resolves itself into contiguity in time or place; and according to Mr. Hume's doctrine, the very idea of cause arises solely from these connexions. Essays, vol. ii. pp. 34, 35. 88. 107. It may be remarked that "the association of ideas" is a modern expression. Aristotle did not need it, since the thing meant by it is referred by him to custom. τῳ γαρ ιθει ακολυθουσι αἱ κινησεις αλληλαις, ἠδε μετα τηνδι. De Memor. p. 682.

CHAP. II.

every act of recollection we are conscious of *hunting about, as it were, among our thoughts,* until we hit on some one which is intimately connected with that which we wish to recall; or, in other words, that we produce in succession a multitude of vibrations or motions in our organs, until we hit on some one of them intimately connected with that of which we are in quest; and which has the power of reviving this last, because the one motion is either excited nearly at the same time with the other, or is entirely the same in kind with it, or so nearly the same, that the minute difference between them is speedily overpowered and lost, and from near agreement finally reduced to perfect coincidence. Thus far our author proceeds in unfolding the mechanism of sensation, fancy [y], memory, and recollection; or, in other words, in ascertaining the laws which regulate the union of mind and matter, without attempting the fruitless task of explaining in what manner those totally heterogeneous [z] substances are united.

Every exercise of recollection, he observes, is a species of investigation, in which the mind may be conscious of its own activity in directing the current of its thoughts, in turning them from one channel to another, in rejecting those which hold by no tie to the perception or image of which it is in quest, and in preferring, examining, and contemplating in all their relations

[y] Fancy is here *used* in its strict and original meaning; not, as in books of rhetoric and criticism, for the power of combining ideas or images by creative genius, agreeably to the dictates of correct judgment and refined taste.

[z] Aristotle carefully distinguishes the percipient power from the motions accompanying perception. ἀνάγκη ἄρα ἔν τι εἶναι τῆς ψυχῆς, ᾧ ἅπαντα αἰσθάνεται, καθάπερ εἴρηται πρότερον, ἄλλο δὲ γένος διὰ ἄλλου. De Sensu, c. vii. p. 675. See also De Anima, l. iii. c. x. p. 696.

tions those which, by their connexion with this perception or image, have a natural tendency to rouse the one or to revive the other [a].

It is the characteristic of animals, in contradistinction to the inanimate parts of nature, to be endowed with sensation; and whatever is endowed with sensation must have perceptions of pain and pleasure; and whatever has such perceptions must feel the impulse of appetite; the great moving principle in all animated beings [b]. But in the exercise of reminiscence, which is the immoveable boundary between man and other animals, he, and he alone, recognises the divine principle of reason or intellect co-operating with the coarser powers of fancy or memory; since every act of reminiscence, as above explained [c], implies comparison; and every the slightest comparison, expressed in the simplest proposition, indicates a substance different and separable from matter, a substance totally inconceivable by man in his present state, where the gross perceptions of sense are the only foundation and sole materials of all others, how lofty soever and refined; but a substance, notwithstanding, of whose existence we are assured by our consciousness of its energies [d].

To

Reminiscence the first boundary between man and other animals.

---

[a] τουτο δι γινεται κιυητα πολλα, ιως αν τνι αυτνι κινησι κινωσιν, ἢ ακολουθσοι το πραγμα. De Memor. & Reminiscent. c. 2. p. 682. He adds, anticipating the philosophy of Hobbes and Hartley, τα δι απο τα αιτα ποτε μιν μνησθηναι, ποτε δε μη, αιτιος, οτι επι πλεω ενδεχεται κινηθηναι απο της αυτης αρχης—ωσπερ γαρ φυσις ηδη το εθος, &c. ibid. "But the cause that the same thing recalls sometimes one perception, and sometimes another, is, that different motions may spring from the same principle; for custom is like nature," &c.

[b] De Anima, l. ii. c. iii. p. 633. & seq.

[c] De Memor. & Reminisc. c. ii. p. 683.

[d] Com. De Anima, l. i. c. v. p. 625. and c. ix. p. 629.

CHAP. II.

Proof of an intellectual principle in man.

To illustrate this further by an example, Aristotle says, let the comparison or proposition be one of the simplest imaginable, that whiteness is not sweetness[e]. These sensible qualities which the vulgar ascribe to external objects, the philosopher knows, as above explained, to depend on certain motions communicated to his internal organs, motions vivid and forcible when first produced by sensation, more faint and languid when afterwards revived by imagination or memory[f]. But the comparison of any two objects necessarily implies, that they should be both present in the same indivisible point of time, to one and the same comparing power. Yet their presence to the senses, the fancy, or the memory, is known to consist in nothing else but certain motions produced in our bodily organs. If the comparison, therefore, could be made by any of them, it would follow that this organ was susceptible of different and contrary motions,

[e] De Anima, l. iii. c. ii. p. 649.

[f] De Memor. & Reminiscent. c. i. p. 680. and De Anima, l. iii. c. iv. p. 652. Sensible qualities as perceived by the mind, Aristotle calls, therefore, παθηματα τη ψυχη, of which, he says, words are the signs: De Interpret. c. i. p. 37: Meaning, thereby, that language expresses things as they are perceived, not as they really are. Το μεν ει μητι τα αισθητα ειναι, μητι τα αισθηματα, ισως αληθες· τα γαρ αισθανομενα παθος τουτο εςι.· το δε τα υποκειμενα μη ειναι α ποιει την αισθησιν αδυνατον. η γαρ δη η αισθησις αυτη εαυτης εγειρει, αλλα εςι τι ετερον παρα την αισθησιν, ο αναγκη προτερον ειναι της αισθησεως. το γαρ κινεν τε κινουμενε φυσει προτερον εςι· καν ει λεγεται προς αλληλα ταυτα αυτα, ηδεν ηττον. Metaph. l. iv. c. v. p. 879. "To say that things perceptible by sense, and the objects of our perceptions, do not exist, is perhaps true; for these are merely the affections of the percipient: but that there should not be certain causes producing sensation, and existing independently of it, is impossible; for sensation is not its own work, but there is something beside sensation necessarily prior to it, since the principle of motion is necessarily prior to the movement communicated; and not the less, that these things are relatives." The existence of imperceptible, and therefore unknown causes of our sensations, is maintained by Aristotle against the ancient sceptics; in whose errors he refuted, by anticipation, those of Hobbes, Berkeley, Hume, &c. as we shall see hereafter.

motions, precisely at the same indivisible instant; for it is necessary that the same simple power should comprehend at once the sweetness and whiteness, or whatever else be the sensations compared, since if it comprehended them distributively, by its parts however minute, or successively in particles of time however short, it could no more draw the result of the comparison, than if the one sensation was recognised by one man, and the other by another, or one of them recognised in the last century, and another in the present. The perception of truth, therefore, being altogether unrelated to time and space, must be totally dissimilar to any corporeal operation, and so essentially one simple energy, that it cannot without absurdity be supposed capable of division. But all the motions and actions of body being performed in space and time, are therefore indefinitely divisible; and although their smallness or quickness soon escapes the perception of sense, and soon eludes the grasp of fancy, yet the intellect still pursues and detects them, knowing that they can never vanish into nothing by their indefinite minuteness. By our divisions and subdivisions without limit, we still leave, in the smallest particle, body with its properties; and after all the steps that possibly can be taken, remain precisely as distant from the goal, as at our first setting out. This goal, therefore, it is impossible for us ultimately to attain; but in the language of geometers, infinite will be still interposed between operations divisible and indivisible, between perceptions of sense and perceptions of reason, between the nature and properties of mind and the nature and properties of matter. It is not sense or fancy, but mind alone, that recognises itself; and this intellectual substance of which we must be contented in our present state merely to know the existence,

CHAP.
II.

and to exercise the energies, is that which characterises and ennobles the creature man, and which gives him a resemblance to his Maker. It is this which, separated from body, is then only, properly what it is[g], immortal and divine; which does not

[g] De Anima, l. iii. c. 6. which passage is commented by Plutarch from Aristotle himself. Vid. Plut. de Consol. ad Apollon. p. 115. Where he says, that the dead are happy and blessed; and that to speak ill of them falsely is to blaspheme against those far superior to ourselves. This work of Aristotle's was a Dialogue, written in honour of Eudemus of Cyprus. It is mentioned by Plutarch in Dion. p. 967. The passage above alluded to in the work De Anima is strangely perverted by Aristotle's commentators; whose erroneous interpretation is adopted by Warburton in the following passage, as bold in assertion as defective in proof. "Aristotle thought of the soul like the rest, as we learn from a passage quoted by Cudworth [*] out of his Nicomachean Ethics; where having spoke of the sensitive souls, and declared them mortal, he goes on in this manner: 'It remains that the mind or intellect, and that alone pre-existing, enter from without, and be only divine [†].' But then he distinguishes again concerning this mind or intellect, and makes it two-fold, agent and patient, the former of which he concludes to be immortal, and the latter corruptible. The agent intellect is only immortal and eternal, but the passive is corruptible. Cudworth thinks this a very doubtful and obscure passage, and imagines Aristotle was led to write thus unintelligibly by his doctrine of forms and qualities, whereby corporeal and incorporeal substances are confounded together. But had that great man reflected on the general doctrine of the το ἑν, he would have seen the passage was plain and easy; and that Aristotle, from the common principle of the human soul's being part of the divine substance, here draws a conclusion against a future state of separate existence, which, though it now appears all the philosophers embraced, yet all were not, as we said, so forward to avow. The obvious meaning of the words then is this: "The agent intellect (says he) is only immortal and eternal, but the passive corruptible, *i. e.* the particular sensations of the soul will cease after death, and the substance of it will be resolved into the soul of the universe; for it was Aristotle's opinion, who compared the soul to a *tabula rasa*, that human sensations and reflections were passions. These, therefore, are what he finely calls the passive intelligent, which he says shall cease, or is corruptible. What he meant by the agent intelligent, we learn from his

[*] Intellectual System, p. 55.
[†] λειπεται δε τον νουν μονον θυραθεν επεισιεναι, και θειον ειναι μονον.

commentators,

not decay with our corporeal powers; and whose energies are so totally different from those of organised matter, that whereas our commentators, who interpret it to signify, as Cudworth here acknowledges, the divine intellect; which glofs Aristotle himself fully justifies, in calling it θεος, divine*." On this passage I would first observe, that though I had frequently read the *Nicomachean Ethics*, I could not meet with the words cited by Warburton; and for this good reason, that such words are not there to be found. In the first edition of Cudworth's Intellectual System, that great Author is very negligent in citing his authorities; and in the second edition published by Birch, we are referred to Aristotle de Generatione & Corruptione, l. ii. c. 3. The passage quoted, however, is not to be found there, nor in any part of the work on Generation and Corruption. It is to be found, indeed, in the Physical Auscultations; and words to the same purpose occur in the fifth chapter of the first book de Anima. ὁ δὲ νες τοικεν εγγινεσθαι, ουσια τις ουσα, και ε φθειρεσθαι. "It is likely that the mind is a substance existing in the body, and not liable to be destroyed with the body." From this and several other passages, where Aristotle always speaks with the greatest modesty on the subject of the human intellect, qualifying his words with a "perhaps," "it is likely," Warburton had no right to conclude that Aristotle maintained the pre-existence of the mind as a part of the Divinity. The argument which he brings in support of this assertion, "that Aristotle calls the active intelligent, Divine," is not conclusive, because Aristotle, with other Greek writers, might use the epithet "Divine" as synonymous with excellent, as the Lacedæmonians, when they admired any one greatly, called him Σιος (instead of θειος) ανηρ. Ethic. Nicom. l. vii. c. 1. But the Stagirite seldom uses any word which he does not accurately define, and when he calls the intellect *divine*, or what *is most divine in us*; Ethic. Nicom. l. x. c. 7; sub init. he tells us plainly what he means by these expressions, which he says can have no other sense, but either that thought, *i. e.* the energy of intellect, from which only it derives its excellence and dignity, exists most perfectly in the divine nature; or, secondly, because intellect enables us, imperfectly indeed, to comprehend that nature. The learned Reader may compare the following passages, Aristot. Metaphys. l. i. c. ii. p. 841. De Anima, l. i. c. v. p. 625. and Metaphys. l. xiv. c. ix. p. 1004. That *intelligence in capacity is prior in time to intelligence in energy, in the individual, but not absolutely*, means merely that the human mind is capable of intelligence before it becomes actually intelligent; but that all intelligence in capacity is derived from intelligence in energy, that is, from God.

---

* Divine Legation, vol. i. book iii. sect. 4.

our senses are easily fatigued, overpowered, and destroyed by the force and intensity of objects sensible[h], the intellect is roused, quickened, and invigorated by the force and intensity of objects intelligible; instead of being overstrained or blunted, it sharpens and fortifies amidst obstinate exertions; and finds

in

Metaphys. l. ix. c. viii. p. 938. & seq. and the last chapters both of his Physics and Metaphysics. That the mind when separated from the body *is only what it is*, means that it then assumes its true nature, activity, and dignity, and is then better and happier than it was before, in which Aristotle says that many agreed with him. ωσπερ ϐελτιον τῳ ιῳ μη μετα σωματος ειναι, καθαπερ ιωθι λεγισθαι, και ωολλοις συνδοκει. Aristot. de Anima, l. i. c. iii. p. 623. That it then *perpetually energises*, not needing the assistance of memory, is explained by what Aristotle says on memory, in his book on that subject, c. ii. p. 681. & seq. in which he shews that memory depends on association of perceptions, and that association again depends on motion; whereas the intellect is simple, impassive; and, existing independently of space, incapable of motion; except by way of accession or appendage, as a sailor is moved in a ship. De Anima, l. i. c. 3.

Since writing the above note, I find that Lord Monboddo cites and translates part of the passage which I have endeavoured to explain; but his Lordship, I think, construes it wrong. On the words ου μνημονευομεν δι, οτι τυτο μεν απαθες· ὁ δε παθητικος της φθαρτος και ανυ τυτυθεν νοει, he observes, "that what Aristotle here says of the mind's thinking of nothing without the passive intellect refers to the progression from the state of mere capacity in which the intellect is, before it is impressed by external objects; which impression is absolutely necessary for its operating in this our present state." His Lordship here condescends to speak rather like a follower of Locke or Hume than as the disciple of Aristotle; and the text will not at all bear his interpretation, for the ανυ τυτυ can only refer to the active intellect, without which Aristotle says the passive thinks of nothing. Plutarch expresses Aristotle's meaning in popular language. παιδεια δε των εν ἡμιν μονον εστι αθανατος και θειον, &c. "That of all things belonging to man, the improvement of his mind alone is immortal and divine; —neither to be assailed by fortune nor shaken by calumny; not to be destroyed by disease nor weakened by old age." Plutarch de Liber. Educand. p. 5. Edit. Xyland. My explication of the obscure passages in Aristotle concerning the soul is confirmed by what he himself says on the subject of education in the 15th chapter of the seventh book of his Politics. The Reader will find the passage in the following translation, book iv. c. 15. Ancient Metaphysics, v. ii. b. iii. c. iv. p. 165.

[h] De Anima, l. ii. c. xii. p. 646.

in such alone its best improvement and most exquisite delight[i].

Having recognised the dignity and the powers of man, Aristotle, in his works throughout, examines how those powers have been exercised in rearing the fair fabric of science, which it was his own ambition to complete and to adorn. Adverse accidents interrupted, as we have seen, from posterity the full benefit of his labours; yet the treatises which emerged amidst the general wreck of his writings, best arrange themselves under the three-fold division of the objects of human thought; God, Nature, and Man: which division he himself seems continually to keep in view. Whatever reasonings relate to theology, though scattered in different treatises, may be referred, therefore, to his Metaphysics; a name unknown, indeed, to Aristotle, but given to his theological works by his editors, and importing that the fourteen books which bear it, should immediately follow his numerous treatises on the subject of physics or natural philosophy; that we may not rest satisfied with the knowledge of bare effects, but proceed to the investigation of causes, and of the Deity himself, the primary cause of all[k]. His histories of the heavens and of the earth; of animals, plants, and minerals; and even of man, considered merely as a material and sentient Being, may conformably with modern language be arranged under the head of Nature; though, in Aristotle's own acceptation, that term has a more limited sense; and, for a reason which will appear

CHAP. II.

Aristotle's Works referred to three heads.

I. God.

II. Nature.

---

[i] De Anima, l. iii. cc. 5, 6, 7, 8. p. 653. et seq. and Ethic. Nicom. l. x. cc. 7 and 8.

[k] Metaph. l. xiii. c. 7. p. 988.

CHAP. II.

III. Man.

appear hereafter, is confined to terrestrial objects, and those existing between this earth and the lunar sphere. Upon the Philosophy of Man¹, as our Author calls it, that is, of Man considered as a social and rational Being, endowed with sentiment, affection, and intellect, Aristotle's writings are as clear and copious as they are solid and satisfactory. His treatises on Logic, Ethics, and Politics, as well as his books on Rhetoric and Poetry, may all be referred to this one head, and viewed as connected parts of one great system of knowledge, to which, after the most patient examination, it will be found that the labours of his successors and detractors have made but slender additions.

The proper subject of his Organon.

In endeavouring concisely, but clearly, to communicate to my Readers the result of our Author's reasonings and discoveries under the three heads above mentioned, I shall begin, for a reason which will presently appear, with that work of his, recently the most decried of all, but long extravagantly magnified as the great engine of discovery, and sole instrument^m of universal science. Aristotle himself never viewed it in this false and flattering light, nor ever bestowed on it those pompous titles. The various tracts composing the Organon, as it is called, are not even given by him as parts of one and the same work.

---

¹ ἡ περὶ τὰ ἀνθρώπινα φιλοσοφία. Ethic. Nicom. l. x. c. ult.

ᵐ The word ὄργανον, organum, is found in Diogenes Laertius (l. i. sect. 28.); where Aristotle's philosophy is divided into practical and speculative: the practical comprehending his Ethics and Politics; the speculative, Natural Philosophy and Logic. Diogenes, however, does not use the word in the sense in which it was afterwards taken by Aristotle's commentators. Besides, when Laertius says, that logic is a part of speculative philosophy, he contradicts Aristotle himself, who divides speculative philosophy into the three branches of Mathematics, Physics, and Theology. Metaph. l. vi. c. i. p. 904.

work[n]. They all relate, however, to one and the same subject; since dialectic[o], in the strict and proper sense, is merely the art of dialogue, that is, the art of conversing. Aristotle's Organon, therefore, rightly understood, is nothing more than an endeavour to teach the rational and skilful employment of that characteristic faculty of man, by which he expresses, through appropriate signs[p], not only his perceptions of sense, but what is indefinitely more various, the comparisons, abstractions, and conclusions of his own mind concerning them. It is in this sense that logic, or dialectic, in the order of communicating liberal and universal knowledge, ought to precede the more abstruse and loftier branches of philosophy, because, by carefully analysing the signs by which internal operations, as well as external objects, are expressed, we remount at once to the origin and source both of our notions and of our perceptions; discover their intimate connections with each other; and unfold, even to the unexperienced minds of youth, a vast intellectual

---

[n] Even the different works must have been arranged otherwise than they now stand, since in some of the first of them we find references to those now published as the last.

[o] Dialectic is the word often used by Aristotle himself to denote what is commonly called his Logic, or the subject of the books composing his Organon. Vid. Metaph. l. xiv. c. 4. Rhetor. l. i. c. ii.

[p] των δε ονοματων εκαστον συμβολον εστι. "Each word or name is a symbol or sign." De Sensu & Sensili. l. i. c. i. p. 663. The whole passage, beginning with αιτων δε τουτων χρησεως, and ending with the words just cited, may be abridged as follows: "Hearing is the sense most instrumental to knowledge, not essentially or in itself, for the sense of seeing discovers to us more of the differences of things; but because sound, which is the object of hearing, is the vehicle of language; which is composed of words, each of which is a sign." Vid. etiam De Interpret. l. i. c. i. p. 36 and 37.

CHAP. II.

intellectual treasure, of which, without being aware of it, they were already in possession [q].

His analysis of language.

Agreeably to these principles, the Stagirite defines discourse, or speech, to be found significant by compact, of which the parts also are significant [r]; all discourse which simply affirms or denies, he resolves into arguments, arguments into propositions, and propositions into words; which last are the ultimate elements of language, because, though significant themselves, their parts are not significant [s]. Sounds significant by compact are either nouns, that is, names denoting things without any reference to time; or verbs, whose signification is accompanied with the appendage of time [t]. Nouns are either proper names or appellatives; a proper name denotes one individual only; an appellative denotes various individuals, and often various kinds or classes of individuals. The formation of appellatives is, according to Aristotle, the united work of abstraction and association [u]; abstraction, by which we separate the combinations

Origin of general terms.

---

[q] Comp. Aristot. Topic. l. i. c. ii. p. 181. & Aristot. de Anima, l. iii. c. ix. p. 656.

[r] De Interpret. l. i. c. iv. p. 38.

[s] To obviate objections arising from the significant parts of compound words, Aristotle says, ἐν δὲ τοῖς διπλοῖς σημαίνει μέν τι, αλλα ο καθ' αυτο ... The syllables are significant, but not essentially; since the whole word is significant by compact; for however subtilely words may be analysed, they will ultimately resolve themselves, not into ιεγατα, but into συμβολα; not into natural instruments, but into conventional signs. De Interpret. c. iv. p. 38.

[t] Ibid. c. iii. Those parts of verbs, therefore, which do not imply time are merely nouns. Ibid.

[u] Compare Metaph. l. xi. c. 2. pp. 955, 956. Ibid. c. xii. pp. 957, 958. Analyt. Posterior, l. ii. c. xix. p. 179. & seq. De Memor. & Reminisc. p. 181. & seq.

tions of sense, and consider a complex object in one view, without attending to the other aspects under which it may be examined [w]; association, by which perceptions that are similar naturally revive each other in unbroken succession; and, in consequence of their similarity, are expressed by a common name, or appellative, which is equally applicable to them all [x]. In reference to this common name, which is merely a sign that different objects have been compared together, and found to agree in one or more respects with each other, different individuals are said to belong to the same species, and different species are said to belong to the same genus; for in order to explain the nature of things, and to see their agreements and differences, it

---

[w] Metaph. l. xi. c. iii. pp. 956, 957.

[x] δηλον δη οτι ημιν τα πρωτα επαγωγη γνωριζειν αναγκαιον· και γαρ και η αισθησις ουτω το καθολυ εμποιει. The author here maintains, that even general principles can only be gathered by induction from perceptions of sense, or from repeated acts of memory coalescing into one experience (αι γαρ πολλαι μνημαι τω αριθμω εμπειρια μια εστι). And the comparison by which this intellectual operation is explained equally applies to that by which "τα καθολυ," "abstract notions," gathered from repeated sensations, are generalised and embodied in language. "In a flying army, when one man stops, the next to him will often stop also, and so on in succession, until the whole will sometimes stand firm. The same thing happens in the irregular flow of our thoughts. The steady contemplation of any individual object in that aspect in which it agrees with other individuals, will recall many similar objects to the mind; the stability of the one will communicate stability to the others, and thus give birth to what are called Universals, that is, to general terms, equally applicable to an indefinite number of individuals." παντος γαρ των αδιαφορων ενος, πρωτον μεν εν τη ψυχη καθολυ· και γαρ αισθανεται μεν το καθικαστον, η δε αισθησις τω καθολυ εστι. When Aristotle says that we perceive, by sense, the universal, he means that we view the object under that aspect in which it agrees with other objects; and the contemplation of it under that aspect only, or, in other words, the considering certain appearances of it apart from the rest, produces in the mind an abstract notion, of which, though itself be particular, the name is general. Metaph. ibid.

CHAP. II.

it is not necessary to suppose the existence of general ideas, but it is necessary that one word or term should, in the same sense, be applicable to many individuals, and also that one word or term should, in the same sense, be applicable to many species'.

Their importance.

Independently of this power in man, of expressing things that are alike by a common sign, his knowledge would be confined to the coarse and complex intimations of sense; he could not form even the most common notion of all, namely, that of number, since objects could not be enumerated, unless they were previously referred to the same genus or class, that is, unless they were expressed by one common sign. They must be so many trees, so many animals, or at least so many beings; and thus generically united, before they can be specifically or even numerically distinguished. For this reason Aristotle observes, that "one" and "being" are, of all terms, the most universal; they are applicable to all other general terms; they can be said in the same sense of them all, but no other term can be correctly said of them, because no other term expresses the full extent of their meaning [2]; or, in other words, is used as a sign for all the variety of things which they are employed to denote. Next to them, in point of universality, the ten categories immediately follow. These most comprehensive signs of things are called, in Latin, Predicaments, because they can be said, or predicated, in the same sense of all other terms, as well as of all the objects denoted by them; whereas no other term can be correctly said of them, because no other is employed

The categories.

[1] Analyt. Poster. l. i. c. xi. p. 141. ibid. c. xxiv. p. 155.

[2] Metaph. l. x. c. 2. p. 945. The το ἓν και το ὂν, "unity and being," agree, he observes, in the universality of their signification. They contain all the categories, but are not included in any of them.

employed to express the full extent of their meaning. They are; substance, quality, quantity, relation, time, place, action, passion, position, and habit [a]. All the objects of human thought that can be expressed by single words, arrange themselves under one or other of these general terms. Aristotle (not indeed in his "Categories," but in his works collectively) explains the nature and properties of each; and thus opens to the inquisitive mind a wide field of various knowledge, since the properties of each predicament belong to all the objects, or classes of objects, comprehended under [b] it, and the properties of the whole united extend to all things in the universe. But to avoid the reproach of bewildering his reader in barren generalities, the philosopher frequently applies his reasonings concerning signs to the things signified by them; perpetually inculcating, that individuals only have a real existence, and that what are called in the Pythagorean

[a] ετι δε ταυτα τον αριθμον δεκα· τι εστι, ποσον, ποιον, προς τι, που, ποτε, κεισθαι, εχειν, ποιειν, πασχειν. Topic, l. i. c. 9. p. 285. What is here called τι εστι, the author elsewhere calls substance, as Categor. c. iv. p. 15; where he says, that all single words denote either substances, or quantity, or quality, &c. This tenfold division had been made before Aristotle's time, and explained by the Pythagoreans, particularly by Archytas of Tarentum, in his book περι τυ παντος, "concerning the Universe." A great part of that work, in its primitive Doric, is preserved in Simplicius' Commentary on Aristotle's Categories. But Archytas and the other Pythagoreans considered as "the principles of things," what Aristotle calls σχηματα κατηγοριας, "figures or forms of predication," and λογυς καθολυ, "universal denominations." Thus also they were considered by Archytas the Peripatetic (Boeth. in Predicam. p. 112.), whom Mr. Harris (Philosoph. Arrangements, c. ii. p. 31.) confounds with Archytas the Pythagorean. The considering of these comprehensive genera as the principles and causes of the universe with the Pythagoreans, or merely as universal denominations with Aristotle, constitutes as wide a difference as that between a visionary and a philosopher.

[b] Categor. c. v. to c. ix. inclusively.

CHAP. II. Pythagorean or Platonic philofophy, numbers, ideas, immutable and eternal effences, are merely the work of human thought expreffed and embodied in language [e]. This doctrine is nearly allied

[e] Categor: c. v. p. 17. "That if individuals, or the firſt fubſtances, were not, nothing elfe could be;" fo that, inſtead of ideas, &c. making them, every thing that exiſts is made by and from them. And again, ιδη μιν ω ιναι, η ι τι παρα τα πολλα, ηκ αναγκη, ει αποδιξις εςαι· ειναι μεντοι εν κατα πολλα αληθες ειπειν αναγκη ... δη αρα τι εν και το αυτο, επι πλειοναι ειπειν, μη ομονυμον. "For the purpofe of demonftration, it is not neceffary to fuppofe the exiftence of general ideas, but only that one general term can be applied with truth, and in the fame fenfe, to many individuals.". Analyt. Pofter. l. i. c. xi. p. 141. Compare cxxiv. p. 155. Ετι δε εδεμια αναγκη τι ιναι τυτο παρα ταυτα, ετι εν δηλοι, εδεν μαλλον η επι των αλλων, ὁσα μη τι σημαινει, αλλ' η ποιον, η προς τι, η ποιειν· ει δε αρα, εχ η αποδειξις αιτια, αλλ' ὁ ακεων. "It is not neceffary to fuppofe, that the general term, denoting any claſs of fubſtances, expreffes any thing befide the different particulars to which it applies, any more than the general terms denoting qualities, relations, or actions. One general term ſtands as the fign for a variety of particulars confidered under one and the fame afpect; but to fuppofe that this term requires one fubftantial archetype, or idea, as general as itſelf, is the hearer's fault; fuch a fuppofition not being neceffary for the purpofe of demonftration." The fimplicity and folidity of Ariftotle's philofophy was early deftroyed by confounding it with Platonifm. The evil has been perpetuated from age to age, by his commentators and pretended followers; not excepting the lateſt of them all, Mr. Harris and Lord Monboddo, who perpetually afcribe to the Stagirite the doctrine of general ideas, which, in the paffages above cited, he formally denies. Thofe laſt-mentioned writers acknowledge that Ariftotle oppofed Plato, in denying the feparate and fubftantial exiftence of ideas, but maintain, that he afferted their exiftence originally in the divine intellect, forming what we call the intellectual world. "From thence proceeds the material world, which is a copy of thefe forms or ideas. The firſt kind of ideas, the Peripatetics called προ των πολλων, "before the many;" the other kind they called ν τοις πολλοις, "in the many;" and thefe laſt are the fubftantial forms of the Peripatetics; that is, the form which gives the fubftance or effence to the thing. And, laſt of all, come the ideas in our minds, which, being formed from the many, and only in confequence of their exiſting in the many, are faid to be επι τοις πολλοις, "after the many." Monboddo Ancient Metaph. vol. i. p. 466. Mr. Harris, in defcribing this triple order of ideas, fpeaks to the fame purpofe. "By mind we mean fomething which, when it acts,

allied to another of Aristotle's above explained, that all our direct knowledge originates in perceptions of sense; and in both

acts, knows what it is going to do; something stored with ideas of its intended works, agreeably to which ideas these works are fashioned. Hermes, book iii. c. iv. p. 380. Again, To work and to know what one is about is to have an idea of what one is doing; to possess a form internal, corresponding to the external, to which external it serves for an exemplar or pattern. Here then we have an intelligible form which is prior to the sensible form." Ibid. p. 376. The same authors abound in repetitions of the same doctrine, which seems indeed to have been universally that of Aristotle's commentators. But what says the author himself. I shall repeat his own words, lest I should incur the reproach of speaking harshly. το δε λεγειν παραδειγματα ειναι και μετέχειν αυτων τα αλλα, κενολογειν εςι, και μεταφορας λεγειν ποιητικας. Τι γαρ εςι το εργαζομενον προς τας ιδιας αποβλεπον; ενδεχεται τε ειναι και γιγνεσθαι ότιουν και μη εικαζομενον. Metaph. l. xi. c. 5. p. 959. "To call ideas exemplars or patterns, and to say that other things are made in imitation, or by participation of them, is mere empty sound and poetical metaphor. Whoever considered in working an idea as his model? Things may exist or be made that never had an exemplar or archetype." According to Aristotle, "the definition is the idea of the thing, and the definition is composed of words." ὁ λογος ειδος τε πραγματος; ... και ὁ λογος συνκειται εξ ονοματων. Comp. De Anima, l. i. c. i. p. 618. and De Sensu, c. i. p. 663. I cannot conclude this note without observing, that something nearly akin to Aristotle's doctrine concerning the categories or universals was revived, in the darkness of the eleventh century, by the sect called Nominalists, which had for its author Roscellinus, a native of Brittany and Canon of Compiegne. But the Stagirite's genuine tenets were generally unknown in that century, and so little understood afterwards, (being studied only in corrupt versions, Arabic and Latin,) that the sect of the Nominalists, after the complete triumph of the supposed Aristotelian philosophy in the twelfth and succeeding centuries, were regarded as rash innovators and philosophical heretics. Their opinions, however, agreed more nearly with those of Aristotle than the opinions of those who believed themselves the Stagirite's most obsequious followers; although the language of the Nominalists seems to have been extremely liable to be perverted to the purposes of scepticism, as taking away the specific distinctions of things; and is in fact thus perverted by Hobbes, Berkeley, Hume, and their innumerable followers. But Aristotle's language is not liable to this abuse; he every where maintains the stability of truth, and the reality of those specific distinctions which general terms are employed to express. He agrees with the Nominalists, for example, that the words "horse" and "dog" have not any correspondent archetypes or ideas in the mind,

as

CHAP. II. both these capital points, the Learned, after innumerable disputes, carried on with singular eagerness through many centuries, have generally embraced his opinion; and, what is most remarkable, chiefly since the time that undue deference ceased to be paid to his writings, and that his name was no longer superstitiously venerated by those who either read what they did not understand, or who affected to admire what they had never taken the trouble to read.

The

as general as themselves, but he maintains that these words imply the result of the comparison of different individuals agreeing in the same ιδος, the same show or appearance; for the sight, as he observes, is that of all the senses which enables us to perceive the greatest number of the agreements and differences of things, and is therefore most generally useful in classing them; or, in other words, in distinguishing those which are alike by a sign common to them all; that is, by a general name. Metaph. l. iv. c. 7. p. 881. Comp. De Sensu, c. i. p. 662. and Metaph. l. i. c. i. p. 838. To prevent the possibility of mistake or obscurity in the above note, it is necessary to observe, that the word "idea" in English is popularly used, not merely to denote an object of thought, but thought itself. To deny ideas in this latter sense is to deny thinking. But this is not the philosophical meaning of the word, as understood by the pretended followers of Aristotle, any more than by Locke in his Essay on the Human Understanding; by whom, ideas are said to be the objects immediately present to the mind in thinking. Essay, b. i. c. i. p. 13. Now Aristotle, in the following passage, expressly denies the presence or existence of any object in the mind, when it theorises or thinks, distinct from the act of the mind itself. επι των θεωρητικων, ὁ λογος το πραγμα, και ἡ νοησις· ουχ ἑτερου εν οντος τῃ νοημειν και τῳ τῳ, ὁσα μη ὑλην εχει, το αυτο εστιν· και ἡ νοησις τῃ νοημενῃ μια. Metaph. l. xiv. c. ix. p. 1004. In another passage he says, ἡ ψυχη πως εστι τα παντα. "The mind is after a sort all things." De Anima, l. iii. c. ix. p. 656. What is meant by τα καθολυ, "generals, universals, ideas," as the words are translated by his pretended followers, he states clearly thus: Επει δ' εστι, τα μεν καθολυ των πραγματων· τα δε καθ' ἑκαστον· λεγω δε καθολυ μεν, ὁ επι πλειονων πεφυκε κατηγορεισθαι· καθ' ἑκαστον δε, ὁ μη· οιον ανθρωπος, των καθολυ· καλλιας δε, των καθ' ἑκαστον, &c. De Interpret. c. vii. p. 39. "The distinction is to be made between universals and particulars; universals, which can be predicated of many, as the term "Man;" particulars, as "Callias," the proper name of an individual."

ARISTOTLE's WORKS.

The reduction of things to genera or classes, by applying to them common names, is the foundation of division and definition, which have been called by a just metaphor the firm Handles of Science. Each of the categories, or classes, above mentioned, that of substance for example, may be variously divided according to the intent of the division, which may be undertaken for explaining the works of art or of nature; for delineating the institutions of civil policy, or describing the structure of plants and animals; in a word, for examining any object, whether material or intellectual, about which human thought is conversant. But for whatever purpose the division is intended, it can be perspicuous and satisfactory only when it descends from the more general classes, or terms, to those which are less general, until it arrives at the lowest species of all, which rejects all further partition but into individuals only[d]. The intermediate terms between the highest genus and this lowest species, stand each of them in two distinct relations, and therefore receive two different names; that of genus with respect to the less general terms which they contain, and that of species with respect to the more general terms under which they are contained[e]. Such is Aristotle's own doctrine concerning classification

CHAP. II.

Division and definition.

---

[d] Analyt. Poster. l. ii. c. xiii. p. 175.

[e] Compare Categor. c. ii. p. 15. and Analyt. Prior. c. i. p. 52. The subject has been strangely perplexed by mistaking Aristotle's language, which is in itself highly perspicuous. το δ᾽ εν ὁλῳ ειναι ἑτερον ἑτερῳ, και το κατα παντος κατηγορεισθαι θατερου θατερου, τ᾽ αυτον εστι· λεγομεν δι το κατα παντος κατηγορεισθαι, ὁταν μηδεν ῃ τῳ ὑποκειμενῳ λαβειν, κατα ὁ (ατερου ῥηθησεται. "To say that one term is contained in another is the same as saying, that the second can be predicated of the first in the full extent of its signification; and one term is predicated of another in the full extent of its signification, when there is no

CHAP. II.

classification and division; a doctrine continually exemplified in his works throughout, moral as well as physical; and admirably illustrated by some modern writers, especially on the subjects of natural history.

Propositions.

Having explained the uses and functions of single words, the author proceeds to examine their combinations into propositions, and the combinations of propositions into reasoning or discourse. According to the measure of our desires or exigencies, our power or inability, language is variously moulded into commands, prayers, or wishes; but for the purposes of instruction or argument, it requires the form of an enunciative proposition, which is defined by Aristotle " the affirming or denying one thing of another." But all that can be directly affirmed of any subject is, either that it belongs to a certain class, or that it is possessed of certain qualities. Those qualities are either such as necessarily inhere in the thing itself while it remains what it is, or retains its distinctive name; or secondly, qualities necessarily proceeding from the former; or thirdly, qualities which do not uniformly belong to the subject, nor proceed from those uniformly belonging to it, but which accede to it

---

no particular denoted by the subject, to which the predicate does not apply." This remark, which is the foundation of all Aristotle's logic, has been sadly mistaken by many. Among others, the learned and truly respectable Dr. Reid writes as follows: " The being in a subject, and the being truly predicated of a subject, are used by Aristotle in his Analytics as synonymous phrases. And this variation of style has led some persons to think that the Categories were not written by Aristotle." See Kaim's Sketches, vol. iii. p. 316. But the two phrases of "being in a subject," and "being predicated of it," are so far from being used as synonymous, that the meaning of the one is directly the reverse of the meaning of the other.

it merely by way of adjunct or appendage[f]. Thus we can say of man, that he is an animal, which is the class to which he belongs; that he is an animal capable of reason, which is the quality necessarily inherent in him, while he deserves his distinctive name; that he is capable of learning grammar or geometry, which are qualities necessarily flowing from the former; but when we proceed farther, and ascribe to him qualities not necessarily flowing from those inherent in the species, although they may be found in many individuals, and even many nations, it is plain that these qualities are mere accessions or appendages to his distinctive name or specific character.

To define a thing, or to define a term, (for when words are considered as signs, these expressions are synonymous,) is to tell, as precisely and perspicuously as possible, what that thing is, or what that term signifies. This can only be done by ascertaining the class to which the object to be defined immediately belongs, and the quality or qualities which, necessarily inhering in it, uniformly distinguishes that object from other objects belonging to the same class or genus. That quality, therefore, or those qualities form what is called the specific difference, because they distinguish the species in question from the other species in the same genus, or the object in question from the other objects that most nearly resemble it. Thus, to define

The specific difference.

---

[f] Topic. l. i. c. viii. p. 285. The Greek word συμβεβηκος is, as far as I know, universally translated "accident;" συμβεβηκοτα, in the plural, "accidents;" from which, "Accidence," denoting the little book that explains the properties of the eight parts of speech, is generally held to be a corruption. But accident, in its proper sense of what is casual or fortuitous, has nothing to do with the one or the other; and Aristotle's meaning of συμβεβηκος ought to be expressed by a Latin or English word derived, not from 'accido,' but from 'accedo.'

CHAP. II.

define the number three, or the triad, we may say or predicate of it, that it is a quantity, and that kind of quantity called number, and that kind of number called an odd number; but each of these predicates, and all of them united, have a signification far more extensive than that of the subject; since there are other quantities beside number, and other numbers beside odd numbers, and many other odd numbers beside three. How then are we to proceed to find the exact definition of the triad? We must continue to combine still more of those predicates, until the whole of them unitedly will apply to the number three, and to it only; although each of them taken separately, and even any number of them short of the whole, have a far more extensive signification. Thus, with the predicates "number" and "odd" we must join that of "first," defining the triad " the first odd number ;" for though the predicate " first" applies to the number "two" as well as to " three," yet " the first odd number" applies to "three" only [g]. It may be necessary here to remark, that, in the accurate language of Aristotle, unity is not number, but the element of number [h]; all numbers are composed of units, but they themselves are indivisible and ultimate elements, incapable as units of farther resolution [i]. For coarse practical purposes, arithmeticians talk of the parts of unit; but when they do this, they have always previously converted unity into number; as when we speak of the tenth of an inch, we must necessarily have first changed the one inch into ten portions; the inch therefore, before it can be divided, ceases to be an unit, and is converted into ten.

Ac-

[g] Analyt. Poster. l. ii. c. xiii. p. 173. & seq.

[h] ὅτι τὸ ἓν ἀριθμῶν ἀρχή, ἢ ἀριθμός. Metaph. l. x. c. i. p. 943.

[i] οὔτε γὰρ τῆι ἐσχάτηι, ἐσχατώτερόν τι ἂν εἴη τι. Ibid. c. iv. p. 946; and again, αἰτίκηται γε ἡ καὶ τὰ πολλα, ὡς ἀδιαίρετοι καὶ διαιρετόν. Ibid. c. iii. p. 945.

ARISTOTLE's WORKS.

According to Aristotle, definitions are the fountains of all science[k]; but those fountains are pure only when they originate in an accurate examination and patient comparison of the perceptible qualities of individual objects; for it is in that case only, that our words being the correct signs of things, the conclusions drawn from our intellectual operations on the signs, exactly apply to the things signified by them. We must cautiously proceed, therefore, from particulars to generals[l], that we may not be cheated by words[m]; endeavouring to discover, in each object of our examination, that principal and paramount property in which all its other inherent qualities unite and terminate[n]. To this property we must assign a name, when an appropriate name for it is wanting; and in the invention of this name, we must respect the analogies of language[o], that the same relations may be preserved among words which subsist among the things which they denote[p]. The name, thus invented, is called the specific difference; which, in the objects to which it applies, is not always that quality which is most palpable or most striking; for many other qualities are often actually

---

[k] αι αρχαι των αποδείξεων, οι ορισμοι. Analyt. Poster. l. ii. c. 3. p. 164. Compare Analyt. Poster. l. ii. c. xvii. p. 178.

[l] δια δει απο των καθεκαςων επι τα καθολυ μεταβαινειν. Analyt. Poster. l. ii. c. xiii. p. 176.

[m] αι ομωνυμιαι λανθανουσι μαλλον εν τοις καθολυ. Ibid.

[n] Analyt. Poster. l. ii. c. xiv. p. 176. & Topic. l. i. c. iv. p. 182.

[o] ισως δε ραον αν ισως τις λαβοι ως μη κειται ονοματα, ει απο των πρωτων, και τοις της αντιςρεφουσι, τιθειη τα ονοματα. Categor. c. vii. p. 23.

[p] Comp. Metaph. l. iv. c. vii. p. 881. ο γαρ λογος, ου το ονομα σημαινει, ορισμος γινεται του πραγματος, & Metaph. l. vii. c. iv. p. 908. c. vi. p. 911. & seq.

CHAP. II.

actually discovered in them, before we distinguish that most important and most general one, which is implied in all the rest, and which forms, as it were, the basis on which they all stand[q]. This paramount property exists independently in its subject; but none of the other properties can subsist independently of the specific difference, which is therefore the principle in which they originate, and the source from which they flow. In many objects with whose sensible qualities we are most conversant, this source is concealed; yet to remount to it, when possible, is the main business of philosophy, since the more our knowledge is generalised, it will be the more satisfactory, and therefore the more delightful[r].

Syllogism.

The patient examination of objects, and the accurate definition of terms, are continually employed by our philosopher, as the best means for arranging perceptions into science. These, and not syllogisms, are the sole instruments used by himself in the deepest and most various researches that ever exercised the ingenuity of man. Yet his art of syllogism (an art ignorantly depreciated in the present age, and more absurdly magnified in preceding times beyond its real worth) is not therefore useless, although its real uses, as will presently appear, are altogether different from the purposes to which it was long most injudiciously applied. The art of syllogism was entirely Aristotle's invention; and in appreciating his merit as a philosopher, it becomes

[q] Το δε ταξαι ως δει ισχι, επι το πρωτον λαβη. τουτο δε ιται, εαν ληφθη, ο πασιν ακολουθει, επομη δε μη παντα. Analyt. Poster. l. ii. c. xiii. p. 175. The word ακολουθει is used in the same sense, when he says (as quoted above) that ἓν & ὂν, "unity and being," is implied in all the Categories.

[r] Analyt. Poster. l. i. c. xxiv. p. 155.

comes neceſſary to examine his firſt Analytics, in which that art is contained, that we may be enabled to decide whether the ſuppoſed improvements of his ſyſtem by ſome writers be not ignorant perverſions, and the objections made to the whole of it by others be not ſenſeleſs cavils.

It was formerly obſerved that every propoſition, affirming or denying one thing of another, muſt affirm or deny that the ſubject of which we ſpeak belongs to a certain claſs, or that it is endowed with certain qualities [s]. But to affirm one term of another, when both of them are taken in the full extent of their ſignification, is merely to ſay that there is not any ſpecies or any individual contained under the name of the ſubject, to which the name of the predicate does not apply. It matters not whether thoſe names denote ſubſtances or qualities, or any other of the ten predicaments. Whatever they denote, the name of the ſpecies, according to the principles on which all languages are conſtructed, may ſtill be predicated of every individual, and the name of the genus of every ſpecies. When the definition of any term is predicated of that term, the definition and word defined, having exactly the ſame ſignification, they

[s] The Author proves this by obſerving, that every ſubject muſt either reciprocate with its predicate, or not. If the ſubject reciprocates with the predicate, that is, if the ſubject can in its turn be predicated of it, then the predicate muſt have been either the definition or the property of the ſubject: if the ſubject does not reciprocate, then the predicate muſt have been either ſomething contained in the definition, namely the genus or ſpecific difference, or ſomething not contained in the definition, but acceding to it as an appendage. Theſe relations of genus, difference, &c. which the predicates can ſtand in to their ſubject are called, in the Scholaſtic Philoſophy, the Predicables. They are the only things that can be affirmed or denied of any ſubject, categorically; which means, in the language of Ariſtotle, that can be affirmed of any ſubject merely by the interpoſition of the ſubſtantive verb between two terms. Topic. c. viii. p. 285.

they both necessarily apply to exactly the same number of things, and are therefore of exactly the same extent. But in all propositions not identical, but which affirm or deny one thing of another, the predicate is according to the structure of all languages, naturally more extensive than the subject[f]; because, as before observed, to predicate one term of another is merely to say that there is not any thing contained under the name of the subject to which that of the predicate does not apply. The predicate, therefore, in every proposition is called the major term; the subject, the minor term; and these terms are conjoined in discourse by the substantive verb "is," called therefore the copula. When we say "the wall is white," the substantive verb is expressed; the same verb is understood, when we say "Achilles runs;" because the word "runs" may be resolved into "is running;" being in fact merely an abbreviation of it for the purpose of communicating the rapidity of our thoughts with suitable rapidity of speech[u]. To prevent imposition arising from the abuse of words, it is necessary to be able quickly to discern whether one term can be justly predicated of another. Aristotle, for this purpose, invented the syllogism, which consists in comparing both the subject and the predicate of any proposition with what is called the middle term, because its natural place is the middle between the other two terms, called therefore the extremes. Let the question be proposed, whether temperance be a habit? I readily find a middle term which is contained under the more extensive appellation of habit, and which itself contains the more limited appellation of temperance. The terms, therefore, stand

in

[f] Categor. c. v. p. 17.

[u] ὁδι γαρ διαφερει το αιθρωπος υγιαινει ετι, η το ανθρωπος ὑγιαινει, &c. Metaph. l. v. c. 7. p. 889.

in this order : Habit, virtue, temperance ; or, in the form of propofitions,

Virtue is a habit,
Temperance is a virtue ;
therefore temperance is a habit. Now the whole cogency of this argument depends on that great principle which prefides in the formation of language, that things, which have a common nature, receive a common name. They may differ in many important particulars, yet having received one common appellation from the particular in which they all agree, the term denoting the genus may be predicated of every fpecies, and every individual contained under it. Whatever is affirmed or denied of a more general term, may therefore be affirmed or denied of all the more particular terms, as well as of all the individual things to which its fignification extends. In the language of Ariftotle, this is exprefled by his calling thofe things fynonymous which have the fame name in the fame fenfe. Thus " man" and " ox" are, according to him, fynonymous, becaufe the name of animal is equally applicable to both[a] ; an obfervation which muft found harfhly to thofe Englifh readers who have derived their knowledge of Greek through the circuitous channel of France.

On the bafis of this one fimple truth, itfelf founded in the natural and univerfal texture of language, Ariftotle has reared a lofty

Wonderful variety in a fubject feemingly fo fimple.

---

[a] Categor. c. i. p. 14. Words, fynonymous in the modern fenfe, have nothing to do with philofophy, whofe terms, if accurate, cannot be interchangeable. Their proper place is poetry ; accordingly we find that Ariftotle, in his now imperfect treatife on that fubject, had treated of συνωνυμα ὧν πλιω τα ονοματα, λογος δε ὁ αυτος, that is, " of various words meaning the fame thing;" which agrees with the modern acceptation Simplicius in Categor. fol. viii.

CHAP. II.

lofty and various ſtructure of abſtract ſcience, clearly expreſſed, and fully demonſtrated. To convince ourſelves of the wonderful variety in a ſubject, ſeemingly ſo ſimple, it is ſufficient to obſerve, that the middle term may either be the ſubject of both the premiſſes; or the predicate of both; or, as in the ſyllogiſm given above, the ſubject of the major premiſs, in which it is compared with the major extreme, and the predicate of the minor premiſs, in which it is compared with the minor extreme. Theſe various arrangements form what are called the three figures of ſyllogiſm[y]; and in each of theſe three figures, every one of the three propoſitions may be either affirmative or negative; and each of the affirmative and negative propoſitions may be either univerſal or particular; univerſal, when their ſubject is taken in the full extent of its meaning, as "all men are mortal;" particular, when their ſubject in its ſignification is reſtricted to a part of the things which its name properly denotes, as "ſome men are wiſe." If we expreſs theſe four kinds of propoſitions, the univerſal affirmative, the univerſal negative, the particular affirmative, and the particular negative, by the four vowels, a, e, i, o, we ſhall find that they will afford ſixty-four different combinations by threes, which are called the different modes in each figure; and therefore one hundred and ninety-two combinations in the three figures collectively. But the variety does not end here; for propoſitions themſelves are either

---

[y] It may be proper to remark, that in books of logic there is a fourth figure which is ſaid to have been invented by Galen the phyſician. In this Galenical figure, as it is called, the middle term is predicated of the major, and the minor term is predicated of the middle. In this abſurd figure, the more general term is placed as the ſubject of the more particular. The natural arrangement of the terms is thus totally reverſed. But every ſyllogiſm in this figure, when properly expreſſed, naturally falls under Ariſtotle's firſt figure.

either pure or modal. A pure propofition fimply affirms or denies one thing of another; a modal propofition affirms or denies with the addition of neceffity or contingency, poffibility or impoffibility. When we confider, therefore, the numerous combinations that will refult from thefe new elements varioufly joined with the old, and that every new combination forms a diftinct fyllogifm, it is impoffible not to admire the perfevering induftry that could contemplate each feparately, and examine how the truth of the conclufion was affected by each fpecific arrangement.

CHAP. II.

From this induction, the moft copious and complete that any fpeculation ever exhibited, Ariftotle infers that all conclufive fyllogifms whatever may be reduced to conclufive modes in the firft figure[z]; of all which, the truth refts immediately on the grammatical principle above explained; and of which, therefore, the fyllogifm already given may ferve for an example. When the three terms of a fyllogifm, therefore, are accurately defined, and the three propofitions compofing it are properly arranged, the juftnefs of its conclufion may always be perceived by a rapid glance of the mind difcerning, by means of the minor premifs, or the propofition in which the fubject of the conclufion is compared with the middle term, whether the major premifs, or propofition in which the predicate of the conclufion is compared with the fame middle term, neceffarily infers the conclufion. For enabling the mind readily to draw this inference in the cafe of all fyllogifms whatever, whether their conclufions be affirmative or negative, univerfal or particular, and how awkwardly foever their terms may have been arranged, the Author

All fyllogifms reduced to thofe of the firft figure.

[z] Comp. Analyt. Prior. c. vii. p. 60. and c. xxiii. p. 79.

CHAP. II.

Rules of converſion.

Author has recourſe to no other rules or axioms than thoſe which concern what is called converſion and oppoſition; and that moſt extenſive principle of reaſon which infers the truth of any propoſition by ſhewing, that to ſuppoſe it falſe leads to an abſurdity. To convert a propoſition, is to make its ſubject and its predicate change places. This may often be done ſafely, becauſe in many propoſitions the converſe will retain that truth which was in the propoſition to be converted. All univerſal negatives, for example, can always be completely converted. If no A is B, no B is A; for if B could be predicated of any thing called A, for example of C, then C would fall under the names both of A and of B, which is contrary to the firſt ſuppoſition, that no A is B; or that B cannot be predicated of any thing called A [a]. When one term, therefore, is univerſally denied of another, that other may, without heſitation, be univerſally denied of the firſt. An univerſal affirmative propoſition does not admit of a complete converſion, becauſe, according to what was formerly obſerved, in every ſuch propoſition the predicate muſt apply to all the ſpecies and individuals expreſſed by the name of the ſubject, but the ſubject needs not therefore apply to all the ſpecies and individuals contained under the name of the predicate. But an univerſal affirmative, though it rejects a complete, yet admits of a partial converſion. Thus if every A is B, ſome B muſt be A; for if no B is A, then no A is B, as juſt proved in the caſe of univerſal negatives. Particular affirmatives admit of a complete converſion; for if ſome A is B, then ſome B is A; ſince, when no B is A, no A is B, as formerly proved in the caſe of univerſal negatives. Particular negatives do not at all admit of converſion, either complete or partial

[a] Analyt. Prior. c. ii. p. 52

partial. Thus, some A is not B cannot be converted by saying that some B is not A, because, though the name of a species does not apply to some things comprehended under the name of its genus, it does not thence follow that the name of the genus does not apply to all the individuals comprehended under the name of the species [b]. The rules concerning conversion then are, that universal negatives, as well as particular affirmatives, may be converted completely; that universal affirmatives can only be converted partially; and that particular negatives are totally incapable of conversion. These rules, perhaps, may all be resolved into one and the same primitive truth, of which they are only different expressions; yet these different expressions will on many occasions render the perception of that truth more distinct, and the application of it more easy as well as more expeditious. The same thing holds here, as with respect to the axioms of geometry, concerning the whole and its parts, equality and inequality, greater and lesser, since the comprehension of any one of those terms necessarily implies the comprehension of them all. Yet geometers find it useful to represent the same elementary truth under a variety of forms, that it may be more forcibly impressed, and more readily applied; and

---

[b] The doctrines of Aristotle's Organon have been strangely perplexed by confounding the grammatical principles on which that work is built with mathematical axioms. All the modern systems of logic that have fallen into my hands, employ in demonstrating the theory of syllogism these two axioms, "Things agreeing with the same third agree with each other:" "When one thing agrees with the third, and the other does not, they do not agree with each other." But Aristotle tells us, that these axioms do not at all apply to the predication of terms, the one of the other; except when those terms denote mathematical quantities. The reason why they do apply to mathematical quantities he says is, because in them, ἡ ἰσότης ἑνότης, "equality is sameness;" and in them, equality is sameness, because ὁ λόγος ὁ τῆς πρώτης κατὰ τὸ ἕν ἐστι. The definition of any particular object denoted by the one, is precisely the same with the definition of any particular object denoted by the other. Metaph. l. x. c. iii. p. 845.

CHAP. II.

Rules of opposition.

and the indefinite number of mathematical theorems ultimately resolve themselves into a few simple propositions, which may themselves perhaps be considered as only different expressions of one and the same original conception of the mind.

Upon this great principle of translating the same truth into different words, in order to render it more familiar to our thoughts, Aristotle next examines the doctrine of opposition. Propositions may be opposite or contrary, which are not contradictory; because the truth of the one does not always infer the falsehood of the other. Thus, "all men are white," "no man is white," are contrary propositions, and both of them false. "Some men are white," "some men are not white," are contrary propositions, and both of them true. But if I say, "all men are white," "some men are not white," the truth of the one proposition infers the falsehood of the other; because in this last case only the predicate "whiteness" is affirmed of the whole species, and denied of some individuals belonging to it; which is inconsistent with the great principle on which all language and all reasoning is founded [e].

In

[e] De Interpret. c. vii. p. 39. & seq. and Analyt. Prior. c. xv. p. 117. & seq. To shew how grossly Aristotle's logic has been mistaken, and with what contempt of reason and grammar, as well as of good manners, the character of this philosopher has been assailed, I shall cite the following passage from a late author (Lord Kaims) of considerable reputation, and of very considerable merit: "His (Aristotle's) artificial mode of reasoning is no less superficial than intricate. The propositions he attempts to prove by syllogism are all self-evident. Take for example the following proposition, 'that man has the power of self-motion.' To prove this, he assumes the following maxim, upon which indeed every one of his syllogisms are founded, 'that whatever is true of a number of particulars joined together holds true of every one separately." Lord Kaims' Sketches, vol. iii. p. 306. It would have been charitable in this acute author to have pointed out the passage where Aristotle maintains, that because it is true of a number of particulars joined together, that they are an hundred or a thousand, the same holds true of every one of them separately. It is impossible to restrain indignation at such unmeaning jargon, poured out against the most accurate of all writers.

In the first Analytics, Aristotle shews what is that arrangement of terms in each proposition, and that arrangement of propositions in each syllogism, which constitutes a necessary connection between the premisses and the conclusion. When this connection takes place, the syllogism is perfect in point of form; and when the form is perfect, the conclusion necessarily follows from the premisses, whatever be the signification of the terms of which they are composed. These terms, therefore, he commonly expresses by the letters of the alphabet, for the purpose of shewing that our assent to the conclusion results, not from comparing the things signified, but merely from considering the relation which the signs (whether words or letters) bear to each other. Those [d], therefore, totally misconceive the meaning of Aristotle's logic, who think that, by employing letters instead of words, he has darkened the subject; since the more abstract and general his signs are, they must be the better adapted to shew that the inference results from considering them alone, without at all regarding the things which they signify.

CHAP. II.

The design of Aristotle's first Analytics misunderstood.

The *form* of syllogisms may be perfect when there is much imperfection in their *matter*; that is, in the premisses from which the conclusion is derived; and which may be either certain or probable, or only seem to be probable, as a face may seem to be beautiful which is only painted. In his second Analytics, Aristotle treats of what he calls Demonstrative Syllogisms, because their premisses are certain. In his Topics, he treats of what he calls Dialectical Syllogisms, because their premisses are only

His second Analytics.

---

[d] A truly respectable philosopher says, in speaking of this subject, "Aristotle's rules are illustrated, or rather in my opinion purposely darkened, by putting letters of the alphabet for the several terms." Reid's Appendix to Kaims's Sketches, vol. iii. p. 631.

only probable; and, in his Refutations of Sophistry, he treats of those deceitful syllogisms whose premisses seem to be, but which are not really, probable. As sophistry consists, not only in reasoning from false principles, but in reasoning unfairly from principles that are true, the Author refers all such erroneous deductions to one head, which he calls "a mistake of the question;" because, in all of them, the "conclusion or answer" will be found to come out otherwise than it ought to do when drawn agreeably to the rules of just inference [c].

His Topics. The four classes of predicates above explained, Genus, Difference, Property, and Appendage, are applicable to single things or single terms, considered separately; there are other predicates which are applicable only to more things or more terms than one, considered conjunctly. These conjunct predicates the Author reduces to four classes; Agreement, Diversity, Opposition, and Order; under which heads, as well as those first-mentioned, he examines in his Topics all the probable arguments by which our affirmations or negations may be either confirmed or invalidated; thus supplying a vast intellectual magazine, which, when compared with the slender additions made to it by subsequent writers, attests both the unwearied ardour of his application, and the incomparable richness of his invention.

His Organon perverted and misapplied. In as few words as seemed consistent with perspicuity, I have thus endeavoured to explain the nature and design of Aristotle's Organon; a work which has often been as shamefully misrepresented, as it was long most grossly misapplied. In that scholastic jargon, which insolently usurped during many centuries the name

[c] De Sophist. Elench. c. vi. p. 287.

name of Philosophy, syllogisms were perverted to purposes for which their inventor declares them totally unfit, and employed on subjects in which his uniform practice shews that he considered them as altogether useless. Our acquaintance with the properties of things, he perpetually inculcates, must be acquired by patient observation, generalised by comparison and induction; but when this foundation is once laid, the words by which our generalizations are expressed, deserve not merely to be regarded as the materials in which our knowledge is embodied, or the channels by which it is communicated, but to be considered in the two following respects, as the principles or sources from which new knowledge may be derived. First, by means of a skilful arrangement of accurate and well-chosen terms, many processes of reasoning may be performed by discerning the relations and analogies of words, with a certainty as great, and with a rapidity far greater, than these processes could possibly be carried on, were we obliged, in every step of our progress, to fix our attention on things. Every general term is considered by Aristotle as the abridgment of a definition[f], and every definition is denominated by him a Collection[g], because it is the result always of observation and comparison, and often of many observations and many comparisons. The improvements in mathematics have advanced from age to age, chiefly by improving the language, that is, the signs, by which mathematical truths are expressed; and the most important discoveries have been made in that noble science, by continually simplifying the objects of our comparisons; or, in other

Its real uses.
1. As an analytic art.

---

[f] διαφέρει δε ὐδέν, ἐὰν τι σλέω τις φαίη σημαίνειν, μόνον δε ὡρισμένα· τεθείη γαρ αν ὑπ' ἑκάστῳ λόγῳ, ἕτερον ὄνομα. Metaph. l. iv. c. iv. p. 873.

[g] εἰ δε μη τιθέιη, αλλα άπειρα σημαίνειν φαίη, φανερὸν ὅτι οὐκ αν εἴη λόγος. Ibid.

CHAP. II.

other words, by finding clear expressions for ratios, including the results of many others. In all other sciences, this investigation is of the utmost importance; and, in many of them, our knowledge will be found to advance almost exactly in proportion to the success with which our language is improved. When terms, therefore, are formed and applied with that propriety which perpetually shines in the Stagirite's writings, his general formulas of reasoning afford an analytic art, which may be employed as an engine for raising new truths on those previously established; and if modern languages do not afford the same advantage precisely in the same degree, it is not from the inefficacy of words as signs, but from the inefficacy of signs ill chosen and ill arranged; from impropriety of application, contempt of analogy, and abuse of metaphor.

As strengthening the associating principles, and thereby multiplying the energies of thought.

Under another aspect, nearly connected with the former, yet really distinct from it, Aristotle's Analytics, and still more his Topics, have the most direct and most efficacious tendency to invigorate and sharpen the understanding; and even to animate and cherish the seeds of invention and genius. The properties and relations of external objects, whether actually present to the senses, or treasured up in the memory, are confined, both as to their kind and number, within narrow limits. But our abstractions, comparisons, and conclusions respecting those objects, expressed and embodied in words, are of a much wider and almost boundless extent. According to that law of mental action by which our Author proves that the current of thought is moved and regulated [h], the relations and analogies of words

---

[h] See the remarks above made concerning what is commonly called "the association of ideas." "Ideas are more powerfully associated," (to use modern language,) "in proportion to the attention with which they are simultaneously examined and observed."

words, therefore, will appear to form the main spring of intellectual energy; and their connections and dependencies, as compared and classed by Aristotle in his Topics, must have a direct tendency to invigorate and expand the thinking faculty; to revive and brighten those associating bands that might otherwise have been effaced; to suggest those principles of reasoning which would not otherwise occur; and thus to prevent that deception and error which most commonly proceeds from partial and incomplete views of our subject; from weakness of combination, and narrowness of comprehension. To say, therefore, that this part of our Author's Works is conversant entirely about *words*, is not to depreciate or reproach it; for Aristotle well knew that our knowledge of *things* chiefly depending on the proper application of language as an instrument[1] of thought, the true art of reasoning is nothing but a language accurately defined and skilfully arranged; an opinion which, after many idle declamations against his barren generalities and verbal trifling, philosophers have begun very generally to adopt. Let it always, however, be remembered, that the Author who first taught this doctrine, had previously endeavoured to prove that all our notions, as well as the signs by which they are expressed, originate in perceptions of sense; and

observed." In Aristotle's language, the action of thought depends on the attentive examination of things, and of words which are their signs. When not only the things themselves, but the signs expressing them, are thus examined, the connections between these things will take faster hold of the mind; the perception of them will be more vivid, and the recollection of them more easy and more expeditious. But words are the signs not merely of perceptible objects and their qualities, but of the comparisons, abstractions, and conclusions of the mind with respect to those objects and their qualities. An attentive examination of the relations and analogies of words serves, therefore, not only to strengthen old associations, but to produce many new ones.

[1] Topic. l. i. c. 15. Metaph. ubi supra, and l. v. passim.

CHAP. II.

and that the principles on which languages are firſt conſtructed, as well as every ſtep in their progreſs to perfection, all ultimately depend on inductions from obſervation; in one word, on experience merely.

Of Truth Demonſtrative.

To abridge Ariſtotle's Works is to treat them unfairly, becauſe (where his text is correct) no author expreſſes his meaning in fewer or more appropriate words. Yet, as it is the purpoſe of this diſcourſe to afford ſuch ſpecimens of every part of his writings, as may ſatisfy the curioſity of one claſs of readers, while it augments or inſpires that of another, I ſhall collect within a narrow compaſs his obſervations on Truth Demonſtrative, that is, on Science; and follow him in his application of thoſe principles to the loftieſt, and, as commonly treated, the moſt abſtruſe ſcience, that ever exerciſed the human intellect.

All inſtruction, and all intellectual diſcipline, he obſerves, proceeds on principles already known and eſtabliſhed. This is manifeſtly the caſe in mathematics, in the arts, and in every kind of reaſoning, which is univerſally carried on either by ſyllogiſm or by induction; the former proving to us, that a particular propoſition is true, becauſe it is deducible from a general one, already known to us; and the latter demonſtrating a general truth, becauſe it holds in all particular caſes. Orators perſuade by examples or arguments, examples being a rhetorical or coarſer kind of induction, as arguments are a rhetorical or coarſer kind of ſyllogiſm.

Wherein it conſiſts.

Truth is the exact conformity of human conception with the real nature of things[k]. Demonſtrative truth, therefore, can

apply

---

[k] το δι κυριωτατω ως αληθες η ψευδος· τουτο δ' επι των πραγματων εςι συγκεισθαι η διαιρεισθαι . . . . η τα πραγματα ωστι εςι, η ως εςι. Metaph. l. ix. c. x. p. 94. Vid. etiam Metaph. l. v. c. xxix. p. 901.

apply only to those things which necessarily exist after a certain manner, and whose state is unalterable: and we know those things when we know their causes: thus, we know a mathematical proposition, when we know the causes that make it true; that is, when we know all the intermediate propositions up to the first principles, or axioms, on which it is ultimately built. Demonstration cannot be indefinitely extended, because the certainty, and even probability of every kind of reasoning would be destroyed, were we to call in question those first principles which, in matters of science, are recognised by what Aristotle calls Intellect, and in matters of practice by what he calls Common Sense [1].

In demonstration, the premisses are the causes of the conclusion, and therefore prior to it. We cannot, therefore, demonstrate things in a circle, supporting the premisses by the conclusion; because this would be to suppose, that the one proposition could be both prior and posterior to the other. In all demonstration, the first principles must be necessary, immutable, and therefore eternal truths, because those qualities could not belong to the conclusion, unless they belonged to the premisses, which are its causes. An affirmative demonstration is preferable to a negative one, and a direct demonstration of any truth to that drawn from the absurdity of supposing it false; because, other things remaining the same, the shortest demonstration is always the best. Aristotle debates the question, whether an universal demonstration is better than a particular one; and, as his remarks on this subject form an apology for the universality and abstractedness of his own reasonings in many parts of his Works,

[1] ἀλλὰ αἰσθήσεις ἐχ ἡ τῶν ἰδίων. Ethic. Nicom. c. vi. p. 8.

CHAP. II.

Universal and particular; which preferable.

Works, I shall subjoin a translation, or paraphrase, of the whole chapter[m]. "1st, To some a particular demonstration may seem preferable, because we know any object better by examining itself, than by examining the class to which it belongs. Thus, that the three angles of an isosceles triangle are equal to two rights, may be thought more convincing when proved with regard to the isosceles itself, than when proved with regard to triangles in general, to which class of figures the isosceles belongs; and therefore the particular demonstration may appear better than a general one. 2d, If individuals only have a real existence in nature, and every demonstration supposes the existence of its subject, a general demonstration must be worse than a particular one, because it leads us to suppose the existence of nonentities.

The former more informing and more satisfactory.

In answer to these objections let it be remarked, that the first does not apply, because if the property of having the three angles equal to two rights belongs to the isosceles, not as it is an isosceles, but as it is a triangle, he who demonstrates this truth respecting the isosceles only, less examines the object in itself, than he who demonstrates the same truth respecting triangles in general: for the definition of a triangle enters into that of an isosceles; and because it is a triangle, the isosceles has its angles equal to two rights; so that he who demonstrates universally, better shews the cause and reason of the conclusion, than he who demonstrates particularly; and he shews it from considering the object itself, that is, the definition of the object, and that part of the definition from which the conclusion results. Again, if universals are merely words, denoting certain classes or species, to all the individuals of which they equally apply,

---

[m] Analytic Posterior, l. i. c. xxiv. p. 154, &. seq.

apply, there is no reason to say that they are nonentities when applied to those objects or individuals. Their existence is even firmer than that of any *portion* of the individuals signified by them, which is continually liable to corruption or change; whereas the general name denoting the whole species is not liable to either, but has a precise and permanent meaning as long as any objects of that species continue to exist. But to suppose that universals, because they are employed in demonstration, have any existence independently of the objects or individuals which they denote, is a mistake chargeable, not on those who employ such terms, but on those who misconceive their use[n].

The more universal the demonstration of any proposition is rendered, it becomes at the same time the more informing and the

---

[n] Had the learned Lord Monboddo proceeded to read this sentence, perhaps he would not have quoted that immediately preceding it, to prove that Aristotle thought, that "ideas, considered as in the divine mind, have an existence, and an existence more real than particulars, because they are eternal and unchangeable." Monboddo's Ancient Metaphysics, vol. i. p. 470.

Aristotle speaks with great caution concerning the divine mind, nor ever says that any thing exists *in* it. Of ideas or examplars he speaks often, and always contemptuously, as of metaphors and vain flourishes. Analyt. Post. l.i. c. xxii, p. 151. Metaph. l.i. c. vii. p. 853. So that it is plain what he would have thought of the distinction, περι των πολλων, εν τοις πολλοις, επι τοις πολλοις; which was adopted by his followers, and is so much insisted on, as the great doctrine of the Peripatetics, by Lord Monboddo and Mr. Harris. The following passage may be quoted to shew what Aristotle thought of the περι των πολλων, "those eternal examplars." αυτο γαρ ανθρωπον φασιν ειναι, και αυτο ιππον και υγιειαν, αλλο δε ειδ.' παραπλησιον μεν ποιουντες τοις θεοις μεν τισι φασκουσιν αιδ'η. ποιιδεις δε. ατε γαρ εκεινοι ουδεν αλλο εποιουν η α.θρωπος αιδιους, ατε ουτοι τα ειδη αλλα η αισθητα αιδια. "They who maintained the eternal existence of such examplars, as the ideas of man, horse, health, acted exactly like to those who maintained there were Gods, but that the Gods were of a human shape. The Gods of such theologians were nothing more than eternal or incorruptible men; and the ideas of such philosophers nothing more than eternal or incorruptible objects of sense." Metaphys. l. iii. c. xi. p. 861.

the more satisfactory; the more informing, because it comprehends the greater number of particular truths; and the more satisfactory, because it demonstrates these truths from their first and ultimate cause; at least, approximates nearer to this cause in exact proportion to its greater universality. To descend from generals is also more natural; because, in matters of science, they are the source and fountain of particulars. It has also more dignity, because generals are the work of intellect, whereas the more particular propositions are, the more nearly they approach to perceptions of sense, in which, when strictly particular, they ultimately terminate.

Aristotle's Metaphysics

From this part of Aristotle's Logic, there is an easy transition to what has been called his Metaphysics; a name unknown, as above observed, to the Author himself, and given to his most abstract philosophical works by his editors, from an opinion that those books ought to be studied immediately after his Physics, or Treatises on Natural Philosophy. Considered under one particular aspect, those books may be properly thus arranged°; because, as we shall see hereafter, the study of nature, conducted according to Aristotle's principles, necessarily leads to Deity, and to the most delightful of all contemplations, that of the Divine Goodness. But, viewed in the full extent of their relations, Aristotle's Metaphysics are intimately connected with every branch of human science, whether natural or moral, since their real subject (which has been grossly mistaken through a preposterous arrangement of the treatises which they comprise) is the vindication of the existence and nature of truth against the cavils of Sophists, and those now called Metaphysicians;

extend to every branch of human science.

° Topic, l. i. c. 2.

ficians; and this doctrine concerning truth illustrated in the demonstration of the being of one God, in opposition to Atheists on one hand, and Polytheists on the other. The whole of Aristotle's metaphysical works may be referred to one or other of those two heads; since to them the greater part of his treatises relate immediately, and the smaller part will appear to be merely preparatory, to their discussion.

CHAP. II.

The unskilfulness of his editors [p] has placed near the middle of the work, a book plainly preparatory, since it merely exhibits the different acceptation of the terms of which he has occasion afterwards to make use. This fifth book of his Metaphysics, which ought undoubtedly to stand as the first, contains in thirty chapters, an accurate philosophical vocabulary, which Aristotle thought peculiarly requisite as an introduction to the first and most comprehensive [q] of all sciences, that of which truth in general was the subject, since the terms employed in it having necessarily a variety of meanings, it was impossible to use those signs properly, without precisely ascertaining the things which they signified. Wonder and admiration, he observes, are the passions naturally excited by the contemplation of the universe, whose sublime obscurity, while it fixes the attention, inflames the curiosity of man, and makes him ambitious to know and comprehend so interesting and magnificent a spectacle. But it is impossible to know any thing without

Begin with a Philosophical Vocabulary,

---

[p] Dr. Morton of the British Museum, who has long studied the writings of Aristotle with equal diligence and success, first shewed to me, that Samuel Petit, in the fourth book of his *Miscellanea*, had already placed Aristotle's Metaphysics in nearly the same order in which I also had arranged them.

[q] αλλα η μεν γεωμετρια και η αστρολογια περι τινα φυσιν ιδιαν εισιν· εκεινη δε (η πρωτη φιλοσοφια) περι θεολογικη) καθολου πασων κοινη. Metaphys. l. vi. c. i. p. 904.

without knowing its causes and principles. Aristotle, therefore, begins his vocabulary with an explanation of those terms; he observes, that all causes are principles; and defines a principle to be that from which any thing exists, is made, or is known. The notion of a cause always includes that of priority, which is the specific quality belonging to all the different acceptations of the word principle. Aristotle enumerates four kinds of causes, the same word being taken in Greek in four different meanings. 1. The material cause, that is, the matter from which any thing is made; as brass of the statue, and silver of the goblet; and which are evidently causes, since, independently of them, neither the statue nor the goblet could exist. The brass and the silver have also their material causes, namely the substances from which those metals are composed; and in the works both of nature and of art, the first component substances, which are so simple as not to admit of any further resolution, are called Elements. 2. The formal cause, which is that specific form or shape, or quality, most commonly distinguished by sight, which characterises each particular object, and gives to it an appropriate nature and essence. It is from their agreement in the same form or essence, that different objects receive a common name; of which name, this form or essence is therefore the proper definition. In losing their appropriate form, objects lose their name and nature; this form, therefore, is a cause of those objects, since, independently of it, they would not be at all, or would not continue to exist. 3. The efficient cause is the principle of motion or change; or, in other words, the maker; which term sufficiently explains itself. 4. The final cause, that is, the end or purpose for which any thing is made, and, independently of

[Marginalia: CHAP. II. Illustrated in words, cause or principle. The material, formal, efficient, final.]

which end or purpofe, the maker could not have exerted his power or fkill; and therefore his work would never have commenced; that is, the thing made would never have exifted[1]. Of thefe four caufes, the two firft are always inherent in the object caufed: in works of art, the two laft caufes are always feparate from this object; we fhall fee in the fequel, whether this is alfo the cafe with refpect to the works of nature.

Ariftotle's enumeration of the different meanings of the word "caufe," which muft be carefully diftinguifhed in all parts of his philofophy, may ferve as a fpecimen of that book, which was intitled "An Explanation of Words with various Significations." That book is naturally followed by the tenth, which ought therefore to ftand as the fecond; becaufe, in it, words are confidered, not fimply in themfelves, but as ftanding in the relation of oppofition or contrariety to each other. It is briefly intitled "The Selection of Contraries," and treats of one and many; likenefs and unlikenefs; contraries in the fame genus, as "white" and "black;" and contraries which are not in the fame genus, as "corruptible" and "incorruptible." The firft kind of contraries may fubfift at different times in the fame fubject;

The fecond book confiders words as ftanding in oppofition to each other.

---

[1] Juftnefs of thought is infeparably connected with propriety of language. The feveral caufes enumerated by Ariftotle, the names of which found awkwardly in Englifh, were expreffed briefly in Greek, each by a particular prepofition. The material was the ἐξ οὗ; the formal, the καθ' ὅ; the efficient, the ὑφ' οὗ; and the final, the δι' ὅ: befides which, the Greeks indicated the means, or inftrument, by which any thing is done, or made, by διὰ οὗ; and the model after which it was made, by πρὸς ὅ. This model, or exemplar, was confidered as a caufe by the Pythagoreans and Platonifts; the former of whom maintained, that all perceptible things were imitations of *numbers*; and the latter, that they owed their exiftence to the participation of *ideas*: but wherein either this imitation or this participation confifted, thefe philofophers, Ariftotle obferves, omitted to fhew.

CHAP. II.

The third book treats of science.

subject; the second, never can; because the first kind are merely appendages to the subject in which they subsist, and may therefore be separated from it; but the second are essentials[¹].

The second and fourth books treat of truth and science; they ought to be considered as one, and to stand the third in order; since they naturally follow the definitions laid down in the first and second. His treatise on science opens with great modesty. Its difficulty, he observes, arises not merely from the subject, but from ourselves, whose intellectual sight (as happens to the eyes of bats) is blinded by what is brightest. Much thanks are due, not only to those who have established truths worthy of being adopted, but to those also who have given us opinions worthy of being considered. They set our faculties to work; and even their errors are useful to their successors. Had Phrynis never lived, we should not now enjoy the charming melodies of his scholar Timotheus[¹].

Of speculative philosophy, truth is the end; and each object participates of truth more or less, in proportion as it more or less participates of reality. Truth, therefore, is to be found in things eternal and unalterable, rather than in their contraries; because such things are not dependent for their reality on other things, but all others on them.

There cannot be an infinite progression of causes.

There must be some principle or first cause of whatever really exists; for if this were not the case, there would be an infinite progression of causes. But this infinite progression is impossible: 1. With regard to material causes; that flesh, for instance, should be made of earth, earth of air, air of fire; and that to this

[²] Metaphys. l. x. c. ix. and x. p. 951. & seq.   [¹] Metaphys. l. ii. c. i. p. 856.

this series of productions there should be no end. 2. As to the efficient cause or principle of motion; that man, for instance, should be actuated by the air, the air moved by the sun, the sun by strife, in endless succession. 3. As to the final cause; that exercise, for instance, should be taken for the sake of health, and health chosen for the sake of happiness, and happiness itself for the sake of some farther object. 4. As to the formal cause; that the characterising properties of things should be derived one from the other without ultimately terminating in one common source. For in all those four cases alike, to suppose an infinite succession of causes, is to say that things exist without any cause at all; since, in this infinite chain, every link is merely the effect of the link preceding it, and when the chain is endless, there is no first link, and therefore no cause. Were we desired to tell which of three things is the cause of the other two, we should name the first of the three. We could not say the last, for it is the cause of nothing; neither could we say the second, for it is the cause of one thing only; and though considered in relation to that one, it be really a cause; yet considered in relation to the whole, it is merely an effect; and in the same manner all the intermediate links are effects, how numerous soever they may be supposed. The very term "final cause" expresses an end and boundary; and if there was not something ultimately desirable on its own account, for the sake of which other things are desirable as means, all desire and all volition would necessarily cease; and all intellection would be destroyed, if the properties of things could be continually traced up to other properties still more essential; that is, if formal causes might be traced back in infinite progression, there

CHAP. II.

The existence of truth vindicated.

would be no firmness for the intellect to rest on; in other words, no understanding ⁱ.

Democritus had said, that truth either did not exist; or that, by man at least, it was not to be discovered. In the same spirit of scepticism, Protagoras maintained that man was the measure of all things; which were true or false, good or bad, merely according to his conception of them. It is melancholy, Aristotle observes, to hear those who might be expected best to see what is true, since they most sought and loved it, maintain such opinions; because, were they well founded, to aim at philosophy would be to court disappointment, and to pursue truth as puerile a folly as that of attempting to catch birds in their flight. But the misfortune of those philosophers is, that they confine their inquiries merely to sensible and sublunary objects, which from their own nature, as well as that of the senses by which they are perceived, are indefinite and variable, liable to decay and corruption, and continually appearing under different aspects to different men; and even to the same man, according to the point from which he views them, and the actual disposition of his organs. But these variations as to the objects of perception by sense, take place chiefly in sublunary things, the whole mass of which is so inconsiderable in magnitude, that it bears not any proportion to the universe at large, where all is permanent and invariable, and the stability of whose arrangement ought to convince us, that there is an eternal arranging cause ʷ, and some manner at least of firmness and constancy in the

---

ⁱ ἡ νοησις ἐοικεν ηρεμησει τινι και επιςασει, μαλλον η κινησει. De Anim. l. i. c. 3. νοησαι δι ουκ ἐστι μη στασαντα. Metaphys. l. ii. c. ii. p. 857.

ʷ πως γαρ ἐσται ταξις, μη τινος οντος αιδιου, &c. p. 983. Natural. Auscult. l. ii. c. vi. p. 335. and c. iv. p. 332.

the world by which we are furrounded[x]. Even here, it belongs to the eye to judge of colours, to the ear to judge of founds, and to the other fenfes to judge of their refpective objects; and they judge exactly alike, when fimilarly difpofed and fimilarly circumftanced. If fublunary things are generated, and perifh, there muft be fome material caufe from which they are generated; and fomething that exifts immutably, even while the deftruction of one fubftance is the production of another. The fceptics are not convinced by their own arguments. None of them, while in Libya, becaufe he can conceive himfelf in Athens, thinks of walking into the Odeum[y]. They confide more in their eyes, with regard to near than remote objects. As to taftes and colours, they prefer the judgment of perfons in health to thofe of perfons in ficknefs; and when they are themfelves indifpofed, they will have more confidence in the prediction of a phyfician than in that of a perfon ignorant of the healing art. But fenfible objects are neither the whole nor the principal of things. There are, as fhall be proved hereafter, exiftences firm and immoveable, and altogether imperceptible to corporeal organs. That our fenfes do not fhew us things as they really are, is perhaps true, but that there fhould not be fome caufe of our fenfation, exifting independently of the fenfations themfelves, is impoffible; becaufe, whatever is produced by motion fuppofes a moving power[z], which exifts independently, and is prior to the thing moved, in the order of caufality and nature[a].

It

[x] Metaph. l. iv. c. v. p. 879.
[y] The Theatre of Mufic at Athens.   [z] Idem ibid.
[a] The moving power does not infer the exiftence of the thing moved, μη αντιςρεφις κατα την τε ειναι ακολυθησιν, but the latter infers the former. Ariftot. Predicam.

CHAP. II.

It is the misery of the sceptics still vainly to reason, while they destroy the only base on which all solid reasoning must stand. Some of them do this through ignorance, and others through obstinacy. The latter stand in need, not of conviction, but correction, for the opposers of some truths ought to be chastised, not confuted; as those who deny that we ought to reverence the Gods, or to respect our parents. But it is the grossest ignorance not to know, that all truths cannot be demonstrated; for it is impossible that demonstrations should run back to infinity, without stopping at certain principles or first truths, which are called self-evident, because more certain and more necessary in themselves than any arguments that could be produced in proof of them. To deny a first cause, we have already proved, is to deny all causation: to deny axioms, is, for the same reason, to deny all demonstration, and to subvert the principles on which both reasoning and language are built [b]. The very nature of words infers, that the things signified by them, have a certain determinate mode of existence; for words, even the most comprehensive, are nothing else than signs denoting that certain properties are characteristic of certain subjects. How numerous soever these properties may be, provided they be not infinite, they are still capable of being collected under one name; but if the properties were totally indefinite, there could not be any collection. Each term, therefore, affirms something definitely respecting the object which it denotes [c]; and to say with the sceptics, truth is merely apparent, or that the same thing may be both affirmed and denied

---

[b] Metaph. l. iv. c. iv. p. 874.

[c] ὁ γαρ λογος, εν τε ονομα σημαινον, ορισμος γιγνεται τε πραγματος, p. 881.

denied concerning the same object at the same time, is to maintain that it is impossible for man, either to reason within himself, or to discourse with his fellow-creatures [d].

The existence of truth may be evinced, from the various shades of error, which gradually receding from the regions of light, finally darken into perfect obscurity. As truth consists in the agreement of human conception with the nature of things, the brightest truths result from those sciences which treat of things simple and invariable. In this view, arithmetic and geometry have long held the pre-eminence. The geometer abstracts from body heat and cold, hardness, softness, gravity, levity, and all other perceptible contrarieties; and contemplates it only under the two properties of magnitude and continuity; concerning which he demonstrates innumerable affections, ascertaining either the magnitudes themselves, or their proportions to each other. His theorems therefore are more convincing than those of the natural philosopher, whose speculations are more complex [e], as comprehending a greater variety of objects. But there is a science preceding geometry in simplicity as well as dignity; which, instead of contemplating properties and their affections, contemplates being and its

CHAP. II.

The subject continued.

---

[d] δει τοινυν των σωματων εκαστον ειναι γνωριμον, και δηλουν ει τι, και μη πολλα, μονον δε εν και ολιγα σημαινη, φανερον ποιειν εφ' ο φερει τουνομα τουτων· ο δη λεγων ειναι τουτο, και μη ειναι, τουτο ο ολως ειναι φησιν, ου φησιν. ωστε ο σχημαινει τουνομα, τουτο ο φησι σημαινει, p. 984. When it is said that each name should denote one, Aristotle means ἑν, as explained p. 883. τα δε πρωτως λεγομενα εν, ων η ουσια μια· μια δε η συνεχεια η ειδει η λογῳ. That unity is ascribed to things whose substance is one; one in continuity, form, or definition; one in form or appearance, is what our eyes tell us is one; one in definition, is what our reason tells us is one; the specific quality being sometimes visible, sometimes intelligible. See above, p. 66.

[e] ακριβεσταται των επιστημων αι μαλιστα των πρωτων εισιν· αι γαρ εξ ελαττονων ακριβεστεραι των εκ προσθεσεως λεγομενων, οιον αριθμητικη γεωμετριας, &c. p. 842.

CHAP. II.

its properties ᶠ. This science may be juſtly called the firſt philoſophy, and theology: it may be called the firſt philoſophy, becauſe all other ſciences imply it, and borrow from it their principles ᵍ; and it may be called theology, becauſe all the claſſes of being, as quantity, quality, and relation, finally reſt on ſubſtance; and God is the firſt, the one neceſſary and independent ſubſtance, whoſe non-exiſtence implies a contradiction, and from contemplating whoſe nature our knowledge of being and its properties is ultimately derived ʰ.

Ariſtotle's introduction to his hiſtory of the firſt philoſophy, or theology.

Having given to his readers a glimpſe of this ſublime ſubject, our author proceeds in examining the principles of things according to his uſual method; firſt explaining the ſentiments of his predeceſſors in ſcience, before he endeavours to eſtabliſh his own ſyſtem. The book publiſhed as the firſt, and that publiſhed as the third, treat of principles; and together form only one diſcourſe, which ought to ſtand as book the fourth. The elaborate exordium of this book ſeems to account for its being conſidered as the beginning of the whole treatiſe. " That all men," our author obſerves, " are naturally fond of knowledge, is proved from the pleaſure which they univerſally take in the exerciſe of their ſenſes; which exerciſe they love on its own account, independently of any end or uſe. But of all our ſenſes, the ſight is that which we moſt delight to exerciſe, and that independently of its aſſiſtance in the buſineſs of life; for even when we have nothing to do, we prefer this exerciſe to all other employments; the cauſe of which is, that the eye affords to us more knowledge, and makes us acquainted with more of the

---

ᶠ Metaph. l. iv. c. i. p. 869. and Metaph. l. xiii. c. iii. p. 983.
ᵍ Metaph. l. iv. c. ii. p. 871. & ſeq.   ʰ Metaph. l. iv. c. iii. p. 872.

the differences of things, than any of the other senses. All animals are endowed with sensation; but in some only, sensation is followed by memory. Those who are endowed with memory, are susceptible of instruction; and even without instruction, (since incapable of hearing,) attain a wonderful degree of sagacity, as appears in bees, and in some resembling tribes. The powers of hearing and remembering infer the capacity of being taught by instruction as well as by experience; of which capacity inferior animals participate in a small degree, but which in man is exalted into art and science. His experience, also, arises from memory; many particular remembrances combining into our experience. From experience, again, both art and science are derived; art being nothing more than the general result of various experience; as when we observe that a certain medicine is beneficial to Socrates, to Callias, and many others, we infer that it will also be so, to all others labouring under a similar malady. In each particular case, therefore, we can assign a cause why the medicine should be administered; and the man of art is preferred to the mere empiric, because he can thus explain the reasons of his practice, and communicate his skill to others. The practice of the empiric, however, may often be far more successful; and even his skill in the healing art may be far greater; for if his knowledge is derived only from individuals, it is with individuals only he has to do. Arts, therefore, are admired rather for their ingenuity than utility; and the farther they are removed from the common uses of life, our admiration of them is the greater. Such arts, indeed, are the latest in invention; for men must be provided with necessaries and accommodations, before they can attain that freedom of mind which is requisite for

for speculation. The mathematical studies, therefore, first assumed a systematic form among the priests of Egypt, who enjoyed independent leisure. We make these observations to show how men are led from sense and memory to experience; from experience to art, and from practical arts to speculative sciences; till they finally reach the most lofty speculations of all, concerning the first principles of the universe.

The nature and dignity of this science.

The science containing these speculations is called wisdom; and those by whom it is cultivated, are eminently distinguished as the wise. The particulars in which it differs from other sciences are, that it is the most universal, the most difficult, the most accurate; and, merely for its own sake, of all sciences the most desirable. It is the most universal, because the knowledge of first principles is the source of all other knowledge; it is the most difficult, because it is of all sciences the farthest removed from sensation; it is the most accurate, because its object is the most simple, being unaccompanied with any accessaries; as geometry is more simple than physics, and arithmetic than geometry. It is also the most desirable on its own account, since in proportion as men possess all other goods of the mind and body, they become most ambitious of attaining this knowledge; which is coveted, loved, and sought merely for itself, independently of any further end than the pleasure of enjoying it. A freeman, in opposition to a slave, lives for himself, not for another; so this science is of all the most liberal, terminating completely in itself. It may therefore be deemed above the rank of humanity, (since men are naturally slaves to innumerable wants,) and a science fit only for gods; so that if the gods, as the poets say, are capable of envy, this science ought to draw down the divine displeasure on those

who

who cultivate it. But the Divinity cannot possibly be subject to envy; and the poets, even by the common proverb, are acknowledged to be liars. This science, therefore, is most valuable, because, in two respects, the most divine; first, as the Divinity being a cause or principle, is therefore its object; secondly, as the Divinity, to whom the universe is but one great truth, alone fully comprehends it. Although all other sciences are more necessary than this, yet none is better.

With this preface Aristotle introduces his history of what he calls wisdom, theology, and the first philosophy; and then proceeds to show that of the two great schools, the Ionian and the Italic, the philosophers of the former were attentive solely to gross material causes, whereas those of the latter wandered in the chimerical regions of ideas and numbers; substituting for the real causes of things metaphysical abstractions, which were the mere creatures of their own intellect. The materialists differed widely from each other. Thales maintained water to be the first principle of things; probably, as our Author says, observing that the nourishment, as well as the seeds, of most natural objects are moist; and that heat, perhaps life, is produced by fermentation. He might also allege the opinions of divines and poets long before his own age, who considered Oceanus and Tethys as the fathers of generation; and who make the gods swear by Styx, that is by water, as the most to be revered of all things, because the most ancient. Anaximenes and Diogenes perceived that water might be resolved into air; and therefore maintained air to be the original principle of bodies. The cause of fire was defended by Hippasus and Heracleitus, who saw all things expanded, animated, and revived by heat; and differing from each other in proportion as they

CHAP. II.

participated of the different degrees of the caloric, from the extreme of condensation to that of rarefaction. Empedocles considering all these three substances as principles, added to them earth as a fourth principle; and called these four the elements, because he supposed that all things were composed of them, that all things might be resolved into them, and that they themselves were simple, indestructible, and totally incapable of farther resolution[1]. Anaxagoras introduced the obscure doctrine of the omæomeria, or the production of bodies from indefinitely small organic particles, exactly resembling the bodies themselves; and therefore maintained principles to be infinite.

In this investigation, which respected only the material cause, philosophers were naturally led to inquire what made these principles or elements (whether one, many, or infinite) change their actual state. In works of art, they perceived that the materials were totally inactive; that the iron did not make itself into a saw, nor the brass into a statue. To answer this question, some maintained, contrary to experience, that all things were one, and unalterable. Others ascribed an active power to fire, which produced all the changes which we behold, by its operation on the other elements. But of the order and beauty which prevail in the universe, neither fire nor any similar substance could be suspected of being the cause; nor was it possible that such regular effects should result from blind chance. Philosophers were again compelled therefore, by the force of truth itself, to look for some higher principle; when one, far wiser than the rest, like a sober man among drunken babblers, pronounced mind to be the primary cause of the

[1] Metaph. lib. i. c. iv. p. 844, & seq.

the beauty and harmony of the universe. This opinion was asserted in plain language by Anaxagoras of Clazomene; but the first author of it was his countryman Hermotimus[k]. Yet Anaxagoras himself, though he employs mind as a machine for making the world, introduces it, however, only when compelled by necessity; and prefers having recourse rather to every other cause in explaining the phænomena of nature[l].

CHAP. II.

We shall not follow Aristotle further in examining the tenets of the Ionian school; much less are we inclined to enter into his sixth, seventh, and eleventh books; where he examines, with a degree of attention, of which the subject would now appear totally unworthy, the *numbers* of Pythagoras, and the *ideas* of Plato; those intellectual abstractions which the wildness of philosophy had converted into the primary causes of the universe; thus substituting shadows for realities. These three books properly constitute one, which ought to stand as the fifth, and be intitled, Concerning Ideas or Universals considered as Causes of the Universe.

Fifth book, concerning ideas as causes of the universe.

In his eighth book, he explains his own doctrine concerning natural philosophy; that is, concerning things liable to motion or change; which subject is treated more fully in his eight books of Physicks, and in his treatise concerning Generation and Corruption. This eighth book ought therefore to stand as the sixth. The seventh book, which is now printed as the ninth, treats of Energy; a word, as we shall see, of mighty import in the Aristotelian philosophy; from the explanation of which he naturally passes to the three concluding books of his Metaphysics, the thirteenth, fourteenth, and twelfth, which treat of a being totally distinct from matter; necessary, eternal, infinite in

The proper arrangement of the five remaining books.

---

[k] Metaph. l. i. c. iii. p. 844. [l] Ibid. l. i. c. iv. p. 844.

CHAP. II.

in perfection; one substantially and numerically, the primary cause of motion, himself immoveable[m]. These three last books, which ought to stand as the eighth, ninth, and tenth of what is now called his Metaphysics, are intitled, by Aristotle himself, his Works concerning Philosophy[n]; meaning thereby, as he elsewhere explains it, the first philosophy or theology[o].

Aristotle's natural philosophy.

In travelling over the vast space which still lies before us, we shall follow the order prescribed by our Author; beginning therefore with the Philosophy of Nature, which is treated in various parts of his works, where the same doctrines are repeated nearly in the same words. In his Analysis of Material Objects, his researches penetrate far beyond those vulgar and spurious elements, first proposed by Empedocles, earth, water, fire, and air; which are so far from being simple and unalterable, that they may be converted with great facility, and are in fact perpetually changing the one into the other[p]. But, in relation to human perception, Empedocles' division is not without merit; since the sense of touch, the most sure and scientific of all our senses, acquaints us with only four different qualities of bodies, distinguished by the names hot, cold, moist, and dry. Aristotle endeavours to prove, by induction, that all other differences perceived by the touch, resolve themselves into these four; whereas no one of these four can be resolved into any of the other three.

His analysis of the supposed elements.

The qualities, therefore, above mentioned, may be regarded as the fittest for distinguishing the different kinds of bodies from each other; and these four qualities, in their most simple combination with each other, will thus form the characteristics [q] of the elements

---

[m] ἐν μὲν ἄρα καὶ λόγῳ καὶ ἀριθμῷ, τὸ πρῶτον κινοῦν ἀκίνητον ἐστ. See p. 1001 and 1003.

[n] Ethic. Eadem, l. i. c. viii.   [o] Metaphysics, l. vi. c. i. p. 904.

[p] Degenerat. & Corrupt. l. ii. c. iii. p. 517.   [q] Ibid. p. 515, 516.

elements as discovered by the sense of touch. But these qualities combined by two, that is, in the manner the most simple, form only four combinations. The elements, therefore, are four. The combination of coldness with dryness is called earth; of coldness with humidity, water; of heat with dryness, fire; of heat with humidity, air. Those elements are most easily convertible, which have one quality in common. Thus water is changed into air, when the quality of cold is destroyed by the caloric [r]. What was before water has now the two characteristics of air, viz. humidity and heat; and, when the latter is added in due proportion, the water evaporates, and mounts to the sky, where it remains, until a new cause again deprives the air of its heat, and makes it fall to the ground in rain. In the same manner, fire may be converted into air, and air into fire; for fire is warm and dry, and air is warm and moist; and the element will therefore be denominated either fire or air, according to the prevalence of the dryness or humidity. Water, too, will be easily converted into earth; since both being cold, but the former moist, and the latter dry, the moisture need only to be overcome by the dryness to make water earth; and dryness need only to be overcome by moisture to make earth water. When the elements possess not any common quality, their transmutation is more slow and difficult. To make water into fire, it is necessary that both its cold and its moisture should be overcome by the contrary principles of heat and dryness; and to make air into earth, or earth into air, the two characteristic qualities of both elements must also be changed. These changes, however, are continually happening around us; the air being first converted into

Their continual transmutations.

[r] More properly calorific. Το θερμαντικοι—Το δε δυναμενον θερμον ειναι, παροντος τα θερμαντι κα και πλησιαζοντος, αναγκη θερμαινσθαι. "What has the capacity of receiving heat, must be heated by the approach and presence of the caloric." P. 508.

CHAP. II.

into water, and the water into earth. Fire alfo is vifibly generated; for flame, which is a fpecies of fire, confifts of nothing but burning fmoke, which itfelf is compofed of air and earth[s].

The perpetual changes of the elements and their compounds produce the ever-varying fpectacle which we behold around us, and are themfelves produced by the revolutions of the heavenly bodies acting in concert with thofe laws of motion which God has impreffed on his lower works[t]. Earth naturally tends to the centre of the univerfe; water rifes above earth; air above water; and fire above air. A gravitating principle, therefore, belongs properly to earth; and an anti-gravitating, to fire; which always feeks the extremities; and is therefore the great minifter of the Almighty in moulding the forms of things[u]. The intermediate elements of air and water have only a relative gravity, being heavier than fire, and lighter than earth[w]; and this relative gravity difappears when they are either in, or below, their proper place[x]: yet that air itfelf is heavy, appears evidently from this, that a bladder filled with air is heavier than when it was void of that element[y].

From

[s] De Generat. et Corrupt. l. ii. c. iv. p. 518.

[t] συμπληρωσι το ιδοι ο θεος εντελιχεια ποιησας την γενεσιν· ουτω γαρ μαλιστα συνειροιτο το ειναι, διο το εγγιστατω ειναι της ουσιας το γιγνεσθαι αει την γενεσιν. Ibid. p. 525.

[u] De Generat. & Corrupt. l. ii. c. viii. p. 523.

[w] De Cœlo, l. i. c. viii. p. 444.   [x] De Cœlo, p. 490. et feq.

[y] De Cœlo, l. iv. c. iv. p. 490. The brevity of the expreffion renders it doubtful whether the experiment was made by exhaufting or by accumulating the air. While writing this paffage, a book fell in my way of a very eminent profeffor, Dr. Adam Smith, in which I met with the following paffage: "Thofe facts and experiments, which demonftrate the weight of the air, and which no fuperior fagacity, but chance alone, prefented to the moderns, were altogether unknown to them (the ancients before the time of Archimedes)." Smith's Effays on Philofophical Subjects, p. 101.

From the active principles of heat and cold, and the paffive ones of dryness and humidity, the denfity, rarity, hardnefs, foftnefs, tenacity, friability, in one word, all the mixed properties of bodies are derived[b]; and from them are compounded the higheft meteors of heaven[c], as well as the metals and minerals in the bofom of the earth[d]. The hardeft of thofe foffils are produced from dry exhalations or humid vapours; which are the material caufes of thofe permanent fubftances, and the efficient caufes of the moft tremendous convulfions; for the earthquakes are not caufed, as Democritus fufpected, merely by the agency of water burfting the too narrow caverns in which it had been accumulated and pent up, but by the agency of heat, which, converting this water into vapour, gives to it a power of overthrowing the weightieft mountains which refift its expanfion[e].

Ariftotle's doctrine concerning the tranfmutation of the elements, vulgarly fo called, (a doctrine long held vifionary by his pretended followers,) is countenanced by recent experiments[f], which

CHAP. II.

The immediate caufes of the mixed properties of bodies, and of natural phænomena.

Refutation of the doctrine of atoms.

---

[a] Meteor. l. iv. c. i. p. 584.
[b] De Generat. & Corrupt. p. 515.
[d] De Meteor. l. iii. c. vi. p. 583.
[c] Ibid.
[e] De Meteor. l. ii. c. iv. p. 558.
[e] Ibid. p. 566. & feq.

[f] I have juft read a fmall German volume, intitled, "Antiphlogiftifche Chemie," by Johann. And. Scherer, Vienna, 1792, 8vo. which is written with the purpofe of proving, that the moft important of the difcoveries which have eftablifhed the antiphlogiftic fyftem, called on the Continent the fyftem of Lavoifier, had been made by our countryman Mayow upwards of an hundred years ago. This wonderful young man, for he died at the age of 34, was acquainted (as his words are quoted by Scherer) with the compofition of the atmofphere; the nature of what is now called vital or dephlogifticated air; the origin and common nature of acids; the doctrines of combuftion, fermentation, refpiration, &c. as explained by Lavoifier, and other authors of the antiphlogiftic fyftem of chemiftry. Scherer makes the comparifon with great fairnefs, ftating the modern doctrines in his own German text, and placing Mayow's Latin in notes at the bottom of the page, from an edition of his works publifhed at the Hague

which show that water may be resolved into different gases, or airs; that atmospheric air itself is capable of resolution; and that the most subtile fluids enter into the composition of solid bodies, which may again, by the agency of the calorific, be changed into fluids. But our Author did not rest satisfied with any discoveries that mere experiment could make, nor with any analogical deductions from such discoveries, of which the most celebrated was the System of Atoms, as explained by Democritus. That philosopher, whom Aristotle often cites and refutes, but on whom he bestows the just praise of unextinguishable curiosity and indefatigable industry[a], thought it an invincible argument in favour of his atoms, that if body was infinitely divisible, it would finally vanish into nothing. Aristotle denies both the position and the inference. The error of Democritus, he observes, arose from thinking, that, because a body might be divided *any where*, it might therefore be divided *every where*. In a line, a point may be taken *any where*, but points cannot be taken *every where*, because one point cannot be contiguous to another[b]. Bodies, therefore, cannot actually be divided to infinity, and therefore cannot vanish into nothing; but as the minutest

in 1681, intitled, " Johannis Mayow, Londinensis, &c. Opera omnia Medico-Physica." Mayow was born in London in 1645, where he died in 1679. He was a Fellow of All Souls College, Oxford. In 1668 he published there " Tractatus duo de Respiratione & de Rachitide;" and, in 1674, he published the same five Treatises, which were afterwards republished at the Hague. This work contains, besides the two tracts above mentioned, I. " Tractatus de Sal-nitro et Spiritu Nitro Aerio," (which he calls Spiritus Vitalis Igneus, p. 1. and Aer Purus Vitalis, p. 281, the name which is likely to prevail.) II. " De Respiratione Foetus in Utero." III. " De Motu Musculorum & Spiritibus Animalibus."

[a] ὄντος δὲ Δημόκριτος ἰσικε μὲν περὶ ἁπάντων φροντίσαι, p. 494. De Generat. & Corrupt. p. 2.

[b] De Gener. & Corrupt. l. i. c. ii. p. 497.

minutest particle still possesses all the properties of body, it is still capable of division, and therefore not an atom [i].

According to our universal experience respecting the vicissitudes of sublunary things, our Author observes, that there are no realisings of non-entity, and no absolute reductions of existence into nothing. These vicissitudes or changes may all be reduced to the four following [k]: 1. A change of place, called lation, the first and most simple species of change, which is implied in all the three following kinds. 2. A change of quantity, which must consist either in augmentation or in diminution. 3. A change of quality, called alteration; as from hard to soft, from health to sickness. 4. A change in substance, which consists in generation and corruption [l]; and which is sufficiently exemplified in what is above observed concerning the transmutations of the elements. When any regularly organized object changes its place, its quantity, or its quality, the object itself, it is plain, still remains the same essentially, though altered in its accessories. But when it changes in substance, that is in the unknown cause from which all its preceptible qualities proceed, is there reason to believe that the continuity of existence is broken, and that one thing is totally annihilated, and another actually created? Aristotle thinks not; and that in this change, as well as in every other, there is something that departs, something that accedes, and

something

CHAP. II.

Of change, and its different species.

Lation.

Change as to quantity.

Alteration.

Generation and corruption.

---

[i] The obscurity of this passage will be removed, by considering what he afterwards proves, that our notion of infinity is entirely negative; and that to suppose body actually divided to infinity, implies a contradiction, κατα ενεργειαν μεν ελη ετι απειρη, δυναμει δε επι την διαιρεσιν. Ibid. p. 499.

[k] De Generation. & Corrupt. l. i. c. xxxiv. p. 493. &. seq. & Physic. Auscu'lt. l. iii. c. i. p. 340.

[l] Idem ibid.

CHAP. II.

The first matter.

something that still remains; a something, indeed, that escapes sense, and even eludes fancy, but of which we get a glimpse [m] from reason, as of a shadowy and obscure existence, susceptible of all qualities, but unendowed with any. What iron is to the saw, or marble to the statue, precisely the same is this *first matter* to all the natural productions which diversify and adorn the earth. It possesses not in itself any characteristic or essentiating quality; never existing therefore apart; but before it quits one form, constantly assuming another [n]. As the secondary elements, and all the compounds formed of them, are moulded into works of art by the hand of man, that instrument of instruments, to which human nature owes so much of its accommodation and comfort, so this primary element is moulded by the hand of God into what are called the works of nature; none of which exist in a rude chaotic state, but of which each is distinguished by its peculiar characteristic; and all admirably adapted

---

[m] ἐξ ἁπάντων τῶν γιγνομένων τοῦτο ἐστι λαβεῖν, ἂν τις ἐπιβλέπῃ, ὥσπερ λέγομεν, ὅτι δεῖ ἀεί τι ὑποκεῖσθαι τὸ γιγνόμενον. Natural. Auscult. l. i. c. viii. p. 324.

[n] ἡμεῖς δὲ φαμὲν ὕλην τινὰ τῶν σωμάτων τῶν αἰσθητῶν, ἀλλὰ ταύτην ἢ χωριστὴν, ἀλλὰ ἀεὶ μετ' ἐναντιώσεως, ἐξ ἧς γίνεται τὰ καλούμενα στοιχεῖα... ἢ γὰρ τὸ θερμὸν ὕλη τῷ ψυχρῷ, ἢδὲ τοῦτο τῷ θερμῷ· ἀλλὰ τὸ ὑποκείμενον ἀμφοῖν. ὥςτε πρῶτον μὲν τὸ δυνάμει σῶμα αἰσθητὸν ἀρχὴ δεύτερον δὲ, αἱ ἐναντιώσεις· λέγω δὲ οἷον θερμότης καὶ ψυχρότης· τρίτον δὲ ἤδη πῦρ καὶ ὕδωρ. ταῦτα μὲν γὰρ μεταβάλλει εἰς ἄλληλα· αἱ δὲ ἐναντιώσεις, ἢ μεταβάλλουσι. De Generat. & Corrupt. l. ii. c. i. p. 515. "We say that perceptible bodies have for their principle a certain stuff or matter, which exists not separately, but is always endowed with some one of the contraries, hot or cold, moist or dry; and from these two, matter and one of the contraries, the elements are composed. For heat supplies not the materials for cold, nor cold for heat; but there is a certain subject susceptible of either of these contraries. So that this subject-matter is the first constituent principle, or element of perceptible bodies; the second, the contraries of which this matter is susceptible; the third, the compound elements of fire, water, &c.; which, as we have said, change into each other; but the contraries do not so change." See also De Generat. & Corrupt. l. i. c. 6.

adapted to anſwer their reſpective ends. This peculiar characteriſtic, by which objects are diſtinguiſhed, Ariſtotle calls their appearance or form, becauſe the ſight, of all our ſenſes, is that which gives us moſt information concerning the differences of things.

CHAP. II.

Works of art are eaſily diſtinguiſhed by their outward ſhape; but the primary form of phyſical productions lies within; for all their ſenſible differences reſult from that internal principle determining their motion to or from a certain ſtate, and of reſt during a certain time in that ſtate; which principle is called their nature. Of this nature we ſee, for example, the effects in plants, when they fix their roots in the earth, rear their ſtems, expand their leaves, and ſcatter their ſeeds; which operations, were theſe organiſed bodies endowed with intelligence, could not be more ſkilfully performed for the preſervation of the individual, and the propagation of the kind[o]. Plants, therefore, act,

What is meant by the works of nature.

---

[o] Natur. Auſcult. l. ii. c. viii. p. 336. &. ſeq ατοπον δε το μη οιεσθαι ενεκα τυ γινεσθαι εαν μη ιδωσι το κινυν βυλιυσαμενον· και τοι και η τεχνη ε βυλιυεται· και γαρ ει ενην εν τω ξολω η ναυπηγικη, ομοιως αν τη φυσει εποιει· ωςε ει εν τη τεχνη ενεςι η ενεκα τυ, και εν τη φυσει ενεςι. μαλιςα δε δηλον, οταν τις ιατρευη αυτος εαυτον· τυτω γαρ εοικεν η φυσις. Ibid. p. 338. "It is abſurd to think, that becauſe we do not ſee the moving principle actually deliberating, that it therefore acts at random, and not with an end in view. Art, then, we muſt ſay, acts at random; for if the art of ſhip-building was in wood, it would not act more judiciouſly *for making a ſhip*, than nature *does for nouriſhing, preſerving, and propagating a tree*. If there is deſign in art, there muſt alſo be deſign in nature. This is moſt plain when a man, being a phyſician, cures himſelf. Nature acts like this man. But nature, as well as art, ſometimes acts beſide or beyond her intention; and ſometimes fails in the execution of her own purpoſes. De Republica. l. i. c. vi. p. 302. By the compound word αυτοματον, (οταν αυτο ματεν γενηται,) Ariſtotle expreſſes nature effecting either more or leſs than the ſpecific ends or purpoſes to which her reſpective operations invariably tend. Natural. Auſcult. l. ii. c. vi. p. 335. This, he obſerves, happens through the concurrence or acceſſion of cauſes or circumſtances, (indefinite in number, ſince things innumerable may accede

CHAP. II.

act, not indeed with, but by intelligence, in consequence of that nature or form which they have received from the first cause of motion and order[p]. The constituent principles of things, therefore, are matter and form; and in all the changes which they undergo, there is a form which departs, a form which accedes, and a substance which remains, namely the first matter. Unless this doctrine is admitted, the continuity of existence would, in this lower world, be perpetually interrupted; each destruction would be an annihilation, and each production an evocation of non-entity into existence. The first matter being totally inactive, all change must proceed from matter endowed with form. But things exactly similar cannot produce any change on each other, because having all properties in common,

to the same thing, and causes innumerable may concur with the same cause; Natural. Auscult. l. ii. c. iii. p. 331.) vitiating Nature's operations and deforming her works. Nature operating κατα συμβεβηκος, and thereby producing effects not in her intention, is called αυτοματον, or chance; and art operating κατα συμβεβηκος, and producing effects not in her intention, is called τυχη, or fortune. Chance, or fortune, therefore, cannot have any existence independently of intention or design. Aristotle, therefore, concludes sublimely, that " if the heavens themselves were the work of chance, this would only prove that intelligence had been the cause of many still nobler works, and was the cause of the universe itself." Natural. Auscult. l. ii. c. vi. p. 335. Chance and fortune, therefore, are merely abridged expressions to denote nature and art producing unintentional and therefore unusual effects. Comp. Natural. Auscult. l. ii. c. iv. v. vi.; Metaph. l. v. c. xxx. and l. vi. c. ii. Ethic. Nichom. l. vi. c. iv. Magn. Moral. l. ii. c. vii. How unjustly is our Author treated by modern writers, (vid. Brucker. Histor. Philosoph. in Aristotel. passim, & Voyage du Jeune Anacharsis, vol. v. c. lxiv. p. 349.) when they arraign his impiety, on account of his doctrine of chance and fortune! Our inimitable Poet far better expresses the sense of his philosophy:

    Shall burning Ætna, if a sage requires,
    Forget to thunder, and recall her fires.
                          Ethic. Epist. iv. ver. 123, & seq.

[p] Τω χρονω αιει προλαμβανει ενεργεια ετερα προ ετερας εως της του αει κινουντος πρωτως. " There is a continual progression of efficient moving principles up to the first mover." Metaph. l. ix. c. viii. p. 939.

common, the one cannot communicate any thing to the other, nor act on that other any more than on itself[q]. Neither do things disparate, that is, totally dissimilar, admit of any reciprocal action. Whiteness has no action on straightness, any more than hardness has on bitterness; because neither of those qualities tends to exclude the qualities to which they are respectively opposed; and both the whiteness and straightness, as well as the hardness and bitterness, may subsist harmoniously in the same subject. By the accession of whiteness, therefore, the subject is not altered as to its straightness, nor by the accession of any one quality is it altered as to any other quality totally dissimilar to the former. To effect this alteration or change, the qualities or forms must be incapable of remaining in the same subject, which no sooner admits the one, than it rejects the other. But this is the nature of what are called contraries, heat and cold, moist and dry, black and white, straightness and crookedness, order and confusion; and of all those things which belong to one common genus, but are of a different species, that is, as formerly explained, which are similar in one respect[r], and dissimilar in another. By the reciprocal actions and sufferings of those contraries, in their utmost extremes and their intermediate states, all the changes are effected which we behold in the world around us. One flavour destroys

CHAP. II.

How her operations are performed.

Contraries.

---

[q] ὑπὸ ἀλλήλων γὰρ παθεῖν ταναντία ἀδυνατον. Natural. Auscult. p. 325. De General. & Corrupt. l. i. c. vii. p. 506. The subject in which the contraries inhere is properly acted upon, and changed from the one contrary to the other; from cold to hot, white to black. When Aristotle speaks of the actions and passions of forms, qualities, or contraries, he always supposes them clothed with matter. Ibid.

[r] The materials of white, black; order, confusion, &c. are the same. ετι δη των οντων τα μεν ποιητικα, τα δε υπο τουτων παθετικα. τα μεν εν αντιστρεφει, ὁσοις ἡ αυτη ὑλη εστι, και ποιητικη αλληλων, και παθητικη υπο αλληλων. De Generat. & Corrupt. l. i. c. x. p. 507.

CHAP. II.

Form, and privation.

destroys a flavour that is contrary to it, one colour its contrary, and complexly one body acts on a body endowed with many contrary qualities. Aristotle claims not for his own discovery, that contraries are the elements of generation and corruption, and of all the lesser changes observable in material objects. That doctrine, he observes, was first established by the school of Pythagoras [o], which arranged contraries into two classes; the better, and the worse: as light, darkness; good, evil; finite, infinite: and thenceforth adopted by all philosophers, compelled thereto by the force of truth [t]. One of these contraries, it was observed, departs as soon as the other accedes; three things, therefore, are concerned in every mutation or change, the matter which still remains one and the same; the contrary which accedes, called in general form; and the contrary which departs, which Aristotle calls in general privation [u]. This term, like many others employed by our author, is merely a sign to mark a thing indefinite and unknown; for the contrary which accedes, or, in other words, the characterising quality, is something certain and definite; but the form which departed in order to make room for this characterising quality, and without the departure of which the change could not have been effected, is, in a great measure, uncertain and indefinite: thus there is but one form of health, and innumerable forms of sickness; one form of order, innumerable forms of confusion; or in things more simple, each body has its definite colour or colours; but it may have been changed to any of these colours, for instance,

[o] οἱ δὲ Πυθαγορειοι, και ποσαι και τινες αἱ εναντιωσεις, απεφηναντο, &c. Metaphys. l. i. c. v. p. 846.

[t] Natural. Auscult. l. i. c. v.

[u] Ibid. l. i. c. viii. p. 325. των εναντιων ἡ ἑτερα ευτυχια στερησις. Aristot. Metaph. passim.

instance, to black, either from its contrary white, or from any of the intermediate shades between those opposite extremes [*].

In the changes which material substances undergo, they reciprocally act on each other; in other words, both substances are agents, and both patients. This is illustrated by what happens in mixture; which, according to Aristotle, consists in this, that two substances, acting on each other, produce a third substance specifically different from either; and of which each, the minutest part, is specifically different from each, the minutest part, of either of the composing ingredients. Leucippus and Democritus, the fathers of the mechanical philosophy, endeavoured to explain mixture as well as all other natural appearances by atoms and a vacuum, commensurate pores, the motions, figures, and positions of the minute particles of matter. But Aristotle justly observes, that if mixture depended merely on mechanical causes, there would be no such thing to the keen sight of Lynceus, which could always distinguish these composing ingredients, how minutely soever they were subdivided, from each other; and easily perceive that what, to our obtuse senses, appeared to be the production of a new substance, was nothing more

---

[*] Natural. Auscult. l. i. c. vi. p. 331. Aristotle maintained a definite number of colours against the atomic philosophers, who made them depend on the indefinite variety of the figures and dispositions of minute corpuscles, τα δε τα χρωματα εν ωρισμα και εκ παντος. De Sensu & Sensili, c. iii. p. 667. He considered colours also as bearing the same relation to light, which sharpness and flatness do to sound: ἔστι γαρ και ϕως εν αυται τα χρωματα; εστι δη και ωσπερ το οξυ και το βαρυ. De Anima, l. ii. c. viii p. 641. How strangely were his doctrines perverted by the scholastics! And how nearly did they in themselves approach to inductions from experiments with which he was not acquainted!

CHAP. II.

Transition to his theology.

more than the minute subdivision and new arrangement of two old ones [x].

The form, species, or light.

Substances endowed with different characterising qualities, in other words, different forms which have the same matter, are fitted for reciprocally acting on each other. But there is a higher order of forms, which act, without suffering; and of which, the highest of all must *necessarily* be impassive. A patient is said, with equal propriety, to be cured, either by the physician's skill, or by the medicines prescribed. The medicines, while they act, are also acted upon; are warmed, cooled, or undergo some such alteration. But the physician's skill suffers nothing from the effect produced on the patient; and by this comparison, Aristotle says we may conceive why, of substances not immerged in the same matter, the one may produce a change on the other, without being reciprocally affected by it.

To know physical objects is to know their causes; the efficient and final, which are principles external to those objects; and the material and formal, which, existing in the objects themselves, are the elements into which they must intellectually be resolved. The formal cause is that by which each object is characterised and distinguished; and from which, as from a perennial and abundant spring, its sensible qualities, as well as latent powers, perpetually flow. Aristotle did not think that, in the present state of our existence, we could remount to this fruitful source, and behold things as they are [y]; but in all his inquiries it is constantly his endeavour to approximate as nearly as possible to

---

[x] De Generat. & Corrupt. l. i. c. x. p. 507. Aristotle illustrates his doctrine by observations on the mixture of metals, one of which is noticed by my ingenious friend Dr. Pearson. See Philosoph. Transf. for the year 1796, p. 432.

[y] Metaph. l. ii. c. i. p. 856.

to this *species*, *form*, or *sight*, which words he often employs merely as signs for things sought; and to discover in each object that essentiating characteristic, whether substance or property, on which its perceptible qualities depend[a]. Familiar with the correct geometry of his times, he discerned the concatenation of truths, which being linked indissolubly together, unite the most distant and seemingly unconnected extremes. Of each object he investigates the true definition; and of each science, the *principal* theorem; because the foundation and bond of union of its parts; justly thinking, that the variety of our apparent knowledge is often the proof of our real ignorance; and that true science improves in proportion as many particular propositions resolve themselves into one general truth. Under the influence of this generalising spirit, the true spirit of philosophy, he is carried sometimes beyond the bounds prescribed to the human intellect; but his errors are always those of a man of genius; and what adventurer in science ever successfully contended in the field of truth, without sometimes being tempted to launch on the ocean of conjecture?

Nothing in nature, he observes, exists in a totally crude and absolutely unorganised state; but it is the inward organization, or invisible form, which moulds the external shape of bodies; and imposes on the motion, producing their various figures and appearances,

---

[a] Metaphys. l. vii. c. ii, xi, xiii. It is worthy of remark, that Aristotle did precisely that which he is blamed by Bacon, Hobbes, Malbranche, &c. for not doing; and declared it impossible to do that which he is blamed for having attempted. By examining, comparing, and classing the perceptible qualities of things, he endeavoured to make them known by a definition, affirming this examination to be the only method by which they could be known and defined. ... Ibid.

CHAP. II.

appearances, the laws and limits of its action. In exerting this inherent power of forms, fire seems to be their principal minister^a; for fire, the most subtile of material principles, and of which light seems to be a modification^b, always diffuses itself through bodies, and seeks their extremities, by which their outward conformation is delineated and defined. There are forms of a peculiar nature, as we shall prove hereafter, that seem to be totally separable from matter, because they are capable of energies and pleasures totally unrelated to any of its properties; but the forms of most physical objects are inseparably combined with the material principle, because independently of it, they would not answer any possible end. Of what use would be the nutritive power of plants, were there not some material substance to be nourished? To what purpose would serve the fierce instincts of the lion, separated from his fangs, his paws, and his brawny members? It is highly unreasonable, therefore, to believe the Pythagorean and Platonic doctrine concerning the separate existence of those substantial forms^c; and not less unreasonable to admit the opinion so strongly inculcated by some poets and philosophers, that such forms migrate from one body to another^d.

In

---

^a De Part. Animal. l. ii. c. vii. p. 986.

^b πυρος η τοιαυτη τινος παρουσια ιν τη διαφανει. De Anima, l. ii. c. vii. p. 638.

^c Natural. Auscult. l. ii. c. ii. p. 329.

^d De Anima, l. i. c. iii. p. 624. It is pleasant to find Hobbes, in the 4th chapter of his Leviathan, and in many other parts of his works, combating, under the name of Aristotle's philosophy, abstract essences, substantial forms, and innumerable other doctrines, metaphysical as well as moral and political, with nearly the same arguments by which Aristotle, their supposed author, had long before victoriously refuted them. Malbranche and the French philosophers in general treat the Stagyrite with not less unfairness, and speak of his opinions with not less ignorance. I scarcely except Rapin,

In the language of Aristotle, the word "nature" is confined to that part of the universe situate within the lunar sphere; which, according to a philosophy preceding his own times, was regarded as the intermediate isthmus separating terrestrial and perishing, from celestial and immortal, things[e]. In its primitive and proper sense, nature peculiarly applies to this lower world, which is the region of perpetual change, and in which all things are continually fluctuating between the extremes of generation and corruption; whereas the heavenly bodies, whether originally created, or the eternal production of an eternal cause[f], appear, as far as our experience reaches, to perform their unwearied motions exempted from the vicissitudes of renovation or decay. Every thing therefore in nature, that is, in this lower world, may be conceived as existing in two different states; so called, though variable, because relatively more stable than the other changes to which they are liable. The first state of their existence, both absolutely[g], and in the order of human conception,

CHAP. II.

The state of capacity and energy between which all objects in it fluctuate.

Rapin, whose account of Aristotle, hitherto regarded as the best, is disgraced by great inaccuracies. It is not easy to conceive how a writer, who had not acquired his notion of Aristotle's writings at second hand, should so totally mistake their aim as Rapin does in speaking of the Ethics to Eudemus. See Comparaison de Platon & Aristotle, p. 345. Edit. Amsterdam. 1686.

[e] Gale's Opuscula Mythol. p. 516.

[f] ὥστε τὸ τῇ γενέσει ὕστερον, τῇ φύσει πρότερον εἶναι. Natural. Auscult. l. viii. c. x. p. 422.: and we shall see hereafter that things existing in capacity must proceed universally from things existing in energy.

[g] No tenet of the Peripatetic philosophy is thought more clearly ascertained than the eternity of the world; and this tenet, I believe, is universally ascribed to Aristotle by all writers whatever, both ancient and modern. The brevity and energy of our author's style, often gives to him indeed the appearance of dogmatising where he is only investigating; but, in the following passage, he speaks concerning the eternity of
the

CHAP. II.

ception, is that of their maturity and perfection; in the state of a tree, a horse, and a man. But with respect to the individuals of those, as well as all other classes, though they always universally proceed from other individuals in a state of maturity, it will be found that they all undergo innumerable changes, before they attain, by slow and insensible degrees, the perfection of their nature. As the rude marble is gradually formed by art into a beautiful or majestic statue, so seeds and embryos, scarcely perceptible to the senses, expand, by assimilating their proper nourishment, into the wonderfully organised productions called plants and animals. Such progressive and ever varying natures may be considered therefore as existing either in a state of capacity for attaining a certain form and maturity, a thing as different from absolute incapacity as sleep is from death; or in a state of actuality and perfection, which qualifies them for performing their respective functions, and exerting their peculiar energies. What then is change or motion in its most comprehensive and philosophical sense? It is the passage from a state of imperfection to perfection, from capacity

---

the world with the same becoming modesty that he shows on other subjects unfathomable to mere reason. Having mentioned that principle in the works of nature, analogous to art in the productions of man, which makes the stems of plants shoot upwards, while their roots fix deeply in the earth; which gives to animals their determinate organisation and proper shape, distinguishable in their respective members, adapted to specific and salutary purposes, he proceeds thus: μᾶλλον εἰκὸς τὸν οὐρανὸν γεγενῆσθαι ὑπὸ τοιαύτης αἰτίας, ἢ γίγνει, καὶ ἴσαι διὰ τοιαύτην αἰτίαν μᾶλλον ἢ τὰ ζῶα τὰ θνητα· τὸ γε μὴν τεταγμένον καὶ ὡρισμένον πολὺ μᾶλλον φαίνεται ἐν τοῖς οὐρανοις, ἢ περὶ ἡμᾶς. De Part. Animal. l. i. p. 970. "It is more likely that the heavens were produced by such a cause, if indeed they were produced, and that they subsist through the efficacy of such a cause, than perishing animals, since definite arrangement and regular harmony are conspicuous far more in celestial than in terrestrial things." Besides this, when Aristotle's doctrine of time is understood, we shall see that he means by the eternity of the world something very different from the sense commonly affixed to those words.

ARISTOTLE's WORKS.

pacity to energy; or, the reverse of this, from energy to mere capacity. For this reason Aristotle, anticipating the subtile principles which gave birth to the sublime geometry of Newton and Leibnitz, expresses an object in itself too fugitive for words to represent, by the limits or extremes between which it fluctuates; calling motion the perfection of mere capacity, because the immediate end at which mere capacity aims; and an imperfect energy or actuality, because until the productive motion stops, the object is only approximating to its most perceptible and most perfect state [b].

Aristotle observes, that the four kinds of change or motion, formerly described, all finally resolve themselves into lation, or change of place [i]; and that place is only a modification of space, that

CHAP. II.

Motion defined.

Space and time.

---

[b] Aristot. Natural. Auscult. l. iii. c. i, ii, iii. p. 339. & seqq. Had Mr. Locke known what Aristotle meant by motion, his candour would not have allowed him to speak of this definition as he does in the following passage: " What more exquisite jargon could the wit of man invent than this definition, ' the act of a being in power, as far forth as in power ?' which would puzzle any rational man, to whom it was not already known by its famous absurdity, to guess what word it could ever be supposed to be the explication of. If Tully, asking a Dutchman what *beweeginge* was, should have received this answer in his own language, that it was " actus entis in potentia, quatenus in potentia," I ask whether any one can imagine he would thereby have understood what the word *beweeginge* signified, or have guessed what idea a Dutchman ordinarily had in his mind, and would signify to another, when he used that sound?" Essay on the Human Understanding, vol. ii. b. iii. c. 4. p. 26. But Aristotle, who had taught before Mr. Locke that, what the latter calls simple ideas, could not be defined, (" Φανερον τοινυν, ὁτι ἐπι των ἀπλων ὐκ ἐστι της ζητησεως ἡδε διδαξις, ἀλλα ἑτερος τροπος της ζητησεως των τοιουτων." Metaphys. l. vii. c. xvii. p. 935. Vid. etiam, pp. 910 & 929.) would have more easily explained to Mr. L. his own definition of motion, than Mr. L. could have explained to Aristotle what he meant by the idea of a triangle, which is neither rectangular, obtusangular, nor acute-angular, but at once none and all of these together—the supposed existence of which ideas, and an infinity of others of the same kind, is the principal basis of the whole Essay on Human Understanding.

[i] Natural. Auscult. l. viii. c. x. p. 421. Metaph. l. xiv. c. vii. p. 1001.

that unsubstantial being of which no other definition can be given but that it is the recipient of body[k]. As our conception of space originates in that of body, and our conception of motion in that of space, so our conception of time originates in that of motion; and particularly in those regular and equable motions carried on in the heavens, the parts of which, from their perfect similarity to each other, are correct measures of the continuous and successive quantity called Time, with which they are conceived to co-exist. Time therefore may be defined the perceived number of successive movements; for as number ascertains the greater or lesser quantity of things numbered, so time ascertains the greater or lesser quantity of motion performed[l]. An instant is not a part, but the boundary of time[m]; whose elements are the perceptible intervals bounded by instants[n]. If body, therefore, had a beginning, so must space, motion, and time, which are conceived merely as affections of body, or of each other[o]. If body cannot be supposed infinitely extended, without supposing a contradiction, (for what quantity can actually exist of which the magnitude cannot be ascertained and expressed?) so neither can any of its properties; and therefore motion cannot be infinite; nor time, which is conceived solely as the measure of motion, a mere fiction of the fancy, possessing no real existence independently of us and our thoughts. The very essence of infinity, again, consists in privation; it is a word denoting not a conception, but the negation of all conception; so that the errors committed on this subject by the ancients, and repeated by some modern philosophers,

and

---

[k] Natural. Ausc.'t. l. iv. c. i, ii. &c. p. 351—364.   [l] Ibid. p. 367.
[m] Phys. Ausc. p. 397.   [n] Ibid. l. iv. c. xiv. &c. p. 364—373.
[o] Metaph. l. v. c. xiii. p. 894.

and even some modern mathematicians[p], proceed from their realising a non-entity, and assigning a positive archetype, or what they call an idea, to a word, which is merely a sign that no such archetype or idea exists. Body and space cannot be conceived as infinite either in greatness or littleness; and although its adjunct of motion or time is imagined to be so conceived, this arises from a mere illusion of the fancy, which, not retaining the parts of time first taken, continually adds new parts, but without increasing the whole; since the former parts are continually annihilated, as the latter are created[q]. To realise infinity must, in all our reasonings, necessarily lead to absurdity; thus, to give our Author's example, to suppose an infinite progression of causes in making and arranging the world, is the same thing as supposing it made or arranged without any cause at all[r].

It

---

[p] " La grandeur (says the admired Fontenelle) est susceptible d'augmentation sans fin. Elle n'est donc pas & ne peut être supposée dans le même cas, que si elle n'étoit pas susceptible d'augmentation sans fin: or si elle n'étoit pas susceptible d'augmentation sans fin, elle resteroit toujours finie; donc étant susceptible d'augmentation sans fin, elle peut être supposée infinie." See the same reasoning throughout his treatise, intitled, Elémens de la Geometrie de l'Infini. It is easy to perceive how much this ingenious man, and his innumerable followers, might have been benefited by reading the third book of Aristotle's Physics, c. iv. to chapter xiii. both inclusive, p. 342—350. αν αφαιρειται δὲ ὁ λογος, οὐδὲ της μαθηματικης την θεωριαν, αναιρων οὕτως τοιαι το απειρον, ὡς ἐνεργεια ειναι ἐπι την αὐξησιν ὡς αδιεξιτητον· οὐδὲ γαρ του διωνται τω απειρω, οὐδὲ χρειται, ἀλλὰ μονον ἰναι ὁσον ἂν βωλωνται πεπερασμενον· τῳ δὲ μεγιστῳ μεγεθει του αὐτου ἐςι τετμησθαι λογον ὁπηλικονων μεγεθος ἑτερον, ὡςε προς μὲν το δειξαι ἐκεινοις οὐδὲν διοισει· το δὲ εἶναι, εν τοις οὐσι ἐςαι μεγεθεσι. Ibid. c. xii. p. 350. " We do not destroy the speculations of mathematicians, when we assert that infinite magnitude cannot exist. For in these speculations, they neither employ nor need to employ infinite, but only a finite magnitude as great as they please; and the smallest may be divided in the same proportions with the greatest. For finding proportions, therefore, it is not necessary to suppose the existence of what is impossible."

[q] Metaph. l. v. c. xiii. p. 350.   [r] Ibid. l. ii. c. ii. p. 857.

CHAP. II.

Aristotle's astronomy.

It is both the glory and the shame of Aristotle's abstract philosophy, that his general conclusions are correct, when some of the arguments, by which he maintains them, are faulty. This is peculiarly manifest in the use which he makes of the erroneous system of astronomy, which prevailed in his own age, to vindicate the doctrines contained in his books of Physics. His treatise concerning the Heavens, indeed, describes with perspicuity and precision the celestial phænomena; while, at the same time, it informs us of the sublime notions given by the first Pythagoreans and their contemporaries, of the distances, figures, motions, and magnitudes of the planets [s]; that the moon abounded with inhabitants; that the milky-way consisted of contiguous clusters of stars [t]; and, conjecturing what it is the boast of modern astronomy to have confirmed, that the same principle which makes the heavenly bodies approach to their centre, perpetually impels them in their orbits, by proportionably increasing their celerity [u]. Aristotle's own sagacity led him to perceive that, in the revolutions of the heavenly bodies, all was regular, easy, and harmonious; and to reject with disdain those childish fictions, by which the moving principles of the universe were degraded by a supposed analogy with the laborious exertions of mortals in sublunary and perishing scenes [w]. But he did not think the astronomical theory of the Pythagoreans sufficiently justified by observation: telescopes were not to be invented till a far later period; and to those who held Aristotle's doctrine concerning space and time, the argument in favour of the earth's motion, resulting from the otherwise inconceivable velocity of the heavens,

---

[s] De Cœlo, l. ii. c. xiii. p. 465.   [t] Meteor. l. i. c. viii.
[u] De Cœlo, l. ii. c. i. p. 452.   Comp. c. xiii. p. 465. & l. i. c. viii. pp. 443, 444. & l. ii. c. ix. p. 462.   [w] Ibid. p. 451. & c. vi. p. 458.

heavens, is not calculated to afford conviction. The earth, therefore, as the heaviest of bodies, he places at the centre; around which, the sun, moon, planets, and fixed stars perpetually performed their respective revolutions [x]; the only kind of motion or change to which these etherial [y] substances, unchangeable in their essence, were supposed to be liable; whereas the earth and all its productions, the metals and minerals in its bowels, the plants and animals on its surface, together with the vapours and meteors between that surface and the lunar sphere, were obnoxious to a great variety of complicated motions, which changed their characterising qualities or essence, and rendered the dissolution of one object the production of another. On the hypothesis, therefore, of the stability of the earth and the daily revolution of the heavens, Aristotle argues, that the material universe cannot be infinite; because, could a radius be infinitely extended from the earth's centre to the remotest body in the universe, that body could never perform a complete circular revolution [z]; since an infinite extent of space could not be passed over in a definite time. Space therefore cannot be infinite, because space is only the receptacle of body, the place where body may subsist; and, if space is not infinite, neither is motion, which depends on space; nor time, which depends on motion. Unalterable and divine substances exist, therefore, in a manner totally unfathomable to our present faculties. In this manner, the first Supreme Deity exists *necessarily* [a]; neither generated in

space,

---

[x] De Cœlo, l. ii. passim. [y] Meteor. l. i. c. iii. p. 530.
[z] De Cœlo, l. i. c. v. p. 437.
[a] καθαπερ εν τοις εγκυκλιοις φιλοσοφημασι περι τα θεια πολλακις προφαινεται τοις λογοις, οτι το θειον αμεταβλητον αναγκαιον ειναι το πρωτον και ακροτατον, p. 446.

CHAP. II.

space, nor growing old in time, unchangeable and impassive, enjoying the best and most perfect life through all eternity[b].

Aristotle makes amends for his airy speculations in astronomy, by well explaining, in opposition to Democritus, the true principles of corpuscular attraction, which gives to the earth its globular form[c]. This, he observes, is further ascertained by the phænomenon of lunar eclipses, in which the bounding line is always perceived to be circular. The earth therefore, he says, is plainly a sphere, and but a small[d] one, compared with many others, its periphery not exceeding 37,000 miles[e]. He speaks with such raptures, as the calmest of philosophers could feel, of the beauty and grandeur of the heavenly motions, whose celerities, how frightful soever to fancy, yet being harmonised by proportion, might be steadily contemplated by the intellect[f]. Had he known the discoveries of Galileo and Kepler, he might perhaps have been a Newton. But astronomy being one of those sciences which requires long-continued observation for its basis, was left by Aristotle in the same imperfect state in which he found it; and yet, by the perverseness of stupidity, it was that part of his works which, in the ages of darkness, was most warmly admired, and most obstinately and most superstitiously defended.

His doctrine concerning the earth and its productions.

From the magnitudes and motions of the heavenly bodies, Aristotle descended to a humbler subject, the productions of the earth; which are connected, however, with man, by far more numerous[g] and powerful relations, namely, those of his daily wants. This globe which we inhabit seems to have undergone various

---

[b] De Cœlo, c. ix. p. 446. [c] Ibid. l. iv. c. vi. p. 492. & l. ii. c. xiv. p. 470.
[d] Meteor. l. i. c. iii. p. 529. [e] Ibid. p. 471. [f] Ibid. p. 451 & 463.
[g] De Part. Animal. l. i. c. v. p. 974.

various revolutions, to have been overwhelmed by inundations and shattered by convulsions, which swept away nations with their cities and their arts; so that the most valuable inventions have innumerable times been lost, and times innumerable been recovered. Of the productions with which our earth abounds, many give indications of these direful vicissitudes; and many appear to have emerged from the wreck of some dreadful catastrophe. Both as the historian and the interpreter of nature, our Author endeavoured to embrace and exhaust the complete science of the globe; and if we may judge of those parts of his works which are lost or imperfect, by those which have come down to us entire, it must have been no easy matter to determine whether most admiration was due to his descriptions of the great masses of nature, seas, rivers, mountains, and meteors [h], or to his minute diligence in treating the several objects of the animal, vegetable, and mineral kingdoms. His books on plants and minerals no longer remain [i]; but both his history of animals, and his philosophy respecting that history, have come down to us in a far more perfect state than any other portion of his writings concerning natural knowledge.

On the subject of Zoology, his treatises are comprised in fifty books, of which twenty-five are happily preserved among his works. The history of animals occupies nine books; the following sixteen are employed in explaining their general affections or properties, and their principal parts or members. Four books

His history of animals and other works relative to that subject.

---

[h] Meteor. l. i. c. i. p. 518. See the great views which he there gives of his undertakings.

[i] The two short books on plants, p. 1007—1030. vol. ii. edit. du Val. are spurious. In the last chapter of the third book of his Meteorology, he says he is to proceed to give an account of all the different fossils and metals; but that account nowhere appears.

CHAP. II.

books treat of their parts; five treat of generation; the remainder, of their sensations and motions, inspiration and respiration, sleeping, waking, youth, old age, life, and death; in the knowledge of which particulars, the liberal study of Zoology, or, in Aristotle's language, its philosophy, appears to him principally to consist. As he extends that term to its full and proper sense, denoting by it the knowledge of whatever has animal life, the first four books of his history, beginning with what is most striking and palpable, the outward conformation of animals, divides and distinguishes, in relation to this complex object, and in comparison with the human form, as that which is most familiarly known, the inhabitants of the earth, the water, and the air, from the enormous whale and massy elephant to the scarcely perceptible productions of dust and rottenness[k], enumerating and defining with incomparable accuracy the agreements, differences, and analogies that prevail, in point of external organization, among all living tribes, and sometimes referring to his treatises on Comparative Anatomy, which are now unfortunately lost. In the three following books, he examines the different classes of animals with respect to the commencement, duration, and term of their generative powers. His eighth book examines their habitation and nourishment; and the concluding

[k] Buffon (vol. iii. p. 223.) carries Aristotle's system of spontaneous generation much farther than the author intended, when he makes him say that " the first men sprung from the earth in the form of worms." Our author is constantly misrepresented by being made to speak absolutely, when he speaks merely hypothetically. His words are ωπερ εγιγνοντο ποτε γηγενεις. De General. l. iii. c. ii. And we shall find hereafter, that the result of all Aristotle's inquiries into nature is a conclusion directly opposite to the following of Mr. Buffon, namely, " qu'il y a peut être autant d'êtres, soit vivans, soit végétaux, qu'il se reproduisent par l'assemblage fortuit de molecules organiques, qu'il y a d'animaux ou de végétaux qui peuvent se reproduire par une succession constante de générations." Supplement à l'Hist. Nat. tom. viii. p. 18.

cluding book of the history contains their manners and habits, enumerates their friends and enemies, and explains the ordinary means by which each class provides for its preservation and defence. In taking this wide survey of animated nature, Aristotle pretends not to comprehend its indefinitely varied branches (since infinites of every kind spurn the limits of science); but in the multitude of important and well-ascertained facts which he relates, and which is incomparably greater than can be found in any work of equal compass, it is his main purpose to illustrate the general heads above mentioned, and to explain the properties or affections common to the greatest or most distinguished portion of the whole animal kingdom. To these general heads or common properties, he constantly has respect in the historical part of his work; so that his minutest observations respecting the minutest insects and least-organized animals, will be often found to elucidate or confirm some important law of the animal œconomy[1].

His System, that is, in the popular sense of the word, his nomenclature, is indeed imperfect. The world created by a microscope, had not any existence for the philosophers of antiquity; and, by the improvements of this invention, new worlds perhaps may be brought to light in endless succession. But in the chain of being, mortal eyes, however assisted, can contemplate only the middle links, of which, though our glasses have shewn to us a greater number than were seen by Aristotle,

His philosophy of natural history.

---

[1] Take the following example: The *cremx* is a species of the Mollia, (fishes so called because their soft parts are without, and their hard within,) which was long degraded by modern naturalists to the rank of sea plants. Aristotle remarks, with regard to this species, that when the female is attacked, the male boldly defends her; but when an attack is made on the male, the female consults her own safety by flight. Females, except in defence of their young, are less courageous than males, and less forward to give assistance. Histor. Animal. l. ix. c. i. p. 922. & seq.

CHAP. II.

Aristotle, yet have they not brought us nearer to what ought to be the result of beholding the extremity of the chain. This result, the history of nature in animals, the Stagyrite, by the intellectual eye of reason and analogy[m], endeavoured to reach and reveal; analysing, defining, demonstrating; sometimes penetrating deeply into nature's mysteries; sometimes encountering difficulties which the human intellect is unable to surmount; often foiled in his exertions, yet always renewing the combat with reanimated hope. Knowledge, he thought, was more likely to be struck out from the collision of error than to emerge spontaneously from confusion[n]; and while his theories are attacked and defended, exploded and revived, the facts which he collected with unexampled diligence, and which he relates with inimitable precision, will for ever support his fame, and instruct the most distant ages of posterity. Our wider survey of the globe has indeed increased our acquaintance with quadrupeds; and the invention of glasses has multiplied to our eyes the ever-diminishing tribes of insects, and enabled us to examine more accurately their germs and organs; yet it will not be easy to prove that modern writers have added any thing of importance to Aristotle's observations on birds, or that any of their works display even an equal degree of knowledge on the subject of fishes[o].

It

[m] The expression of an anonymous writer preserved in Suidas, is bold in the extreme: Αριστοτελης γραμματευς ην της φυσεως, τον καλαμον αποβρηχων εις νουν. "Aristotle was Nature's secretary, having dipped his pen in intellect." Suid. in Αριστοτελης.

[n] Metaph. passim.

[o] In proof of this, I shall cite the testimony of an author, which derives great weight from the accuracy of his own observations, and the importance of his own discoveries. "Questi fatti finora rapportati in ordine allo suiluppo delle ouva nei pesci spinosi, sono

It may seem extraordinary that, on a branch of science, which, like all other parts of natural history, is naturally progressive, our author should have attained such accurate and extensive knowledge in so early an age of the world. But Aristotle was the friend of a man as extraordinary as himself, from whom he received two favours, which, to a mind like his, must

CHAP. II.

By what means he was enabled to render this philosophy so complete.

sono quelli pochi che ho potuto osservare nelle rare occasioni che mi si son presentati delle loro covate gattate, & gia suiluppantisi. E percio la serie di tali fatti e di multo interrotta, ne' continuata come a giorni nostri e' quella dello sviluppo del feto nelle uova della gallina. E quando io reflettendo su di questa mancanza, scorro la Storia degli Animali di Aristotele, non posso non essere da stupore preso, in esso leggendo veduti quei fatti, che a noi non si son potuti che a stento manifestare; & relevati poi con tutta la nettezza, & posti in parallelo coi fatti gia' riconosciuti nel feto di gallo: & tanto maggiormente in me cresce lo stupore, quanto che allora uso non vi era degli instrumenti microscopici, che a tempi nostri abbiamo grandemente perfezzionati. E quindi non posso che di sdegno accendarmi contra dei moderni Izziologi, vedendo per lor balordaggine trascurato quanto la veneranda antiquità avea scritto su questo particulare, & a quello sostituite false osservazioni, illuzioni assurde ed incoerenti." " These are the few observations concerning the development of the eggs of shell-fish, which I have been able to make on the few occasions on which I found the impregnated gems in the act of disclosure; observations of which the series has been greatly interrupted, nor continued to the present times, like those which relate to eggs of birds. When I consider this defect, and turn to Aristotle's History of Animals, I am seized with astonishment at finding, that he should have fully and distinctly seen the facts which we have been able only very imperfectly to perceive; that he should have described them with the utmost precision, and compared them with the well-known observations concerning the eggs of birds. My astonishment is the greater, when I reflect that he was unassisted by microscopes, which instruments have in our days been greatly perfected; and I cannot therefore repress my indignation against those modern Ichthyologists, whose stupidity, neglecting the lights thrown on their subject by venerable antiquity, has substituted in their stead false observations, absurd and incongruous inferences." Memorie Sulla Generazione dei Pesci, di Philippo Cavolini. Compare p. 55. and p. 92. with Aristotle's History of Animals, b. vi. c. viii. and c. xiii. To the petulant questions in Athenæus, l. viii. p. 352. " From whom did Aristotle learn the minute particularities which he tells of fishes? From Proteus or Nereus?" No, (we may answer with Is. Casaubon.) but from fishermen. Vid. Casaubon Animadvers. in Athenæum, l. viii. p. 388.

CHAP. II.

must have been of inestimable value. Alexander enabled him to rebuild and adorn his native city, for the benefit of his contemporaries[p], and to improve science for the benefit of posterity[q]. Upon his first entering Babylon, that inimitable prince eagerly demanded, for the use of his preceptor, the astronomical tables preserved in that ancient capital above nineteen centuries, and remounting 2234 years beyond the Christian æra[r]; and Pliny labours to describe with what ardour and zeal the same illustrious conqueror, during the course of his expedition, collected as presents to be sent to Aristotle, at the expence of 200,000 l.[s], and by the activity of several thousand men, whatever rarities were to be found in parks or ponds, in aviaries or hives, or were to be procured by hunting, fishing, and fowling, in the wide extent of Asia. Such were the resources of Aristotle for writing the history of animals, besides the assistance of a great library, which Strabo says that, to the best of his knowledge, he was the first person that knew properly how to arrange[t]. By combining with the descriptions in his books the observation of those living wonders transported from the East, Aristotle, who preferred a philosophical residence in Athens to the honour of personal attendance on the master of the world, composed, in the tranquillity of the Lyceum, his immortal work, which a Pliny professes to abridge[u], and a Buffon despairs to rival[w].

In the wide survey which our author takes of the heavens and of the earth, as well as in the minute diligence with which he

[p] Plin. l. vii. c. 29. [q] Idem, l. viii. c. 16.
[r] Porphyrius apud Simplicium in Aristot. de Cœlo.
[s] Comp. Plin. ubi supra, & Athenæum, p. 398. edit. Casaub.
[t] πρωτος ὡν ισμιν συναγαγων βιβλια, και διδαξας τυς ν αιγυπτῳ βασιλιας βιβλιοθηκης συνταξιν. Strabo, l. xiii. p. 609.
[u] Plin. ubi supra. [w] Histoire Naturelle, t. i. p. 63. & seq.

he examines the productions of the latter, whether inanimate or living, it is his perpetual aim to remount from effects to causes, and to lead us from perceptible qualities to those invisible principles by which they are produced. These principles, not being objects of sense, can be discovered only by making fair inferences from observation and experience. In this manner Aristotle treats, in three books, a subject which naturally follows his history of animals, investigating those principles on which their nutrition, sensation, and appetite, with all their perceptible powers and actions, depend. In this treatise, intitled "Concerning the Soul," his language is perpetually and necessarily metaphorical, because words, in their origin, being universally expressive merely of perceptions of sense, metaphors become indispensable in expressing the deductions of reason. Of material as well as intellectual substances our knowledge, he observes, results entirely from their perceptible qualities, that is, from what our universal experience teaches us to regard merely as the effects of hidden causes, scarcely conceivable to ourselves, and of which our notions are totally incommunicable to other men but by images and comparisons drawn from sensible objects. When Aristotle speaks philosophically of fire, he calls it "the power of communicating heat." In the same manner, the hidden causes necessary for explaining the properties and actions of animals, he calls "the nutritive, sentient, motive, and rational," that is, the collecting "power;" and as, from the phenomena of body, he inferred the existence of a substance called Matter; so, from the phenomena of sensation, reason, and intelligence, he inferred the existence of a substance called Mind; of which latter substance our knowledge is equally

The soul or mind in its most general sense.

certain

CHAP. II.

certain with that of the former [x]. But as some of the most noted philosophers before him had attempted to explain every thing by matter and its properties [y], Aristotle, on the other hand, thinks that it is by mind chiefly that all natural productions are characterised and distinguished; meaning, by mind, that inward principle and invisible form whose effects are displayed in the external organization of things, as well as in their perceptible properties and actions. In this sense, therefore, the terms "form" and "mind" are applied to whatever characterises and distinguishes, whether that be merely a specific and principal quality; or whether it be a substance inseparable from matter, because separately unfit for any end or use [z]; or whether it be a substance capable of actions and pleasures peculiar to itself, and so totally different from those of body, and any of its variable affections, that, when separated from this mortal frame, it will then, and then only, assume its natural activity, perfection, and dignity [a].

The book intitled "Concerning Energy," connects his natural philosophy with his theology.

The doctrine of the mind naturally brings Aristotle to what is published as the ninth book of his Metaphysics, but which, as above mentioned, ought to stand as the seventh. It is intitled "Concerning Energy," a word of mighty import in our author's philosophy, since his doctrine on that subject is a link in the grand chain, by which he connects the earth with the heavens, and nature with the Deity. The state of energy, as opposed

---

[x] δηλον δὲ καὶ ὅτι ἡ μὲν ψυχὴ οὐσία ἡ πρώτη, τὸ δὲ σῶμα ὕλη· ὁ δὲ ἄνθρωπος· ἢ τὸ ζῶον τὸ ἐξ ἀμφοῖν. Metaph. l. vii. c. xi. p. 919. and l. i. De Anima, c. v. p. 625.

[y] Metaph. l. viii. c. ii. p. 927.   [z] Ibid. l. viii. c. iii. p. 929.

[a] De Anima, l. i. c. iii. p. 623. and c. v. p. 625. and Metaph. l. xiv. c. ix. p. 1004.

opposed to that of capacity, was already explained; but it may be a matter of some curiosity more minutely to examine distinctions, independently of which this great philosopher thought it impossible to mount up from things visible and perishing to things invisible and eternal. Energy, then, as the word denotes, is always said in reference to action; and that is said to exist in energy, which executes its peculiar work, or performs its peculiar function [b]. The state of energy is the most perfect state of existence in which any object can be exhibited; as a master thinks he has perfected his scholar when he shews him performing skilfully the proper work of the art in which he was instructed [c]. Though energy always implies action, yet all actions are not energies. The actions of building, carving, healing, learning, respectively terminate i a house, a statue, health, and science. But the actions of thought, of life, and of happiness, (which is a kind of life,) have not any natural limit, but may proceed eternally revolving on themselves, perfect without addition, complete in every instant [d]. That things essentially different may be distinguished by different names, Aristotle calls limited actions, motions; the unlimited, energies; observing, that in the scale of being there is a continual ascent from mere powers and capacities to motions or imperfect energies, properly so called, because terminating in nothing more excellent than themselves [e]. Those operations, which terminate in a certain work, are only perfect in the work or production in which they are fixed and concentrated; as painting

The nature of energy explained.

[b] Metaph. l. ix. c. viii. p. 339. Comp. Metaph. l. ix. c. vi. p. 936.
[c] Idem ibid. [d] Metaph. l. ix. c. vi. p. 937.
[e] Comp. Metaph. l. xiii. c. ix. p. 990. & p. 991, and Metaph. l. ix. c. viii. p. 938.

CHAP. II.

The first energy eternally and substantially active.

painting in the picture, building in the edifice [f]. But energies not terminating in any work or production, are complete and perfect in themselves. The former belong in a certain sense to the work in which they are embodied [g]; the latter can belong only to the energising principle, which, when unceasingly active, as the first efficient cause was proved necessarily to be, is simple, unmixed, and pure energy [h].

On such a principle as this, eternally and substantially active, both the heavens and the earth depend [i]. He is the spring of motion, the fountain of life, the source of order and of beauty [k]. All our observations and all our reasonings lead us irresistibly to this conclusion; for in all the motions or changes of body or matter, there must always be one part acted upon as well as another that acts, otherwise no action, and therefore no motion, could possibly take place. But when we separate this acting part from the inert mass with which it is united, the same reasoning will still apply to it; it cannot be self-moved wholly [l], and the part which gives the impulse must always be different from that which receives it [m]. By our divisions and subdivisions without end, we shall therefore never come nearer to a solution than at first setting out, but shall always be compelled to consider matter as something fit to be moved, changed, or acted upon, but

[f] Comp. Metaph. l. xiii. c. ix. p. 990. & p. 991. and Metaph. l. ix. c. viii. p. 938.

[g] Metaph. l. ix. c. vi. p. 936.

[h] ὁ γὰρ νοῦς ἐνέργεια. Metaph. l. xiv. c. vi. p. 999.

[i] ἐκ τοιαύτης ἀρχῆς ἤρτηται ὁ οὐρανὸς καὶ ἡ φύσις. l. xiv. c. vii. p. 1000. and Physic. Auscult. l. viii. c. vii. p. 418.

[k] τὸ πρῶτον πάντων κινοῦν πάντα. Metaph. l. xiv. c. iv. p. 998. Comp. c. vi. p. 999. and l. xii. c. iii. p. 975. and l. ix. c. viii. p. 930.

[l] Physic. Auscult. l. iii. c. i. p. 340.

[m] Ibid. l. viii. c. vi. p. 417.

but constantly deriving its motion, change, or activity from some foreign cause[n]. The prime mover, then, is necessarily "immaterial; and therefore indivisible, immoveable, impassive, and invariable[o]; ever actuating this visible system, as is plain from the phænomena, according to the best principles both of intellection and volition, which exactly coincide[q], when traced up to Deity, their ultimate source. The phenomena of the universe are not unconnected and episodical, like an ill-written tragedy; but all of them regulated and adjusted with consummate harmony[r]. The Divinity, who comprehends and directs the whole, is not himself divisible in parts, nor comprehensible by magnitude, since all magnitude may be measured[s]; and what finite magnitude can exert infinite power[t]? He ever is what he is[u], existing in energy before time began, since time is only an affection of motion, of which God is the author[w]. That kind of life which the best and happiest of men lead occasionally, in the unobstructed exercise of their highest powers, belongs eternally to God in a degree that should excite admiration in proportion as it surpasses comprehension[x].

This

CHAP. II.

His attributes.

---

[n] Physic. Auscult. l. viii. c. vi. p. 417.

[o] Ibid. l. viii. c. vi. p. 416. & seq.

[p] Metaph. l. xiv. c. vii. p. 1000. and 1001.

[q] τυτων (in reference to the οριχτοι and νοητοι) τα πρωτα τα αιτια. Comp. Metaph. l. ix. c. ix. and l. xiv. c. vii.

[r] ουκ εοικε η φυσις επεισοδιωδης ... ωσπερ μοχθηρα τραγωδια. Metaph. l. xii. c. iii. p. 975.

[s] Metaph. l. xiii. c. x. p. 991.   [t] Ibid. l. xiv. c. vii. p. 1001.

[u] δει αρα ειναι αρχην τοιαυτην ης η ουσια ενεργεια. Metaph. l. xiv. c. vi. p. 999. Comp. De Cœlo, l. ii. c. xiii. p. 466.

[w] Metaph. l. xiii. c. viii. p. 992. and το κινειν αιδιον, και προτερον τε κινεμενε, και το προτερον ουσιας, ουσιαν αναγκαιον ειναι. Metaph. l. xiv. c. viii. p. 1002.

[x] ει δε μαλλον, ετι θαυμασιωτερον, l. xiv. c. vii. p. 1001.

CHAP. II.

That Deity the source of Being handed down from antiquity.

This doctrine was delivered down from the ancients, and remains with their posterity, in the form of a fable; which, with many additions to it, has been employed for the service of legiflation, and for bridling the paffions of the multitude [y]. The Gods have thence been reprefented as endowed with human forms, and agitated by human paffions; from which ftrange fuppofitions, many confequences not lefs ftrange have very naturally been derived. Yet, from the motley mafs of fiction, if we feparate this fingle propofition, that Deity is the firft of fubftances, it will appear to be divinely faid; and to have been faved, as a precious remnant, in the wreck of arts and philofophy, which, it is probable, have often flourifhed, and often fallen to decay [z].

Ariftotle refutes the materialifts and metaphyficians.

Such is Ariftotle's doctrine in his books intitled "Concerning Philofophy;" the far greater part of which is employed in refuting two claffes of writers, who may very properly be called the Materialifts and the Metaphyficians. The former contenting themfelves with the properties and laws of matter and motion, beyond which they thought it impoffible to penetrate, miftook effects for caufes, and confounded the maker [a] with his works: The latter, who were the more modern, and alfo the more fafhionable of the two, perverted logical analyfis by applying it to phyfical fubjects [b]; and fubftituting words for things, fought

---

[y] Metaph. l. xiv. c. viii. p. 1003.   [z] Idem Ibid.

[a] το κινῶν πρῶτον, l. xiv. c. x. p. 1006. This muft found harfh to thofe who do not underftand Ariftotle's notion of the eternity of the world, in the fenfe in which it is above explained.

[b] Compar. Metaph. l. xii. c. iv. p. 977. l. xiii. c. ii. p. 981. & feq. and l. xiv. c. i. p. 995.

sought for first causes in numbers, ideas, contraries, and other metaphysical abstractions; or, in Aristotle's language, general terms; which, the more general they become, diverge the wider[e] in their nature from energies, the only substantial and efficient principles in the universe[d]; and all proceeding from the first energy or substance, who is both specifically and numerically one[e]. This doctrine perfectly agrees with that beautiful harmony discernible in the works of the first mover; which are all of them connected by the most intimate relations[f]; and whose arrangements uniformly conspire to one great and salutary end[g]: For the perfection, excellence, and beauty, discernible in the universe, are to be ascribed to its Maker, not less than the regular arrangement of a well disciplined army is ascribed to its general[h]. This doctrine only is consistent:

CHAP. II.

Goodness of God.

"One rules alone, one, only one, bears sway;
" *His* are the laws, and Him let all obey[i]."

This

[c] Compar. Metaph. l. xiii. c. ii. p. 982. and l. xiv. c. v. p. 998.
[d] Comp. l. xiii. c. vii. p. 988. and l. xiv. c. ii, iii. p. 996.
[e] ἐν μὲν ἄρα καὶ λογῳ καὶ ἀριθμῳ τὸ πρῶτον κινοῦν ἀκίνητον ὄν. l. xiv. c. viii. p. 1003. Things are one specifically or λογῳ, when they are collected into one count, and expressed by one word or κατηγορημα, the definition of which applies equally to them all. Material things may be one specifically, though many numerically: but this cannot hold as to energies; so that if there were as many different heavens as there are different men, the first necessary being would still be numerically, as well as specifically, one. Compar. Phys. Auscult. l. viii. c. vii. p. 418. & seq.
[f] οὐχ οὕτως ἔχει, ὅτι μὴ εἶναι θάτερον θατέρῳ, l. xiv. c. x. p. 1005. & Phys. Auscult. l. viii. c. vii. p. 418.
[g] πρὸς μὲν γὰρ ἓν, ἅπαντα συντέτακται, Ibid.
[h] Comp. l. xii. c. iv. p. 976. & l. xiv. c. x. p. 1004. Pliny, l. ii. c. i. & l. xxvii. c. ii. strangely mistakes his great master in natural history. The same errors he commits elsewhere in speaking of God, Nature, the world, &c.
[i] Iliad, l. i. v. 204. quoted Metaph. l. xiv. c. ult. p. 1006. Cicero greatly misrepresents

CHAP.
II.

The same doctrine inculcated in his exoteric or popular works.

This syſtem of theology, not leſs ſatisfactory than ſublime, Ariſtotle tells us that he had often inculcated, not merely in his acroatic works, which were lectures confined ſolely to his pupils, but alſo in his exoteric or popular writings, intended for the inſtruction of the public[k]. If this aſſertion cannot be diſproved, his character will be reſcued from the charge of diſhoneſty, in teaching a double doctrine, one to his pupils, and another to the world. Cicero[l] indeed ſays, that the Greek philoſophers (meaning our author in particular) did not "ſeem always to hold the ſame language in their popular and in their more accurate works;" which variation was, ſurely, to be expected; ſince, in the former, they often reaſoned, as Ariſtotle himſelf tells us, looſely or according to vulgar conception, and in the latter ſtrictly or philoſophically. But as to the fundamental points of his moſt important doctrines, Ariſtotle frequently refers from thoſe of his books, " which were diſtinguiſhed by pregnant brevity, cloſeneſs of thought, and quickneſs of tranſitions[m]," to his more expanded, more perſpicuous, and more popular productions[n]. Much circumſpection indeed became

repreſents his original, "Inde deinde illi tot Dij ſi numeramus etiam Cœlum, Deum," &c. De Natur. Deor. l. i. c. xiii.

[k] καθαπερ εν τοις εγκυκλιοις φιλοσοφημασι περι τα θεια πολλακις προφαινεται τοις λογοις ὁτι το θειον αμεταβλητον παν το πρωτον και ακροτατον. De Cœlo, l. i. c. ix. p. 446.

[l] De Fin. l. v. c. v.

[m] Simplicius (ad Categor. in Prooem.) thus characteriſes the acroatic, in contradiſtinction to the exoteric works, " ἡ βραχυλογια, ἡ των νοιων πυκνοτης, και το της φρασεως ευπεριγραμμον. To the laſt clauſe I have given a ſenſe more conformable to truth than that which the words naturally preſent.

[n] Simplicius Comment. in Ariſtot. de Cœlo, fol. 67. Ethic. Nicom. l. i. c. iii. & c. xiii. l. vi. c. iv. Ethic. Eudem. l. i. c. viii. l. ii. c. i. De Republ. l. iii. c. vi. & l. vii. c. i.

became a philosopher, detesting superstition and detesting democracy, yet living and teaching in the bosom of Athens; a city shamefully deformed by whatever is most abject in the one, and most wild in the other. But there is not a shadow of proof that, in any part of his writings, he encouraged or approved either of those gross popular delusions; though it is highly probable that he arraigned their folly and absurdity with more freedom in the Lyceum, than his prudence would have allowed him to express in the Pantheon or the Forum.

An objection very commonly made to Aristotle's philosophy is, that he is regardless of experience, and too fond of hypothesis. In the whole extent in which this reproach is usually urged by his detractors, it betrays ignorance in the extreme; since the principles of every one of his treatises are drawn solely from experience; and, in almost every step that he takes, to experience he continually recurs for trying and confirming his conclusions. That he was not sparing of experiments, in the modern sense of the word, upon those subjects on which he thought that a philosopher might consistently make use of them, is evident from his mechanical questions, his problems, his discourses on the general properties or affections of animated nature, and, above all, from his doctrine of sensation, memory, recollection, and other powers of the soul or mind; which is entirely experimental. But Aristotle was contented with catching Nature in the fact, without attempting, after the modern fashion, to put her to the torture; and in rejecting experiments operose, toilsome, or painful, either to their objects or their authors, he was justified by the habits of thinking, almost universally prevalent in his age and country. Educated in free and martial republics, careless of wealth, because uncorrupted by luxury,

The objection made to Aristotle's philosophy, as not built on experiment.

CHAP. II.

His philosophical language

luxury, the whole tribe of ancient philosophers dedicated themselves to agreeable only and liberal pursuits, with too proud a disdain of arts merely useful or lucrative. They ranked with the first class of citizens; and, as such, were not to be lightly subjected to unwholesome or disgusting employments. To bend over a furnace, inhaling noxious steams; to torture animals, or to touch dead bodies, appeared to them operations not more misbecoming their humanity, than unsuitable to their dignity. For such discoveries as the heating and mixing of bodies offers to inquisitive curiosity, the naturalists of Greece trusted to slaves and mercenary mechanics, whose poverty or avarice tempted them to work in metals and minerals; and to produce, by unwearied labour, those coloured and sculptured ornaments, those gems, rings, cups, and vases, and other admired but frivolous elegancies, of which (in the opinion of good judges º of art) our boasted chemistry cannot produce the materials; nor, were the materials at hand, supply us with instruments fit to shape. The work-shops of tradesmen then revealed those mysteries which are now sought for in colleges and laboratories; and useful knowledge, perhaps, was not the less likely to be advanced, while the arts were confined to artists only; nor facts the more likely to be perverted, in order to support favourite theories, before the empiric had yet assumed the name, and usurped the functions, of the philosopher.

To the Stagirite, it appeared to be the proper business of philosophy, not to multiply or collect facts, but to arrange and

to

º I remember a strong expression of the late Mr. Wedgewood, in speaking of the Portland Vase, that the making of it " implied a science of chemistry, of which we have not yet the elements."

to explain them. This can only be done through the medium of a well-defined and highly cultivated language; and the language of Aristotle will be found the most copious and complete, and at the same time the most precise and elegant, ever employed by any philosopher; serving at once as the readiest channel of conveyance, and the fittest instrument for discovery. In his physical, as well as in his moral works, facts known and ascertained are reduced to their simplest expressions, and those doubtfully inferred, or barely suspected, are, according to the true spirit of analysis, denoted by words merely expressive of relations to things previously known. It is true that, in ages of ignorance, when Aristotle's supposed tenets were read in barbarous and disgusting translations, the terms employed by him, as signs of things sought, and which, unless marked by signs, could never possibly be discovered, were as grossly mistaken, as they have been since shamefully misrepresented. In the scholastic philosophy, that useless mass of insipid dulness, which insolently arrogated to itself the name of Aristotle-ism, the schoolmen rested in the names of occult qualities for explaining the phenomena both of mind and matter; and neglecting the repeated warnings of him whom they called their great master, and who well knew how liable the best things are to abuse, they perverted the study of nature into metaphysical subtlety and vain logomachy. But the same stupid ignorance which made them incapable of appreciating the Stagirite as a philosopher, rendered them prone to worship him as a god. This imaginary divinity and his adorers were assailed by the giants of the sixteenth century; who, in their rage to punish such gross intellectual idolatry, confounded the master with his disciples, arraigned Aristotle for opinions which he had never held,

mistaken, and perverted.

degraded

degraded him from honours which he had never ufurped; and adopting his favourite method of analyfis, endeavoured ungratefully and infidioufly to deftroy his well-earned fame with the inftrument which he himfelf had formed and fharpened. But whatever unmerited difgrace may have been thereby reflected on fome fpeculative doctrines, which I have here attempted briefly to explain, his practical philofophy, which may be read in the following tranflation, will ftill vindicate his fair claim to be regarded as one of the beft inftructors of mankind, on the more important fubjects of Ethics and Politics.

ARISTOTLE's ETHICS.

BOOK I.

INTRODUCTION.

THE poet Gray writes thus in a letter to a friend: "For my part I read Aristotle, his poetics, politics, and morals; though I do not know well, which is which. In the first place, he is the hardest author by far I ever meddled with. Then he has a dry concisenefs, that makes one imagine one is perusing a table of contents rather than a book: it tastes for all the world like chopped hay, or rather like chopped logic; for he has a violent affection for that art, being in some fort his own invention; so that he often loses himself in little trifling distinctions and verbal niceties; and what is worse, leaves you to extricate him as well as you can. Thirdly, he has suffered vastly from the transcribers, as all authors of great brevity necessarily must. Fourthly and lastly, he has abundance of fine uncommon things, which make him well worth the pains he gives one." See Gray's Letters.

In this first book, our Author fays "abundance of fine uncommon things," on the subjects of human nature, virtue, and happiness. His mode of composition, however, is so totally different from that to which the caprice of fashion has given

BOOK I.

given its temporary sanction, that much labour and much skill must be employed, to adapt the form of his work to the taste of modern readers; to whom both his method and his style, which formerly appeared to deserve admiration [a], may now seem to demand apology. His method requires, that every subject of discussion should be accurately defined, and completely divided; and that, how complex soever its nature may be, the compound should be resolved into its constituent elements; viewed in its birth and origin; and examined, in all its changes, varieties, augmentations, and diminutions. This mode of proceeding appeared to him peculiarly useful in moral and political questions, whose connections and relations are so intimate and so extensive, that erroneous conclusions, on such subjects, proceed far more frequently from narrowness of survey, than from inaccuracy of reasoning. In practical matters above all, this full and comprehensive examination seemed indispensably necessary, to prevent hasty decision, to inspire cautious distrust; and thus to arrest the progress of passion and frenzy in a career which might leave them without retreat.

But, with whatever other advantages a treatise written with this strictness and severity of method may be accompanied, it certainly is not calculated to afford *gratuitous* information. To apprehend its meaning distinctly, and to perceive its full scope, demands much attention and much reflection on the part even of the reader. His patience is likely to be soon exhausted by the too painful task; especially if his taste has been corrupted by those flowery and fallacious productions of the times, whose authors (men of narrow views and selfish minds, and so long
habituated

---

[a] Cicero Topic. c. i. p. 171. Edit. Olivet. & passim.

habituated to party politics, that they have loft all relifh, and almoft all perception of truth,) are contented to confound and darken a whole region of fcience, provided they can throw a falfe glare on one favourite and fafhionable fpot. This darling topic they exert themfelves to beautify and illumine; adorning with eloquence and metaphors, and all the embroidery of declamation, the dangerous inference that is drawn from their erroneous, becaufe imperfect, argument. Nothing can be more fmooth, or more eafily followed by the reader, than the whole progrefs of their difcourfe. But the very circumftance which renders it fo eafy and fo popular, alfo makes it of no value. The fubject has been confidered under one partial afpect; a different view of it is taken; the incomplete theory is affaulted by another equally imperfect; and both of them fo flimfy and cloud-built, that they are unable to withftand even the foft impreffions of their adverfe debility. Yet each party triumphs for a while in the bubble of its own creating, and vainly deems it irrefiftible; a falfe confidence, that often gives birth to the greateft practical errors. Ariftotle's method is directly the reverfe: his works require attention, but they repay it; they will fully compenfate, in folid inftruction, for their defect (if it may be called one) in point of delufive entertainment.

The Stagirite's ftyle is not lefs unfafhionable than his method. It difplays not any allurements to catch the reader's fancy; it difdains every attempt to excite furprife, to provoke mirth, to inflame, footh, or gratify paffion. The thirft for knowledge is the only want which the Author profeffes to fupply; and this thirft, he was of opinion, will ever be beft quenched

BOOK I.

in the clear stream of unadorned reason; as that water is the purest and most salutary, which has neither taste nor colour.

Aristotle did not, like his master Plato, banish poets from his Republic. He himself courted the Lyric muse, and reached her loftiest flights. But he never understood by what perversity of purpose the agreeable illusions of poetry could be associated and mixed with the sober science of politics. In all practical matters, he knew the danger of saying any thing to the heart and passions, which would not bear to be examined by the light of the understanding. In translating incomparably the most valuable part of his works, I have attempted therefore to imitate his precision and energy, as far as that can be done without leaving the faintest trace of his obscurity. My aim throughout is to adhere rigidly to his sense; to omit nothing which he says; to say nothing which he has omitted; but to endeavour, to the best of my abilities, to express his meaning, agreeably as well as forcibly; since a mere verbal translation would convey not only an inadequate, but often a very false, impression of the Greek original.

Words, as our Author teaches, are both the signs of things, and the materials in which our comparisons, abstractions, and conclusions concerning those things are embodied. The words of one language, therefore, will often be very imperfectly expressed by those of another; and the more complex their significations are, the diversities between them will naturally be the wider. To the terms employed in the sciences of Ethics and Politics, this observation is peculiarly applicable. The original term, and that by which it is translated, not comprehending

hending exactly the same identical notions, the English word which corresponds to the Greek in one of its meanings, will often not express it in another. The phraseology, therefore, must be occasionally varied; and the ambition to attain propriety and excellence, will thus sometimes give to a translation, the appearance of looseness and inaccuracy. In many cases, exact equivalents to single Greek words, are not to be found either in English, or in any other language. One term, therefore, must frequently be rendered by several; and the translation necessarily degenerating into a paraphrase, will often gain in perspicuity and popularity, what it loses in precision and energy[b]. From the philosophical arrangement of the Greek tongue, and the singular fondness of Greek writers for abstract and universal conclusions, words denoting the higher genera or classes, are employed by them on many occasions, when terms more specific would answer the purpose better, and sound more gracefully, in English. With regard to this particular, I have sometimes ventured to prefer to strictness of version, a compliance with the genius of modern tongues, and with the taste of modern readers.

My

[b] When the Greek language was more familiarly known than it is at present, Aristotle's style was acknowledged by the best critics to possess the highest of all merits, that of expressing his deep and various wisdom always in the fittest terms. Dicendi quoque incredibili quadam cum copia, tum etiam suavitate. Cicero Topic. c. i. p. 171. Edit. Oliveti. Quintilian speaks to the same purpose: Quid Aristotelem? quem dubito scientia rerum, an scriptorum copia, an eloquendi suavitate, an inventionum acumine, an varietate operum, clariorem puto. "Why need I mention Aristotle? concerning whom I am in doubt, whether he is rendered more illustrious by the magnitude and variety of his writings, his universal science, the acuteness of his inventions, or the suavity of his diction." Quintil. Inst. Orat. l. x. c. i. p. 224. Edit. Bipont.

BOOK I.

My principal design and only ambition is to convey, in the present state of public opinion with respect to fundamental principles, a clear notion of those writings of the Stagirite which he intitled his " Philosophy concerning Human Affairs [c]." His Ethics, I believe, no man can read without becoming the better; and his Politics, I think, no statesman can study, without becoming the wiser. But the corrupt and mutilated state of his works compelled me, reluctantly, to use some freedom with their form, in order the more completely to preserve their substance. In different books, and even in different chapters of the same book, the same thoughts often recur in nearly the same words. These useless repetitions, proceeding commonly from the fault of unskilful editors, I thought it my duty to retrench; and continually to aim at selecting that expression in which the sense is most fully conveyed. A translation is a portrait; but that the portrait may please, the original should be shown with its most becoming expression, and in its best attitudes.

[c] ἡ περὶ τὰ ἀνθρώπινα φιλοσοφία.

BOOK I.

ARGUMENT.

Human action—Operations and productions—Happiness—Opinions concerning it—It consists in virtuous energies—Proved by induction—Solon's saying concerning it explained—Analysis of our moral powers.

SINCE every art and every kind of knowledge, as well as all the actions and all the deliberations of men, constantly aim at something which they call good; good, in general, may be justly defined, "that which all desire." But among the various ends and purposes of our activity and pursuit, there is this important difference, that some consist merely in operations, and others chiefly in productions. Of those arts or actions of which production is the chief end, the work is more valuable than the operation by which it was produced; and, as there is a wide variety of arts and actions, there must be a correspondent variety of ends: of the medical art, health; of shipbuilding, a vessel; of generalship, victory; of œconomy, riches. It often happens that arts rise one above another in dignity, and that all those of an inferior sort are subservient to one principal, their natural and acknowledged sovereign. Thus bridle making is subservient to horsemanship; and horsemanship to war; and the end of the subservient art is plainly less valuable than that of the art to which it ministers, because the former is pursued merely for the sake of the latter. This holds universally, whether

BOOK I.
Chap. 1.

Human action terminates either in operations or in productions.

BOOK I.
Chap. 2.

It belongs to politics to investigate the chief end of man.

ther the ends of human action consist in operations or in productions.

But if there be an ultimate end of all human pursuit, an end desirable merely in itself, (and unless there be such an end, desire, proceeding to infinity, will terminate in a baseless vision,) this ultimate end must be what is called good; and of goods, the best. The knowledge of it, also, must greatly contribute to the benefit of life; serving, as a butt to bowmen, for the direction of our views and actions. Let us, therefore, endeavour to delineate it carefully, first premising that the investigation of it belongs to that master-science called politics; a science which regulates and appoints what are the other sciences, as well as what are the arts that ought to be introduced into cities, what kinds of them the different classes of citizens ought respectively to learn, and to what extent each in particular ought to be known and cultivated. The most honourable functions of a civil or military nature; those of the orator, financier, or general, are but instruments employed by politics for promoting human happiness; which, if precisely one and the same in states and individuals, must, with regard to the former, be more difficult both to produce and to maintain. How delightful is it to make individuals happy! but to effect the happiness of states is an employment still more divine. Such then is the aim of this work, which is entirely of a political nature [d].

It

---

[d] In the Magna Moralia, l. i. c. i. p. 145. the following reason is given why Ethics should be considered as a part of politics, ἔτι δὲ οὐθὲν ἐν τοῖς πολιτικοῖς δυνατὸν πρᾶξαι ἄνευ τοῦ ποιόν τινα εἶναι, &c. "That it is impossible to do any thing in politics, without having men endowed with certain habits; wherefore Ethics," he observes, "are likely to be a part as well as the principle and source of politics."

It will be our endeavour to attain that accuracy which the nature of the subject admits; for perfection is not required in all the labours of the mind, any more than in all the works of the hand. Political justice or virtue seems liable to this uncertainty, that it depends rather on law than on nature. The good, or end, at which this virtue aims, seems to be not less doubtful; since much evil is frequently its result. Many are ruined by their wealth, and many by their courage. In matters so little stable we must be contented, therefore, with catching the general resemblance of truth; and our conclusions will deserve to be approved, if in most cases they are found to hold true; for it is the part of wisdom to be satisfied in each subject with that kind of evidence which the nature of the subject allows; it not being less absurd to require demonstrations from an orator, than to be contented with probabilities from a mathematician. Of performances in each science, those only can appreciate the merit by whom that science has been studied. From a work on politics, therefore, those alone can derive much benefit who have acquired a general and practical knowledge of human nature. Youth is not the season for such a study; for youth is unexperienced in the business of life, which is both the source and the object of all sound political reasoning. It makes not any difference whether a man is young in point of years, or in point of character; for his inaptitude arises entirely from his boyish pursuits, and childish opinions. But to those whose passions have been disciplined by the maturity of years and reason, this kind of knowledge will afford both pleasure and profit. Thus much concerning our subject, the mode of treating it, and the character of those to whom our discourse is addressed.

BOOK 1.
Chap. 3.
The proper method of treating moral and political philosophy, and the fit character of its hearers.

Let

BOOK I.
Chap. 4.

Different opinions concerning happiness.

Let us resume, therefore, by inquiring, since all our thoughts and desires aim at some kind of good, what is the end of the science called politics: or, in other words, what is the principal of all those goods resulting from the proper direction of human action? Its name is universally [e] acknowledged; both the learned and the multitude call it happiness [f]. But as to the thing itself, there is a wide diversity of opinion between philosophers and the vulgar. The latter place happiness in things visible and palpable: in pleasure, wealth, honour; and, often changing their minds, they place it, when sick, in health; when poor, in riches; and when they reflect on their own ignorance, they deem those most happy who can boast their attainments in science. Some philosophers again think that besides all these particular and relative goods, there is a good in itself absolutely, the cause of this quality in other things, which deserve to be called good merely because they participate of this absolute goodness. It would be useless to enumerate all the opinions on this subject; let it suffice to mention the most prevalent, or the most reasonable. It ought not to escape our notice that, in all our inquiries, we may either proceed from principles, or mount up towards them. Plato, therefore, doubted which of the two was the best mode of investigation; as, in Olympic Stadium, whether the proper course proceeded from the judges to the goal, or from the goal to the judges [g]. In other sciences, we ought to begin from the things best known; either absolutely in themselves,

from

---

[e] σχεδον υπο των πλειρων ομολογειται. "Almost acknowledged by the most," which seems merely a modest way of speaking, not tolerable in English.

[f] το δε ευ ζην και ευ πραττειν ταυτον υπολαμβανει τω ευδαιμονειν. "To live well and to act well, they reckon synonymous with being happy." This sentence is omitted.

[g] See History of Ancient Greece, vol. i. c. v. p. 228.

from the simplicity and stability of their nature; or relatively to the inquirer, because most familiar to his senses, his observation, and experience ᶠ. But in Politics, we ought to begin by operating on the moral nature of man, since the first requisite is to have disciples habituated to the practice of virtue. Such persons either know, or will soon understand, principles ʰ. But those of a different character may attend to Hesiod.

BOOK I.

> The best and noblest of the human kind
> Are those endow'd with a deep-thinking mind;
> Nor are *they* useless, who such men obey,
> Submitting still to wisdom's lawful sway;
> But he, who though unfit his ways to rule,
> Yet will not to a wiser go to school,
> That man is, sure, a good-for-nothing fool ⁱ.

To return from this digression, men's notions of happiness may easily be conjectured from the lives which they lead. The gross vulgar of mankind think of nothing but pleasure, and therefore lead a life of mere sensual enjoyment; constrained like slaves, and stupid as cattle. Their error is excusable, since many of the great set them an example, which themselves seem

Chap. 5.
Those opinions examined.

ᶠ For the sake of perspicuity I have here expanded Aristotle's thought by borrowing expressions frequently repeated in his Analytics and Metaphysics.

ʰ Aristotle says, they know that the thing is, and therefore need not be taught its cause; they have a practical knowledge of virtue, which is better than its theory; and this practical knowledge is itself a principle instilled and confirmed by experience and custom. See the end of chapter vii. It may be further observed, that our author, with his usual modesty, says, *perhaps* we ought to begin with the things best known to ourselves; and *therefore* those only are qualified to study politics with advantage, who have been previously trained to good morals. I have inverted the order, because the latter is proved in chapter iii.

ⁱ Hesiod, Ἔργων, i. 293.

BOOK I.

seem to have copied from the sottish Sardanapalus. A second plan of life is that pursued by men of activity and enterprise, who eagerly engage in the public concerns of their country, and have honour for their object. But this honour is a thing too superficial and flimsy to be the happiness of which we are in quest. It seems to depend not less on those who confer honours, than upon those on whom they are conferred. But happiness, we foresee, must be something independent and permanent. Besides, these troublesome honours are courted chiefly for the purpose of flattering self-love, for removing our suspicions of our own unworthiness, and for rendering us in our own conceit virtuous and happy. For this reason we take most pride in being honoured by men of sense, by those who best know us, and for meritorious actions. Virtue, therefore, is plainly more valuable than honour, even in the estimation of those by whom honour is most coveted; since the latter is pursued merely as the sign and shadow of the former. But virtue alone does not constitute happiness. A man possessed of virtue may be asleep or inactive; he may never, through life, have an opportunity of exhibiting his good qualities; and notwithstanding these qualities, he may frequently be involved in the greatest disasters. Such a man was never, except for argument's sake, pronounced happy. But enough on this subject, which has been already treated in our popular discourses. A third plan of life is that of the speculative philosopher, which shall be examined in the sequel. A life of money-making and commerce is plainly a state of toil and trouble; and riches cannot be the good inquired after, because they are desired, not on their own account, but for the purposes which they answer; and are valuable, not as ends, but merely as instruments. The other schemes of

happiness

happiness are, therefore, preferable to that of the money-maker; but even those, it appears, are defective; in confirmation of which many arguments may be produced, which we shall not at present urge.

<small>BOOK I.</small>

It may, perhaps, be better to consider good, absolute and universal; which, according to some philosophers, is the only real good, by the mere participation of which other things are entitled to this epithet. To me the task of examining this opinion is unpleasant and arduous, because the doctrine of universals and ideas was introduced by those for whom I have the greatest friendship[k]. Yet a philosopher ought to demolish even his own systems, when they stand in the way of truth; nor ought the sacred name of friendship ever to obstruct a thing still more sacred than itself. Those who introduced the doctrine of ideas allow that it is not applicable to things prior in order the one to the other[l], and therefore not applicable to number. But the word "good" applies equally to substances, to modes, and to relations; although substances are certainly prior in order to modes and relations, which are the affections or appendages of substances. The word "good" therefore, when applied to both, is not taken in the same sense; and therefore it does not

<small>Chap. 6.

Examination of Plato's opinion concerning the chief good; and refutation of the doctrine of ideas.</small>

---

[k] The author means Plato. He says, in his Magna Moralia, p. 145, that Pythagoras first treated of virtue, but improperly; since he explained the science of Ethics by that of numbers, confounding speculations altogether heterogeneous. Socrates spoke better and more perspicuously: but his theory is imperfect, because he makes the virtues matters of science; whereas science belongs only to the intellect or rational part of the soul, while the virtues belong not only to that, but (as will be fully explained hereafter) to the irrational part, consisting in the passions and appetites. Plato followed, well distinguishing the rational and irrational principles, but perplexing and darkening the subject of Ethics, by mixing with it the doctrine of ideas.

[l] Eudem. Ethic. l. i. c. viii. p. 201.—See also Analysis, p. 84, & seq.

BOOK I.

not denote any common idea. Good, indeed, is said in as many ways as being: thus it is applied to God, and the human mind, which are substances; to the virtues, which are qualities; to utility, which is a relation; to mediocrity, which is a quantity; to the critical moment, which is time; and to a fit residence, which is place [m]. It is plain, therefore, that the word "good" applied to things so different, does not denote any one idea common to all those classes or categories. If it did, all kinds of good would belong to one and the same science. But we find that various sciences are requisite for ascertaining the different kinds of good, even in one and the same category. Thus, the critical moment in war is ascertained by a general; in disease, by a physician. The medical science determines what is mediocrity with respect to diet; and the gymnastic, what is mediocrity in point of exercise. It is difficult to know wherein consists the difference between the idea of a man and a man, since both must be defined by the same terms. The same observation applies to good, and the idea of good. The eternity ascribed to the latter does not make any difference; for that which is white now, is as much white, as what has continued white for an indefinite length of time. The Pythagoreans reason better when they distinguish various kinds of good and evil[n]; in which they seem to be followed by Speusippus[o]. But of this subject we shall treat hereafter. Some uncertainty seems still

---

[m] Aristotle says, ετερα τοιαυτα, meaning the other categories, See above, p. 58.

[n] Aristotle says, they placed one in the co-arrangement of good. See above, p. 112.

[o] Aristotle is supposed to have taken it amiss that Plato should have preferred to him his own nephew Speusippus, as his successor in the academy; and this private pique is thought to have influenced him in his philosophical opposition to his master's doctrines. Were this true, it might be expected that his opposition would not have been less marked to Speusippus, whom he here goes out of his way to commend.

still to adhere to the observations above made, because we have not sufficiently distinguished the two kinds of goods; those which are loved and pursued for their own sake only, and those which are loved and pursued merely because they are fitted to produce or preserve the former, or to ward off the contrary evils. Let us separate therefore from things merely useful to some further end, things called good in themselves, and consider whether this epithet is bestowed on all of them precisely in the same sense. What are these goods in themselves, unless such things as we wish to obtain and enjoy for their own sake only; pleasures, honours, the exercise of our sight or understanding? Such things may be useful, but they are not merely useful, since, independently of any purpose which they answer, they are desired on their own account. Are all such things then called good, for the same reason that snow and ceruse are both called white, because they excite one and the same simple perception of whiteness? This is not true; for pleasure is good in one sense, honour in another, intellection in a third; in each of the three, the word "good" has a different meaning; which would not be the case if the idea of good was as simple and uniform as that of white; a doctrine that totally confounds the specific distinctions of things. Why then is the same appellation applied to such different objects? Not surely by chance; but because those objects are somehow related to each other, as proceeding from one cause, tending to one end, or connected by some analogy; as the understanding is called the eye of the mind, having the same relation to it, which the eye has to the body. But such nice speculations belong not to the present subject [p]; for if there be

[p] Aristotle says, that it is not necessary at present accurately to ascertain why different things are called good, any more than to treat accurately concerning the general idea of goodness.

ARISTOTLE's ETHICS.

BOOK I.

be a general idea of goodness, common to all things called good, and separable from them, it is plain that this separate goodness cannot be an object of human attainment, and therefore need not be an object of human pursuit. None of the arts or sciences contemplate this general idea as their example or pattern[q]; or consider it as affording the smallest assistance for attaining the different ends at which they respectively aim. Of what benefit would such a contemplation be to the embroiderer or the architect? The physician does not consider good in general, but the good, or health of man, or rather of that particular man who happens to be his patient; for with individuals only he has to do.

Chap. 7.

A delineation of the supreme good;

Let us return again to the sought-for good, and try to find out what it can be. We see that it is a different thing in different arts and actions: one thing, for example, in the art of physic; another in the art of war. What then is the good peculiar to each? Is it not that for the sake of which all the other operations of the art are performed; as in physic, health; in war, victory; in architecture, a house; and in all our actions and deliberations, the end at which they aim? If then there is an end or purpose in life itself, the good sought for must consist in this; and if more ends than one, in these. This investigation therefore brings us back to the same conclusion as before; but we must endeavour, if possible, to render the matter still more perspicuous. Since there are various objects of our pursuit, some of which are desired merely for the sake of other things, and never rationally for their own, such as riches, a flute,

---

[q] The author says, that though this general good be neither πρακτον nor κτητον; neither an object of human practice nor human attainment, yet it may be thought to serve as a παραδειγμα, or pattern; and therefore removes this objection, which he had proposed to himself.

ARISTOTLE's ETHICS.

flute, and whatever comes under the description of means or instruments, it is plain that none of these can be the good of which we are in quest, and which must be something complete and perfect in itself; for we call that more perfect which is desired on its own account, than that which is desired as a means towards some further end: and that more perfect which is never desired but as an end, than that which is desired both as a means and as an end. Happiness is never desired but for its own sake only. Honour, pleasure, intelligence, and every virtue, are desirable surely on their own account, but they are also desirable as means towards happiness. But happiness, we have said, is never desired as a means, because it is complete and all-sufficient in itself, which the good sought for ought to be; and all-sufficient, not merely for the individual, but for his parents, children, family, friends, and fellow-citizens, since man is by nature a social being; yet to this social principle limits are assigned, for if it diverged to infinity [r], there would be a desire without an object [s]: but of this we shall speak hereafter. That is all-sufficient, which, taken by itself, renders life an object of desire. Such we say is happiness, which, separate and alone, is the most desirable of all things; and therefore united with the least of other goods, still entitled to pre-eminence [t]; complete and perfect in itself, and the ultimate end of all our designs and actions.

But to call happiness the best thing in the world, (which none will dispute,) does not clearly explain wherein human happiness consists. This will best appear, if we consider what is the peculiar work and proper business of a man. A musician, a sculptor,

BOOK I.

which consists in virtuous energies.

---

[r] Aristotle says, to his children's children, and the friends of his friends, in endless succession.
[s] See above, p. 91.
[t] The good added to happiness is ὑπεροχη των αγαθων, superabundant.

BOOK I.

sculptor, and every other artist, has his respective operation and work, in the performance of which his main excellence lies; and can it be imagined, while shoemakers and carpenters have their proper tasks assigned to them, that Nature intended man for idleness? His eyes, and hands, and feet, and all his other parts, have their peculiar functions; and shall there be no function different from any, or all, of these, belonging to the whole? Wherein does this function consist? To live, is common to him with plants. The mere power of growth and nutrition belongs not therefore to the present question. The sensitive life follows next, which is common to man with horses, oxen, and the whole animal kingdom. There remains then a life of rational action; whether he exercise reason himself, or obey the reason of another. In such a life his real business consists; and that man does his business the best[t], who acts most rationally through life; the virtue of each individual of a species, depending on the excellence with which he performs the work peculiar to that species alone. The proper good of man consists then in virtuous energies[u], that is, in the exercise of virtue continued through life; for one swallow makes not a summer; neither does one day, or a short time, constitute happiness. Let this serve for a sketch of good—that universally coveted object, which will afterwards be more fully delineated: for, it should seem, that an accurate outline may easily be filled up; especially with the assistance of time,

from

---

[t] The author illustrates this, by saying that the business of a harper, and of a good harper, is the same; the difference between them arising only from the superior excellence with which the latter performs his work.

[u] Aristotle here introduces his distinction between virtue and the energy of virtue. See above, p. 133. This sense is expressed in the text, in language more familiar to the modern reader.

from which arts derive their improvement. Let us remember
also what was before observed, that more accuracy should not
be expected from an author, than is consistent with the nature
of his subject, and his design in treating it. Both the bricklayer and the mathematician are conversant with perpendiculars;
but the former considers them only as useful in his work; the
latter examines their nature and properties, because abstract
truth is the object of his study. Unless the example of the
bricklayer be followed in other matters, the principal subject
will often be exceeded and obscured by the mere accessories.
Let it also be remembered, that we ought not to be over curious
in the investigation of causes; concerning some things it is
sufficient to know that they are, without knowing their reason.
This is the case with those first principles which result from perceptions of sense, from induction, and from custom [a]. We ought
carefully to draw them from their respective sources, and exert
our utmost care that they be correctly ascertained. This is of
the highest importance in all our inquiries; in which, that
which is begun well, is more than half ended; since much
light is thereby diffused through every subsequent part of our
speculations.

BOOK I.

We shall examine this chief good or happiness, not merely
in its definition, but in the properties rightly ascribed to it.
Truth only is consistent; and if our notion of happiness be
just, it will not be discordant with those properties. Goods
are

Chap. 8.

This opi-
nion consist-
ent with the
properties
ascribed to
happiness.

[a] Our author adds, αλλα δι αλλως, which may be translated, " and other principles
arise from other sources." But this does not appear to me to be his meaning, because
I do not find any other sources mentioned in any part of his works: The αλλα αλλως
must then mean that some of those principles arise from one of those sources, and some
from another, which is implied in the translation.

VOL. I.   Y

BOOK I.

are divided into three kinds: those of the mind, those of the body, and those consisting in externals. We give the preference to the first of the three, which we regard as the sovereign good; placing happiness in mental energy; an opinion ancient and universal among philosophers. We do right also in placing the chief end and main purpose of life in action. From this, it results that happiness is seated in the mind; a truth confirmed by the common sense of mankind embodied in language; "living well," or "doing well," being expressions synonymous with happiness. In all their inquiries on the subject, men seem to have been led to conclusions nearly resembling the notion of happiness above given. Some place it in virtue, others in prudence, others in wisdom; some join pleasure; others add externals; and those different opinions have either been long held by the greater part of mankind, or more recently introduced by most respectable philosophers. It is not credible, that either party should totally mistake the truth. Our notion nearly agrees with theirs who place happiness in virtue; for we say that it consists in the action of virtue; that is, not merely in the possession, but in the use[y]. The mere possession is consistent with a state of sleep, or listless apathy, from which no good can result. But the virtuous man, when he acts, must act well, and be happy; as, in the Olympic games, the prize is gained only by the combatants; not by those, whatever their merits may be, who decline entering the lists. To such men virtue is the highest pleasure; for pleasure resides in the mind, and each is most pleased with what he most loves. Thus the lover of horses is pleased with horses; the lover of shows, with shows; and the lover of justice is no less pleased with justice;

and

---

[y] Aristotle here opposes habit to energy, as well as possession to use.

and the lover of virtue, with virtue. The multitude, indeed, purfue different pleafures, becaufe they do not rightly apprehend in what true pleafure confifts. But pleafure, ftrictly fo called, is the delight of a virtuous man, whofe life needs not an appendage of falfe joys, containing the perennial fpring of true pleafure in itfelf. For he is not a good man who delights not in good actions; and vain is the praife of juftice, liberality, and other virtues, by thofe who feel no gratification in their practice. In the eftimation of a wife man, virtue is pleafant becaufe it is honourable and good; his happinefs is one regular whole; not broken and disjointed like that in the Delian infcription:

"The faireft good is juftice; health, the beft;
"The fweeteft far, to tafte of what we love."

All thefe qualities belong to the beft energies, in which, we fay, happinefs confifts. The opinion of thofe who add externals, is not ill-founded; fince, independently of them, it is often impoffible, at leaft very difficult, to exhibit virtue in its full luftre [*]. Many operations muft be performed by inftruments; under which name I include friends, wealth, and political power. The want of fome advantages; for example, of honourable defcent, of promifing children, or of dignity of prefence;

---

[*] In the Ethics to Eudemus, b. i. c. ii. p. 196., Ariftotle makes an important diftinction between the things in which human happinefs confifts, and thofe without which it cannot be completely enjoyed; ιν τοι ταν ημετερων το ξην ιυ' και τινων ανιυ, τοις ανθρωποις ουκ ενδεχεται ποιω, &c. "Healta is different from the things by which it is upheld, and life from thofe by which it is rendered comfortable. The fame holds with regard to all the actions and habits of men." The confounding happinefs with the externals, without which, in our dependent ftate, it cannot be completely enjoyed, is confidered by our author as one of the great fources of immoral practice, as well as of erroneous theory.

BOOK I.

Chap. 9.
───
Which depends on our own exertions.

presence; deprives happiness of its splendour: and the man seems less qualified for attaining it, who is deformed in body, friendless, childless, and forlorn [a]. Wherefore some place happiness in external prosperity [b].

It comes then to be considered, whether happiness is acquired by instruction, custom, or some other kind of exercise; or merely by the dispensation of fortune and the gods. There is not any gift surely that might more reasonably be expected to descend from heaven, since, of all human possessions, happiness is the most valuable. But this question will be more fitly examined in another place. For happiness, even though it descend not from heaven, but be attained by study and exercise on earth, is yet most divine in itself; the end and prize of virtue, which all may gain by due exertion, who are not maimed in their minds. The acquiring of happiness by ourselves, is preferable to owing it to fortune [c]; it most probably therefore is thus acquired; since nature always effects her purposes by the best means; a point aimed at by art, and every intelligent cause, and which the best cause always attains: and to leave happiness, the fairest and best of things, to the disposal of fortune, would be a mark of negligence not discernible in any other of the arrangements of nature [d]. That happiness is acquired by ourselves,

[a] Aristotle adds, "or who having had good friends and promising children, has lost them."

[b] What is added, τινι δι την αριτην, "and some place it in virtue," seems superfluous.

[c] For this he assigns two reasons in the Ethics to Eudemus, b. i. c. iii. p. 197. ει δ'εν τω, αυτοι ποιω τινα ειναι, και τας κατ' αυτοι πραξεις, κοινοτερον αν ειη το αγαθον και θειοτερον, &c. "If good or happiness consists in the quality of our actions and characters, it must be both more common and more divine; more common, because a greater number may attain it; and more divine, because it will depend upon our own exertions." Idem ibid.

[d] There is, perhaps, an intentional obscurity in the whole of this passage. Aristotle does

ourselves, agrees also with its definition, "that it consists in virtuous energies." Other things, we have said, are necessary, as a certain length of time; and others are serviceable, as instruments. The same conclusion corresponds with what we said in the beginning, namely, that politics aimed at promoting the highest felicity of man; the principal care, therefore, of all good statesmen has always been, to form their fellow-citizens to virtue. Neither an ox nor a horse, nor any other animal, is denominated happy; because virtuous energies cannot be ascribed to them. Nor is this epithet bestowed on children, whose imperfect age affords only a promise of happiness. But many are the vicissitudes of life; and those who have long been prosperous, may, towards the conclusion of their days, be involved in calamities rivalling the far-famed disasters of Priam. None will call those happy, who, after suffering such evils in life, die a wretched death.

Ought we, then, to adopt the sentiments of Solon, "that no man can be called happy while he lives?" Is he therefore happy when he dies? or is not this too absurd to be said, especially by those who place happiness in action? It does not appear that Solon had this meaning, but only that a man might, at death, be congratulated upon his escape from the evils and calamities of life. Yet this opinion is liable to contradiction; for a man when dead, is, with regard to prosperity and adversity, in the same state with a man who meets with either of them when alive,

BOOK I.

Chap. 10.

Solon's saying, that none can be pronounced happy till dead.

does not expressly deny the interference of the gods; but afterwards, confounding this interference with fortune, says, that it is not reasonable to believe that nature, or (as explained in other passages) the God of nature, should commit such an important object as human happiness to the direction of so blind a guide as fortune. But in the strict philosophical sense, happiness, as well as all other things, is ultimately to be referred to the Deity as its cause. Metaphys. l. i. c. ii. p. 841.

alive, without being fensible of them; and is in this manner still within the reach of the good or bad fortune which befals his children and their defcendants. And how unftable is the profperity of families? What vaft degeneracy in the fons of happy and illuftrious fathers? Yet it feems abfurd to fuppofe the ftate of the dead affected and altered by thefe revolutions, and not lefs abfurd to fuppofe that the happinefs of children fhould not be fhared by their parents. But the folution of the queftion firft propofed, will enable us to folve the other difficulties. Solon faid that we muft look to the end; meaning thereby, that we might then juftly fay, not that a man was, but that he had been, happy. Is it not therefore abfurd to think that, while he actually was happy, this epithet could not be applied to him, becaufe of the viciffitudes of life to which he was expofed? If happinefs changes with fortune, it will be as variable as the colours of the camelion. But this is not true: for the propriety of our conduct depends, not on our fortune, but on our manner of ufing it; and virtuous energies are the genuine fource of happinefs, as the vicious are of mifery. This is attefted by the queftion juft ftarted concerning the importance of ftability to happinefs. Of all human things, habitual energies of virtue are the moft ftable; they are more permanent than even the fciences; and of the virtues themfelves, the moft valuable are the firmeft; forming the continual meditation and delight of thofe whom they adorn. For this reafon, they alone are not liable to be forgotten or loft; but are an immoveable property in the thoughts and life of a good man; who, whatever may befal him, will behave gracefully; approving his conduct exact, fquare, and blamelefs. Slight misfortunes are unable to fhake his well-balanced happinefs; but,

This faying explained.

The peculiar ftability of virtuous energies.

in the use of a great prosperity, his excellence will shine more conspicuous; and when persecuted by painful and afflicting calamity, which not only impedes his present exertions, but darkens his future prospects, his worth will irradiate the gloom, while he resists and surmounts the severest sufferings, not by stupid insensibility, but by generous magnanimity; for, if our own actions be the sovereign arbiters of our lot, a virtuous man can never be wretched; because he will never render himself an object either of hatred or contempt. Of the circumstances in which he is placed, he will always make the best and most honourable use; as a good general, and a good artist, employs the forces, and the materials, with which they are respectively entrusted, always to the best advantage. A happiness founded on such a basis, can never sink into misery; although it must be shaken by tragic misfortunes, from which it will not soon recover its natural state. Yet, in consequence of virtuous exertions, continued through a sufficient length of time, a good man, competently furnished with the accommodations of life, will resume his wonted serenity; and may be pronounced happy, notwithstanding the vicissitudes to which he is still exposed; at least possessed of such happiness as is consistent with the condition of humanity.

We are not therefore to ascribe happiness only to the dead, (for thus Solon's sentiment is commonly understood,) especially since to suppose that the dead are totally insensible to the misfortunes of their kinsmen and friends on earth, is neither conformable to common opinion, nor consistent with the social principles belonging to human nature. It would be endless to enumerate and describe the various forms of calamity and woe, by the differences of which even the living are very differently

Chap. II.

How the dead are affected by the condition of the living.

BOOK
I.

differently affected; but the sympathy of the dead with such miseries, bears less proportion to that of the living, than the sympathy of spectators at the theatre bears to that of spectators in the real tragedies of life. It may deserve consideration, whether the dead at all participate in the good or bad fortune of their living friends; but if they do, it is reasonable to think that the events of this world affect them too slightly, to render such of them as are miserable happy, or those that are happy miserable.

Chap. 12.

That happiness is above praise.

Let us proceed then to determine whether happiness be the object of praise, or rather of honour; for it is plain that its nature is not doubtful, and that it never can be blamed or despised. That only is an object of praise which is endowed with certain qualities or habits, that naturally terminate in some salutary effect. For this reason we commend justice and courage, as well as strength and swiftness, and every virtue; but the praises which belong to men, are ridiculous when applied to the gods, whose perfections are the objects of emotions of a higher nature; we bless and honour and magnify them; and even those things which, from some resemblance to them, are called divine. Happiness, therefore, is exalted above praise, by the excellence and divinity of its nature. Wherefore Eudoxus[e] ingeniously defended the pretensions of pleasure to be called the sovereign good; saying, that it was confessedly not the object of praise, and therefore something better. But praise properly belongs to virtue, the only source of those exertions of mind or body on which just encomiums are bestowed; to examine which particularly, belongs to the subject of Rhetoric.

[e] Eudoxus, the scholar of Plato, and legislator of his countrymen, the Cnidians.—He is again mentioned by our author in the tenth book of his Ethics.

toric. This, then, is clear, that the value of happiness is not relative, but absolute; it is complete and perfect in itself; and, being the ultimate end to which all praise-worthy things are referred, is itself the object, not of praise, but of veneration and honour [f].

But since happiness results from virtuous energies, by examining the nature of virtue, we shall be more likely to understand that of happiness. The true statesman is chiefly solicitous about virtue, exerting himself to the utmost to inspire his fellow-citizens with a respectful deference for good laws. Such were the legislators of Crete and of Sparta; and others, perhaps, who were animated by the same enlightened principles of public spirit. To investigate the nature of virtue belongs to every liberal system of politics, and therefore to our present subject, of which human happiness is the end, and human virtue the means; understanding, thereby, the virtue of the mind, in the exercise of which happiness consists. The true statesman therefore ought to know the mind, as much, or rather more, (because his pursuit is still more excellent,) than the physician does the body; and we see that the more liberal sort of physicians bestow no small pains in gaining an accurate knowledge of the latter. To enter into speculations, not connected with practice, is

Chap. 13.

The knowledge of the mind a necessary preparation for moral science.

[f] This subject is explained more clearly in the Ethics to Eudemus, b. i. c. i. p. 203. The author discriminates the words ενεργειν πραξις and αποτελεσμα: the first of which applies to particular actions; the second to habits; and the third to the ends and enjoyments which are thereby accomplished or attained. The English language does not admit of such nice distinctions; and αποτελεσμα, "beatification," is an appropriate term in the Romish church, which could not, without doing violence, be distorted to a philosophical sense.

BOOK I.

is beside our present purpose. We shall make use of that distinction between powers rational and irrational, which is sufficiently explained in our popular discourses, without inquiring whether these two are separable from each other, like the parts of the body and every thing divisible, or whether they be two merely to the intellectual eye, though as incapable of corporeal division as are the convexity and concavity of the same circle [a]. The irrational powers of the soul are distinguishable into different kinds. Those which contribute to nutrition and growth are the same in man arrived at maturity, and in the child unborn, and even in plants. Any virtue belonging to them cannot be dignified with the epithet of human, since their energies are most perfect in sleep, during the total inactivity of those higher powers, by which men are peculiarly characterised and individually distinguished; wherefore it is said, that for nearly one half of their lives, the same lot befals the good and the bad, the happy and the miserable; except that, in consequence of some remains of wakeful motions, the dreams of the former will commonly be more agreeable. But enough of this, which is foreign to our present subject. There is another part of the soul, which, though irrational itself, is capable of combining with reason;

Our moral powers compounded of the rational and irrational principles of our nature.

[a] διαφέρει δι ειδεν καὶ τι μέρος ἡ ψυχη, ὥς τι αμερες· εχει ταυτα δυνάμεις διαφόρους. Eudem. l. ii. c. i. p. 204. Aristotle says, that it makes not any difference as to the present subject, whether the soul be divisible or indivisible; it is sufficient that it have distinct powers or faculties; that is, distinct principles to which all the complicated operations of the mind, and all the wide variety of human action may be traced. It will not be easy to point out what improvement has been made since the days of Aristotle, either in the investigation of those principles from the phenomena, or in the application of them when discovered, to explain the highly-diversified operations observable in the intellectual and moral world.

4

reason; and, when thus combined, is virtuous and praise-worthy. This appears in persons endowed with self-command, but not completely confirmed in that habit. Reason exhorts them to prefer the better part, but another power impels them to the contrary side, and violently resists reason; in the same manner as limbs affected by the palsy refuse obedience to our determinations, and assume one direction when we wish them to move in another. A similar resisting power exists in the mind, though the false motion impressed by it is not perceptible to the senses. This power, though irrational[h], is capable of combining with reason, and submitting to its control, as appears in men endowed with self-command[i] or continency, and still more in those whose minds are harmonised by temperance. The appetites therefore are of a higher order than the mere powers of growth and nutrition, because they are capable of listening to reason, as children do to their parents, whose admonitions they understand and obey, in a sense quite different from that in which they afterwards understand and know mathematical truths. If we choose to call also this part of the soul rational, there will then be two different principles of reason in the mind, the first of which possesses reason absolutely in itself, whereas the second is only capable of harkening to the reason of another. On this distinction,

[h] This power, he says, is something different from reason, but how different it is unnecessary to inquire; which relates to what is explained above.

[i] Self-command or continency, in Greek ἐγκρατεια, implies that a man is impelled by corrupt appetites, which he has strength of mind sufficient to resist; temperance, in Greek σωφροσυνη, implies that his appetites have been so thoroughly subdued by custom and reason, that they no longer have any tendency to rebel. This latter, in its highest perfection, is that delightful harmony of soul in which our moral improvement terminates.

distinction, the division of the virtues into the intellectual and moral, is founded. Wisdom, intelligence, and prudence belong to the former class; liberality and temperance to the latter. In reference to morals, we do not say that a man is wise or intelligent, but that he is meak or temperate. Good men are praised for good habits; and all praise-worthy habits are called virtues.

ARISTOTLE's ETHICS.

BOOK II.

INTRODUCTION.

THE moſt profound as well as the moſt elegant of all modern writers on the ſubject of political Ethics, the immortal Grotius, in his treatiſe on the laws of war and peace, obſerves, that Ariſtotle holds the firſt rank among philoſophers, whether we eſtimate him by the perſpicuity of his method, the acuteneſs of his diſtinctions, or the weight and ſolidity of his arguments[a]. This criticiſm is fully juſtified by the book before us, in which our author treats of the nature of moral virtue, ſhews by what means it is acquired, proves by an accurate induction that it conſiſts in the habit of mediocrity, and lays down three practical rules for its attainment. This part of his work will bear that trial which he regards as the teſt of excellence; " it requires not any addition, and it will not admit of retrenchment." The objections made to it, as falling ſhort of the purity and ſublimity of Chriſtian morality, will equally apply to all the diſcoveries of human reaſon, when compared with " that divine light which, coming into the world, gives, or offers, light to every man in it[b]. But the critics who make objections[c] to Ariſtotle, would urge

---
[a] Grotius in Prolegom.   [b] John, c. i. v. 9.
[c] See ſome of them ſtated in Grotii Prolegom. de Jure Belli & Pacis.

urge them with less confidence, if they attended to two remarks on which our author often insists; first, that practical matters admit not of scientific or logical accuracy; secondly, that the virtues of which he is in quest, are all of them merely relative to the condition and exigencies of man in political society, being those habits, acquired by our own exertion, in which, when confirmed, we shall uniformly act our parts on the theatre of the world, usefully, agreeably, and gracefully. In Aristotle's philosophy, man is the judge of man; in Christianity, the judge of man is God. Philosophy confines itself to the perishing interests of the present world; Christianity, looking beyond those interests, takes a loftier aim, inspires the mind with nobler motives, and promises to adorn it with perfections, worthy of its inestimably valuable rewards. Yet to the man of piety, it may be a matter of edification, to compare the virtue of philosophical firmness with the grace of Christian patience; and to observe how nearly the rules discovered by reason and experience, as most conducive to the happiness of our present state, coincide with those precepts which are given in the Gospel in order to fit us for a better.

BOOK II.

ARGUMENT.

Moral virtues acquired by exercise and custom—Consist in holding the mean between blameable extremes—Test of virtue—The virtues, habits—The nature of these habits ascertained—Why vices mistaken for virtues, and conversely—Practical rules for the attainment of virtue.

VIRTUE being twofold, intellectual and moral, the former is produced and increased chiefly by instruction, and therefore requires experience and time; the latter is acquired by repeated acts or custom, from which, by a small change[d], its name is derived. None of the moral virtues, therefore, are implanted by nature; for properties given by nature, cannot be taken away or altered by custom; thus the gravity of a stone, which naturally carries it downward, cannot be changed into levity, which would carry it upward, were we to throw it in that direction ten thousand times; and fire, which naturally seeks the extremities, cannot be brought by custom to have a tendency towards the center: nor, in a word, can any law of nature be altered by custom. The moral virtues, therefore, are neither natural nor preternatural; we are born with capacities for acquiring them, but they can only be acquired by our own exertions. Powers, implanted by nature, precede in the order of existence their operations; which is manifest with regard to the senses. The powers of seeing and hearing are not acquired by repeated operations of those faculties; but, on the contrary, they existed in us before we exercised them, and continue to exist

BOOK II.

They are acquired by exercise and custom.

exist in us, though they should cease to be exercised. But the habit of moral virtue, like all other practical arts, can be acquired or preserved by practice only. By building, we become architects; by harping, musicians; and, in the same manner, by acts of justice, we become just; and by acts of courage, courageous. This is attested by what happens in whole nations; whose characters result from their conduct. All legislators wish to make virtuous and happy citizens: but they do not all attain this end; for the virtues are like the arts, acquired by a right, and destroyed by a wrong, practice. Architects and musicians thus become good or bad; and if this were not the case, instruction would be superfluous. The same holds in the virtues. By correctness, or the contrary, in our transactions with mankind, we become just or unjust; according to our behaviour in circumstances of danger, our characters are formed to courage or cowardice; and in proportion as we indulge or restrain the excitements to anger and pleasure, we become adorned with the habits of meekness and temperance, or deformed by those of passionateness and profligacy. In one word, such as our actions are, such will our habits become. Actions, therefore, ought to be most diligently attended to; and it is not a matter of small moment how we are trained from our youth; much depends on this, or rather all [c].

Chap. 2.

What are the rules by which our actions ought to be shaped in order to attain virtue.

Since the present treatise is not merely a theory, as other parts of our works, (for the inquiry is not "wherein virtue consists," but "how it may best be attained," without which the speculative knowledge of it is not of the smallest value,) we must begin by examining, by what rules our actions ought to be shaped, because by them our habits and characters are moulded. That our conduct ought to be agreeable to right reason, may be

[c] The same subject is treated in the Magna Moralia, l. i. c. vi.; and in the Eudemian Ethics, l. ii. c. ii.

be here assumed as an axiom; but it will afterwards be shewn what this right reason is, and what reference it has to the other virtues. Let us not forget, what was formerly observed, that practical matters admit not of logical precision; and that greater accuracy of language ought not to be expected, than is consistent with the nature of the subject. The propriety of action admits not of definite rules, any more than the exact quantity of food or exercise conducive to health. This observation holds true with regard to the science of morals as well as of medicines; but is peculiarly applicable to the particular cases belonging to both sciences; which cases are so dissimilar to each other, that it is impossible to include them under any common precept; and the man of morals, like the pilot and the physician, must comply with the exigencies of the moment, and vary his behaviour with the variation of circumstances. Notwithstanding this instability in the nature of the subject, we must endeavour to give some assistance to those who aim at virtue. First, then, it is worthy of remark, that propriety of conduct always consists in a mean or middle between two vicious extremes; and as the health and strength of our bodies visibly depend on a due proportion of food and exercise, equally remote from superabundance or penury; so is the health and vigour of our minds destroyed by superabundance or penury of those very things or qualities, by the due proportion of which those excellencies are acquired, maintained, or augmented. This we may perceive holds true with respect to courage, temperance, and every other virtue. He who flies from every danger, is a coward; he who rushes on every danger, is a madman; the man who indulges in every pleasure, is a voluptuary; and the man who, with rustic austerity, rejects the most allowable pleasures, may be justly charged with an insensibility misbecoming his nature. The virtues of courage and temperance, which are destroyed

BOOK II.

That it consists in holding the mean between two vicious extremes.

This proved by induction.

BOOK II.

stroyed by excess or deficiency, are therefore preserved by mediocrity; and on observing this golden mean depend not only the origin and increase of the virtues [f], but the energy or operation by which their proper work is effected; for as a strong constitution, which is produced or confirmed by much food and much exercise, enables a man to bear with safety a great measure of either; so, by resisting the temptations of pleasure, we acquire temperance; and having become temperate, we can resist such temptations: by resisting the emotions of fear amidst dangers, we acquire courage; and having become courageous, we are able to face dangers.

Chap. 3.

The surest test of virtue is the pleasure felt in exercising it.

The pleasure or pain resulting from acts of virtue, affords the best criterion concerning the confirmation of the habit. He who abstains from bodily pleasures, and rejoices in his temperance, is truly possessed of this virtue; he who grieves at his abstinence is, on the other hand, a voluptuary. A man of courage faces dangers with pleasure, at least without pain; a coward, always with the latter. Moral virtue is therefore occupied about regulating our pleasures and pains; for the love of pleasure stimulates us to profligacy, and fear of pain withholds us from the path of honour. Plato says well, that right education consists in teaching us to rejoice, and to grieve, at such things as are the proper objects of those emotions. Virtue is seen in affections and actions, all of which are accompanied either with pleasure or with pain; and therefore virtue is necessarily conversant about pains and pleasures; as is proved also by the necessity of rewards and punishments, which are moral medicines; and, like all other medicines, in their nature contrary to the diseases which they are fitted to cure. Besides, every

---

[f] Aristotle adds, "their destruction," which is produced by a departure from this mean, so that their energies have the same causes with their generation, augmentation, and destruction; only with regard to the last, these causes act in a contrary direction.

every habit of the mind is intimately connected with those things by which it is rendered better or worse; which happens to virtue with regard to pleasure and pain; for our morals are vitiated by pursuing or avoiding either of them with undue ardour; at improper times, in improper places, or on improper occasions. The virtues, therefore, have been supposed to consist in apathy; erroneously indeed, because they consist in the due regulation, not in the total extinction, of passion; and passion properly directed, is productive of happiness; improperly, of misery. For, as there are three objects naturally preferred, namely, honour, profit, and pleasure; and three naturally shunned, namely, disgrace, loss, and pain; a virtuous man knows practically how to estimate the value of all those things in their relation to human happiness; a knowledge, of which the man enured to vicious habits is totally unsusceptible. But the two characters are principally distinguished by their various degrees of sensibility to the different kinds of pleasure; the love of which is implanted in all animals, and of which one kind or other necessarily accompanies every object of preference; both profit and honour being pursued as pleasures. Our natures indeed are deeply tinged, and as it were engrained, with the love of pleasure, which, being nourished and growing stronger with our frame, is most difficultly moderated; especially when it has become the standard by which things and actions are appreciated. The great business of morality, therefore, lies in restraining the undue pursuit of pleasure, and the undue aversion to pain. As Heracleitus says, it is more difficult to contend with pleasure than with anger; but the most difficult part is that best fitted for shewing the excellence of the performer. The moralist and statesman, therefore, must bend their utmost attention towards regulating the behaviour of those intrusted to their care, in those particulars on which their merit or demerit chiefly depends. But enough has been said to shew, that moral virtue is conversant about pains and pleasures; that the actions from which it originally springs, either augment or destroy it, according as they are well or ill directed; and that the same good works to which its existence is due, are those in which it continues to be constantly employed.

Chap. 4.

Solution of a difficulty respecting the mode of acquiring virtue.

A doubt arises, why we should say that men acquire justice by doing just actions, or become temperate by observing the rules of temperance; since, if they perform such actions and observe such rules, it should seem that they must be already endowed with those virtues; in the same manner as a man who writes or who performs according to the rules of grammar and music, is already a grammarian and a musician. But this does not hold true even with respect to the arts; for a man may write grammar, merely by imitation, by chance, or by the direction of another; but to be a grammarian, he must himself understand the art. Besides this, the perfection of works of art is in themselves; but the whole merit of virtuous actions depends on the disposition of the actor:

Four things requisite to constitute a virtuous character.

first, that he performed them with knowledge; secondly, with deliberation and preference; thirdly, that he preferred and performed them on their own account; and lastly, that he is firm and immovable in his virtuous resolutions. The first of these requisites only, viz. that of knowledge, is essential to the artist; but in constituting the character of a virtuous man, mere knowledge is of little avail, and the other three particulars of the greatest: stability in virtuous practice results from repeated acts of virtue; in consequence of which, not only those acts are such as a virtuous man would perform, but he who performs them is rightly disposed, and virtuously affected. It is therefore truly said, that we acquire justice and temperance

temperance from acting justly and temperately; since, independently of our own actions, we never could acquire those virtues. But the multitude, neglecting practice, think to acquire virtue by theory; like those patients who consult physicians, but use none of their prescriptions. Such physic will not benefit the body; nor such philosophy the mind.

We must next examine, whether virtue be a passion, a faculty, or a habit; for these are three distinct principles in the mind. By passion, I mean every emotion accompanied with pain or pleasure; as love, anger, fear, courage, envy, joy, friendship, hatred, tenderness, emulation, pity. By faculty, I mean, in this place, the capacity of being affected by those passions; by anger, grief, or pity. By habit, I mean the habitude or relation which our minds bear to those passions; as whether we are affected too much or too little by anger, both which are wrong; or affected by it moderately, on proper occasions, which only is right: the same observation applies to all other passions. Neither the virtues nor the vices therefore can be passions; because it is not in reference to the passions that we are denominated good or bad, and are regarded as the objects of praise or of blame. It is not our fear or anger simply, but the degree of those passions, that constitutes the propriety or impropriety of our conduct; and renders us the just objects of commendation or reproach. Besides, fear and anger, and all other passions, are emotions independent of our own deliberation and preference; but the virtues always imply an act of comparison, and the preference of one sort of conduct to another. Farther, we are said to be moved and impelled by passion, but our characters are disposed and settled by virtue; for which reason the virtues cannot be called capacities; and also, because we are neither praised nor blamed in reference to

our

BOOK II.

Chap. 5.
That the virtues are neither passions nor capacities, but habits.

our being fusceptive or capable of paffion. Thefe capacities, befides, are implanted by nature; which the virtues, as we have already proved, are not. Since then they are neither paffions nor faculties, it remains that they fhould belong to that clafs called habits [f].

Chap. 6.

The nature of this habit afcertained.

It is not enough to fay that virtue is a habit; we muft further afcertain what is the nature of that habit. Every virtue, then, tends to conftitute the perfection of that object to which it belongs, and to fit it for performing properly its peculiar functions. Thus, the virtue of the eye conftitutes the perfection of that organ, and qualifies it for feeing diftinctly: and the virtue of a horfe conftitutes the perfection of that animal, and qualifies him for running fwiftly, for bearing his rider, and for difdaining fear at the approach of an enemy. The virtue of a man, therefore, muft be that habit which conftitutes the perfection of his nature; and fits him for performing properly his peculiar functions. How this habit is to be attained, we have explained already; but the matter will be rendered more perfpicuous by further examining the nature of virtue. From every thing continuous and divifible, we may take the half, a greater part, or a leffer. The half may be confidered as the mean proportional between the extremes of too much and too little, from which it is equally remote; and confidered in relation to the object itfelf, this mean proportional is always one and the fame; but confidered in relation to man, this juft mean continually varies, becaufe the middle between the two vicious extremes of too much or too little is, in reference to him, that which is neither more nor lefs than propriety requires. Thus, if ten be the greater extreme, and two the leffer, fix muft be the

arithmetical

[f] The fame fubject is treated in Magna Moral. l. i. c. v.; and in the Eudemian Ethics, l. ii. c. iii.

arithmetical mean, becaufe it exceeds the leffer, as much as it is exceeded by the greater. But in regulating human actions, which, like all other motions, are things continuous and divifible[h], the fame fimple rule will not apply: for two pounds may be too fmall an allowance, and ten too large; yet he who directs the regimen of the wreftlers, will not therefore prefcribe univerfally fix pounds, which might be too little for Milo the wreftler, though far too much for one beginning his exercifes: the fame thing holds as to the quantity of labour which he enjoins to be performed, in running, wreftling, and the other branches of the gymnaftic. Thus, he who is fkilful in directing actions of any other kind, will carefully avoid excefs or defect, but find out and prefer the golden mean; which is the object that every good artift always keeps in view, fince the higheft commendation of works of art confifts in faying that they admit neither of addition nor retrenchment. But virtue, which is the perfection of nature itfelf, is far fuperior to art, which only imitates her operations, in aiming at the juft mean between two vicious extremes. I fpeak here of moral virtue, which is converfant about paffions and actions, all of which admit of mediocrity, as well as of excefs or defect. Thus we may be too much or too little affected, with defire or averfion, courage or fear, anger or pity, pain or pleafure. Both extremes are bad; and the paffion is then only proper and correct, when we are affected fuitably to its caufes, its objects, and its ends: when this is the cafe, both the paffion, and the action proceeding from it, are juftly praifed as virtuous; becaufe they do not deviate from the mark at which they ought to aim. The Pythagoreans, therefore, did well in affigning definite to the co-arrangement of

BOOK II.

That the virtues do not admit of excefs or of defect, nor the vices of mediocrity.

[h] ἡ μὲν γὰρ κίνησις συνεχής· ἡ δὲ πρᾶξις κίνησις, Eudem. l. ii. c. iii. p. 205.

of good, and indefinite to that of evil[h]; for there is but one right road; but the ways of error are innumerable. The former is as difficult as the latter is easy; it is difficult to hit the mark, but easy to miss it;

"Virtue is still the same, but vice has various forms."

The former, therefore, is the habit of preferring and observing mediocrity in our passions and actions, agreeably to the rules of right reason: virtue then, in its essence, is mediocrity; in its effect, it is excellence, and the highest excellence [i]. But neither all passions nor all actions admit of mediocrity; for there are many whose very names infer excess and blame; as the passions of impudence, malice, and envy; and the actions of adultery, theft, and murder. Such passions and such actions are in themselves detestable excesses: and for the same reason, there cannot be any mediocrity in cowardice, injustice, or intemperance; nor any excess or defect in the virtues of courage or wisdom; nor universally can mediocrity or virtue admit of excess

[h] See Analysis, p. 112.

[i] This is the clearest meaning I can affix to κατα το εν ακροτης. But Aristotle when he calls virtue, in one sense, an extreme, seems to allude to what is said in his second Analytics concerning the ὁροι συμπερασματικοι, the termini conclusorii, and the difference between them and definitions, shewing the essence, that is, the cause which makes any thing to be what it is. Thus, What is it to square an oblong? This question may be answered, or in other words, the squaring may be defined by saying, either that it is to find a square equal to an oblong; or, that it is to find a line which is a geometrical mean between the sides of the oblong. The former definition is called συμπερασματικη, because when the mathematician demonstrates, that the square constructed on a line, which is the mean proportional between the sides of the oblong, is equal to that oblong, he draws the conclusion, "a square, therefore, is found equal to an oblong:" but the second definition tells, not only that the square is equal to the oblong, but the cause which makes it to be so. In the same manner, when we call virtue the highest excellence or perfection of any object, we only tell, in other words, what is meant by virtue; but when we call it mediocrity, we define it by its essence, and shew the cause which makes it to be the highest excellence.

excefs or defect; nor the vices, which are all of them extremes, admit of a virtuous mediocrity.

In practical morality, general principles are of little ufe, unlefs they be applied to particulars, in which all practice confifts, and by which all general principles muft, if true, be confirmed. Let the various paffions or emotions therefore be arranged in a diagram[k], and we fhall fee that the degree of them confiftent with propriety always lies in the middle between two blamable extremes. Thus, in encountering or avoiding dangers, courage holds the middle place between rafhnefs and timidity: in obeying or refifting folicitations to pleafure, temperance holds the middle place between voluptuoufnefs, and a vice which, being uncommon, is namelefs, but which we fhall call unfeeling apathy. In pecuniary matters, liberality is the mean between extravagance and parfimony. The prodigal is too carelefs in throwing away money, and at too little pains to acquire it. The mifer pays exceffive attention to the acquifition of money, and exceffive attention to the keeping of it. There are other qualities relating to money, as magnificence with its contrary extremes of niggardlinefs and wafteful profufion; which diftinctions will be afterwards explained[l]. As to honour and difhonour, magnanimity is the middle term between boaftful pride and mean-fpirited abafement; and there is another quality or habit which bears the fame proportion to magnanimity which liberality does to magnificence, confifting in the propriety of our affection with refpect to fmall and ordinary marks of honour,

BOOK II.

Chap. 7.

That all the virtues confift in mediocrity, proved by induction.

---

[k] The diagram, or delineation, which is here wanting, may be partly fupplied from Ethic. Eudem. l. ii. c. iii. for even there it is extremely incomplete.

[l] In the firft chapters of the Fourth Book.

nour, whereas magnanimity confifts in the propriety of our affection with refpect to thofe which are great and extraordinary. In the common intercourfe of life, men are diftinguifhed by too much or too little defire of honour; the excefs and the defect are both marked by names [m], but the intermediate and praifeworthy degree of the affection is namelefs; wherefore the extremes contend with each other about the middle place; and, as either happens to obtain it, we praife a decent pride or a becoming humility. The reafon of this incongruity in our judgments will be afterwards explained: we proceed at prefent according to our propofed plan. With regard to anger, fome men are too fufceptible, and others too unfufceptible of this paffion; and others commonly indulge it only in that degree which is laudable. Thefe different difpofitions or habits are not accurately diftinguifhed by names. We fhall call the intermediate and proper degree of the affection meeknefs; which inclines, however, more to the extreme of phlegmatic endurance, than to that of immoderate irafcibility. There are three other virtues or proprieties, which, though different, are yet nearly allied to each other, and all of them diftinguifhable in the ordinary intercourfe of words and actions; bearing different relations, the one to truth, and the other to pleafure; and that which relates to pleafure, either confined to matters of paftime and amufement only, or comprehending all the complicated bufineffes of life, whether they be gay or ferious. Neither thefe proprieties themfelves, nor the various and contrary deviations from them, are accurately diftinguifhed by names; but it is neceffary that they

---

[m] The perfons diftinguifhed by the excefs and defect, were called φιλοτιμοι and αφιλοτιμοι: but there was only one of thefe adjectives, which afforded an abftract φιλοτιμια, denoting the difpofition or habit.

they should here be considered, in order to shew that the praise-worthy habit in trivial as well as in important actions, always lies in the middle between two blameable extremes; and as names are wanting, we must, as in other cases, take the liberty of making them, both for the sake of perspicuity, and to keep unbroken the connexion of our discourse. In the habit or disposition relative to the true exhibition of our characters in word and action, let the propriety or virtue which lies in the middle be called plain-dealing; and the impropriety or vice, by which we assume good qualities which do not belong to us, be called ostentation; and that, by which we divest ourselves of the good qualities with which we are really endowed, be called dissimulation or irony. In matters relating to pleasure and merriment, there is a virtue in facetiousness; buffoonery is the impropriety on the one side, and rustic simplicity on the other. In the more serious concerns of life, but which have still pleasure for their object, the virtue of companionable friendliness is distinguished, on the one hand, from quarrelsome moroseness; and, on the other, both from unmeaning officiousness, and interested flattery. Even in mere affections which do not exert themselves either in words or deeds, modesty is praised as holding the middle place between bashful timidity, and frontless assurance. An honest indignation at the prosperity of the worthless is easily distinguishable, both from envy which pines at the prosperity of all alike, and from that depraved pleasure which none but the most vicious can receive from beholding the unmerited success of artful villany or ruffian violence[n]. But concerning those habits,

---

[n] επιχαιρεκακια in the Latin versions is translated *malevolentia*, which does not at all express Aristotle's meaning: malevolence wishes ill to all mankind, even to the good, and therefore is grieved at their prosperity; but the vice here spoken of is that depraved

BOOK II.

Chap. 8.
───
Why vices are often mistaken for virtues; and conversely.

habits, we shall treat more fully hereafter, and also concerning justice, which must be divided into two kinds, before we can distinguish wherein the propriety of each kind consists; and likewise concerning the intellectual virtues.

Of those three dispositions or habits, of which that in the middle is only right, the extremes are contrary to, and at variance with, each other, and also with the virtue which lies between them. For as in a line divided into equal, and also unequal, parts, the half is great when compared with the smaller division, but small when compared with the greater; so of human passions and actions, their proper and moderate degree appears an excess or defect just as it happens to be compared with either extreme. To the fool-hardy, courage appears cowardice; and to the coward, rashness°. The voluptuary deems temperance insensibility; and the spendthrift calls liberality avarice; each pushing the extreme, which happens to form part of his own character, into the place of honour. It is worthy of remark, that the extremes are not only more contrary to each other than either of them is to the middle, but also that one of them often bears a false resemblance to this middle, and is frequently mistaken for it. Thus rashness often passes for bravery, and profusion for liberality: but cowardice is never mistaken for courage, nor voluptuousness for temperance; although temperance
is

depraved pleasure which wicked men take in beholding the success of arts like to their own. In this sense only, Aristotle could say νεμεσις εϛι μεσοτης φθονα και επιχαιρεκακιας, that indignation was the middle between envy and the vice here specified: for envy grieves at prosperity well merited, but επιχαιρεκακια rejoices at prosperity unmerited; which are two extremes equally remote from that affection by which we rejoice at the prosperity of good men, and grieve at the prosperity of the wicked.

° Aristotle says, that the courageous man, compared with the coward, seems foolhardy, and therefore the coward calls him rash.

is sometimes called insensibility, and insensibility temperance. This irregularity proceeds from two causes; first, the one extreme is really nearer than the other to that proper affection which lies between them. Rashness is nearer than cowardice to the virtue of courage; and therefore cowardice, the most distant extreme, is most properly opposed to courage. The second cause is, that mankind in general being more inclined to one extreme than the other, those vices to which we are naturally most prone, are most the objects of our blame as well as of our attention. Thus, with regard to pleasure, most men are prone to err rather on the side of indulgence, than on that of abstinence. Voluptuousness therefore is the vice naturally opposed to temperance [p].

Enough has been said to shew that virtue consists in mediocrity. But this middle point, either in passions or actions, it is not easy to hit; for, as a man must have some knowledge in geometry to find the centre of a circle, so it belongs not to those ignorant of Ethics to observe the rules of propriety. Every one is capable of being angry, or of giving away money; but how much, when, to whom, in what manner, and for what end or purpose, are questions which it is not easy for every one to resolve; and of which, as the proper solution is extremely rare, so it is highly praiseworthy. He, therefore, who would not err widely from the point of propriety, must make it his first care to keep at a distance from the most blameable extreme; and as **Calypso** advises,

"Steer by the higher rock; lest whirled around
We sink, beneath the circling eddy drown'd [q]."

In

BOOK II.

Chap. 9.

Practical rules for the attainment of propriety of affection and action.

[p] The same thoughts are expressed in other words, and illustrated by other examples, in the Ethics to Eudemus, l. ii. c. v.
[q] Pope's Iliad, b. xii. v. 263, 264. But Ulysses, and not Calypso, says this, Il. xii. v. 108.

In doing this we shall imitate the skilful pilot who, when he cannot hold the course which he desires, sails the nearest to it possible; and of two evils prefers the least. We ought next to consider to which of the two extremes or faults we are most prone; for different men are more or less easily beset by different faults or vices, and what these are by which each is most liable to be entangled, he will best discover by attending to the pleasure which he has in indulging, or the pain in restraining them. In order to correct his character, he must bend it, in a contrary direction, as we straighten a crooked stick; but, above all, he must beware of the blandishments of pleasure, of which we are seldom impartial or uncorrupt judges: treating this fair enchantress, as the aged senators in Homer did the beautiful Helen, whose words on this occasion cannot be too often repeated, nor their example too strictly imitated.

> "They cry'd, no wonder, such celestial charms
> For nine long years have set the world in arms;
> What winning graces! what majestic mien!
> She moves a goddess, and she looks a queen!
> Yet hence, Oh, Heaven! convey that fatal face,
> And from destruction save the Trojan race[r]."

By thus banishing pleasure, we shall be less liable to error. Such, briefly, are the precepts by which propriety of affection and action may be attained; a thing for which it is extremely difficult to lay down general rules, which are at all applicable to the indefinite variety of particular cases; and to ascertain, for instance, with whom we ought to be angry, how long, to what degree, and for what reasons or purposes. Sometimes we praise the defect, and call insensibility meekness; sometimes we praise the excess, and call irascibility manhood. He who deviates

---

[r] Iliad, iii. v. 203, &c.

deviates but a little from the middle point, commonly escapes blame; great deviations become perceptible, but the precise degrees of blame which they respectively merit cannot be accurately expressed in words; and in such practical matters [s], common sense is the sole and ultimate judge. This only is certain, that mediocrity is always praiseworthy; and that, in order to attain it, we must, for the reasons above given, incline ourselves, according to circumstances, sometimes to the one extreme, and sometimes to the other.

[s] In things perceptible by sense, or objects of sensation, as contradistinguished from objects of intellection; in which latter only, accuracy is attainable. See above, p. 141.

# ARISTOTLE's ETHICS.

BOOK III.

INTRODUCTION.

In this Book, Ariſtotle examines the ſpecific diſtinctions between moral virtue and other habits of the mind. The habit of moral virtue implies the deliberate preference of one kind of conduct to another; and deliberate preference implies freedom of choice. Thoſe actions are voluntary, which have their principle in ourſelves; thoſe are involuntary, which proceed from an external cauſe. Building on accurate definitions and ſolid diſtinctions, the philoſopher proves, with equal perſpicuity and energy, that our moral conduct is the proper object of praiſe or blame, of reward or puniſhment. His reaſonings and ſpeculations ſoar above and ſuperſede the abſtruſe, or rather the frivolous queſtion, introduced by his perverters the ſchoolmen, concerning the freedom of the human will; a queſtion which continued to be agitated, long after their other ſubtilties were condemned to oblivion. With Ariſtotle, all will is free-will; ſince nothing can be more free than that which is voluntary: and although ſome actions originating in ourſelves are conſidered as of a mixed nature, becauſe they are performed reluctantly, though ſpontaneouſly, this happens merely becauſe, of two evils, we naturally chooſe the leaſt: ſuch actions, how contrary ſoever to our will in their own nature, being nevertheleſs voluntary in reference to the unfortunate circumſtances in which we happen to be placed.

His work, hitherto, proceeds with great regularity. He began by proving that the happineſs of man conſiſts in the exerciſe of the moral and intellectual virtues; or, in his own technical language, "that happineſs is energy directed in the line of virtue." As his definition of happineſs implies an acquaintance with the nature of virtue, and the knowledge of virtue implies that of the mind in which this habit reſides, he explains the different parts or principles of the mind, whether rational or irrational; ſhewing that both principles neceſſarily cooperate in the acquirement of good moral habits, as well as in the approbation of good moral characters. This ſyſtem is totally different from that which regards morality as founded ſolely or ultimately on feeling; whether a moral ſenſe, ſympathy, or any other modification of merely ſenſitive nature; an abſurd doctrine, liable to groſs and dangerous perverſion; and which has often been employed to juſtify, and even to produce the wildeſt practical errors. Having explained his theory of Ethics, the Author proceeds to the practice; and concludes this Book with the examination of courage and temperance.

BOOK III.

ARGUMENT.

Moral election and preference.—Our habits voluntary.—Courage. —Its different kinds distinguished.—Temperance.—Natural and adventitious wants.—Comparison of intemperance and cowardice.

VIRTUE is relative to passions and actions; of which, those only which are voluntary, are the objects of praise or blame; and those which are involuntary, are the objects always of pardon, and sometimes of pity. In treating of virtue, therefore, it is necessary clearly to explain what is meant by the epithets *voluntary* and *involuntary*; the force of which words ought to be fully understood by legislators, when they establish rewards and punishments. Those actions and those crimes, then, are involuntary, which are either done by compulsion, or committed through ignorance. We are said to act or move by compulsion, when the principle of action or motion is not in ourselves, but external; as when we are driven before the force of the wind, or impelled by strength greater than our own. But it is doubtful whether those evils are voluntary which we either encounter through motives of honour, or endure through the fear of greater calamities. Thus, if a tyrant commands us to commit some act of baseness, having in his power our parents and children, whose fate depends on our obedience; and when sailors or merchants in a storm throw their goods overboard to save their lives; such actions are of a mixed nature, but rather voluntary, because, at the moment of doing them, they are matters of choice; and the true motive to any action is that by

BOOK III. Chap. 1.

What is meant by the epithet voluntary as applied to human actions.

BOOK III.

which we are actuated at the time of performing it. Besides, the principle of motion is in ourselves, and may be exerted or not at pleasure. Such actions, therefore, are voluntary in reference to the unfortunate circumstances in which we are placed, though independently of those circumstances they are much against our will; and therefore, considered absolutely, are involuntary.

Actions of this mixed kind are sometimes the objects of high panegyric, when we boldly encounter pain and disgrace for the sake of great and honourable advantages: and when we decline this conflict, we often render ourselves the objects of reproach. But to encounter difficulties and disgrace without the expectancy of honour or advantage, is the part only of a fool. On other occasions, though we receive not any praise, yet we meet with pardon, when our virtue yields to terrors too powerful for the weakness of humanity: but the degree in which it yields, is still in our power; for there are some criminal acts to which neither threats nor violence can ever compel those who, rather than commit them, would suffer the most wretched death. In Euripides' Alcmæon, the reasons for which that hero says he is forced to commit matricide, are only worthy of ridicule.

It is difficult to determine what goods are to be preferred, and what evils are to be encountered; and still more difficult in time of action and danger to adhere firmly to our predetermined resolutions. For the most part, men are forced to suffer disgrace, only for the sake of avoiding pain; and as these evils are of a different kind, it is not easy fairly to compare, and exactly to appretiate them: but when pain is preferred to disgrace, our manliness is praised; when disgrace is preferred to pain, our effeminacy is blamed. On the whole then, what actions are compulsory? Are they those only whose principle is external, and in which the immediate agent has not any voluntary share? Or, shall we call those actions compulsory, which, though matters of choice relatively to the unfortunate circumstances in which we are placed, are yet, when considered in themselves, absolutely against our will? We say, that such acts ought to be considered rather as voluntary, because all actions being conversant about particulars only, must depend on circumstances, and leave room for the preference of one motive to another. If it should be said that pleasures and honours consisting in things external to ourselves, the actions performed for their attainment, are also compulsory, all actions whatever would then deserve this epithet, because all proceed from such motives. But it is absurd to accuse pleasure, which cannot be the object either of punishment or blame; and not ourselves, who are too easily seduced by it; and equally absurd to consider ourselves as the cause of our good actions, and pleasure as the cause of our bad ones. Those actions only, therefore, are properly compulsory, whose principle lies without, and which are totally independent of our own voluntary co-operation.

We said that crimes committed through ignorance are involuntary. But this assertion is not universally true; for those only are involuntary, which produce pain and repentance. He who has committed a wickedness through ignorance, and feels no compunction for the act, cannot be said indeed to have done voluntarily what he did not intend; nor, on the other hand, is his action involuntary, since he feels not any uneasiness for the commission of it. But as *his* action is *involuntary* who repents; *his*, who repents not, may be called *not voluntary*: that things of different natures may be expressed by different names. A distinction is also to be made, between acting *through* ignorance and

BOOK III.

and *with* ignorance. A man drunk, or in a paffion, is guilty of violence *through* intoxication or anger, not *through* ignorance, though ignorantly; and every bad man is ignorant of what things it is his duty either to do or to avoid; an ignorance profound and univerfal, infeparably connected with his pravity of will and election, and therefore inexcufable. But in the particular actions, which, becaufe committed through ignorance, feem entitled to pardon or pity, it will often be ufeful to diftinguifh, between the agent and the action, its fubject, end, the manner how, and the inftrument with which it is performed. None but a madman can be ignorant with regard to all thofe particulars. In whatever he has done, every one in his fenfes muft know that he himfelf was the agent; but he may not know that he was doing wrong; as thofe who blab in fpeaking, beg pardon for words which efcaped them unintentionally; or, as Æfchylus[t] profaned the myftical terms, not knowing them to be fuch; and, in actions, a man fhowing a catapult, difcharged that formidable engine; and Meropé would have flain her own fon, taking him for an enemy; poifons have been given inftead of remedies; fome perfons have been killed by thofe who inftructed them in their exercifes; and others have been flain with fpears thought to be blunted, or with ftones miftaken for pumice. The refult of fuch actions being totally different from what the agents intended, they are juftly deemed involuntary, when accompanied with pain and repentance; whereas thofe actions feem moft voluntary, which not only proceed from our own movements, but which are begun, carried on, and terminated

[t] Æfchylus was acquitted by the Areopagus for divulging fome expreffions ufed in the myfteries, having proved that he was not initiated, and therefore did not know what he faid. Clemens Alexandrin. ftrom. ii.

terminated with a clear perception or knowledge of their real nature and end. To which of the two classes then shall we ascribe things done through anger or appetite? If we call them involuntary, brute animals, and children, who are yet incapable of reason, can never act voluntarily. But appetite and anger are principles of human nature, as well as reason itself; and when they prompt us to act amiss, are not less voluntary than when they prompt us to act properly; to repel injuries, and to defend our persons; to gratify hunger which promotes health, or to gratify curiosity which promotes knowledge. That which is involuntary is painful, but the gratification of our natural appetites is highly pleasing. Besides, what does it import us to say, that things done in passion are less voluntary than those done on reflection, since guilty transports of passion ought to be as carefully avoided and shunned as deliberate villainy? The actions of man too often proceed from anger or concupiscence; which irrational impulses, being moving principles in the human frame, cannot, without absurdity, be considered as involuntary ".

BOOK III.

Having thus distinguished actions and passions as voluntary and involuntary, we next proceed to treat of that intentional election or preference of one plan of conduct to another, which seems, still more than actions themselves, to compose the nature and essence of virtue, and to constitute the distinction of characters. This election or preference is not only voluntary, but something more '; for it belongs not to brute animals and children,

Chap. 2.

Of moral election and preference.

" See Magna Moralia, b. i. c. xiii.; and Ethic. Eudem. b. ii. c. vii.

' επι πλιον το εκουσιον. " Voluntary," is an epithet of more extensive application. It applies to actions that are not " deliberate." Moral election therefore implies something more than merely what is " voluntary."

BOOK III.

children, whose actions are voluntary; nor to voluntary acts done suddenly, with such precipitate haste as leaves not any time for comparison, election, or choice. Those who name it inclination, passion, or opinion, seem to mistake its nature. For the passions, whether founded in anger or concupiscence, are common to man with the brute creation; but this election or preference is peculiar to himself. The intemperate man acts from passion, without election; but the man of true temperance acts from election, without passion[Y]. The calm motive, by which he is actuated, is a thing so different from passion or desire, that it is frequently set in direct opposition to them: but desire cannot be opposed to desire, nor any one passion to itself. Pleasure and pain are the ultimate moving principles which set all the desires and passions to work, but the actions of good men depending on a higher cause, do not obey their impulse. Neither ought this intentional preference or election to be confounded with mere inclinations or wishes, though it appears to be nearly connected with them. We may wish for things impossible, as immortality; or things not depending on ourselves, as that such a player or wrestler may gain the prize. But to prefer impossibilities, is the part only of a madman; and moral election or choice implies, that the goods preferred may be obtained by our own exertions. Besides, our wishes relate principally to ends; our preferences, to means: we wish for health,

---

[Y] ὁ ἀκρατὴς ἐπιθυμῶν μὲν πράττει, προαιρούμενος δὲ ὔ· ὁ ἐγκρατὴς δ' ἀνάπαλιν, προαιρούμενος μὲν, ἐπιθυμῶν δ' ὔ. "The intemperate man acts desiring, not preferring; the temperate man (quite the reverse) acts preferring, not desiring." The full sense of this passage will appear hereafter, when we come to treat of the important distinctions between temperance and self-command on the one side, and intemperance, or weakness and wickedness, on the other: distinctions essential to a complete theory of Ethics, but which Aristotle is the only author that clearly explains.

health, we prefer the means necessary for attaining it; "to wish for happiness," is correct language; "to prefer happiness," is an expression highly inaccurate: our preferences seem universally to relate to things within our own power. Moral preferences, therefore, are not merely opinions; which latter may relate to things impossible, eternal, and unchangeable; and which are characterised by the epithets "true" and "false," not by those of "good" and "bad;" which apply only to our preferences or elections. These last differ not only from opinion in general, but from every opinion in particular; for by no opinion whatever, and which is merely an opinion, are our characters marked as good or bad. Our preferences ascertain the morality of our actions and habits. But our opinions merely tell us what it is that we choose or reject; wherein it may be useful or hurtful; and how it may prove either the one or the other. Our opinions are estimated by their truth, our preferences by their propriety; the former are unstable like their causes, the latter are regulated by our own experience; and what opinion tells us to be the best road, is not always that which we choose to follow, our vices dragging us in an opposite direction[*]. To determine whether this moral preference is either preceded by, or accompanied with opinion, belongs not to the present question, which consists only in deciding whether these two be one and the same. We see that they are not. What then can this moral preference be, since it belongs not to any of the classes above mentioned? It plainly is voluntary, but also something more, since it implies deliberation and reason; and, as its name indicates, is that which, after due

---

[*] ——— Video meliora proboque
Deteriora sequor.   Hor.

BOOK III.

Chap. 3.

About what objects it is conversant.

due comparisons made by the understanding, the will prefers as best [a].

But it is worthy of consideration, whether all questions be the objects of such deliberations and comparisons, or some questions only. There are some points concerning which none but a fool or madman would hesitate a moment; and we are not said to deliberate concerning things eternal and unalterable, as the existence of the universe, or the incommensurability of the sides of a square with its diagonal. Neither do we deliberate concerning things merely fortuitous, as the finding of a treasure; nor concerning those which either naturally or necessarily always happen after the same manner, as the seasons of draughts and tempests; the rising, setting, and motions of the planets. Nor do all human affairs, that is, all those depending on the exertions of man, form a fit subject for our deliberation. The Lacedæmonians do not deliberate what is the constitution of government most suitable to the Scythians; because the conduct of the Lacedæmonians cannot have any efficacy in establishing it. The proper object of deliberation, therefore, consists in those practical matters, which depend on our own exertions; since these are the only things that remain unmentioned. Nature, necessity, fortune, intellect, are all of them considered as causes; but our deliberations bear a reference to those causes only which it is in our own power to influence and control. Things subjected to strict rules, admit not of deliberation; for example, in writing the letters of the alphabet, we have only to follow the practice prescribed. But the great field for deliberation

[a] See Ethics to Eudemus, b. ii. c. vii, viii, ix, x.; and Magn. Moral. b. i. c. xiii, xiv, xv, xvi, xvii, xviii.

beration lies in those practical arts which are uncertain and doubtful; physic, œconomy, and navigation, rather than the gymnastic; because the more precarious their operations are, the more patient deliberation is requisite ; it is more necessary therefore in arts than in sciences ; and must be constantly exercised about those things which, as they are not fortuitous, happen, for the most part, after the same manner ; but concerning which, it is not easy for human wisdom to foresee how they will, in any given case, fall out. In matters of this kind, which are of high moment, we do not choose to act without the advice of counsellors, mistrusting our own sagacity. It was before observed, that we do not deliberate concerning ends, but concerning the means by which they may be attained. A physician never examines, whether he shall cure his patient; nor an orator, whether he shall persuade his audience ; nor a statesman, whether he shall promote public prosperity. But the means through which those several purposes may be best attained, are the proper objects of their respective deliberations; which often extend to a long series of reasoning: for the immediate instruments, or agents, through which their designs may be effected, must often be procured by means of others more remote, and those, by others naturally prior ; until they arrive finally at the first efficient cause ; which, as in a mathematical investigation or analysis, is frequently the last in the order of discovery. The statesman, too, as well as the mathematician, when he comes to an impossibility, there stops ; and tries some other road, which may lead to the end in view : as for example, if money be wanted, and cannot possibly be found, his schemes, which must be ineffectual without it, are immediately laid aside; but he does not desist from his purpose until he has

examined

examined not only his own resources but those of his friends; for what may be done by our friends, is in our own power, since they may be set to work by a principle in ourselves. Our deliberations, therefore, relate to instruments, to agents, to materials, and to means; and not only to the causes by which, but to the manner in which, our actions are to be performed, our conduct regulated, and our purposes effected. On the other hand, our ends and purposes themselves are never subjects of deliberation; neither are we said to deliberate concerning those particulars, which are merely perceptions of sense, as whether this bit of bread be well baked; neither can our deliberations be indefinite or endless, because this would imply a desire without an object. Moral preference, then, is not deliberation, but that which, after mature deliberation, is preferred as most agreeable to the commanding principles in our nature. In this preference, deliberation terminates; and from it, action commences. This natural progress appears in the Heroic Polities, faithfully delineated by Homer. The wisdom of the senate deliberates, and prefers, and declares its resolves to the people; who immediately carry them into execution. Moral preference, then, relates to those things only which may be accomplished by our own exertions; it is appetite or affection, combined with, and modified by, reason [b]; and, as above observed,

[b] The sagacious Polybius analyses with Aristotle the moral principle or faculty into reason or intellect, operating on the social and sympathetic nature of man. The passage is in the part of Polybius translated by Hampton, in whose words I shall give it. " From the union of the two sexes, to which all are naturally inclined, children are born. When any of these therefore, being arrived at perfect age, instead of yielding suitable returns of gratitude and assistance to those by whom they have been bred, on the contrary, attempt to injure them by words or actions, it is manifest that those who behold the wrong, after having also seen the sufferings and the anxious cares that were

observed, conversant, not about ends, but about the best means by which they may be attained.

Volition, on the contrary, is, as above said, conversant only about ends; which consist, according to some, in real, and, according to others, in seeming, good. The opinion of those who think that the will is moved only by what is really good, involves this contradiction, that the volitions of a bad man are not voluntary; and the opinion of those who think that

were sustained by the parents in the nourishment and education of their children, must be greatly offended and displeased at such proceeding. For man, who, among all the various kinds of animals, is alone endowed with the faculty of reason, cannot, like the rest, pass over such actions with indifference; but will make reflection on what he sees; and comparing likewise the future with the present, will not fail to express his indignation at this injurious treatment; to which, as he foresees, he may also at some time be exposed. Thus again, when any one who has been succoured by another in the time of danger, instead of shewing the like kindness to this benefactor, endeavours at any time to destroy or hurt him; it is certain that all men must be shocked by such ingratitude, through sympathy with the resentment of their neighbour; and from an apprehension also, that the case may be their own. And from hence arises, in the mind of every man, a certain *notion* of the nature and force of duty, in which consists both the beginning and the end of justice. In like manner, the man, who, in defence of others, is seen to throw himself the foremost into every danger, and even to sustain the fury of the fiercest animals, never fails to obtain the loudest acclamations of applause and veneration from all the multitude; while he who shews a different conduct, is pursued with censure and reproach. And thus it is that the people begin to discern the nature of things honourable and base, and in what consists the difference between them; and to perceive that the former, on account of the advantage that attends them, are fit to be admired and imitated, and the latter to be detested and avoided." Polybius, l. vi. c. 6. The doctrine contained in this passage is expanded by Dr. Smith into a theory of moral sentiments. But he departs from his author in placing the perception of right and wrong in sentiment or feeling ultimately and simply. This also was the doctrine of Hutcheson, who ascribes our notions of virtue and vice to what he calls a moral sense *. Polybius, on the contrary, maintains with Aristotle, that these notions arise from reason or intellect operating on affection or appetite; or, in other words, that the moral faculty is a compound, and may be resolved into two simpler principles of the mind.

* Hutcheson's Moral Philosophy.

that the will is moved only by seeming good, destroys all natural motives to volition, and makes it dependent merely on human caprice. If such opinions must at first sight be rejected, let us, then, say, that real good is the natural cause of volition, but that each individual prefers what seems good to himself; a good man, what is truly good; and a bad man, what he happens to think so; just as we see, in different habits and constitutions of body, the same things are not equally conducive to the health of all alike, but wholesome things agree with healthy constitutions, whereas the sickly often delight most in things naturally unwholesome. In the same manner the moral constitution of a virtuous man, being congenial with truth, appreciates things by their real worth; for such as our habits are, such will be the estimates which we form of honour, pleasure, and every object of desire. This perhaps is the chief excellence of virtue, that it enables us to see the true value of things, and to measure them by a correct standard. But the multitude, deceived by appearances, pursue pleasures as the only good, and shun pain as the only evil.

Chap. 5.
That our habits are voluntary.

Ends are, then, the objects of volition; and the means of attaining them are the objects of deliberation and preference; which, being conversant only about such things as are in our own power, the virtues immediately proceeding from them must also be in our own power, and voluntary, as well as the contrary vices. The poet's sentiment therefore is but partially true:

" None chooses wretchedness, or spurns delight^e."

The

---

^e ουδις ικων πονηρος ου' ακων μακαρ. " Nobody is willingly wicked, or happy against his will." The sentiment is ascribed to an ancient tragedian. Ethic. Nicom. edit. Oxford, p. 108. and to Hesiod, " ιν ταις μεγαλαις." Eustrat. in Moral. Aristot. p. 62. The verse originally meant that nobody was willingly *miserable*, &c. that sense being given to the word πονηρος in Hesiod. Suidas says, that Hesiod wrote a catalogue of illustrious women in five books, from which work Eustratius conjectures this verse may be copied.

The latter clause cannot be disputed; but the former must be denied, otherwise we must reject the doctrine just established, that man is the author of his own actions; and that those things, whose principles or causes are in ourselves, are also in our own power. Yet these truths are attested by common sense and universal experience. Criminal actions are punished by law, when not committed either through compulsion or ignorance; in which cases they are pardoned, as not proceeding from ourselves. Praise-worthy actions, on the other hand, are encouraged and honoured; that as men are deterred from vice by the dread of punishment, they may be excited to virtue by the hope of reward. But were not our conduct voluntary, such persuasives to virtue would be useless and absurd; and there would be no more sense in exhorting a man to his duty, than in persuading him not to feel cold or heat, thirst or hunger. Crimes committed through ignorance are only excusable when the ignorance is involuntary; for when the cause of it lies in ourselves, it is then justly punishable; as in that ancient law which inflicts a double penalty on crimes done in drunkenness [d]. The ignorance of those laws, which all may know if they will, does not excuse the breach of them; and neglect is not pardonable, where attention ought to be bestowed. But perhaps we are incapable of attention. This however is our own fault; since the incapacity has been contracted by our continual carelessness; as the evils of injustice and intemperance are contracted by the daily commission of iniquity, and the daily indulgence in voluptuousness. For such as our actions are, such must our habits become; a truth confirmed by such universal experience, that to be ignorant of it betrays the grossest

---

[d] This, and other laws of the same tendency, will be considered in the " Politics."

BOOK III.

grossest stupidity. It is plain therefore that our vices are voluntary; since we voluntarily do those things which we know must produce them. But does it depend merely on our own wills to correct and reform our bad habits? It certainly does not; neither does it depend on the will of a patient, who has despised the advice of his physician, to recover that health which is lost by his own profligacy. When we have thrown a stone, we cannot restrain its flight; but it depended entirely on ourselves, whether we should throw it or not. The villain and the voluptuary are therefore voluntarily such; because the cause of their turpitude lies solely in themselves. Not only the vices of the mind, but even the imperfections of the body, are just subjects for reproach, when they are not natural, but produced through our own indolence or neglect. We pity blindness, lameness, or deformity, when they proceed from causes independent on those afflicted with them; but they are just objects of reproach, when contracted through drunkenness or any other species of debauchery; and, in the same manner, all vices and imperfections are blameable which originate in ourselves [e].

Objections answered.

But should any endeavour to excuse their wickedness, by saying that all men aspire after apparent good, but that the appearances or phantasms which make us assign to things this important epithet, arise not from our own suggestion, but depend on our constitution and character, it may be answered, that in as far as we ourselves are the causes of this constitution and character, we also must be the causes of these phantasms or appearances. But if the two former depend not at all on ourselves, and villains, when they commit wickedness, do it merely through ignorance of the ends at which they ought to aim; and

[e] The Magna Moralia, and Ethics to Eudemus, as above.

and virtuous men, on the contrary, when they perform virtuous actions, do them merely through Nature's bounty in furnishing them with a moral or intellectual eye, which enables them to discern what is truly good; this surely would, in the latter, be the best and fairest of pre-eminences, a prerogative not adventitious but innate [f], not acquired by instruction or example, but growing up spontaneously with the admirable frame of their natural constitution. First of all, if this were the case, virtue would not be voluntary any more than vice, since both would solely depend on the original organization of our minds. But if we ourselves are in any degree the artificers of our own characters; and if it depends on our own voluntary acts, what sort of habits we shall form; and, if not entirely what ends we shall pursue, at least what means we shall use for their attainment; then both our virtue and our vices will be voluntary; and, as such, the former will be the objects of praise and reward, and the latter of blame and punishment.

BOOK III

We have thus given a sketch of the virtues in general, shewing that they are practical habits, consisting in mediocrity, dependent on ourselves, voluntary, and agreeable to right reason. Actions and habits are not precisely in the same sense voluntary; the former are voluntary throughout, from beginning to end; but the beginnings only of habits, which gain force, like maladies, by degrees, until they become irresistible; even these

Transition to the consideration of each virtue in particular.

[f] This word is used in other parts of Aristotle's works to distinguish natural powers from those acquired by our own exertions. Thus in his Metaph. l. ix. c. v. Ἁπασων δ. των δυναμεων ουσων, των μεν συγγενων, οιον των αισθησεων, των δε εθει, οιον της του αυλου· των δε μαθησει, οιον της των τεχνων. "The most general division of powers is into three, which are innate, like the senses; those acquired by custom, like the power of playing on the flute; and those acquired by instruction, like many of the arts."

ARISTOTLE's ETHICS.

BOOK III.

these however are also voluntary, since their causes were such, namely, the actions by which they were formed. We now proceed to consider the several virtues in particular; wherein each consists, to what object it relates, and in what manner it relates to them; whence their number will be manifest:—and first, concerning courage.

Chap. 6.

The definition and nature of courage.

This virtue, as we formerly observed, consists in the moderation and propriety of our affections and actions in reference to those causes and circumstances which either excite fear, or inspire confidence. Since whatever is evil is in some degree formidable [f], fear is defined "the dread of evil," and of evil of every kind, infamy, poverty, disease, friendlessness, and death. But courage is not displayed in universal fearlessness; for not to fear infamy is the part of impudence and baseness; whereas the worthy and respectable character has always the keenest sense of shame, and the strongest aversion to disgrace. Yet impudence sometimes passes for courage; and may be so called, by a metaphor; since it resembles that virtue in being equally fearless. Neither poverty nor disease, nor whatever proceeds not from any voluntary turpitude, ought, perhaps, to be much dreaded by those who aspire to the dignity of virtue; yet fearlessness, as to such objects, does not constitute what is properly called courage, though it sometimes receives metaphorically that name: for those who tremble at the sound of war, may be liberal of their money, and fearless of poverty; those, surely, are not cowards, who dread the insults likely to fall on their wives or children; nor are those to be dignified with the epithet of courageous, who, with the calm intrepidity of slaves, endure

---

[f] φοβούμεθα δὲ δηλονότι τα φοβερα· ταυτα δ' ιϛι, ὡς απλως ιπειν, κακα. "We fear things formidable, which, to express them in one word, are evils."

endure the prospect of disgraceful stripes. To what kind of terrors, then, does courage render us superior? To the greatest of all, the fear of death; for death seems of all things the most formidable; because, in common opinion, it is the ultimate limit of all our pains and pleasures, beyond which there is neither good nor evil. Yet courage is not alike shewn in contempt for every form of death. This virtue appears not conspicuous in disease or shipwreck, but in an honourable death in the field of battle, which is, of all, the fairest and most illustrious; as is attested by the honours with which it is rewarded, both by republics and kings. Courage, therefore, is peculiarly displayed in encountering death in battle, and in setting warlike dangers at defiance: not but that a brave man will be fearless during a storm at sea, or on a sick-bed; but his fortitude is different from that of sailors, who are rendered fearless through experience and custom; whereas he, perceiving no means of safety, submits with indignant [h] intrepidity to a death, from which no honour can be reaped, and in which no exertion of manhood can be displayed.

The

---

[h] *εν ταις τοιαυταις δε φθοραις ωλτιφυ υπαρχει.* Both Ulysses and Eneas thought with our author.

  With what a cloud the brows of Heaven are crown'd?
  What raging winds? What roaring waters round?
  'Tis Jove himself the swelling tempest rears;
  Death, present death, on every side appears.
  Happy! thrice happy, who in battle slain,
  Prest, in Atrides' cause, the Trojan plain, &c.   Odyss. V. v. 390.

And Æneas,
    O ter quaterque beati,
  Queis ante ora patrum, Trojæ sub mœnibus altis,
  Contigit oppetere, &c.   Æneis, l. i. v. 98.

Chap. 7.

The same evils which terrify one person are not formidable to another; though there are some of such an irresistible nature, as to shake the firmest minds, and to inspire fear into all possessed of understanding. But those objects of terror which surpass not the strength of human nature, differing from each other in magnitude, as well as do the grounds of confidence, courage will discriminate between real and apparent dangers; and make us meet the former as brave men ought, unshaken and dauntless, subjecting the instinctive emotions of fear to the dictates of reason and of honour. For we betray our weakness, not only when we fear things really not formidable, but when we are affected in an undue degree, or at an improper time, by objects of real danger. A brave man avoids such errors; and, estimating things by their real worth, prefers the grace and beauty of habitual fortitude to the delusive security of deformed cowardice. Yet he is not less careful to avoid that excess of intrepidity, which, being rarely met with, is, like many other vices, without a name; though nothing but madness, or a most stupid insensibility, can make any man preserve, amidst earthquakes and inundations, that unshaken composure, which has been ascribed to the Celts[1]. An overweening estimate of the causes of confidence, and a consequent excess of courage, is called audacity; a boastful species of bravery, and the mere ape of true manhood. What the brave man *is*, the rash and audacious man wishes to *appear*; he courts and provokes unnecessary dangers, but fails in the hour of trial; and is, for the most part, a blustering bully, who, under a semblance of pretended courage, conceals no inconsiderable portion of cowardice.

[1] Alexander, who perhaps knew them better than his preceptor, considered the "πελται or καλαται, or γαλαται," the Celts or Gauls, as an arrogant and boastful nation. Arrian. Exped. Alexand. l. i. p. 5.

cowardice. But the complete and genuine coward easily betrays himself, by fearing either things not formidable, or things formidable, in an undue degree; and his failing is the more manifest, because it is accompanied with plain indications of pain; he lives in continual alarm, and is therefore spiritless and dejected; whereas courage warms our breasts, and animates our hopes. Such then is the character of true courage, as opposed to audacity on one hand, and cowardice on the other. It holds the middle place between those vicious extremes; it is calm and sedate; and though it never provokes danger, is always ready to meet even death in an honourable cause. But to die, rather than endure manfully the pressure of poverty, or the stings of love, or any other cruel suffering, is the part of a coward; who basely flies from an enemy that he has not spirit to encounter; and ignominiously quits the field, where he might have sustained a strenuous and honourable conflict.

There are five kinds of courage, besides that properly so called. The first kind is the political, which most resembles that above described; because it is inspired by legal honours and rewards, and upheld by legal punishments and infamy. Courage therefore chiefly prevails, where cowardice is most stigmatised. Homer will supply us with examples; hear those of Hector and Diomed:

> Shall proud Polydamas before the gate
> Proclaim, his counsels are obeyed too late,
> Which timely followed but the former night,
> What numbers had been saved by Hector's flight[k]?

And Diomed,

> But ah, what grief! should haughty Hector boast,
> I fled inglorious to the guarded coast[l]?

[k] Il. xxii. v. 110. & seq. [l] Il. viii. v. 179. & seq.

This political courage moſt reſembles genuine valour, becauſe it originates in the love of glory and the ſhame of reproach, which are virtuous and honourable motives. Nearly alike to it, is that bravery which is inſpired into ſoldiers by their generals; but inferior in merit, ſince engendered not by ſhame, but by fear; and by the dread not of diſgrace but of puniſhment. For generals compel by threats; as Hector:

> " On ruſhed bold Hector, gloomy as the night;
> Forbids to plunder, animates the fight,
> Points to the fleet; for by the Gods, who flies,
> Who dares but linger, by this hand he dies;
> No weeping ſiſter his cold eye ſhall cloſe,
> No friendly hand his funeral pile compoſe.
> Who ſtops to plunder at this ſignal hour,
> The birds ſhall tear him, and the dogs devour [m]."

Thoſe who advance, fearful of ſtripes, ſhould they retreat; and thoſe who ſtand their ground, in conſequence of obſtacles to their flight, all ſuch loſe the merit of bravery, becauſe they are brave on compulſion. Experience and cuſtom may produce likewiſe an artificial bravery; wherefore Socrates thought that courage was a matter of ſcience. Each is moſt courageous in what he beſt underſtands; and therefore ſoldiers in battle; ſince they know the emptineſs of many of the terrors with which the parade of war is accompanied. To the ignorant, therefore, they appear truly valiant; beſides, their experience has taught them ſkilfully to employ their weapons, and by what means they may beſt defend themſelves, and moſt effectually aſſault their enemies. They contend therefore with all the advantage which a practiſed prize-fighter enjoys over an ignorant ruſtic;

[m] Il. xv. v. 194. & ſeq.

ruftic; or that men completely armed enjoy over naked troops; for in such combats, spirit and manhood yield to armed dexterity. But when the odds are against them, the courage of disciplined mercenaries speedily fails, and they are the first to fly; whereas the national troops remain and are slain; which recently happened at the Hermæus, where the Theban citizens preferred death to an ignominious safety, while their auxiliaries, though they behaved valiantly in the beginning of the action, no sooner discovered their inferiority in strength, than they basely betook themselves to flight; fearing death more than disgrace. Anger is often called to the assistance of manhood; and men seem courageous through passion, like wild beasts which turn, when wounded, and attack their pursuers; for both valour and anger makes us regardless of danger.— Whence Homer says:

  Inflaming thus the rage of all their hosts [n];

And

  Each Trojan bosom with new warmth he fires [o].

These passages imply, that the excitement of anger is auxiliary to courage; which, however, in man, ought to originate in a sense of honour, whereas in beasts it springs only from the smart of pain; for they turn on their pursuers, only when they are afraid or hurt; but, in their native woods or marshes, they venture not to approach human kind. Manly courage, therefore, cannot result from the irritation of pain, or from that blind passion which rushes, improvident, on unknown dangers. Even the unfeeling ass, when hungry, does not, through the fear of blows, forsake his pasture; and adulterers, impelled by lust, have exhibited signal examples of
             boldness;

[n] Il. xvi. v. 658.   [o] Il. vi. v. 626.

BOOK III.

boldness; but such things are far remote from true courage. Yet, of all passions, anger is the most nearly allied to this virtue, and would entirely accord with it, if directed by mature deliberation, and controlled by maxims of honour. Even in men, anger is painful, and revenge is sweet: yet acting under the impulse of such passions, they are not courageous but quarrelsome; for neither reason nor moral principle has any share in their behaviour; which has something in it resembling courage, but is not that virtue. Nor are persons buoyed up by hope courageous; for they are confident of success, only because they have often conquered. This confidence, indeed, resembles that of true courage; but it proceeds from a different principle, the opinion of superiority, and the consequent sense of safety; and like the spurious valour of drunkards, (who are brave while successful,) fails them under the slightest reverse of fortune. But true courage surmounts real and known dangers, because it is honourable to resist them, and base to sink under them.. It is best seen in sudden emergencies, because, on such occasions, undisturbed firmness cannot be assumed, but must be the result of confirmed manly habits. Persons ignorant of the dangers which they encounter, have also a false semblance of courage; they are somewhat allied to those buoyed up by hope, but are of a stamp still inferior, their boldness being founded on mistake, and therefore destitute of merit: for when they either know or suspect the truth, they betake themselves to shameful flight; as the Argives did, after encountering the Lacedæmonians, whom they mistook for Scyonians. We have now described, who are truly courageous, and who only seem to be so.

Though

Though the office of courage confists in moderating the impulse of rash boldness, as well as the excess of cautious timidity, yet its principal business is employed about the latter; because it is more difficult, and therefore more praiseworthy, to endure pain, than to resist pleasure; and we endure pain when we silence the dictates of fear, and encounter real dangers with manly fortitude. Yet the end and essence of courage are truly pleasant, though the pleasure disappears amidst the crowd of painful circumstances with which it is accompanied. In the Gymnastic games, the prize-fighters contemplate with pleasure the crowns and honours with which their victories are rewarded: but their laborious exertions, and repeated wounds, are uneasy and painful. The splendour of the prize, which is small, is lost therefore in the gloomy magnitude of surrounding circumstances. The same thing happens as to courage. Death and wounds are painful to a brave man, and reluctantly encountered; yet he meets and defies them, because it is honourable to do so; and although the more distinguished he is in virtue, and therefore in happiness, he well knows that his loss in death will be the greater, and therefore the more deeply laments the dangers to which he is exposed; yet, on this account, his courage is only the more conspicuous in preferring a glorious death to a happy life. The exercise therefore of laborious virtue is painful in its progress, and only delightful as it approaches the goal. But there are mercenary ruffians, who, though endowed with little true courage, are ready, for their miserable hire, to throw away their lives, which are of still less value. Thus much concerning courage; of which we may delineate the nature, from the observations above made [p].

We

[p] Vid. Magna Moral. l. i. c. xiii.; and Eudem. l. iii. c. i.

BOOK III.
Chap. 10.
Of the definition and nature of temperance.

We now proceed to speak of temperance, which, as well as courage, is employed in regulating the irrational, and merely animal part of our conſtitution. Temperance, we have ſaid, is the habit of mediocrity in our affections with reſpect to the objects which afford pleaſure; and alſo (though in a different manner, and an inferior degree) with reſpect to thoſe which give pain. Ungoverned voluptuouſneſs is the reverſe of temperance. We farther proceed to examine what kinds of pleaſure it is the office of temperance to regulate. Pleaſures are commonly diſtinguiſhed, as either corporeal or mental. Of the latter kind is the pleaſure which we derive from virtue or from knowledge; with both of which we are delighted, becauſe we love them; and that, without any bodily ſenſation, but merely through mental affection. Neither temperance nor voluptuouſneſs are converſant about ſuch pleaſures, nor about any others not originating in the body. Men fond of the marvellous, and who delight in relating idle ſtories from morning to night, are called prattlers, not profligates: nor are thoſe guilty of intemperance who indulge exceſſive grief for the loſs of their fortunes or of their friends. Temperance relates therefore to bodily pleaſures only, but not even to them univerſally. It reſtrains not the gratification which the eye receives from colours, figures, and pictures, nor that given to the ear by declamation or muſic. There is a propriety, doubtleſs, in the affection with which we deſire, and the degree in which we indulge, thoſe pleaſures; but they who act properly in ſuch particulars, are not denominated temperate; nor thoſe who act improperly, intemperate. Nor do temperance and intemperance apply to our reſtraint or indulgence with regard to the pleaſures derived from the ſenſe of ſmell, except by way of acceſſion,

cession, that is, when grateful odours are confidered as an acceffory to agreeable fenfations derived from the tafte or touch. To be delighted with the fragrancy of flowers and fruits, and of thofe aromatics which perfume the altars of the Gods, is never regarded as fenfuality; but a propenfity to vicious indulgence may appear in the pleafures received from thofe artificial fcents which are employed for heightening perfonal allurements, and from the odour of thofe delicacies which form the luxury of our tables; becaufe, in thefe cafes, the perceptions of one fenfe naturally bring into our thoughts the perceptions of other fenfes, which are too often indulged with grofs and beaftly intemperance. The inferior animals, when hungry, are delighted with the fmell of their food; but this delight in them happens alfo, as above explained, by way of acceffion; dogs are pleafed with the fcent of the hare, becaufe they delight in eating that animal; and lions are pleafed, not with the bellowing of the bull, but with devouring him; and the bellowing only pleafes them, becaufe it is a proof that their prey is near to them. The fight of the deer or wild goat alfo delights them, becaufe it affords the expectation of foon tafting their flefh. Temperance, therefore, is converfant about thofe pleafures only, which are common to us with beafts; and in which an exceffive indulgence is therefore juftly deemed the loweft depravity. Thofe pleafures depend entirely on the touch and tafte, but far more on the former; the tafte being properly that fenfe which difcriminates different flavours, as is done by thofe who critically examine wines and fauces. But the beaftly fenfualift has little or no pleafure in any thing except mere corporeal contact in eating and drinking, as well as in venery. Wherefore the voluptuary Philoxenus wifhed his neck as long as a crane's, that his gratification in the act of fwallowing might be the more durable.

BOOK III.

durable. Temperance, therefore, is chiefly conversant about regulating the pleasures of that sense, of which, as it is of all the most common, the improper indulgence is the most blameable and most debasing; since it belongs to us, not as men, but as mere animals. To love and take delight in such gratifications, is to divest ourselves of the man, and to put on the wild beast: for the more liberal pleasures of the touch, such as the warmth produced by friction and exercise in the *gymnasia*, fall not under this head; intemperate voluptuousness in contact, not extending to the whole body, but centering in particular parts of it.

Chap. 11.

Natural and adventitious desires.

Of our desires and appetites, some are common and natural; others, peculiar and adventitious. Every animal needs and desires nourishment, either dry or moist; and sometimes both; and in the vigour of life, every man, as Homer says, wishes for a mate. But all do not desire either the same objects; nor is every particular object alike necessary to the happiness of every individual; the desire of particular objects, therefore, is often considered as peculiar and adventitious. This desire may nevertheless be natural to him who feels it, since different men have different inclinations; and one person may receive much delight from that which cannot afford any gratification to another. In our natural desires, there are few improprieties; the sole error consisting in excessive indulgence. Gluttony, which, instead of satisfying, overloads the stomach, is the vice only of the most abject of the human kind. But in adventitious and unnatural pleasures, there is scope for the wildest and most various errors; which result, not only from the excessive degree, but from the improper and even odious objects, of our desires; as well as from the unbecoming manner and unseasonable occasions on which they are indulged.

dulged. Intemperance, then, is an excefs with regard to pleafure; and juftly reprobated. With regard to pain, the office of temperance is different from that of fortitude. The intemperate man is grieved at miffing pleafure; which, by his perverfity and folly, is thus abfurdly converted into a perpetual fource of pain; fince he defires it with diftreffing anxiety, and both abufes it when prefent, and forrows after it when it is gone. But temperance, which is not to be feduced by pleafures within its power, cannot grieve at the lofs of thofe which are placed beyond its reach. Extreme infenfibility to pleafure is not the lot of human nature: even brute beafts prefer one kind of food to another. The fault therefore of being too little affected by pleafure, as it feldom or never occurs, is not diftinguifhed by a name. But temperance holds the middle place between this namelefs vice and the oppofite extreme. The man endowed with temperance is fo far from delighting in, or enjoying, the pleafures of the voluptuary, that he beholds them with deteftation and difguft. He indulges in none but lawful pleafures, and in them feafonably and foberly; and not being intoxicated by them when prefent, does not painfully long for them when abfent. His health, his fortune, and above all his honour and his duty, prefcribe laws to his appetites. The profligate prefers fenfual pleafures to all things befide: the man of temperance eftimates them at their true value, and that a low one ^q.

Intemperance is more voluntary than cowardice; the former proceeding from the defire of pleafure, the latter from the averfion to pain: and fuch is the nature of pain that it difturbs and deftroys the frame of mind of thofe who behold its approach, and

Chap. 12.

Comparifon of intemperance and cowardice.

^q Magna Moral. l. i. c. xxii. Eudem. l. iii. c. ii.

and anticipate its pangs. Pleasure not producing these effects, the intemperate indulgence in it is therefore more voluntary, and consequently more blameable; especially since there are innumerable opportunities in life for restraining our pursuit of unlawful or improper pleasures, and thereby acquiring a confirmed habit of temperance, the several acts of which are unattended with danger. The reverse of this happens as to cowardice; the opportunities for correcting it are much fewer in number, and the experiment is dangerous. But though particular instances of cowardice are in some measure involuntary, through the invincible terror which produces them, and which impels those affected with it to throw away their shields, and to commit other shameful actions, yet the frame and habit of mind from which such actions flow, seems to be more a matter of choice; whereas the frame and habit of mind from which intemperance flows, seems less voluntary than the particular instances of it; for no one can will or choose, that by his internal constitution he should be the sport of vicious propensities, and ungovernable appetites. The word denoting intemperance in Greek is applicable to the wanton and unchastised petulance of boys, which bears a near analogy to what is called intemperance in men. Which of the two was the primary meaning of the word, it is not material to inquire; for the transition is extremely natural from the one signification to the other, nothing standing more in need of chastisement than depravities which increase by indulgence; to which depravities, passions as well as boys are peculiarly liable. For boys are actuated almost solely by passion, pleasure being their ruling pursuit; the desire of which, unless it be restrained by higher principles and controlled by authority, will transgress all reasonable bounds; and, gaining strength

by

by repeated acts of indulgence, will finally deftroy and extinguifh the light of reafon itfelf. Our defires therefore ought to be few and moderate, and as obedient to the dictates of reafon, as boys to the commands of their mafter. By fuch habitual regulation, they will gradually harmonife with the higher powers of our nature, and at length terminate in the fame excellent and honourable end; exhibiting the fteady luftre of virtue; and exactly conforming, as to their object, degree, time, and all other circumftances, to the ftrict rules of propriety. So much concerning temperance.

ARISTOTLE's ETHICS.

BOOK IV.

INTRODUCTION.

HAVING treated of the virtues of courage and temperance, which, how different soever in many respects from each other, agree in this particular, that they both consist in the proper government of the irrational or merely sensitive part of our nature, the author proceeds in the fourth book, to explain the nature of liberality, magnificence, magnanimity, meekness, courtesy, plain-dealing, and facetiousness. As things are best understood by comparison, he points out and defines the blameable extremes (for example, of niggardliness and profusion) which stand in direct opposition to each other; and which are both of them contrary, though not always in a like degree, to the praiseworthy habit which lies between them. He shows that there is an intermediate, but anonymous habit, highly deserving of approbation, between the extremes of ambition and blameable insensibility to honour: observing on this and other occasions, that many of the virtues, as well as of the vices, are not accurately distinguished by names; and that from this imperfection of language, much confusion results; for when the intermediate and praiseworthy habit is nameless, each of

BOOK IV. the extremes will strive to thrust itself into the middle place, which is the post of honour; and that habit which is approved as virtue by one class of men, will be condemned as vice by another. He examines whether shame can be classed with the virtues, since it seems rather a passion than a habit. He explains what is meant by a conditional virtue, in opposition to virtue simply and absolutely; and proves that shame is at best only a virtue of the conditional and imperfect kind.

BOOK IV.

ARGUMENT.

Liberality.—Vices opposite thereto.—Magnificence, its contraries.—Magnanimity.—Meekness; its contraries.—Courtesy; its contraries.—Plain-dealing; its contraries.—Facetiousness; its contraries.—Shame.

We proceed to speak of liberality, which seems to be that virtue which bears a peculiar relation to property. For the praise of liberality is not acquired by courage in war, moderation in pleasure, or justice in judgment, but by the propriety of our behaviour in receiving or bestowing money, or whatever things can be measured by money; and principally in bestowing them. Of the propriety of our conduct in relation to property, prodigality and niggardliness are the two contrary and blameable extremes. Niggardliness always refers to those who set more than a just value on money: but prodigality is sometimes employed to express extravagant profusion joined with inordinate intemperance; for those are called prodigals, who waste their fortunes in ruinous pleasures, and thus signally debase themselves by complicated worthlessness. Yet prodigality more properly signifies one simple vice, that of ruining ourselves by our own fault; for he ruins himself by his own fault, who wastefully consumes his property, that is, the means by which his life is supported; and in this acceptation we take the word. Property falls under the description of things useful; which may either be used rightly or abused; and he only can use them rightly, who is adorned with the virtue appertaining to them; namely, liberality. The use of money consists in expending or bestowing it: for the taking or keeping of money relates to possession rather than to use. The virtue of liberality therefore is more conspicuous in bestowing handsomely, than either in receiving what is our due, or in refusing what we ought not to accept. For virtue consists rather in acting our part well, than in avoiding what is amiss. This active virtue alone is the proper object of praise and gratitude; for it is more meritorious to part with what is our own, than to abstain from what belongs to another; which latter may be praised indeed as justice, but not as liberality; and to accept what is strictly due to us, is not entitled to any degree of praise. None are more beloved than the liberal, because their virtue is extensively useful, diffusing itself in benefits. But the motive from which their actions proceed, is what chiefly constitutes their excellence; for liberality, like every other virtue, must keep the beauty of propriety in view; selecting its objects, and proportioning its extent, according to those rules which right-reason prescribes. The critical moment for best conferring a favour must also be carefully studied; and they must be conferred cheerfully, at least not painfully: and when any one of these conditions is wanting, whatever acts of bounty a man may perform, he will not carry off the palm of virtuous and graceful liberality. If the gifts bestowed on others occasion pain to ourselves, it is a proof that we prefer money to the beauty

beauty of generous actions; and if we are rapacious in acquiring money, we cannot be truly liberal in employing it. A man of real beneficence will not be importunate in solicitation. He will be delicate as to accepting favours; but will enrich himself by the diligent management of his own affairs, that he may acquire materials for his bounty, which will be distributed with caution, that it may never fail the deserving. It belongs to his character to be more provident for others than for himself; and to extend the measure of his beneficence far beyond those limits which the prudence of selfishness would prescribe. But our liberality is relative to our wealth; it consists, not in the value of our gifts, but in the temper and habit of the giver; and he who gives the least of all, may be the most liberal of all, if what he gives bears the highest proportion to his substance [r]. Men of hereditary estates are more inclined to liberality, than those whose fortunes are their own work; the former have never known the severities of want; and all men are disposed to love and cherish their own works, as parents and poets. It is not easy for a liberal man to be rich, since he is nice in receiving money, not retentive in keeping it; and always ready to give it away, on no other account than that of the proper or beneficent purposes to which it may be applied. Fortune, therefore, is continually accused of enriching those who are least worthy of her favours. But this happens naturally, without the interference of fortune; since wealth cannot well be possessed by those who employ not the ordinary means by which it is acquired and accumulated. Yet true

---

[r] Verily I say unto you, that this poor widow hath cast more in, than all they which have cast into the treasury. St. Mark, c. xii. v. 43.

BOOK IV.

true liberality avoids unnecessary and superfluous expence, lest the source should be dried up, from which only its salutary streams can plenteously flow. Whoever lives beyond his income, is strictly a prodigal, and he only; for kings, how great soever their expenditure may be, are never branded with this appellation; because it seems difficult for their munificence to exceed the measure of their resources. The liberal man, both in great and in small matters, and both in giving and receiving, behaves with cheerful serenity, because his behaviour is always proper, and always consistent with his character. As propriety in giving and receiving depends on the same principle of moderation in our desires with regard to money, he who gives properly, will not improperly receive; since contraries cannot result from the same principle, nor subsist in the same subject. Should it happen that a liberal man consumes more than he ought, and on an improper occasion, he will doubtless lament it, but with that calm and moderate composure which becomes his character; for it is the part of virtue not only to joy and grieve from fit motives, but to assign proper limits to those emotions. The liberal man is, in matters of interest, of an accommodating temper; he is open to imposition and injury, because he does not value money beyond its real worth, and is more uneasy at having omitted to do what he ought, than at doing too much; living in direct opposition to the avaricious rapacity of Simonides [1]. The prodigal, again, is directly the reverse;

[1] A poet of the Isle of Ceos, and the first on record who prostituted his mercenary muse for the vile purpose of gain. He was born 538 years before Christ, and lived ninety years; the companion and favourite of many of the princes and grandees of his time. As his avarice increased with his age, he apologized for it by saying that the pursuit of money was the only delight which time had left to him. Conf. Fragment. Callimac.

reverse; both his joy and his grief spring from improper motives, and both shew themselves in unseemly and immoderate degrees; which will be more manifest in the sequel. Prodigality and avarice are both of them excesses, and both of them defects. Prodigality is excessive in giving, and defective in receiving; avarice is defective in giving, and excessive in receiving, and scraping together the meanest and most sordid gains. The qualities which compose and support prodigality, are not easily united: it is difficult for him who is careless of receiving, to continue lavish in bestowing; for his funds, if he is a private man, will soon be exhausted. The prodigal, therefore, is better than the miser, because his malady is more curable. Age, and the experience of want, will correct his extravagance; and, as he still shows a generosity of nature, though unwisely and unseasonably, custom and good example will convert his thoughtless profusion into decent and graceful liberality; since his deviations from the right path proceed rather from folly than from depravity and turpitude. For this reason such a prodigal is preferable to the miser; and also because the former benefits many, and the latter, no one; not even himself. But those who are prodigal of their own, are for the most part rapacious of what belongs to others; and finding it impossible to supply their wild extravagance by honourable means, abstain from no source of gain, however impure and polluted it may be; so that even their bounties have nothing liberal in them, being with-held from virtue in distress, and lavished on parasites, flatterers, and on the idle retinue of vice and folly. For the greater part of prodigals unite profligacy

with

Callimac. apud Spanheim. v. i. p. 264 and 337. Plutarch. An seni copiend. Respublica, V. ii. p. 785. Athen xiv. c. xxi. Fabric. Bibliot. Græc. V. i. p. 501.

BOOK IV.

with prodigality; and insensible to the beauty of virtue, fall victims to the allurement of pleasure. But though this happens to the undisciplined prodigal, yet, under proper management, he may be brought into the middle and right path; whereas avarice is incorrigible; for it is increased by old age and every kind of infirmity; and it seems more congenial to human nature than the contrary vice, there being in every country more hoarders than spendthrifts. It also extends to extraordinary lengths, and assumes a variety of forms; the immoderate love of money leading some men to daring rapacity, and others to sordid parsimony; for there are niggardly misers, and tenacious scrape-pennies, who either through a sense of justice, or through fear, are careful in abstaining from shameful gains, and meanly sparing of their property, lest they should be forced, as they say, on dishonest expedients for subsistence. Their maxim is, neither to borrow nor to lend, neither to give nor to receive; because, should they accept any thing from others, they think it will be difficult always to avoid giving to others something in return. But rapacious avarice sticks at no expedient by which money may be acquired; submits to the basest drudgery, practises pimping or usury, and thinks no profit too infamous or too minute, which, by frequent repetitions, may accumulate into a great gain. Both kinds are alike disgraced by their false estimate, and inordinate love of money; since, for the sake of profit, and that a small one, they encounter and endure a burdensome load of infamy; which is an evil that even the greatest profits cannot possibly compensate. Those who aspire to great and sudden acquisitions of wealth, such as tyrants who storm cities and plunder temples, are not branded with the reproach

of

of avarice, but of impiety and villany. The pirate, the pickpocket, and the gamester, are guilty of illiberal rapacity; since the two first encounter, for the sake of gain, not only danger but disgrace; and the last plunders and ruins his friends and acquaintances, whom a man of liberal principles wishes always to benefit. They are all equally debased by a shameless preference of wealth to worth; and by bartering things incomparably more valuable, for unjust and illiberal gains. Illiberality, therefore, is the vice most properly opposed to the virtue of liberality; for it is a greater, more extensive, and more universal evil, than the vice of prodigality, which holds the contrary extreme. So much concerning mediocrity in our passions and actions with regard to money, and whatever money can purchase, as well as concerning the vicious extremes which are inconsistent with this praiseworthy and meritorious habit [t].

BOOK IV.

We naturally proceed to treat next of magnificence; for that likewise seems to be a virtue respecting money; but differs from liberality in this, that it relates to money in one view only, namely, the spending of it; and in this, it exceeds the measure which mere liberality would prescribe. The very name of magnificence indicates a certain magnitude, joined with propriety, in expence; and the magnitude or splendour of our expence is estimated by the occasion on which it is employed; for that might be great in a trierarch [u], which would be small in an ambassador to the public solemnities of Greece; and the propriety depends both on the object of the expence, and on the

Chap. 2.

Magnificence, and its contraries.

---

[t] Vid. Magna Moral. l. i. c. xxiv.; et Eudem. l. iii. c. iv.

[u] The rich citizens of Athens were liable to the burden of equipping gallies for the public service; in which they often vied with each other in displaying their patriotism to the ruin of their fortunes. Lys. Orat. passim.

the character and situation of the person who incurs it. He is not called magnificent who spends his money with propriety on small or ordinary occasions, like him

" Who often gave the hungry beggar bread:"

For magnificence is not simply liberality, but something more; the former implying the latter, though the latter does not imply the former. Magnificence holds the middle place between two blameable extremes, of which the one, in matters of expence, falls short of what is suitable to our circumstances or to the occasion, and the other ostentatiously exceeds them. To be truly magnificent requires no small degree of judgment; since it infers a graceful theory of moral propriety, and a skilful harmony in great expenditure; for as we said in the beginning, habits are characterised by the acts and energies from which they spring, and which in a man of real magnificence must be great and decorous; the work worthy the expence, and the expence suiting and rather exceeding the work. A man truly magnificent, is actuated by the love of moral beauty, which is the principle of all the virtues. His generosity is large and liberal, without strictness of accounts; his consideration being, not how much any thing will cost him, but how it may be done most handsomely. For the magnificence is not in the expence, but in the manner of employing it; which must be such, not merely as propriety would dictate, for this belongs to liberality, but such as will strike the spectators with wonder. It is most conspicuous in temples, dedications, sacrifices, and whatever concerns the Gods: and in those honourable benefactions which generous patriots confer on the community; the equipment of gallies, public entertainments, and dramatic exhibitions. As magnificence must be consistent with propriety, it can never be the

the virtue of a poor man, in whom every attempt towards exerciſing it muſt be egregious folly. It becomes thoſe only who poſſeſs great hereditary wealth, or who have enriched themſelves by great and ſplendid exploits; and it is moſt honourably diſplayed on the public occaſions above mentioned. It may be ſhown alſo in matters of private concern, when they are ſuch as occur but once in our lives, as a marriage; or ſuch as intereſt the whole community, or at leaſt the members of the government; as the reception and entertainment of ſtrangers, and the honours and preſents beſtowed on them at their departure: for the expences of a magnificent man are public, not perſonal; and preſents to ſtrangers ſomewhat reſemble dedications to the Gods. To build a houſe ſuitable to a great fortune, is a work of magnificence, for it is a public ornament; and works are magnificent in proportion to their durability, provided propriety always be obſerved, for the ſame monuments will not ſuit Gods and men, nor the ſame ornaments become tombs and temples. Magnificence, we have ſaid, is not meaſured ſimply by the expence, but by the expence in reference to the object on which it is beſtowed. The magnificence, doubtleſs, riſes in proportion to the magnitude of that object; but a beautiful bauble, of little or no value, may be a magnificent preſent to a child; becauſe, though trifling in itſelf, yet being conſiderable with reſpect to the occaſion, it atteſts the noble liberalitty of the donor. True magnificence is far remote from unſeaſonable oſtentation, which makes a parade of wealth on ordinary and mean occaſions; the oſtentatious man receives his gueſt at a friendly dinner, as if he were celebrating a marriage feſtival; and when he exhibits dramatic entertainments, decks, after the awkward faſhion of the Magareans, his comic actors in the purple trappings of tragedy;

BOOK IV.

gedy; catching popular admiration by unseasonable and absurd extravagance; while, on the other hand, he is meanly parsimonious at times when true magnificence might properly be displayed. The vice opposite to magnificence betrays niggardliness throughout, even in the midst of the most profuse expence; for, in some minute particular, an attention to a pitiful saving will be discovered, which ruins the beauty and gracefulness of the whole, as it proves that whatever has been done, was done sparingly and painfully; and that the performance, if great, far surpassed the mind of the performer. These two contrary habits are both of them vices, but not very reproachful ones, since they neither do harm to others, nor evince gross turpitude in the mind which harbours them [x].

Chap. 3.
Magnanimity.

Magnanimity, as the name imports, is conversant about great things; what these are let us first consider; contemplating not the habit itself, but the person actuated by it, which will bring us to precisely the same conclusions. A magnanimous man is he, whose character being of great worth, is estimated by himself at its full value. He who forms a grossly false estimate of himself is a fool; and none of the virtues are consistent with folly: while the man who, conscious of his defects, appreciates his small merits by a fair and just standard, may be praised for his good sense and modesty, but cannot pass for magnanimous; which epithet always implies dignity and excellence; this beauty of the mind requiring, like that of the body, elevation and magnitude; for persons of a diminutive stature, are not called beautiful, but neat and elegant. A mean-spirited [y] man under-rates his own merits; and the vain-glorious boaster arrogates

[x] Eudem. l. iii. c. vi.   [y] Aristotle says "little-minded."

rogates to himself merits, of which he is by no means possessed; but the more solid merit he possesses, his vain-glory is the less; whereas mean-spiritedness is the greater, in proportion to the excellence of the worth which is so improperly appreciated by its possessor; for how contemptible would he be, even to himself, were his real character of little or no value! The magnanimous man estimates himself at the highest rate, yet no higher than he ought; and conscious of his inward worth, thinks himself entitled to whatever is held most precious; to what the most exalted of men claim as the highest of all rewards; and to what all men confer on the Gods as their acknowledged due; in a word, to honour, the greatest and most invaluable of external goods. Magnanimity, therefore, is peculiarly conversant about honour, and its contrary, ignominy; holding the middle place between vain-glory that unfairly courts undue honours, and mean-spiritedness that improperly rejects even those that are due. But though, in point of propriety, magnanimity holds the middle place, yet, in excellence and dignity, it rises to the summit; for it heightens and enlarges every virtue; and the most boastful vain-glory never proudly arrogated more than true magnanimity has fairly claimed. This illustrious habit of the mind cannot bear an alliance with any kind of vice. It is most opposite to cowardice or injustice; for, from what motive can he, who thinks of nothing so highly as of his own character, exhibit himself under such deformities? And if we apply to particular instances, or survey individual characters, we shall find that those who affect magnanimity without real worth, infallibly expose themselves to ridicule. For, honour, which is the meed of virtue, cannot belong to the worthless; and magnanimity forms, as it were, the orna‑

ment

BOOK IV. ment of the virtues, since it cannot subsist without them, yet heightens, extends, and magnifies them, wherever they are found. True magnanimity then is a thing most difficult, since it implies the perfection of moral rectitude. It delights, moderately, in great honours bestowed by the deserving, as meeting with its due, or less: for with perfect virtue no honour can be fully commensurate. It accepts however such honours, because nothing better can be bestowed; but of vulgar honours, or from vulgar men, it is altogether disdainful; and is as insensible to their reproach, as careless of their applause. Wealth, power, good or bad fortune, it will meet and sustain with the same dignified composure, neither elated with prosperity nor dejected by adversity; for to a magnanimous man those things are desirable chiefly as the signs of honour; and, if he bears honour itself with moderation, much more must he thus bear those things which are only its signs, and desired merely on its account; since to him who thinks not too highly of honour, nothing besides can possibly appear great. Magnanimity, therefore, sometimes passes for superciliousness; especially since great external prosperity seems to heighten and increase it; for nobility is honoured; and men of wealth or power, being distinguished by great superiority of advantages, will always find persons ready to do them honour; and though honour belongs properly to virtue alone, yet virtue, adorned with great external prosperity, will seem doubly entitled to pre-eminence. But, in reality, the most prosperous fortune, when destitute of virtue, affords not any just ground for self-applause; it gives to us neither a high opinion of ourselves, nor a fair claim to be highly thought of by others; and as it is incapable of inspiring true magnanimity, it too frequently begets insolence and

supor-

superciliousness; since worthless men cannot bear gracefully the gifts of fortune, but abuse their fancied superiority by treating others contemptuously and unjustly; whereas the contempt shown by the truly magnanimous, is just; their opinions being formed on reflection, as those of the multitude are taken up at random. A man of magnanimity neither courts dangers, nor willingly encounters them on slight occasions. But when a worthy occasion requires it, he is unsparing of his life, thinking that to live is not, under all conditions, eligible. He is eager to confer favours, and ashamed of receiving them; because the former is a mark of superiority, the latter the reverse; he therefore repays every kindness with interest, that the person who first obliged him, may become his debtor. He hears with more pleasure a recital of the good offices he has performed, than that of the favours which he has received. Wherefore Thetis does not expatiate on her benefits to Jupiter *y*, nor the Lacedæmonians on those which they had conferred on the Athenians *z*; but rather on the kindness they themselves had received at their hands; for magnanimity having few wants, seldom needs that assistance which it is always disposed to afford; it is lofty towards the great and prosperous, but behaves modestly towards men in moderate circumstances; to rise above the former, has difficulty and dignity; but to magnify ourselves in company with the latter, betrays a lowness and littleness of mind, not less ungenerous and vulgar, than making a parade of our strength or courage amidst weakness and cowardice. Magnanimity contemns trivial honours; and disdains, even in great things, to act a second part. It is slow in action, and averse to exertion, except when great honour may be obtained, or great actions are

to

---

y Homer. Ilias. l. i. v. 503. & seq.

z Xenoph. Hellen. l. vi. p. 609—613. Edit. Leunclav.

BOOK IV. to be performed: not bufied about many things, but confined to thofe which are great and fplendid. A magnanimous man is as open in his hatred as in his friendfhip; for concealment is the part of fear; he regards truth more than opinion, and fhows himfelf manifeftly in his words and actions, declaring his mind with full freedom; which indicates both his own love of truth and his contempt for the opinions of others; but this opennefs of character is liable to one exception, for he is much given to *irony*, diffembling his merits before the vulgar, who are unworthy to appreciate them. He can fhow undue complaifance for no one's humours, except thofe of his friends; for flattery is a low and fervile vice. He is not prone to admire, for he deems nothing great. He is not mindful of injuries, which his magnanimity teaches him to defpife. He is no man's panegyrift or flanderer; he talks not of himfelf, nor does he blame others; not fpeaking ill even of his enemies, except when their infolence excites his indignation. As to things of fmall import, or even daily ufe, he is no petitioner or complainer; for that would fhew too much concern about them. His poffeffions are diftinguifhed for their beauty and elegance rather than for their fruitfulnefs and utility; becaufe the former qualities are more nearly allied to that independence and all-fufficiency to which he afpires. The gait of a magnanimous man is flow; his tone of voice grave, his pronunciation firm. Hafte and rapidity betoken too much folicitude. *He* therefore is feldom in hafte, who deems few things worthy of his purfuit; nor is he often eager who thinks few things of importance: quicknefs and fharpnefs of voice proceeding from earneftnefs and eagernefs. Such then are the characteriftics of magnanimity, of which mean-fpiritednefs is the defect, and vain-glory the excefs; qualities which, though

not

not very hurtful to others, yet show much imperfection in the minds which harbour them. The little-minded man deprives himself of those advantages to which he is entitled. He is ignorant of himself and of his own worth, otherwife he would aspire to those advantages which he really deserves. His fault however consists rather in sluggishness than folly; he draws back from noble actions and illustrious enterprises, as things much above him; and even excludes himself from that external prosperity which fortune throws in his way. But the vainglorious man is ignorant of himself still more conspicuously; and even to folly. He engages in undertakings the most honourable, but far above his abilities; and in which his signal failure manifestly convicts him of unworthiness. He delights in the ornaments of dress, and all other showy externals. He makes a parade of his prosperity, and boasts of it in the vain hope of being honoured on its account. Yet mean-spiritedness is more contrary than vain-glory to true magnanimity; because the former vice is more frequently met with, and is also attended with worse consequences. Such then is the nature of magnanimity, or that virtue which is conversant about great and extraordinary honours [a].

BOOK IV.

There seems to be another virtue also conversant about honour, and bearing the same proportion to magnanimity, which liberality bears to magnificence. This virtue, as well as liberality, relates, not to what is great and extraordinary, but to what is ordinary and moderate: and as liberality teaches us to behave with propriety in the pursuit of ordinary and moderate profits, so this nameless virtue teaches us to behave with propriety in the pursuit of ordinary and moderate honours. A man

Chap. 4.

Of the propriety of affection and conduct with regard to honour.

[a] Vid. Magna Moral. l. i. c. xxvi.; Eudem. l. iii. c. v.

man may either be more or less desirous than he ought, of glory as well as of gain; he may seek both those objects on improper occasions, and by undue means. An ambitious man is more fond of honour than he ought; an unambitious man, less than he ought; not caring to reap the natural reward even of praiseworthy exploits: the former recommends himself by his spirited manliness and emulation of excellence; the latter, by his moderation and modesty; and from the imperfection of language in not assigning distinct names to the different degrees of our affections, the same word excites either praise or blame, according to the sense in which it is taken: ambition is a subject of commendation, when it denotes a more than vulgar love of honour; it is a term of reproach, when it denotes the same affection in an immoderate and unwarrantable degree; and as a term is wanting to denote that middle state of the affection, which is alone consistent with propriety, the contrary extremes contend with each other for the vacant place of pre-eminence. Whatever things admit of excess or defect, admit also of this middle state, which is alone praiseworthy. This is the case with the desire of honour, which may be too strong, too weak, or in a moderate and proper degree; a degree not marked by any distinct term, and which, by the ambitious, is called low-mindedness; and by the lowminded, ambition; thus appearing to either extreme the vice opposite to itself. This happens with regard to some other virtues; each of the extremes usurping the middle place, because the middle itself is not distinguished by a name.

Chap. 5.

Meekness, with its contraries.

Meekness is propriety of affection with regard to the causes and circumstances which naturally provoke anger; or rather, as names are wanting to denote either a mediocrity or the opposite

opposite extremes of this affection; meekness, though verging towards the anonymous extreme, consisting in defect, is thrust into the middle place. The extreme consisting in excess, may be called irascibility; and anger being a passion excited by a variety of different causes, and under a variety of different circumstances, it can only be commendable when it results from a proper cause, is directed towards proper objects, is seasonable in its commencement, moderate in its degree, and limited in its duration. If meekness be a praiseworthy quality, even the meek man must be affected with anger under the conditions above specified. For meekness denotes freedom from unreasonable perturbation, and a due resistance to passion, in compliance with the higher powers of our nature; inclining, indeed, to the defective extreme; since a meek man is not resentful of injuries, but always prone to pardon them. The incapacity of feeling just provocation is certainly a fault; which, when it proceeds beyond a certain pitch, borders on folly; it denotes a stupid insensibility of character; and he who does not feel wrongs as he ought, cannot be well qualified to repel them; he will submit, with the meanness of a slave, to insults offered either to himself or to his friends. An excessive propensity to anger displays itself in a great variety of ways; it is excited by improper causes, and is determined towards improper objects; it appears in immoderate or excessive degrees; in some men it bursts forth suddenly into intemperate rage; in others, it settles into unjustifiable and permanent resentment. All those extravagancies of passion do not take place at once; for multiplied excesses of vice are destructive of each other; and should they fall with their full weight on one individual, their burden would be intolerable. Irascible men, though moved to passion

BOOK IV.

too suddenly, in immoderate degrees, and on improper occasions, are yet easily pacified; if they be soon angry, they are also soon pleased, which is the best circumstance attending them; and which happens from this, that they do not restrain their passion, but give free vent to it; their quickness of temper plainly shewing their affections and intentions, which they have no sooner made manifest, than they are ready to be appeased. The excess of this disposition, which takes offence against every person, and on every the slightest occasion, receives its name, in Greek, from two words denoting the sharpest asperity of choler. The resentful and implacable temper retains anger long, because it does not give free vent to it; for, to vent anger in vengeance naturally appeases it, by substituting pleasure in the stead of pain; but passion restrained, gathers strength by compression; and as it remains hid within the breast, the gentle power of persuasion cannot be applied for its alleviation; it must be digested by the internal vigour of the constitution, which is a work of time. A fell and savage temper directs its immediate anger against improper objects, and is implacable in its resentment, until it is fully satiated with vengeance. The excesses of anger are more opposite than its defects to the virtue of meekness; because they occur more frequently; because human nature is too prone to be immoderate in its resentment; and because persons of irascible and querulous tempers are the most troublesome to live with. From what was above observed, it is plain that words cannot accurately express all the conditions, as to time, place, person, cause, and degree, which render anger praiseworthy or blameable. He who deviates a little on either side from the exact point of propriety, escapes blame, because his slight error escapes observation.

tion. The incapacity of feeling or resenting an injury, is sometimes praised as meekness; too strong a propensity to anger, is sometimes extolled as manhood, and regarded as indicating a disposition fit for command. The precise middle point, in which alone propriety consists, cannot be accurately ascertained in words, because it is determined only by a perception of sense; and the senses do not perceive minute variations. This however is plain, that the middle habit is laudable, and the extremes blameable, more or less, in exact proportion to their greater or lesser deviations, in point of all, or any, of the conditions above specified. This laudable mediocrity, therefore, ought to be our constant aim; and let this much suffice concerning the dispositions and habits that have a reference to the causes and circumstances that naturally provoke anger [b].

In the intercourse of life and society, there are men of a fawning disposition, ever prone to praise, totally averse to contention, and who think it incumbent on them to give pleasure to all with whom they converse. There are others of so peevish a temper, that they are continually contradicting and crossing all those with whom they have to do; and who feel not the smallest concern for the pain occasioned to others by their churlish asperity. That both these habits are blameable, is manifest; and also that there is an intermediate habit between fawning flattery and savage severity, which is truly laudable, because it distributes its approbation and disapprobation in due measure, according to the circumstances of the case. This intermediate habit is not distinguished by a name; it most resembles friendship, for should affection be added to the companionable qualities of a man endowed with this habit, he would

Chap. 6.

Courtesy, with its contraries.

---

[b] Vid. Eudem. l. iii. c. iii.

would be a most delightful friend: but it differs from friendship in this, that it does not include any peculiar affection towards those with whom we converse; and the person adorned with this laudable habit, does not approve from love, nor disapprove from hatred, but because it is his nature and character to bestow his approbation and disapprobation agreeably to those rules which moral propriety prescribes; whether he has to do with acquaintances or strangers; with familiar friends, or with persons altogether unknown to him; except, that his behaviour to each of those classes of persons will be marked with such distinctions as circumstances require; for we ought not to testify as much pleasure at the merit of mere strangers as at that of our friends; nor to be equally complaisant to the follies of the latter, as to those of the former. The man of courtesy and civility (for these are the words by which the habit in question may most nearly be expressed) will, in the intercourse of society, behave himself universally as he ought: his aim will be, never needlessly to offend; but to gratify and please those with whom he lives, on all occasions on which it possibly can be done consistently with utility and propriety. But the courteous man will not betray his own interest or honour, or even those of the persons with whom he converses, for the sake of affording a small and unseasonable pleasure. He will resist their opinions, when to resist them gives small pain; whereas to approve them would be injurious or disgraceful either to others or to himself. His behaviour will vary with the rank and dignity, with the degree of his familiarity or connexion, and with a variety of other circumstances belonging to the persons with whom he converses, but will be always regulated by propriety. Pleasure, we have said, will be his aim; but without

sacrificing

sacrificing interest or honour to pleasure, or a greater pleasure to a lesser. Such then is this intermediate habit, which is nameless in Greek; and of which the extremes are, on one hand, universal and indiscriminate complaisance, which, when it proceeds from motives of interest, is called flattery; and, on the other, churlish asperity and contentious peevishness. As there is no term to express the intermediate and laudable habit, the extremes only seem to stand in opposition to each other, and alternately arrogate the praise of virtue, though in fact they are both vices; and as such, in direct opposition to the praiseworthy habit above described.

The virtue which lies between the extremes of dissembling concealment and arrogant ostentation is conversant about nearly the same objects with courtesy; except that this has a reference to the pleasure of those with whom we live, whereas that has a reference to truth in our words and actions. It is worth while to consider also this praiseworthy, though anonymous, habit; because by thus shewing that each particular virtue consists in mediocrity, we shall best explain the nature of virtue in general, and most clearly establish the truth of our moral theory. The characteristics of those who give pleasure or pain in the intercourse of society, have already been described; we proceed to speak of those who are adorned by truth and frankness, or degraded by falsehood and dissimulation. There are men who arrogate to themselves good qualities, of which they are entirely destitute, and who amplify the good qualities of which they are possessed, far beyond their real measure and natural worth. The ironical dissembler, on the other hand, either conceals his advantages; or if he cannot conceal, endeavours to depreciate their value; whereas the man of frankness

and

BOOK IV.

Chap. 7.

Plain dealing, and its contraries.

BOOK IV.

and plain-dealing shews his character in its natural size: truth appears in all his words and actions; which represent him exactly as he is, without addition and without diminution. Each of these three habits display themselves either from the spontaneous impulse of our character, or from motives of interest; and when men have not any reason for acting otherwise, they indulge the bent of their characters, either to plain-dealing on the one hand, or to the opposite kinds of deceit above specified. There is a deformity in falsehood, which renders it odious in itself; whereas truth is beautiful and praiseworthy: and plain-dealing is the intermediate habit or virtue between the opposite extremes or vices of him who would pass himself for more than he is worth, and of him who conceals, or dissembles, his advantages. Of those two kinds of deceit the former is the most blameable; we shall treat of both, after having first spoken of plain-dealing. By this word we do not mean the faithful performance of contracts or engagements, nor any of those things which have a reference to justice or injustice in our transactions; for such matters as these belong to another branch of virtue: but we mean the undisguised truth and downright honesty which are apparent in some men's behaviour, when no interest whatever is at stake, merely because such plain-dealing is most agreeable to their character. Such men will naturally be just in their transactions, since they who avoid deceit which is harmless, will still more avoid fraud which is injurious to others and disgraceful to themselves. This habit is praise-worthy, even when it inclines to the defective extreme of disavowing or concealing advantages that really belong to us; it derives a comeliness from avoiding to make a parade of invidious distinctions, and of our own superiority,

which

which is always mortifying to others. The vice of oftentatious
vanity, and falfe arrogation of merit, when it proceeds not from
any interefted motive, fhews great weaknefs and levity; but
its folly is more confpicuous than its turpitude; when it fprings
from a love of honour or praife, which we muft be confcious
that we do not deferve, it is indeed highly contemptible, but is
in that cafe lefs odious than when it has its fource in the love
of money, or of any thing by which money may be gained.
The virtues and vices juft mentioned depend like all others not
on our natural powers or propenfities, but on election and
habit: it is from habit that fome delight in plain-dealing, others
in deceit; and that fome take a pleafure in practifing deceit for
the purpofes of glory, and others for thofe of gain. The
former affume the femblance of qualities, of which the reality
would entitle them to congratulation and praife; the latter arrogate to themfelves qualities, which, if they really poffeffed
them, might be fuccefsfully employed in promoting the pleafure or alleviating the pain of others; and to which qualities it
is not eafy to prove that they are only vain pretenders: to this
clafs of deceivers belong phyficians, fophifts, and foothfayers.
The ironical diffembler has more of the grace of propriety, becaufe he conceals or depreciates his real advantages, in order to
avoid the fwelling pomp of oftentatious arrogance. Such men
cannot appear to be actuated by motives of intereft: they are
fometimes inclined to diffemble even the moft honourable advantages; as happened in the cafe of Socrates. But there is a littlenefs
and affectation in diffembling advantages inconfiderable in themfelves, and too manifeft to be concealed; fuch diffemblers are
contemptible, and that fometimes in point of vanity and often-
tation; witnefs the Lacedæmonians with their fhort beggarly
dress;

BOOK IV.

dress; for an assumed poverty is frequently as ostentatious as the parade of riches. Dissimulation, therefore, to be graceful, must be used with respect to things not too open and visible: but the arrogation of advantages which do not belong to us is the vice commonly opposed to the virtue of plain-dealing; because it is the worst of the two extremes.

Chap. 8.

Facetiousness, and its contraries.

As life requires repose from serious employment, and this repose may be enlivened by amusement, there seems to be a virtue relative to the intercourse of men in their hours of relaxation and merriment, regulating both the matter and the manner of their conversation. The strain of this conversation may be more austere or more ludicrous than it ought, or may flow in that happy medium which is alone consistent with propriety. He who seeks to raise laughter on all occasions indiscriminately, without regard to decency, or to the pain inflicted on the object of his ridicule, is a low and contemptible buffoon: he who is himself totally incapable of exciting mirth, and who is so far from relishing, that he is highly offended with the innocent jests of others, indicates a roughness and savageness of character, unbending hardness, and unsocial austerity; whereas true facetiousness consists in graceful flexibility of mind and manners, which can assume all shapes, and which becomes all; for as the habits of the body are known by its motions, so are those of the mind. An immoderate propensity to ridicule being a more prominent and more conspicuous quality than the contrary extreme of sullen and rustic gravity, and the greater part of mankind being inclined to delight in merriment, without anxiously examining whether it originates in a pure and proper source; buffoonery often passes for facetiousness, although there be the greatest difference between the coarseness of the one, and

the

the elegance of the other; for in facetiousness, which is the middle and proper habit, an easy pliancy of humour is adorned with a graceful dexterity which skilfully avoids whatever is indecent and illiberal; never debasing the delicate gaiety congenial to the character of well educated citizens, by the smallest approximation to the vile raillery of profligates and slaves. The progress of letters and civility has a powerful influence on the refinement of wit and humour; witness the difference between the ancient and modern comedy. In the former, the most shameful reproaches, expressed in the coarsest language, formed a principal source of the public entertainment; in the latter, the audience are taught chiefly to relish the faint insinuation, and the delicate hint: with respect to beauty and gracefulness, the two styles of writing are marked by the strongest differences. But by what circumstance is true facetiousness characterised? Whether does it consist in saying that only which becomes a well educated citizen? or, may it be characterized by the avoiding of offence? or, thirdly, by the communication of pleasure? Or rather is not such a habit in its nature indefinite, since things pleasing to one audience, may be highly offensive to another: for things which we are pleased to do, we will not be much offended to hear; and those which we are pleased to hear, we in some measure seem to do; but persons well educated prescribe just limits both to their words and actions. The laws prohibit certain reproaches, when made seriously; they should perhaps also prohibit malicious raillery. A man endowed with urbanity and facetiousness is a law unto himself. Such then is this intermediate habit; whereas the extreme of buffoonery renders the mind in which it subsists a slave to low humour; for the buffoon neither spares others nor himself;

BOOK IV.

himself; and provided he can excite laughter, condescends to say what no man of an elegant turn of mind would venture to repeat, or even endure to hear. But the austere and solemn character is, on the other hand, totally unfit for the intercourse of society in hours of relaxation; to the entertainment of which he not only does not contribute any thing himself, but glooms by his unseasonable severity the merriment of others. There are then three laudable habits which have a reference to our behaviour in society; the first consists in a fair exhibition of our own characters; the other two relate to the pleasure of those with whom we live; and of these two, the one consists in heightening that pleasure in hours of relaxation; the other, in promoting it amidst the ordinary employments of life [c].

Chap. 9. Of shame.

Shame can scarcely be numbered among the virtues; for it seems to be rather a passion than a habit. It is defined, the fear of disgrace; and, like another kind of fear, it appears on the countenance; for men, when ashamed, blush, and when afraid of death, grow pale: both seem to be affections of the body, and therefore more properly to be classed with passions than with habits. Shame is not graceful in every period of life; it only becomes youth. Young persons, we think, ought to be extremely sensible to shame; because, as they are chiefly actuated by passion, they would be thereby seduced into many disgraceful excesses, were they not restrained by a sense of shame. We praise the blushing modesty of youth, but nobody would think shamefacedness in old age a fit subject of commendation: for persons of mature years ought to be incapable of any action, on account of which shame can be felt; for as shame

can

---

[c] Magna Moral. l. i. c. xxviii.; Eudem. l. iii. c. vii.

can be felt only for things bafe or blameable, it cannot belong to men of confirmed virtue, who will avoid all fuch actions, whether they be really blameable in themfelves, or only of evil report. Bad men alone can be guilty of bad actions; and it is the wildeft abfurdity to flatter ourfelves, that though we do what is wrong, yet we may efcape the guilt thereof by being heartily afhamed of our conduct. Shame is caufed only by fuch actions as are voluntary; and bafe actions a good man will never voluntarily commit. Shame then can at beft be confidered only as a conditional virtue; that is, it may belong to a good man particularly circumftanced; for on the fuppofition, that he fhould have performed a bad action, he certainly would be afhamed of it. But the virtues, properly fo called, are things defirable and graceful on their own account, fimply and abfolutely, independently of any fuppofitions or conditions whatever. Impudence indeed is a vice; but it does not therefore follow, that its contrary is a virtue; for there is not any room for fhame, where nothing fhameful is either done or intended. For a fimilar reafon, felf-command, which is often fo highly commended, is only a conditional virtue, as fhall be proved hereafter. We now proceed to fpeak of juftice.

ARISTOTLE's ETHICS.

BOOK V.

INTRODUCTION.

This Fifth Book is entirely dedicated to the important subject of justice. Aristotle explains the different acceptations of the word, and distinguishes the different kinds of justice strictly so called. Political justice, again, is either distributive or commutative; which last our author, for a reason given in the text, calls corrective. He shews wherein those kinds of justice differ; the one being regulated by proportion, and the other by equality. The difference is pointed out between what our lawyers call the *mala in se*, and the *mala prohibita*; and the distinction clearly explained between *doing harm* and *committing injury*. Aristotle concludes with examining the nature of equity in contradistinction to that of justice; and illustrates his doctrine concerning the latter, by considering the question whether a man can be guilty of injury towards himself. As the author introduces not any thing superfluous, (for his account of the origin and use of money is essentially connected with the subject,) he comprizes within a narrow compass a solid and satisfactory explanation of those great commanding principles which uphold civil society; an explanation exempt from those ambiguities and contradictions, which too often occur in the innumerable volumes

BOOK V. volumes in which his opinions have been unfaithfully reported, or unskilfully commented. Yet had succeeding writers improved and enriched his observations, the present Book would have the fairest claim to attention, as containing the first attempt to treat fully and scientifically the most important subject on which the pen of any author can possibly be employed.

BOOK V.

ARGUMENT.

Difference between intellectual and moral habits.—Different acceptations of the word injustice.—Justice strictly so called.—Distributive justice.—Corrective justice.—Retaliation.—Natural justice, independent of positive institution.—Misfortunes.—Errors.—Crimes.—Equity.

IN examining justice and injustice, we must explain to what kind of actions they relate; what kind of virtue justice is, and what are the extremes or vices between which this virtue may be found. We shall thus follow the same method which has been pursued in the preceding parts of this discourse. All describe justice as that habit which qualifies men to practise just actions with inclination and pleasure; injustice is the reverse; and this general description may suffice for our present purpose. Justice, we have said, is the habit which qualifies men to practise just actions with pleasure; because the moral habits differ essentially from the intellectual in this, that the latter, as well as mere powers and capacities, may be subservient to quite contrary purposes; and those endowed with the intellectual habits, or sciences, may exercise them spontaneously and agreably in producing directly contrary effects. But the moral virtues, like the different habits of the body, are determined by their nature to one specific operation: thus a man in health acts and moves in a manner conformable to his healthy state of body, and never otherwise, when his motions are natural and voluntary; and in the same manner the habits of justice or temperance uniformly determine those adorned by them, to act justly and temperately. Yet habits of all kinds are often known by their contraries; thus, if a good habit of body consists in density and firmness of flesh, a bad habit must consist in its softness and rarity. When the word denoting any habit is taken in different senses, the word denoting its contrary is likewise, for the most part, employed with equal latitude: thus the different meanings of injustice correspond with those of justice; both those words having respectively various significations, which, on account of their near affinity to each other, are seldom accurately distinguished; for when a word denotes two things totally unlike, its separate meanings are manifest; as, for instance, in the Greek word which is applied equally to denote the collar-bone, and the key of a door. Let us examine then in how many acceptations the word injustice is used. A man who violates law is called unjust, as well as he who aspires to any undue advantage, and is not contented with equality: since what is unlawful or unequal is unjust, and justice must be conformable to the principles of law and of equality. Injustice consists in desiring more than our share, not of all things indiscriminately which fall under the denomination of good, but of those only which it is supposed to be good fortune to obtain; and which, though universally deemed good in themselves, are often evils to those who obtain them. Such goods mankind in general wish for and pursue; though, in fact, they ought

ought rather to pray that things absolutely good, may be good in relation to themselves; and always to prefer and choose those only which are likely to be so. An unjust man does not necessarily choose the greater share; sometimes he prefers the lesser; and that always, when the things in his option are evils. But as the lesser of two evils is in some measure a good, he seems always to desire the greater share, and is thence called in Greek an usurper of more than his due; though, in reality, according to circumstances, he chooses sometimes the greater, and sometimes the lesser share, but always an unequal one; so that his real turpitude consists in acting contrary to equality or to law; an opposition to both of which, is common to every species of injustice. Since, then, whatever is unlawful is unjust, justice may be said to consist in acting agreeably to the laws of our country. But laws regulate the transactions of life, either with a view to the benefit of the public at large, or with a view to the benefit of that portion of the state which is invested with sovereignty, whether that has been acquired by pre-eminence in virtue, or attained by any of those other means through which sovereign authority is established. In one sense, therefore, justice comprehends every thing that has a tendency either to produce or to maintain the happiness of men in political society. The law prescribes to citizens who are soldiers, not to leave their ranks, not to fly, not to throw down their arms; that is, it commands them to behave themselves with bravery. The law also prohibits all those subject to its authority from adultery, and every species of debauchery which is injurious to others; which is nothing else than to command its subjects to be temperate. It also pre-

scribes

BOOK V.

scribes meekness, in the injunctions, "thou shalt not strike," "thou shalt not revile:" and in the same manner, partly by precepts, and partly by prohibitions, the law more or less accurately defines the rules and practice of the other virtues; so that justice, taken in the sense of conformity to law, comprehends the whole of virtue, not indeed simply and absolutely, but in reference to those with whom we are connected; being another name for the strict performance of all those relative duties which are essential to the happiness of social life. Viewed in this light, justice is the first and brightest of all the virtues; more worthy of admiration than either Hesperus or Lucifer; since according to the proverb,

"Justice alone comprises every virtue."

It is indeed the perfection of virtue, since it is not only the best constitution of our internal frame, but the external exercise of whatever is praiseworthy in behaviour towards others; and even the whole community, however extensive, of which we are members[d]. There are many capable of acting uprightly within a limited domestic sphere, whose imperfections become manifest

[d] This passage is expanded and adorned by Cicero in language the most glowing and impressive, "Est quidem vera lex, recta ratio, naturæ congruens, diffusa in omnes, constans, sempiterna quæ vocet ad officium jubendo, vetando a fraude deterreat; quæ tamen neque probos frustra jubet, neque improbos jubendo aut vetando movet. Huic legi nec abrogari fas est, neque derogari ex hac aliquid licet, neque tota abrogari potest. Nec vero aut per Senatum, aut per populum solvi hac lege possumus. Neque est quærendus explanator, aut interpres ejus alius: nec erit aliud lex Romæ, alia Athenis, alia nunc, alia posthac: sed et omnes gentes, et omni tempore una lex et sempiterna et immortalis continebit; unusque erit communis quasi magister et imperator omnium Deus ille, legis hujus inventor, disceptator, lator; cui qui non parebit, ipse se fugiet, ac naturam hominis aspernabitur; ac hoc ipso luet maximas pœnas, etiamsi cætera supplicia, quæ putantur, effugerit." Fragment. de Republic. l. iii.

manifest on a wider and more exalted theatre. Wherefore Bias well observed, "that government shows the man;" for he who is entrusted with the exercise of power, is placed in multiplied relations with respect to others, and the whole commonwealth. Justice, therefore, seems to contribute to the benefit rather of those towards whom it is exercised, than of those who are endowed with this virtuous habit; because it is the nature of this habit always to bear a reference to our transactions with the world. The worst of men are those whose vices injure themselves and their friends; the best are those, whose virtues benefit not only themselves and their friends, but the community at large, and the whole society of mankind. This, indeed, is a noble, because a difficult task. Justice, then, considered in this view, is not a part, but the whole of virtue; and its contrary, injustice, is not a part, but the whole of vice. Wherein virtue and justice differ, is evident from the observations above made. They are precisely the same thing viewed under two different aspects; and denominated virtue when considered in relation to the mind adorned by this praiseworthy habit; but called justice when considered in relation to those towards whom it is exercised.

BOOK V.

But our present inquiry is concerning justice taken in a more limited sense, and denoting one virtue in particular; and also concerning injustice as signifying one particular vice, distinct from every other. That such a specific injustice, as well as justice, exists, appears from the following consideration; that he who commits any other baseness, is indeed guilty of wrong, but does not thereby benefit his fortune; which is plain, from the examples of him who throws away his shield through cowardice,

Chap. 2.

Justice properly so called.

comardice, who reviles his neighbour through ungovernable asperity of temper, or who refuses, through illiberality, any pecuniary aid to those who have claims on his bounty. But a man may benefit his fortune by usurping more than his due share of worldly goods, without incurring the blame of all, or any, of these vices. His conduct, however, is culpable, and we arraign his injustice. There is then a particular kind of injustice differing from that above mentioned, and bearing the relation to it, of a part to the whole: in the first sense, unjust is synonymous with unlawful; in the second, it implies the breach of a particular class of laws, namely, that which prohibits any man from benefiting himself at the expence of his neighbour. One man commits adultery for the sake of gain, another pays dearly for his criminal pleasure; the vice of the former, is aggravated injustice; that of the latter, is profligate intemperance. All other wrongs may always be referred to some particular species of vice; the commission of adultery, to intemperance; the desertion of our companions in war, to cowardice; an assault, to unbridled violence of anger: but that wrong which is committed for the sake merely of gain, is referred to no other vice than that of injustice; not that injustice above described, which is synonymous with wrong in general, but a specific vice, bearing the same relation to the former, which the species does to the class under which it is included; for injustice, both in its large and in its limited sense, has always a reference to our transactions with others; its very essence consists in our behaving amiss in those transactions: but injustice, strictly so called, implies that our misconduct results from the desire of promoting our own profit or honour,

or

ARISTOTLE's ETHICS.

BOOK V.

or whatever we think gainful to ourselves[e]; whereas injustice, largely taken, comprehends all those improprieties in our behaviour towards others, which are inconsistent with the character of a virtuous man. We proceed then to explain the nature and properties of justice and injustice, strictly so called. This species of injustice was said to consist, not in what is unlawful merely, but in what is also unequal; for whatever is unequal is unlawful; since laws, properly made, assure to each individual his equal share, that is his due, in his transactions with his fellow-citizens; but many things are unlawful which are not unequal, because laws relate to many other objects besides the distribution and adjustment of interests and honours; enforcing, by authority, the practice of every virtue, and upholding a system of education by which this practice may, through discipline and custom, be rendered easy and agreeable. Whether such an education properly falls under the science of politics, will afterwards be examined[f]; for under all forms of government indiscriminately, perhaps the character of the good man will not be found compatible with that of a good citizen. The particular kind of justice now under consideration, is employed either in distributing to each citizen his due share of honour, wealth, and all other advantages, in the political partnership, or commonwealth, of which he is a member; or in regulating, by the rules of right, those transactions, whether voluntary or involuntary, which happen between fellow-citizens; and where wrong has on either side been committed, in correcting this wrong,

[e] Aristotle says, "for the sake of honour, money, safety, or for that which would include all these in one word."

[f] Aristotle examines this question in his Politics, which work is merely a continuation of his Ethics to Nicomachus.

wrong, by again setting the parties, as far as may be, on a foot of equality with each other. Voluntary transactions are those in which both parties voluntarily concur; such as buying, selling, borrowing, lending, letting, hiring, pledging, depositing. Involuntary transactions are either secret or open; the secret are, theft, adultery, poisoning, seduction of other men's slaves, prostitution for hire of other men's wives, premeditated murder, and the bearing of false witness. The open but involuntary transactions include all violent and manifest aggressions on the persons, property, or reputation of others; such as assault, maiming, imprisonment, death, robbery, slander, insult.

Chap. 3.

Distributive justice.

Justice implies equality; and this equality lies in the middle between two extremes, the greater and the lesser: for whatever admits of division into two unequal parts, may also be equally divided. But equality, being a relative term, always supposes the comparison of two things at least. Distributive justice, therefore, always implies two things, and also two persons between whom those things are divided. If the persons are exactly equal, so ought to be their shares; but if the persons are unequal, the shares ought also to be unequal in the same proportion: for complaints and strife always will arise, when either persons of unequal worth meet with precisely the same treatment; or when persons of nearly equal worth are distinguished from each other by too considerable differences. This is universally acknowledged; but men's notions of worth vary with their political principles. In democracies it is measured by liberty; in oligarchies, by wealth or birth; in aristocracies, by virtue. Justice, however, plainly consists in proportion, which is the equality of ratios; and proportion, whether discrete or continuous,

continuous, always implies four terms; since when continuous, one of the terms must be taken twice. Distributive justice always requiring four terms at least, implies that the shares bear the same proportion to each other as do the persons among whom these shares are distributed; for proportion is applicable to all quantities, and not merely to numbers. If the first share therefore be to the first man, as the second share to the second; then alternately, the first share will be to the second share, as the first man to the second man; and as each of the antecedents is to its consequent, so will both the antecedents be to both the consequents. This is what is called by mathematicians geometrical proportion, consisting, as we have said, in equality of ratios; which equality is in the middle between excess and defect; for if one of the ratios were greater or lesser than the other, the proportion, or, in other words, the justice of the distribution, would be destroyed. In distributive justice, the four terms are all of them distinct, the one from the other; consisting of two persons, and two shares, at least; none of which can be taken twice in the series. The proportion therefore is not continuous, but discrete; and when proportion is violated, injustice immediately follows. This evidently appears in actions: for the injurious person has more, the person injured has less, than their respective shares of good; of evil, the reverse; for the lesser evil is considered as a good [g].

BOOK V.

The remaining species of justice is properly distinguished by the epithet of corrective: it applies to the mutual transactions between men, whether voluntary or involuntary. It differs from

Chap. 4.

Commutative and corrective justice.

---

[g] I thought it unnecessary to subjoin with Aristotle, that the lesser evil is considered as a good because it is to be preferred to the greater; that good is always desirable, and, of two goods, the more desirable is the greater.

BOOK V.

from distributive justice in this, that the latter consists in geometrical proportion, and requires that the shares should have the same ratio to each other as the persons among whom they are divided; so that each citizen may find himself treated according to his deserts, and those who contribute most to the public benefit may meet with proportionally higher remunerations. Corrective justice also implies equality, but an equality of a different kind, founded not on geometrical, but on arithmetical, proportion; for the law does not make any difference in its correction or punishment, whether a good man has injured a bad one, or a bad man a good. It contemplates merely the hurt done or the injury sustained; and endeavours to set the two parties, the one of whom is wronged by the other, on the same foot of equality on which they formerly stood. The words gain and loss are not indeed applicable in all cases where one man is injured by another; they can be properly used only when the injuries done may be estimated in money; but in all cases whatever, he who has committed an injury should be compelled, as far as may be, to make reparation, which, when complete, reduces the parties to that condition of equality from which they set out, by giving back to the loser what had been taken from him by the gainer. Corrective justice, then, holds the middle place between gain and loss. In their disputes with each other, men have recourse to a judge, as to a living fountain of justice; who, as it is his business to adjust differences, and mediate between contending parties, is often styled a mediator. This office he performs by finding the middle term between the unequal extremes of gain and loss; in the same manner as if, a line being divided into two unequal parts, he cut from the greater part its excess above half the line, and

added

added it to the lesser. When the whole is divided equally, each party has his due, because the shares are alike; and this equality is the middle arithmetical term between the greater and the lesser extreme. It is the duty of a judge to find this middle term; from which function, he appears in Greek to have derived his appellation; for justice in this language means an equal division; and a judge, an equal divider. When, from two equal quantities, a part is taken from the one and added to the other, the latter will exceed by two parts: for were the part taken away destroyed, it would exceed by one; it exceeds the middle term therefore by one; and this term exceeds the quantity from which the part was taken away by one. By this means we may learn, that in order to correct inequality, and thereby to do justice, we must take from the greater extreme that by which it exceeds the middle, and add this excess to the lesser. This plainly appears in geometry by means of a diagram; but the same thing holds in all other arts, which would speedily be subverted, and all human society overturned, unless equality and justice were tolerably well maintained in the actions and intercourse of life; and proper correctives applied where these bonds of society are materially violated. The words gain and loss are introduced by the voluntary transactions of men; in which, he who got more than he gave in exchange, was said to gain by the bargain; and he who got less, to lose; as in buying and selling, and all other legal contracts. But when the bargain was equal, each party was said to have his due. Justice, then, even in such transactions as are involuntary, consists in a middle term between a certain kind of gain and loss, and requires that the parties should be reduced, as nearly as may be, to that condition of equality in which they stood

BOOK V.

Chap. 5.

Retaliation does not apply to justice, either distributive or corrective.

stood with regard to each other, before any such transaction took place.

Retaliation seems to some to be the whole of justice. This opinion was held by the Pythagoreans; who defined justice to be " reciprocity of doing and suffering." But retaliation will not apply either to distributive or to corrective justice; although the law of Rhadamanthus says, " The completest justice consists in making a man suffer the same ills that he has committed." This rule, however, is liable to innumerable exceptions. Thus, if a general should strike a soldier, the blow must not be retorted ; but to strike a general, or any other person invested with authority, requires that the offender should be punished more severely than by mere retaliation. The difference also is very great between voluntary and involuntary injuries ; to the latter of which Rhadamanthus' rule is totally inapplicable. Yet the commercial intercourse of nations, and of individuals in the same nation, is maintained by a reciprocation, not indeed of the same, or similar, but of proportional benefits and injuries. When injuries are offered by one set of persons, and cannot be retorted by another, the latter class look on themselves as nothing better than slaves : when benefits, on the other hand, are conferred, but without any prospect of being returned, there is an end to that interchange of good offices, which is the main pillar of civil society ; a truth acknowledged by those commonwealths who have erected temples to the Graces on the most conspicuous situations ; that man might continually be reminded of the duty of gratitude, the favourite virtue of those divinities ; and that those who had received and returned favours, might always be ready to renew the laudable contention among themselves, by mutually provoking each other to works of kindness.

The comfort of life requires an interchange of different works and exertions. The bricklayer, for example, must exchange the production of his labour with the shoemaker; and the bargain will be just, when the works exchanged bear the same proportion to each other, as do the exertions of the artisans by whom they were produced. If the exertions of the bricklayer be more valuable for their duration, or their difficulty, than those of the shoemaker, the works produced by the latter must, to render the bargain equal, bear the same proportion numerically to those produced by the former; thus, if the bricklayer has consumed a thousand times as much labour in making a house, as the shoemaker has done in making a pair of shoes, a thousand pair of shoes must be given for one house. The same thing happens with respect to all other arts, which derive their whole utility from the mutual exchange of different sorts of labour, and which could not long be maintained unless the exertions of one artisan in one way were nearly balanced and compensated by those of another artisan in another. A community could not subsist, composed wholly of physicians, or wholly of husbandmen; it must consist of physicians and husbandmen, and other classes of individuals employed in different trades and different professions. But that operations and works of such different kinds should be fairly exchanged for each other, it is necessary that they should be nearly commensurate; that is, that all of them should be capable of being estimated with tolerable accuracy by comparison with one common measure. Hence the introduction of money; by means of which all those operations and works are compared in value with each other, and their relative excesses or deficiencies ascertained with sufficient correctness for all prac-

tical

BOOK V.

The nature and use of money.

tical purposes. In reality, value depends on the mutual wants of men, which form the great bond of society; for unless their wants were mutual, exchange could not be effected: but money is used by convention as the representative of all things wanted; since it serves as a pledge and surety, that whenever those wants occur, they will be speedily gratified; and its name is derived from the word signifying law, which indicates that it is founded, not on nature, but on convention; and that human laws, which have thought fit to employ it as a measure of value, may, at pleasure, set this use of it aside, and employ some other measure in its stead. Money, which represents the value of all other things, varies in its own; but its variations are less considerable than those of most other substances. It serves therefore to fix their price, and to render them commensurate with each other, thus performing a function essential to the existence of civil society; for communities could not subsist without exchange; nor exchange, without equality; nor equality, without a common measure. The various kinds of labour, and the works thereby effected, cannot indeed be accurately compared, and exactly measured, either by each other or even by money; but they may, by means of the latter, be estimated with sufficient correctness for maintaining that commercial intercourse which is essential to the supply of our numerous exigencies [h].

From

[h] Aristotle illustrates this subject by shewing how the exchangeable value of a house and a bed are compared with each other, by reducing both to the common measure of a certain number of minas. The text is corrupt, and the example superfluous; but it is of importance to observe how well our author explains the nature of traffic, money, labour, exchangeable value or price, on just notions of which all theories of political œconomy ought to be founded. In various parts of his works he makes the important distinction between labour consumed in use, and labour employed in production. That

of

ARISTOTLE's ETHICS.

From the explanation given of justice and injustice, it is manifest that a just action holds the intermediate place between doing and suffering an injury. The doer has more, the sufferer less, than he ought; and justice is mediocrity, not indeed in the same sense with the other virtues, which lie between two contrary and vicious extremes, but because it is productive of equality in our dealings, and gives to each individual that share which truly belongs to him; whereas injustice contains in it two opposite faults, giving to the one party more than his due, and robbing

BOOK V.

Chap. 6.

In what sense justice consists in mediocrity.

---

of a servant or domestic slave is of the first kind; that of a manufacturer or artisan, of the second. The labour of the artisan or manufacturer is concentrated and fixed in his work; the labour of a builder in a house built, of a weaver in the web. (ἡ ωικοδομικη εν τω οικοδομημενω, και ἡ ὑφαντικη εν τω ὑφασμενω, &c. Metaph. l. ix. c. viii. p. 939.) Having distinguished between productive and unproductive labour, he observes that every work or production may be employed in two different ways, either in the way of use or that of exchange. Thus a pair of shoes may either be worn or they may be sold (ὡσει ὑποδηματος, ἡ τι ἐπεδεσις, και ἡ μεταδοσεως, Politic. l. i. c. ix. p. 305.). Every production or commodity has, therefore, in reference to the wants of human life, two different values, a value in use and a value in exchange. These different values ought to be distinguished, because things that have the greatest value in use, have often very little value in exchange, and things that have a great value in exchange have often very little value in use. The exchangeable value of commodities, according to Aristotle, is always relative to the labour requisite for procuring them; and the quantity of productive labour is exactly measured by the work or production in which this labour is fixed and embodied (Metaph. l. ix. c. viii. p. 939.). But commodities or productions are so complex in their nature, that they cannot be compared with each other without some common measure. The metals, in consequence of their usefulness and beauty, their facility of division without injury, and of transportation without much labour, above all, their extreme durability, have been adopted by very general consent as the fittest measures of the exchangeable value of all other commodities. But neither the metals in general, nor any one metal in particular, is an exact measure. At different times and places, their own values are found to vary; and therefore they cannot be an exact, that is, an invariable measure of the value of other things. But though the exchangeable value of the metals varies, Aristotle maintains that it is less variable than that of any other commodity (ταχει μεν ου και τουτο το αυτο, ἡ ἀγαρ αυτο ισον δυναται ὁμως δε βουλεται μενειν μαλλον. De Moribus, l. v. c. viii. p. 6c.).

BOOK V.

robbing the other of his right. The virtue of justice, then, is that by which a man practises by preference and with pleasure fairness in his dealings, not arrogating to himself more than his due proportion of good, nor declining to bear his equal share of evil. He treats other men as he would wish to be treated by them, assigning to each his fair proportion, and following the same invariable rule, when his own interest is at stake, and when he is only adjusting the differences of others. Injustice is directly the reverse; it leads men in all their transactions to give an undue preference to themselves; and when they are entrusted with settling the concerns of others, always to do this unequally, by giving an undue advantage to one of the parties. This much may suffice concerning the nature of justice and injustice.

Chap. 7.

Justice applied to actions in a sense different from that in which it is applicable to persons.

Since the commission of every unjust action does not necessarily make an unjust man, it may be inquired whether, in this respect, there be any distinction between particular acts of injustice, bearing the same name, such as theft, adultery, and robbery; or whether the difference of the external acts is altogether immaterial as to constituting the vice of injustice, even when those acts are performed knowingly; for a man may know that the object of his passion is his neighbour's wife; and yet, if he acts merely from the blind impetuosity of appetite or desire, without deliberate intention, he is not an adulterer. The same holds in all other cases in which wrong is done; the mere perpetration of the act does not infer the vicious state of mind from which such acts naturally flow. The difference between retaliation and justice was formerly mentioned; but, in our inquiries respecting the latter, it must be remembered, that we have in view chiefly

chiefly that kind of juftice which may be called political, fince it is eftablifhed for the comfort and all-fufficiency of fociety among freemen and equals; whether the government, being democratical, require that each citizen fhould be dealt by alike; or whether it admit of thofe diftinctions of birth, wealth, and abilities, which are allowed their due weight under other forms of government. Where fuch equality does not prevail, there is not any room for what is ftrictly called juftice, but only for that virtue which, on account of its refemblance, receives the fame name. Juftice takes place among thofe who being capable of injuring each other, are reftrained by law from mutual encroachments; and thofe encroachments muft be made, before injuftice can be committed; though, as we formerly obferved, the converfe of the propofition does not hold, that injuftice always is committed, when fuch encroachments are made, becaufe injuftice implies the deliberate purpofe of wronging others for the fake of benefit to ourfelves; a propenfity fo ftrong in human nature, that few men are capable of being entrufted with power, without ufing it tyrannically: wherefore law and reafon ought to bear fway, and rulers to be the guardians of equal juftice; contented with thofe rewards and honours which have been affigned to them for upholding the public good by their impartial adminiftration. Their power is of a different kind from that of fathers and defpots, in the exercife of which there is not any room for the virtue of juftice ftrictly fo called, fince no one can, in propriety of language, be faid to commit injuftice againft himfelf, or what entirely belongs to himfelf; becaufe no one ever deliberately propofed to do real harm to either, and could not poffibly do fuch

BOOK V.

such harm for the sake of benefiting himself: but slaves, who are a kind of property, and also children, until they have attained a certain age, are so intimately connected with their masters and parents, that no such relations as those of political justice can subsist between them; for political justice implies laws; and laws suppose an equality, not indeed of ranks and persons, but of rights and obligations. Wherefore something more nearly resembling political justice takes place between husbands and wives; but this, which is called œconomical justice, is also different from the former.

Natural justice independent of positive institution.

Political justice is founded either on nature or on law. The natural, is that which has every where the same force and authority; the legal, is that which depends on human institution, rendering actions just or unjust, which are in themselves indifferent; as that no more than one mina should be required for the ransom of a prisoner; that a goat should be sacrificed rather than two sheep; regulations respecting individuals, as that Brasidas should be honoured with heroic worship; and those that come in the shape of decrees or resolutions. Some are of opinion that all justice whatever depends on positive institution; which they endeavour to prove by observing that the laws of nature remain every where unalterably the same: fire, for example, which burns and warms in Greece, has precisely the same powers in Persia; whereas the rules of justice are liable to perpetual variations. This, however, is true only in a certain sense; for though among the gods in heaven, what is natural is, perhaps, unalterable, yet, in this lower world, many institutions of nature are capable of being changed and modified by circumstances. Yet the distinction between what is natural

and

and conventional, is not thereby destroyed; unless we should
infer that, because some men are capable of using both hands
with equal dexterity, it is not natural for mankind in general
to use one hand more dexterously than the other[1]. Men's
notions of justice are often warped by their interests; and this
great measure of human actions varies like the measures of
wine and corn, which the dealers in those articles have of different sizes; using the larger when they buy, and the smaller
when they sell. Great variations result also from the different
forms of government; although, as we shall shew hereafter,
there is one form of government naturally the best. Justice is
a general term; and differs from an act of injustice, as an universal does from a particular. That is unjust which is contrary
to nature or to law; and the same thing, when done, is an
unjust action. An unjust action is a wrong; and when we
rectify a wrong, we are said to do justice. But the force of
those terms will be afterwards more fully explained.

BOOK V.

Injustice, as applicable to actions, consists in what we have
now said; but it does not belong to persons, unless it be committed voluntarily; for when a man acts without intention,
the quality of his action, as good or bad, just or unjust, is, in
reference to the agent, merely an accessory, not springing
essentially from himself, and neither entitling him to praise,
nor subjecting him to blame. That, therefore, which is unjust,
is

Chap. 8.

Distinction of misfor-
tunes, errors, and crimes.

---

[1] He gives the reason more generally in Magna Moral. l. i. c. xxxiv. p. 167. τὸ
γὰρ ὡς ἐπὶ τὸ πολὺ διαμενον, τοῦτο φύσει δίκαιόν πεφυκὸς. "That which is invariable and
constant is manifestly natural justice." Political justice, on the other hand, varies
with the arrangements and exigencies of men in society. He therefore concludes
ἔστιν ὧν δίκαιον τὸ κατὰ φύσιν, "That natural injustice is the better of the two;" a
conclusion agreeable to his observations in the first Philosophy. See Analysis, p. 92,
& passim.

is not injuftice in the agent, unlefs it be committed voluntarily; that is, as formerly explained, unlefs the action, with all its circumftances, depend entirely on our own power, and be performed knowingly, with intention, and without conftraint. Thus, to make the act of ftriking parricide, we muft know the perfon whom we ftrike, the nature of the inftrument with which the ftroke is inflicted, and the motive through which we are impelled to fuch a horrid crime. The action muft alfo depend entirely on our own power; for in many natural events, we are both agents and patients knowingly, though not voluntarily; witnefs old age and death [k]. The fame happens as to juftice and injuftice. When a man reftores a depofit involuntarily through fear, he cannot be faid to act juftly, fince the juftice of the action is not caufed by himfelf: it is a mere acceffary or appendage, quite foreign to his defign or purpofe. In the fame manner, he cannot be accufed of injuftice, who is conftrained involuntarily not to reftore a depofit. Voluntary actions are performed with, or without election; deliberate actions are performed with election; and thofe that are without deliberation are without election. In the intercourfe of life, one perfon may hurt another in three ways; either ignorantly, in which cafe the hurt done is called an error; as when we are miftaken either in the perfon or the inftrument; or when the action turns out to be of quite a different nature from that which we intended: a man may be hurt by a blow meant merely for roufing him; a wound may be given cafually; and one perfon may receive a blow which was intended for another. When the harm is not only done unintentionally, but happens altogether unexpectedly, it is called a misfortune; when the confequences

[k] See Analyfis, p. 109.

quences of the action might have been foreseen and expected, the harm done, without any mischievous purpose, is properly termed a fault; for a fault is that evil which originates in ourselves; and a misfortune, that of which the cause is external. Harm done knowingly, but not deliberately, is an injustice; as those injuries which proceed from anger and other passions, that are either necessary, or at least natural. Yet the persons who have committed such injuries, are not branded with the reproach of injustice or wickedness; which falls only on wrong proceeding from wilful pravity. The law, therefore, well distinguishes between premeditated crimes, and those committed through passion; for the source of the latter may be traced up rather to him who provoked the passion, than to him who yielded to its violence. In all such cases, the question is, not whether the deed was done, but whether it was done justly; for anger always proceeds from some real or supposed injury. But in all other disputes, the question turns on some fact, which one party affirms, and the other denies; and as to which, either the one or the other, unless his memory deceives him, must plainly be guilty; for every deliberate wrong is manifest injustice, whether it consist, as above explained, in violating the law of equality, or in violating that of proportion. The virtue of justice, on the other hand, is exercised only in such acts as are done voluntarily and deliberately. Involuntary acts are, or are not, entitled to pardon, according to circumstances. Those are pardonable, which proceed from complete and habitual ignorance; those are not, which proceed from a temporary ignorance, occasioned by the blind impetuosity of passion, either extravagantly excessive in its degree, or highly improper in its object.

BOOK V.

Doubts

BOOK V.
Chap. 9.
Solution of doubts respecting justice.

Doubts may arise, whether the doing and the suffering of injustice, have been defined with sufficient precision. First, shall we hearken to Euripides? One of his characters reasons thus:

> I flew my mother; the defence is plain,
> She *with her* will, or *'gainst my* will, was slain.

Can any person be injured willingly? or must every injury be unwillingly suffered as it is willingly inflicted? A man, it is said, may be injured willingly; since an intemperate man willingly hurts himself. But this argument is not conclusive, for the intemperate man does, what he thinks he ought not to do; his passion makes him act against his deliberate will; for no one can deliberately will what he thinks mischievous to himself. To injure then, is not only to hurt knowingly, but to hurt against the will of the sufferer; for when his will consents, he may indeed be hurt, but is not injured. Glaucus was not injured by his disadvantageous exchange of armour with Diomed, because it was voluntary.

> " Brave Glaucus then, each narrow thought resign'd
> (Jove warm'd his bosom, and enlarg'd his mind),
> For Diomed's brass arms of mean device,
> For which nine oxen paid (a vulgar price)
> He gave his own of gold divinely wrought,
> A hundred beeves the shining purchase bought."
>
> Iliad VI. v. 290. et seq.

Secondly, Whether is the injustice in him who makes an unfair distribution, or in him who receives more than his due? If the former is asserted, those persons distinguished by liberality and equity, who are inclined rather to refuse their full propor-

tion, than to arrogate more than their just share, will sometimes injure themselves. It may be answered, that these persons, liberal and equitable as they are as to things of a particular nature, will not decline their full share of goods in general; and of some kinds, such as praise, glory, and whatever is honourable and laudable, will be inclined to arrogate more than fairly belongs to them. But the difficulty is solved by the observation above made, that no one can be the willing victim of injustice; so that men cannot injure, although they may hurt, themselves. Besides, the injustice is plainly in him who makes the unfair distribution; for by him the unjust action is begun and completed; whereas he who holds more than his due share, may often do it ignorantly and innocently. The word action is taken in different senses. It is applied to inanimate things. The sword, or any other warlike instrument, is said to strike or kill, as well as the hand of one man moved by that of another; or a slave, by the command of his master. None of those injure, although they are the instruments of injustice. Unjust judgments may proceed merely from ignorance; but that judge only is unjust, who passes unjust decrees, knowingly, from partiality to one party, or ill-will to the other. Between such a judge and one of the parties, the iniquity, as well as its fruits, are sometimes divided; the latter gets more land than he ought, and the other gets money to which he is not entitled. Injustice, however, in judgment, as well as every other species of injustice, always consists in arrogating to ourselves more than our due proportion of advantage, whether this consists in benefiting our fortune, indulging our partiality, or gratifying our resentment. Men think, because injustice seems to be
always

BOOK V.

BOOK V.

Justice, a matter of more difficulty than commonly imagined.

always in their power, that therefore justice is easy. The thing, however, is far otherwise. To commit vicious actions is indeed always in our power, but to acquire either virtuous or vicious habits is the work of time and custom; and the vice is not in the act, but in the frame of mind and habit of the actor. They think also, that to distinguish between just and unjust transactions requires but small discernment; because it is easy to understand the laws promulgated on this subject. But the justice or injustice is not in those transactions themselves, except by way of appendage or accession, when, together with the simple performance of the act, certain dispositions and affections, and those uniform and habitual, concur in the agent. To know, therefore, what constitutes or contributes to justice, is still more difficult than to know what constitutes and contributes to health. The medicines of hellebore, honey, and wine, as well as the operations of cutting and burning, are indeed easily known; but to understand when, how, and to whom, we ought to administer the one and to apply the other, is a thing of no less difficulty than to be a skilful physician. It is also a false opinion, that a good man is capable of acts of wickedness; because, were he inclined to indulge guilty passions, he is more likely to do it with impunity than any other. But, as we above observed, the vice or wickedness is not in the act itself, but in the frame or habit of mind of him by whom that act is performed. The art of healing does not consist in performing operations and in administering medicines; it consists in doing these things properly, that is, in the intellectual habit or skill of the physician. Justice takes place only among those who are sharers in that kind of goods, of which a certain proportion contributes to their

their happiness; but of which either the excess or the defect has a tendency to destroy it. The Gods, perhaps, cannot have too much power and prosperity; and beings incurably wicked, cannot have too little of either; since, by them, the means of good will always be converted into sources of evil. But men are benefited by a due proportion, and by that only.

BOOK V.

We proceed to speak of equity, and to consider what relation it bears to justice. It is not the same thing, nor yet is it different in kind; for it is a praiseworthy quality as well as justice, but is spoken of as something better than mere justice, and really is so, for it is the correction of strict, that is, of legal justice; which often needs to be modified by equity, because laws being in their nature general, cannot decide rightly in the indefinite variety of particular cases. The lawgiver is contented with making a rule, which fairly applies to the greater part of cases; well knowing that it will not include the whole, and the fault is neither in the law nor the lawgiver, but in the nature of things. When an exception to the rule occurs, which the lawgiver did not foresee, this exception is admitted in equity, which thus supplies the defect of law, as the lawgiver himself would do, were he present in court, and as he would have done by amending his law, had he been aware of the exception. Equity, then, is better than legal justice, being its amendment; and supplying that defect of laws, which arises from their universality. The variety of human transactions cannot be comprised within general rules. Occasional decrees therefore become requisite; which vary with each variation of circumstances, for the measure of what is indefinite must be indefinite itself, like the leaden ruler in the Lesbian architecture, which changes its own shape according to that of the stones to which

Chap. 12.

Of the nature of equity in contradistinction to justice.

it is applied. It is manifest, therefore, that equity is a species of justice, and contrasted with another species to which it is preferable. A man of equity is he who deliberately and habitually exercises this virtue; who prefers it in all his dealings to the rigour of justice; and who, even when the law is on his side, will not avail himself of this advantage to treat others injuriously or unhandsomely.

Chap. 11.

That a man may hurt, but cannot be guilty of injury towards himself.

Whether justice be taken in its larger sense, of disobeying the laws; or in its stricter acceptation, of depriving others of their property, it is plain, from the observations already made, that no one can be guilty of injustice towards himself. A man may spontaneously and knowingly commit an unprovoked injury; he may even destroy his own life, in direct opposition both to the laws and to right reason [k]. He thereby certainly does an injury; but to whom? Not to himself, because he suffers voluntarily. The injury is therefore done to the state; which, on this account, punishes self-murder with infamy. As to the other kind of injustice, which does not comprehend wickedness in general, but which consists, like cowardice, in one specific vice, we cannot, without a total confusion of thought, suppose that a man is guilty of it towards himself; for in that case, the same thing

---

[k] The Oxford edition very properly supplies the word λογω of which ορθω is the ordinary epithet, and of which it must here be the adjunct, to render the passage intelligible. Suicide is always spoken of by Aristotle as a base and cowardly crime, as a mean dereliction of all personal dignity, and a gross violation of all social duty. Cicero sometimes (for on this subject he is not consistent) speaks otherwise. "Atque hæc differentia naturarum tantum habet vim, uti nonnumquam mortem sibi ipse conscisere alius debeat, alius in eadem caussa non debeat." De Officiis, l. i. c. xxxi. Here he speaks of suicide as a duty; probably out of deference for his admired Cato. But his language is very different elsewhere. Confer. Tusc. Disp. l. i. c. xxx. Somn. Scip. c. iii. Had Aristotle's Ethics been equally well known, Cicero's Offices would not have been so long regarded as the purest and most solid production of heathen morality.

thing would be both added to and taken from the same person, at the same time. Injustice, therefore, always implies two persons at least; and if it did not, the distinctions formerly made concerning spontaneity, deliberation, retaliation, and aggression, would be totally destroyed. Retaliation cannot deserve the epithet of injurious; but could a man injure himself, injury would be consistent with the most complete retaliation, namely, the doing and suffering precisely the same thing, under precisely the same circumstances; besides a man might suffer injury voluntarily, which was formerly proved to be impossible. Still further, the commission of wrong always implies some specific act; but by no such act can a man do wrong to himself. He cannot commit adultery with his own wife, he cannot be guilty of housebreaking with regard to his own house, he cannot steal his own property: universally, therefore, he cannot do an injury to himself. It is an evil to suffer, as well as to do, wrong, but the latter is by far the worst evil of the two, because it is blameable and base. The former, however, may sometimes, by concurring with other circumstances not essentially connected with it, be attended with far more deplorable consequences; in the same manner as a fall, by stumbling, may sometimes have worse effects than a pleurisy, because it may occasion a man's capture by the enemy, and, in consequence thereof, his ignominious death. But the science of Ethics, no more than that of Physics, pays attention to consequences not essentially inherent in the subject, and connected with it merely by way of appendage or accession. It is said metaphorically, not indeed that a man can exercise justice towards himself, but that one part of him may exercise justice towards another. This justice, however, resembles, not the political justice above examined, but the justice

tice of fathers and masters towards children and slaves; whose relation to each other bears a near similitude to that of the rational and irrational parts in the human constitution. The passions often rebel against reason, as slaves do against their masters; and as the latter seem guilty of injustice, so do the former. Let thus much suffice concerning justice, and the other moral virtues [1].

[1] The doctrine of justice is explained on the same principles delivered in this Book, Magna Moral. l. i. c. xxxiv.; & Eudem. l. iv.

(285)

ARISTOTLE's ETHICS.

BOOK VI.

INTRODUCTION.

IF philofophy confift in explaining phænomena, feemingly indefinite in number, by a few diftinct principles of action, this Sixth Book affords one of the fineft fpecimens of it ever exhibited. According to Ariftotle, moral virtue is appetite or affection difciplined by reafon and cuftom; which, enabling us to make a fair eftimate of excellence, teaches us to prefer and purfue it[a]. To explain, therefore, the different acceptations of the word reafon; or, in Ariftotle's language, to defcribe the different powers of the underftanding, muft form an effential part of every complete treatife of Ethics. By modern philofophers thofe powers are not accurately diftinguifhed; although, according to our author, the powers of intellection differ as widely from each other as thofe of fenfation. Colours, flavours, founds, and odours, and other objects about which the fenfes are converfant, are not more diftinguifhable from each other, than the different claffes of fpeculative and practical truths, which are perceptible by what our author calls the demonftrative and deliberative faculties of the underftanding[b].

Reafoning

[a] Magna Moral. l. i. c. xxii. p. 161.   [b] Magna Moral. l. i. c. xxxv. p. 169.

BOOK VI. Reasoning on this principle, that powers must differ from each other, which exert themselves in different actions and effectuate different ends, he treats separately of art, science, prudence, intellect, and wisdom; he explains the nature and functions of each of those habits; examines the difference between what are called natural virtues, and those which are acquired by exercise and custom; and proves that none of the acquired virtues can subsist without that intellectual habit which he calls prudence.

BOOK VI.

ARGUMENT.

Sensation, intellect, and appetite.—Their different offices.—The five intellectual habits—Science—Art—Prudence—Common sense—Wisdom.—Quickness of apprehension.—Justness of sentiment.—Importance of the intellectual habits.—Virtue, natural and acquired.—Their difference.

HAVING formerly said that, in moral matters, mediocrity only ought to be the object of our preference, as being alone consistent with right reason, it is proper that this subject should be more distinctly explained. Whoever exercises reason has, in all his habitual actions, a certain aim, according to which he regulates his behaviour; moderating his passions when too strong, invigorating them when too weak, and always bending them to propriety, as a bow is rendered more or less tense in order to hit the mark. This observation is indeed true, but not sufficiently explicit to be practically useful; for, in all other matters in which science is concerned, we ought certainly to do what right reason prescribes, that is, neither too much nor too little. Thus the physician ought to act with regard to his patient; but by knowing that this is his duty, he will not be rendered much the wiser as to what operations ought to be performed, or what medicines ought to be administered. It is necessary, therefore, to speak more definitely concerning the habits

*BOOK VI.
Chap. 1.
Transition to the intellectual virtues.*

BOOK VI.

bits of the mind, to explain what right reason is, and to point out what are the boundaries which it assigns to our passions and actions. The habits or virtues of the mind were formerly divided into the moral and intellectual; concerning the moral we have already treated; it remains to examine the intellectual, having previously spoken of the soul itself. In this, we formerly distinguished two parts, the rational and irrational; and the former may also be divided into two, namely, that faculty by which we understand those sciences whose principles are certain and necessary, and which cannot possibly be otherwise than they are, and that by which we comprehend other branches of knowledge; for if there be any resemblance or affinity between the truths recognised, and the powers which recognise them, it is natural to think that things, so extremely different as are the necessary and contingent, should be perceived and known by different faculties [c]. Knowledge, then, may be divided into that which is demonstrative and scientific, and that which is deliberative and probable; for no one deliberates about things which necessarily exist after one certain manner, and which cannot possibly exist after any other. Let us examine, then, what is the best habit of each of these faculties: the best habit of any thing is, in other words, its virtue; and the virtue of each object is ascertained by its fitness for performing its peculiar function.

Chap. 2.

Sensation, intellect, and appetite, their different offices.

There are three principles in man, which, either single or combined, are the sovereign judges of truth and conduct. These are, sensation, intellect, and appetite. Of these three, mere sensation cannot alone be the foundation of any judgment respecting conduct, that is, the propriety of action; for wild beasts have

---

[c] See also Magna Moralia, l. i. c. xxxv. p. 169.

have perception by sense, but are totally unacquainted with propriety. Affirming and denying are the operations of intellect, desire and aversion are those of appetite; and since moral virtue implies the habit of just election, and election or preference resolves itself into deliberation and appetite, every act of virtuous preference requires, that there should be accuracy and truth in the comparison, as well as correctness and propriety in the desire. Of that intellectual faculty which bears not any relation to life and practice, and which is employed, not in deliberation, but in demonstration, the simplicity of abstract truth is the proper and only object; but deliberative moral wisdom bears in all its operations a reference to human happiness; and terminates, not in the discoveries of speculation, but in the exertions of action[d]. This latter faculty, then, only attains its end, when well-ordered appetite harmonises with sound practical reason; from the combination of which elements, results that moral election or preference, peculiar to man; which may be called either impassioned intelligence, or reflecting appetite; and which is the sole fountain of whatever is laudable and graceful in behaviour and manners[e]. This practical reason is superior to that conversant about production: for production, as we above observed, is imperfect in itself, and continually remains so, until the work, for the sake of which it operated, be produced. But the operation of practical reason terminates in nothing better than the pleasure of its own energies. It is not given to us for the gratification of appetite: but appetite itself is

---

[d] In conformity with what is here said, Aristotle in his Topics, b. v. c. i. p. 226. distinguishes science from virtue, by saying that the former is in one part of the soul, and the latter in more than one.

[e] ἡ δὲ πρόαιρεσις, νοῦς διανοητικὸς καὶ ὄρεξις. De Animal. Motu. c. vi. p. 706.

is implanted in us for the sake of that virtuous moral action, which constitutes an essential part of human happiness. Such, then, is man, an intellectual but impassioned being, exercising his faculties concerning things contingent and future. The past cannot be an object of deliberation or preference. No one chooses, that Troy should not be taken; and Agathon says rightly,

> " All things to God are possible, save one,
> " That to undo, which is already done."

As truth, then, is the object of both our rational faculties, (the speculative and practical,) their excellencies must consist in those habits by which truth is most clearly discerned.

Chap. 3.

The five intellectual habits. First, science.

Let these habits be the five following; art, science, prudence, wisdom, intellect. In matters of opinion we are liable to be deceived; not so in matters of science. The former relates to things variable in their nature, of whose very existence we may doubt, unless when they are actually perceived; the latter is conversant about things unalterable, necessary, and eternal, incapable of being generated, exempt from corruption; the knowledge of which admits not of degrees between total ignorance and absolute certainty. All science may be taught, and all teaching implies principles, namely, those truths which are previously known by experience or reason. The first principles are acquired by induction, that is, by intellect operating on experience[e]. Science, then, may be defined a demonstrative habit, distinguished by those properties which we have ascribed to it in our Analytics[f]. The principles of science must be perceived with the clearest evidence; for unless they be more evident than the conclusions drawn from them, those conclusions will not form

---

[e] See Analysis, p. 57. Comp. p. 161.   [f] See Analysis, p. 77.

form science strictly so called; because their truth does not necessarily proceed from the truth of their premises; with which they are connected, not essentially, but only by way of accession or appendage [f].

Things in their nature variable, and which might either have never been, which may cease to exist, or whose mode of existence is liable to perpetual alterations, are of two kinds; productions or actions. These things are sufficiently distinguished from each other even in popular discourse; so that a rational habit of action must be different from a rational habit of production. Since building, which is a rational habit of production, is an art, and every other such habit is also an art, and every art is also the habit just mentioned, art may be defined the habit of making or producing a certain work agreeably to the rules of right reason. All art is employed in examining and contriving how it may best form and fashion those productions or works of which the efficient cause is in the maker, not in the materials. Things which exist necessarily, are not the subjects of art; nor those which are produced naturally; for the latter have their efficient cause in themselves [h]. Art, then, is conversant after a certain manner about the same things as fortune. Wherefore Agathon says,

" In friendly ties are art and fortune bound."

Artlessness is the contrary of art; it is the producing of such works awkwardly; according to erroneous principles of reason.

In explaining the nature of prudence, let us consider first, who they are that deserve this appellation. It seems to be the part of a prudent man to deliberate wisely about his good or advantage; not in particular points merely, as health or strength, but

[f] See above, p. 65. Conf. p. 115. [h] See above, p. 109.

BOOK VI.

Chap. 4.
Art.

Chap. 5.
Prudence.

but as to the general happiness of life. This is indicated by our calling those men prudent in their affairs, who take proper means for attaining valuable purposes, which are not the proper objects of particular arts. Prudence then implies deliberation; and no one deliberates about things invariable in their nature, and which cannot be otherwife than they are; nor about things which are not in their own power. Prudence then is not science, because the objects of science are things invariable; it is not art, because the object of prudence is action, not production. It remains then, that prudence should be a rational and practical habit, bearing a reference to the happiness and misery of human life. The end of production consists always in the work produced; but action is often its own end; for happiness, which is a kind of action, is perfect in itself. Pericles, and other great statesmen, are called prudent on account of their singular ability in effecting the good of human kind; the great business of œconomy, both political and domestic. The word, in Greek, denoting the moral virtue of temperance, is compounded of two other words, which may be literally translated, " the preservative of prudence;" for temperance tends to preserve this intellectual excellence. Pleasure and pain do not destroy every exercise of the understanding, for instance, that which relates to mathematical truth; but that exercise only which relates to the practical concerns of life. For the excessive love of pleasure, or the excessive abhorrence of pain, substitutes new principles of action quite different from those by which wise and good men are actuated. Prudence, then, is a rational and practical habit, effective of human happiness. We speak of excellence in art, but prudence is itself excellence. In the arts, voluntary errors are the best; but, in matters

matters of prudence, they are the worst; as in all the moral virtues. Prudence, then, is not an art but a virtue; and the virtue of that faculty of the mind which is conversant about opinion and probability, discerning in such things truth from falsehood. As it relates to the practice of life, which, with all men, is a constant object of thought, prudence, when once acquired, is not, like other habits of the understanding, liable to be forgotten or lost.

BOOK VI.

Since the object of science, as above observed, is universal and demonstrable truth, and whatever is demonstrable must be founded on principles, it is manifest that there must be primary principles[i], which are not science, any more than they are art or prudence. They are not science, because all science is demonstrable; they are not art or prudence, because these have for their subject things contingent and variable: neither are they wisdom, because, as we shall see hereafter, wisdom, and the highest wisdom, is conversant about truths susceptible of demonstration. Since then none of the four habits just mentioned; neither science, nor art, nor prudence, nor wisdom, can afford those primary principles; and since all the habits of the understanding are reducible to five, it follows that intellect, operating on experience[k], is the only source from which those great and primary truths can be supposed to flow.

Chap. 6.
Intellect.

Wisdom is sometimes taken for skill in the arts; and applied, for instance, to Phidias, who was a skilful sculptor; or Polycleitus, the skilful statuary. But there is a wisdom of a far superior kind, which does not denote excellence in any of those operations or arts to which Homer alludes in speaking of Margites: " The Gods had not formed him for digging or ploughing,

Chap. 7.
Wisdom.

---

[i] See Analysis, p. 92. & seq. [k] See Analysis, p. 57. Comp. p. 161.

BOOK VI.

ing, nor made him skilful in any other work;" but a wisdom absolute and universal, since it relates to the universe and its principles; contemplating, not merely, like other sciences, the qualities or properties of things, but the things themselves, or substances[k]; and, therefore, of all sciences the most accurate as well as the most sublime; comprehending both the highest demonstrations, and the vindication of those primary truths on which all demonstration is built[l]. To say that prudence is more valuable than wisdom, is to prefer man to all other beings in the universe. One thing may be salutary and good for human kind; and another for fishes: but abstract qualities remain perpetually the same; and in like manner wisdom is permanent and stable, but prudence must vary its maxims with each alteration of the subject about which it is employed. The business of prudence consists in providing for the good of those peculiarly recommended to its care; and whoever best understands how to promote the good of each tribe or of each individual, to him we should be most inclined to commit their direction and management. Wherefore some of the inferior animals seem to be endowed with a kind of prudence, in foreseeing and providing what is necessary for the preservation of their own lives. The unalterable stability of wisdom clearly distinguishes it from civil policy, which, if it would attain its end, the public good, must be guided by circumstances; and the different tribes of animals require, in health as well as in disease, different kinds of management, which are respectively most conducive to their well-being. It will not avail to say, that as man is the noblest of animals, therefore the virtue of prudence,

[k] These are God and Intellect—the best substances, ἡ ἐστι μὴν ὁ θεος και ὁ νες, &c. Moral. Eudem. l. i. c. viii. p. 201.

[l] See above, Analysis, p. 86. & seq.

prudence, which is conversant about human happiness, merits the preference to every other [m]; for that there are many natures more divine than man, is attested by those glorious luminaries, and that beautiful arrangement which adorns the universe. Wisdom, then, comprehends both intellect and science, applied to the highest purposes, the discovery of the most valuable truths. Wherefore we call Thales, Anaxagoras, and others of their character, wise, indeed, but surely not prudent, since they manifestly neglect their private concerns and personal advantage, and apply their thoughts to the investigation of subjects as lofty and difficult as they are completely useless for the ordinary purposes of human life. But the virtue of prudence is directed solely to those purposes; and he is justly deemed the most prudent, whose advice is most conducive to public prosperity. This great object is not to be attained by abstract speculations. Prudence must be conversant about particulars; for all practice relates to particulars only; wherefore many men, ignorant of theory, are more useful than those acquainted with it; for instance, empirics, than physicians. What avails it to know that light food is salutary, unless we also know, for instance,

BOOK VI.

---

[m] According to Aristotle, prudence is, as it were, wisdom's steward, holding a delegated authority in lesser concerns, that the master may have leisure for more important pursuits, ἡ φρονησις, ὡσπερ ἐπιτροπος τις ἐστι τῆς σοφιας, και παρασκευαζει ταυτῃ σχολην, και το ποιειν της αυτης εργον. Magn. Moral. l. i. c. xxxv. p. 172. These more important pursuits consist in speculations concerning God; in meditating on, and worshipping him: ει τις δε η δι' ἡδονην, η δι' ὑπερβολην κωλυει τον θεον θεραπευειν και θεωρειν, αυτη δε φαυλη. Moral. Eudem. c. xv. p. 291. This employment is the chief end of man; the natural exercise of his noblest faculties, ὁυτος της ψυχης ὁ ὁρος ἀριστος, τα ἡκιστα αισθανεσθαι τῳ ἀλλῳ μερει της ψυχης, ἡ τοιουτον. The less we are disturbed by bodily passions, or harassed by worldly cares, the more likely we are to approach to this ultimate term of mental enjoyment. Idem ibid. Religion cannot be eradicated from the mind, unless the understanding be destroyed: μη τους θεους φοβεισθαι ουκ ανδρειος, αλλα μαινομενος. Magna Moral. c. v. p. 151.

stance, that the flesh of birds is light? Prudence being a practical virtue, essentially includes the knowledge of particulars. Yet even here general and superintending principles are not without their use.

Chap. 8.
Policy, general and particular.

Prudence and policy are the same habits, but applied to different subjects. Policy is general or particular: the general consists in legislation; the particular, in deliberations and decrees; for as decrees apply general principles to particular cases, they immediately precede execution; and therefore those who busy themselves about decrees, in proposing or procuring them, are peculiarly considered as workmen in the trade of politics. Prudence chiefly relates to the management of our private affairs, and while directed to this purpose preserves its proper name; but when our prudence extends to the affairs of others, it is called œconomics, legislation, politics; which last is either deliberative or judicial. Yet politics is sometimes contrasted with prudence; too much concern about other people's affairs seeming unfavourable to our own happiness. Wherefore Euripides says, in the person of Philoctetes,

> " How can the name of wife to me belong
> Who might have mingled in the martial throng,
> Unvex'd with business and exempt from care,
> Taking of spoils my honourable share;
> Yet chose by over-anxious thoughts to move
> The direful hate of all-commanding Jove?"

But a prudential regard to our own interest requires, perhaps, that we should not be regardless of politics, since our own good is involved in that of the Public; and many are extremely ill-fitted to provide even for their own. Young persons may become good geometers, and render themselves skilful in the arts

arts depending on the mathematical sciences. But it is scarcely possible for a youth to have the virtue of prudence, because this virtue is conversant about particulars, the accurate knowledge of which requires observation and experience, which must be the work of time. The mathematics are conversant merely about abstractions formed by ourselves; the notions of which are clear and precise. But the knowledge of nature, and of those causes by which nature subsists, is far more complicated, requiring continually the assistance of that experience in which it originates. As to practical truths, resulting from long experience, young men may indeed repeat them, but they seldom feel their full force. In applying theory to practice, errors may arise from mistaking either the general or the particular proposition; for example, that all heavy waters are bad, or that this water is heavy. Prudence is manifestly different from science; being the perception of those particular and practical truths which admit not of demonstration; whereas intellect is employed about those general and primary principles which require not any proof. In the chain of mental faculties, intellect and prudence then form the two extreme links; prudence holding the extreme of individuality, and intellect that of generalization. Prudence then may be called common sense, since it is conversant about objects of sense; but in a manner specifically different from that in which the other senses are respectively conversant about their particular objects.

Prudence implies deliberation, which word has a less extensive meaning than investigation, because deliberation is that species of investigation which relates to the practical concerns of life. It is not science, nor opinion, nor conjecture; not science, because no one deliberates about that which admits of demonstrable proof: not conjecture or guessing, because these are quick and rapid, but deliberation is a work of time; and it is a common maxim, that we ought to be prompt in execution, but slow in deliberation. Deliberation is not presence of mind, any more than happiness of conjecture; it is not science, which cannot err; nor opinion, the rectitude of which consists in truth, whereas that of deliberation consists in utility; since wrong deliberations are hurtful. Besides, every opinion is a proposition either affirmative or negative; whereas deliberation neither affirms nor denies, but investigates and inquires. Good deliberation is rectitude of counsel; but, as rectitude is taken in different senses, it is not every kind of rectitude, particularly it is not that by which an intemperate or bad man may contrive right means for attaining his wicked ends. His right deliberations terminate in much mischief; whereas good deliberation naturally terminates in advantage. This, however, may sometimes be attained without good deliberation, since a right conclusion is sometimes inferred from wrong premises. Good deliberation also must be seasonable: its result must be drawn at a right time, must proceed from right premises, and must terminate in some valuable purpose, whether that be happiness in general, or something thereto conducive. *Good counsel*, then, consists in discovering proper means for attaining those ends which prudence approves as worthy objects of pursuit.

Chap. 10.
Quickness of apprehension.

There is a readiness of apprehension in some men, which makes them be distinguished as intelligent; while others are equally remarkable for their slowness and stupidity. This quickness of thought, or acuteness in decision, is something quite different from science or opinion, since all men are capable of
learning

learning sciences and forming opinions; nor does it belong to any science in particular, as physic, which is conversant about health, or geometry, which is conversant about magnitude; nor does its proper subject consist in things which happen casually, or in those which are unalterable and eternal; but it is most conspicuous in those things which are matters of deliberation and doubt. It is conversant, then, about the same subject with prudence, though not precisely in the same manner; for prudence speaks with a voice of authority, commanding one action and prohibiting another; but the intellectual excellence, now under consideration, is rather critical than commanding; it does not govern and regulate our actions, but enables us to understand the regulations which prudence prescribes; and follows the dictates of this sovereign virtue, as an intelligent youth goes along with the lessons of his teacher.

That justness of sentiment by which some men render themselves so commendable, is nothing more than a nice discernment of the virtue which we called equity; in proof of which it may be observed, that those who are most equitable in their transactions, are also the most distinguished by their fellow-feeling with others, and the most inclinable to excuse their pardonable errors. Pardon is nothing more than an equitable decision; that is, indulgence flowing from right reason. The intellectual habits above described, readiness of apprehension, justness of sentiment, prudence, intelligence, or common sense, are all of them conversant about the same objects, and all of them conspire to the same great end of making men behave well in the practical concerns of life. These concerns are all of them particular, depending on time and circumstances; and the habits that have reference to them, must therefore be different

Chap. 11.

Justness of sentiment.

BOOK VI.

from those which are conversant about general and abstract truth. In practical matters, prudence regulates and commands, sentiment criticises and approves, and intelligence, or common sense, operating on observation and experience, furnishes those first principles, which are equally essential to the due selection of ends, and the proper adjustment of means. As these first principles spring up in the mind, without teaching or reasoning, merely from observation and experience, they seem to be the gift of nature; and justness of sentiment, as well as the other virtues depending on them, seem also to be natural, and to belong to men at a certain period of life, who seem then naturally to attain understanding and sentiment; whereas art, science, or wisdom, (as above explained,) never seem to grow up naturally, but always to be the work of application and study. Common sense, then, that is, intellect operating on experience, being the ultimate judge of whatever is practically good, we ought to respect the opinions of old and prudent men, not less than demonstration itself; because they see with the eye of experience, which alone can discern right principles of conduct. Such, then, is the nature of prudence in contradistinction to that of wisdom; virtues which are conversant about different objects, and which respectively belong to different faculties of the soul.

Chap. 12.

The value of the intellectual virtues, how to be estimated.

Doubts may arise in what respect these intellectual virtues are useful; for wisdom, as above explained, has not any reference to mutable and material things, and therefore seems not to have any tendency to promote human happiness. Prudence, indeed, is conversant about worldly affairs; but wherein consists its utility, since it only deliberates concerning honourable, just, and other actions conducive to happiness, which a virtuous man has learned to practise? If virtue be a habit, how

is

is it to be improved by the reflections of prudence? Persons possessed of health or strength would not be more strong or more healthy, though endowed with the skill of physicians and masters of exercises. But prudence, it will be said, though not necessary for the practice, is useful to the acquisition of virtue. Is skill in physic necessary or useful to the acquisition of health? If this were the case, we ought, when sick, to study physic, instead of calling a physician. Besides these doubts, it is not easy to determine the relative value of wisdom and prudence; and why the latter, which is inferior in dignity, should prescribe rules for the exercise of the former. Having proposed these difficulties, it is our duty, if possible, to solve them. First of all, wisdom and prudence, though they terminated not in any distinct and separate end, would be things highly desirable in themselves, since they are respectively the virtues of two mental faculties. But they are productive causes of human happiness, not indeed as physic is the cause of health, but as health itself is the cause of a healthy habit. The great business of human life is performed by the co-operation of prudence with moral virtue. The latter makes us pursue right ends; and the former makes us employ fit means for attaining them. To that power of the soul, which discovers itself in the growth and nutrition of the body, no such spontaneous function belongs; since its operations are carried on altogether independently of our own wills; and it is entirely beside our power to accelerate or retard them. As to the doubt whether prudence contributes to the practice of just and honourable actions, it will be best solved by tracing those actions to their real source. Acts of virtue, in general, may be performed by those who

Their utility in practice.

are

are not virtuous men, involuntarily, ignorantly, through fear of the law, or through any other motive which does not imply the habitual love of virtue, and the deliberate preference of it merely for its own fake. This habit, then, makes our ends right and good; but how to attain those ends, is the work, not of moral virtue, but of another principle. There is a power of the mind, call it cleverness, keenness, or sagacity, of which the nature consists in enabling us to accomplish our purposes; and which, when the purposes are good, is praiseworthy; when they are bad, this cleverness changes its name, being justly reproached as villany. Prudence, though not the same thing, (since a villain cannot be called prudent,) yet requires for its foundation this natural dexterity, which is determined to the side of honour and propriety by habitual acts of virtue. For reasonings alone cannot supply correct principles of conduct. The ends best to be pursued, appear such to good men only. Vice distorts the judgment; and even in men of naturally keen minds, produces the greatest practical errors: wherefore it is impossible to be prudent without being morally virtuous.

Chap. 13.
Natural virtue different from virtue properly so called.

It is necessary to speak farther of virtue; for, as natural sagacity, though similar, is not the same with prudence, so natural virtue, though similar, is not the same with virtue properly so called. Our capacities and dispositions are the work of nature; and therefore, in some sort, our morals are so likewise; men being born with propensities to justice, temperance, and fortitude. But this natural aptitude is not the virtue of which we are in quest. Strong natural propensities, and striking differences of manners, appear in children, and even in wild beasts; and this native vigour being unenlightened by reason, has a tendency to do much mischief, like the irregular motions of giants when deprived of their eye-sight. But when the intellectual eye opens, and affection is disciplined by reason, then that moral virtue displays itself; which bears the same relation to the natural, which prudence bears to that doubtful quality above mentioned, which, though somewhat resembling it, is yet specifically different. As virtue properly so called implies prudence, some have resolved all the virtues into modifications of this intellectual excellence. Socrates did this; saying, rightly, that none of the virtues could subsist without prudence; which is nothing else than right reason, (which all philosophers now add to the definition of virtue,) applied to the subject of morals; but he erred in thinking that the whole of moral rectitude depended solely on the understanding, and in calling the virtues sciences. Virtuous men, indeed, must act, not only according to right reason, but with right reason; that is, the right reason which regulates their conduct, must be a principle in themselves. The virtues then, though not sciences, cannot subsist without that principle of reason from which all the sciences spring; in other words, prudence is requisite for constituting the character of the truly good man. The question therefore may be answered, whether the virtues can exist separately. It should seem that they may; because the same person not being born with equal aptitude to them all, he may possess some of them, though still deficient in others. This indeed is true with regard to the natural virtues; but with regard to those which constitute the character of the truly good man, it is impossible; for none such can be exercised without prudence, and with this single intellectual excellence, all the moral virtues necessarily co-exist; since prudence not only shews us

how

how best to obtain our ends, but always implies that the ends themselves are good. Yet prudence, extensive and dignified as its function is, ought not to be preferred to wisdom, which is conversant about still higher subjects, and is the virtue of a nobler faculty[x]. Physic is not better than health; though it prescribes rules by which health may be attained[y]. To set prudence above wisdom, is the same absurdity as to set policy above the Gods; because policy regulates the national religion, as well as all other public concerns[z].

---

[x] See above, p. 285.

[y] The art of physic does not make use of health, it only contrives how health may be preserved or restored. It is for the sake of health, and therefore less valuable. See above, p. 149. & seq.

[z] The intellectual virtues are treated of more briefly in the last chapters of the first, and first chapters of the second Book of the work intitled Magna Moralia; and in the fifth Book of the Ethics to Eudemus.

ARISTOTLE's ETHICS.

BOOK VII.

INTRODUCTION.

HAVING examined the virtues and vices, strictly so called, the author proceeds to habits which, though often confounded with them, are yet essentially different; namely, self-command, and its opposite, incontinency; heroic virtue, and its opposite, beastly depravity; which sometimes shews itself in savageness and ferocity, and sometimes in unnatural perversions of the concupiscible appetites. There is not any system of Ethics that accounts so fully and so clearly for the important distinction between weakness and wickedness, as is done in this Seventh Book.

BOOK VII.

ARGUMENT.

Vice.—Weakness.—Ferocity.—Self-command, and its contrary.—Unnatural depravities, different from vices.—Voluptuousness more detestable than irascibility—Reasons of this.—Intemperance and incontinency.—Their difference.

WE now proceed, making a new division, to observe, that in morals three things ought to be avoided; vice, weakness, and ferocity: the opposites to the two first are manifest, namely, virtue and self-command; and to the third, we may set in opposition a virtue more than human, something heroic and divine, such as Homer makes Priam ascribe to Hector;

> " And last great Hector, more than man divine,
> For sure he seemed not of terrestrial line [a]."

So that should we believe what is said of the deification of illustrious men, their pre-eminent worth might be properly opposed to savageness and ferocity: for virtue belongs not to gods, any more than vice to beasts; the excellencies of gods are above virtue, and the depravities of beasts are specifically different from vice. The Lacedæmonians, when they admire any one exceedingly, say, " you are a divine man;" but as such men are seldom to be met with, so beastly depravities are seldom to be found in the human race; they occur rarely, and chiefly

[a] Iliad, b. xxiv. v. 223. & seq.

BOOK VII.

chiefly among barbarians. They are sometimes produced by diseases or wounds; and the excesses of human vice are reproached as beastly. But concerning such enormous depravities, we shall afterwards have occasion to speak; and we have already considered vice properly so called. It remains therefore that we now treat of incontinency and self-command; which seem not to be entirely the same with the habits of vice and virtue, nor yet altogether different from them. We shall first mention the prevailing opinions on this subject, and next state our own doubts: when difficulties are removed, and probabilities established, the theory will be sufficiently correct for all practical purposes. Firmness and self-command appear then to be respectable and praiseworthy habits; and their contraries, weakness and yielding softness, appear to be, in the same proportion, both blameable and contemptible. The man of self-command is steady to the decisions of his reason; the weak man is easily moved from them. The latter, knowing that his actions are bad, yet commits them through passion; the former, knowing that his appetites are bad, yet restrains them through reason. Some confound self-command with temperance, and the want of it with intemperance; others think that those habits are widely different from each other. Prudence appears to some to be totally incompatible with the want of self-command; others think, that men, highly distinguished by their prudence and abilities, are often extremely deficient in this particular. A man is said to lose the command of himself, and to be mastered, not only by pleasure, but by anger, honour, and gain. Such are the prevailing opinions on this subject[b].

It

---

[b] The subjects treated in this Book are explained nearly in the same words in the sixth book of the Ethics to Eudemus.

It seems difficult to explain how a man, who entertains juſt conceptions of things, ſhould voluntarily reſign his independence; and how he who, as Socrates obſerved, has ſcience to direct him, ſhould allow himſelf to be domineered over by inferior principles, and dragged in captivity like a ſlave. Socrates, indeed, maintained, that this could not happen to him who poſſeſſed real ſcience, and that none acted amiſs but through ignorance only. But this opinion is manifeſtly at variance with the phænomena; for if paſſion were cauſed by ignorance, the ignorance ought to precede the paſſion, which is plainly not the caſe; for the man who errs through want of ſelf-command, only does ſo when ſtimulated by paſſion; well knowing, before his paſſion is excited, that the actions to which it moves him are wrong. Some philoſophers maintain that none can err againſt demonſtrative knowledge, but that many daily err againſt that which is only probable; and that the love of pleaſure, though it cannot prevail over ſcience ſtrictly ſo called, may yet be too ſtrong for opinion. But if opinion merely, that is a faint and wavering impreſſion of truth, is the only power that makes reſiſtance to the ſtrength of appetite, it is not wonderful that the latter ſhould obtain the victory; nor ought thoſe to be blamed, in whom the ſtronger principle prevails. But this we find is not true; for men are highly blamed for indulging their corrupt appetites. If neither ſcience nor opinion can take part in this mental conflict, prudence remains as the only antagoniſt. But this is abſurd; for the want of ſelf-command cannot ſubſiſt in the ſame mind with prudence; a prudent man will not voluntarily commit bad actions; and prudence, as we have above ſhewn, is a practical principle, implying the exiſtence of all other virtues[c]. Self-command ſup-
poſes

BOOK VII.

Chap. 2.

Concerning ſelf-command, and its contrary.

Difficulties concerning this quality.

[c] See p. 303.

poses the presence of strong passions, and those blameable either in their nature or in their degree: if they were not blameable, they ought not to be resisted; and if they were not strong, there would be little praise in resisting them. Temperance, as above explained, is inconsistent with the presence of any such passions. Temperance and self-command cannot therefore belong to the same character. If self-command implied an immoveable adherence to every conclusion of the understanding, it would, when this conclusion happened to be false, be nothing better than obstinacy; and if the imperfection opposite to self-command consisted in easily departing from certain opinions or resolutions, it would sometimes be a very respectable quality; as in the case of Neoptolemus, who is represented in Sophocles' tragedy as easily departing from the resolution which he had taken, by the advice of Ulysses, because he could not bear to tell a lie; and those who having once yielded to the seductions of sophistry, continue pertinaciously to adhere to them, are surely not commendable on that account. Great weakness of resolution, when accompanied with great stupidity, might sometimes be a virtue; because through extreme irresolution, a man might be tempted to do directly the reverse of what he foolishly intended. Besides, he who led a life of voluptuousness through deliberate choice, and on conviction of its being the best kind of life that he could pursue, would not be in a condition so totally hopeless, as he who followed the same plan through want of self-command, in direct opposition to the dictates of his own reason. The former having been corrupted by argument, might also, by argument, be reformed; but the latter, resisting the persuasion of his own mind, would be totally incurable; and obnoxious to the proverb,

" Of drinking still, e'en when the water chok'd."

Besides, wherein does self-command, and the weakness opposite to it, properly consist; are the objects about which these habits are conversant, limited to a certain class? Such are the doubts of which we must endeavour to find the probable solution.

We proceed first to examine whether a man gives up the command of himself knowingly; and, if so, how that can happen: we shall also inquire, whether self-command, and the inability to restrain our appetites, have a reference to all pleasures and pains indiscriminately, or to certain definite kinds of them; and whether it belongs to the same habit of mind to resist pleasure, and to encounter pain; with several other questions naturally connected with the present speculation. Does inability to restrain our appetites appear in the improper pleasures that we pursue, or in the improper manner in which we pursue them, or in both these united? Self-command, and its opposite, incontinency, when taken in the strictest acceptation, have a reference to the same things about which temperance and intemperance were formerly proved to be conversant [d]; but the kind of relation which they bear to these things is exceedingly different. The intemperate man obeys his appetites knowingly and deliberately, thinking that he ought always to follow the impulse of present pleasure; the man, merely weak and incontinent, also obeys his appetites, but without thinking that he is thereby acting the part which becomes him. Whether the perceived impropriety of his conduct be the result of certain or only probable knowledge, makes not any material alteration; since some opinions, as Heraclitus proves, hold as firm possession of the mind, as if they were conclusions of science.

BOOK VII.

Chap. 3.

Whether persons deficient in self-command err knowingly.

[d] See above, p. 218. & seq.

BOOK VII.

science. But a man is said to understand, either when he actually exercises this faculty, or when he is barely possessed of it. It is exceedingly difficult to conceive how he should act against his understanding in the former case, though not at all extraordinary that he should do so in the latter. He may understand both the general precept, and the particular case to which it is applicable; but if he does not actually make the application, his knowledge will not avail him. In practical matters, there are general propositions which relate to the agent, and others which relate to the object of his action; and each of these have particular propositions which naturally fall under them. A man may be possessed of the knowledge of all the general propositions, and also of the knowledge of all the particular ones; and yet, if there be any one of the latter, concerning which his understanding does not, in the moment of action, exert its operation or energy, it is not wonderful that he should fall into the greatest practical errors. This operation or energy is manifestly suspended in the case of persons asleep, drunk, or mad; whose condition nearly resembles that of men under the influence of passion. Anger and lust plainly alter the bodily frame, and sometimes produce madness. Such is the state of those unable to restrain their appetites. It is no proof of the contrary, that such persons talk reasonably; for some madmen will repeat the verses and reasonings of Empedocles; and boys may be taught to string together demonstrations, although they know not what they say; for to appropriate truth to ourselves, it must be rendered congenial to the mind; which is the work of time. Such persons no more understand the conclusions which they pronounce, than comedians feel the passions which they fictitiously exhibit. There is also a philosophical

phical cause resulting from the physical nature of man, which may explain why he often through passion acts contrary to the dictates of his understanding. In all practical morality, there is to be considered, besides the general precept or proposition, also the particular one, which results from a perception of sense. When these two propositions coalesce, there is not merely an assent of the mind, but in practical matters, action must immediately and necessarily ensue. Thus, if the general proposition be, " sweet things ought to be tasted ;" and the particular, " this before me is sweet ;" it is necessary that, unless restrained by some obstacle or argument, I should immediately taste what is before me. Although the mind, therefore, may have the knowledge of some general proposition which ought to prevent tasting, yet, if appetite conspires with the two propositions above mentioned, appetite will, in those destitute of self-command, be indulged, in opposition to right reason ; and these propositions will be alleged by them in excuse for their infirmity. They will appear therefore to act licentiously on argument ; but, in fact, argument is not in itself contrary to right reason, but only by way of accession or appendage to appetite, which has the power of moving and changing the whole frame of the body, and thereby distorting the intellects. Beasts, therefore, cannot be blamed for this want of self-command, because they have not any perception of general precepts, their highest powers consisting in imagination and memory. How men enslaved by their appetites resume the exercise of their understandings, needs not here be explained ; this change has nothing in it peculiar ; since it entirely resembles what happens to all mankind when they awake from sleep, or to drunkards when they recover from a fit of intoxication ; subjects which belong to the province

BOOK VII.

vince of the physiologist. Socrates then said true, that science, properly so called, could not be overcome by appetite, which only disturbs our perception of particular and practical truths.

Whether incontinency be a specific imperfection, denoting, without any addition to it, infirmities of a peculiar kind, comes next to be inquired. It is manifestly conversant about pleasures and pains; and as pleasures are either necessary, namely, such as are essential to the health of the body and the preservation of the species; or though not necessary, yet in themselves eligible, such as victory, honour, wealth, and such other external advantages, it is to be remarked that we do not call those incontinent who are too easily mastered by the latter pleasures, and who are inclined to indulge them in a degree not warranted by right reason, without adding the particular cause or object which oversets them, such as gain, honour, anger. They are incontinent, that is wanting in self-command, not simply and absolutely, but as to gain, honour, anger; and the definition of incontinency in general no more applies to them, than the general definition of a man to an Olympic victor. It is doubtless an imperfection in a man's character that he is actuated by too eager a desire of honour or of wealth; but incontinency, taken absolutely, is blamed, not merely as an imperfection, but either as general depravity, or at least as a particular vice; which consists in pursuing with too much eagerness the pleasures of the taste and touch; or in avoiding, softly and weakly, the pains originating in those senses, cold and heat, hunger and thirst. Continency and incontinency, taken simply and strictly, are conversant therefore about precisely the same objects with temperance and intemperance; though the relation which they bear to those objects be extremely different. The intemperate

man

man pursues pleasure willfully and deliberately, thinking it always the proper object of his preference; wherefore his intemperance is more odious in proportion to the debility of his desires; for what excesses might he be expected to commit, were he stimulated by the warmth of youthful passions? Desires and pleasures, as we have already explained, are either natural, (of which some are even highly respectable and honourable,) or unnatural; or thirdly, they hold an intermediate rank, being natural under certain conditions, and unnatural under others; in which last class we may place the desires of gain, glory, or victory. Desires of the first and last kind do not subject those who gratify them to blame, provided they do not indulge them to excess; so that those who delight in their own honours and advantage, or in the honour and advantage of their parents or children, and take proper means to promote objects naturally so dear to them, are justly respected on this account; although even here, extremes are dangerous; as was exemplified in the case of Niobé, whose pride in her children made her contend with the gods; and in that of Satyrus, surnamed Philopater, whose zeal for the honour of his father proceeded to the extravagance of folly. But such desires, being highly natural in themselves, have nothing in them of wickedness or turpitude, only their excesses being hurtful or useless, ought to be carefully avoided. In indulging such desires beyond the limits prescribed by right reason, we are indeed guilty of an error which ought to be shunned, but which is not culpable, like that want of self-command, properly called incontinence. These errors bearing some analogy to each other, fall under the common denomination of weakness; but that word, when applied to the one, does not mean the same thing, as when it is applied

BOOK VII.

to the other, any more than the epithet bad, applied to a player or a physician, means the same thing, as when it is applied to a man. Self-command then, and its opposite weaknesses, are conversant about the same subjects with temperance and intemperance. When the words are applied to other subjects, they are extended by way of simile beyond their strict acceptation, and therefore other words must be added to them in order clearly to express our meaning. To say simply that a man is wanting in self-command, denotes that he is liable to be overcome by the seductions of sensual pleasure, but does not immediately suggest to us that he is liable to be overcome by anger, honour, or gain.

Chap. 5.

Unnatural depravities, their difference from vices.

Some things naturally please all animals; others are naturally pleasant only to certain tribes; and a third class, though not congenial to any species of animals in their sound and natural state, are yet agreeable to some individuals of the species, either through certain bodily defects, through perverse habits, or through pravity of nature. From this last kind result the fierce and beastly propensities incident to some individuals of the human species; witness that savage female who delighted in tearing to pieces women with child, and in devouring their young; and those barbarians around Pontus, who feast, some of them on raw, others on human flesh, and who make mutual presents of their children to eke out their horrid entertainments; witness also the shocking stories told of the tyrant Phalaris. These are beastly depravities, and others, not less abominable, are sometimes produced through diseases and madness, as was exemplified in that wretch who sacrificed and eat his mother; and in the slave who killed his companion that he might devour his liver. Some persons, through disease or custom, cuftom, delight in plucking out their hair, biting off their nails, or in eating coals or earth. In nearly the fame clafs we may place pæderafty. Such depravities, whether originating in natural corruption, cuftom, or malady, exceed the limits of vice, and cannot be reproached with epithets characteriftic of merely human pravity, except by way of metaphor or fimilitude. Thus he who fhould fear even the buzzing of a fly, would be degraded by cowardice more than human, and brutifh. A man was afflicted with a malady which made him tremble at the fight of a cat; and there are fome nations of diftant barbarians who have fo little ufe of their reafon, and who are fo completely guided by their fenfations, that they are fcarcely diftinguifhable from brutes. Madnefs, epilepfy, and other difeafes alfo fubject thofe afflicted by them to ftrange perverfities of defire; and from the fame fource of rational nature vitiated and changed, either by malady or cuftom, we fee fpring thofe exceffes of folly, cowardice, intemperance, and favagenefs, which tranfcend the boundaries of merely human wickednefs. We may fuppofe a man ftimulated by brutal appetites, and yet reftraining them; Phalaris for inftance, reftraining his defire to eat a boy, or to abufe him as the inftrument of an abfurd venereal pleafure; and it may happen on the other hand, that a monfter in a human fhape may not only feel fuch propenfities, but want felf-command to reftrain them. In fpeaking of men, fuch abominations cannot be called vices fimply and properly; they are fomething worfe: depravities originating in difeafe or brutifhnefs, not fpringing from the improper indulgence of natural appetite. It is manifeft then, that felf-command and weaknefs, continency and incontinency, are converfant about the fame fubjects with temperance and intemperance, and that there is another fpecies

of

BOOK VII.
Chap. 6.

Reasons why voluptuousness is more detestable than irascibility.

of continency, so called metaphorically, though conversant about different objects.

Incontinency of anger appears a lesser deformity than incontinency as to pleasure. The reasons of this are, that anger seems to listen to reason, though it does not hear it distinctly; like officious servants, who before they have received their orders fully are in too great a hurry to execute them, and therefore often do it amiss; and dogs which bark at the least noise, before they know whether it proceeds from a friend or an enemy. In the same manner anger, without waiting for reason's last commands, is precipitated through the warmth and quickness of its nature, into over-hasty acts of inconsiderate vengeance; concluding, at every real or supposed insult, that the author of it is worthy of indignation and punishment. The conclusions of anger are indeed often erroneous; but sensuality, without stopping to draw any conclusions at all, at the first prospect of pleasure, rushes to enjoyment; it is therefore the more degrading imperfection of the two, since the sensualist yields to mere appetite, whereas the angry man is led astray by the appearance, at least, of reason. Besides this, it is to be observed, that all our faults seem to be more or less entitled to indulgence and pardon, in proportion as they are more or less natural, or more or less common. But transports of anger are far more natural than excesses in criminal pleasure: the former seem to be congenial to some races of men; as in the family of him who apologized for beating his father by saying, that *he* beat my grandfather, and my grandfather, the father before him; and this little boy, pointing to his son, will beat me when he is able; the fault runs in our blood. Another, when dragged by his son to the door, desired him to stop there, because he had

only

only dragged his own father thither. Anger besides is open and undesigning; but the passion of voluptuousness is artful, and therefore unjust. The cestus of Venus is pregnant with wiles.

> "In this was every art and every charm
> To win the wisest and the coldest warm ;
> Fond love, the gentle vow, the gay desire,
> The kind deceit, the still reviving fire,
> Persuasive speech and more persuasive sighs,
> Silence that spoke, and eloquence of eyes*."

The incontinency of voluptuousness is therefore worse than that of anger ; since it more nearly approaches to deliberate wickedness. It may be observed to the same purpose, that no person afflicted with pain is addicted to insolence ; for insults are committed with pleasure, but anger is always accompanied with pain ; wherefore insolence, which is of all things the most provoking, is incompatible with anger. The different kinds of incontinency have now been sufficiently explained, the human, the brutish, and that originating in diseases; the first kind only is conversant about the same objects with the vice of intemperance ; a thing never ascribed to brutes, except metaphorically, or comparatively ; when any class of animals is remarked as peculiarly obnoxious for its lust, voracity, or mischief. For brutes, being incapable of deliberation and election, cannot be deformed by vice, strictly so called ; their ferocity, how formidable soever it may be, is a less evil than human vice; since they are destitute of that best principle of man, which, by corruption, becomes the worst ; and bad effects flowing from a principle, are thereby rendered more dangerous.

A bad

* Iliad, XIV. v. 247. & seq.

BOOK VII. Chap. 7.

A bad man is capable of doing ten thousand times more mischief than a beast.

With respect to the pleasures and pains of the touch and taste, which it falls within the province of temperance to regulate, we may be so constituted as either to conquer those by which the greater part of mankind are subdued, or to be conquered by those over which the greater part are victorious. The terms, self-command, or continency, and its opposite, incontinency, are most properly applied in speaking of pleasures; the terms, firmness and softness are respectively most applicable to those who shew more than an ordinary strength of mind in resisting pain, or more than an ordinary weakness in yielding to this adversary. The greater proportion of mankind float between the opposite extremes of firmness and softness, continency and incontinency; verging, however, for the most part, rather to the imperfections of incontinency and softness. Since some pleasures are altogether unnecessary, and of those which are necessary, the excesses are carefully to be shunned, he who pursues unnecessary or immoderate pleasures, with deliberate election, and merely for their own sake, is guilty of intemperance; a vice the more incurable, because those who harbour it are not liable to repentance. The vice opposite to intemperance consists in rejecting, through insensibility, even necessary or commendable pleasures: the virtue of temperance lies in the middle between these blameable extremes. With regard to bodily pains, a man may fly from and avoid, even those which ought to be encountered, either through deliberate election, or through mere weakness and infirmity of nature; and as one person is led captive by pleasure, another may be overcome by the painful irritation of desire.

ARISTOTLE's ETHICS.

BOOK VII.

desire. Bad actions are aggravated, when they are committed without impulse from any violent passion. To strike in anger, is an extenuation of the assault; and, in like manner, base actions, done without temptation, are rendered still baser; for, in what shameful excesses would he who commits them be likely to indulge, were he stimulated by fierce desires and headstrong appetites? Intemperance, then, properly so called, is more odious than that weakness which we have called incontinency; and continency, which enables us to conquer pleasures is preferable to that resisting firmness, which merely prevents us from being subdued by pain. Softness, or effeminacy, consists in yielding to slight pains; and is illustrated in him who trails his flowing garments on the ground, rather than submit to the uneasiness of tucking them up; thus exhibiting, without necessity, a picture of disease and infirmity, and thinking that there is no misery in resembling the miserable. That a man should be overcome by great pleasures or great pains, is not a matter of wonder; and his defeat is entitled to pardon, provided his resistance has been vigorous; as is exemplified in the Philoctetes of Theodectes, when bit by the snake, and in the character of Cercyon in Cercinus' play of Alope. The bursts of agonising pain are as natural on such occasions as those of laughter, when long and earnestly suppressed; an instance of which was seen in Zenophantus. But a man is truly contemptible, when he softly yields to slight and inconsiderable sufferings, unless this happens through disease, or through some natural infirmity in his race. In the kings of Persia, effeminacy is hereditary; and manly firmness is not expected in women. A playful character is more allied to softness than to intemperance; for playfulness is the repose and relax-

BOOK VII.

ation of the mind. The want of self-command originates, either in rashness or in debility. Weak men deliberate, but want strength of mind to persevere in their resolutions; rash men are hurried away by passion, without deliberating at all. Our own preparations and exertions have great power even over our bodily feelings; a man may accustom himself to bear tickling without suffering the uneasy sensation which it excites; and, in the same manner, by calling up pains and pleasures to the mind, by rendering them objects of perception and examination, and moderating by reason the affections which they naturally stir up in us, we may acquire the power of resisting and conquering those formidable enemies, whenever we are obliged actually to contend with them in real life. Men of quick tempers, and those disordered by melancholy, are peculiarly deficient in self-command; the former, through their mobility; and the latter, through that vehemence and impetuosity which renders them slaves to their fancies, how wild soever they may be.

Chap. 8.

He that is properly intemperate, is not given to repentance; because, acting with deliberate election, he remains firm in his perverse purposes. He, on the other hand, who sees the right path, but, through weakness of character, does not pursue it, is liable to repent of his misconduct. His faults therefore are curable[f]; and the mental malady under which he labours, resembles rather the epilepsy, which comes by fits, than the consumption or dropsy, which are unremitting and continual. His weakness, indeed, is specifically different from vice; for the latter can conceal itself, and even assume the mask of virtue; but

---

[f] Aristotle says, "contrary to what was stated in our doubts;" he doubted how a man who knowingly erred, could ever be cured of his errors. See above, p. 311.

but the former is always undisguised and open. This infirmity of nature is the less inexcusable in proportion to the strength of passion, and the total absence of reflection; and the persons disgraced by it resemble those who are speedily intoxicated and overcome by such a small quantity of wine, as would produce no perceptible effects on ordinary constitutions. Yet mere weakness of character is attended with as bad consequences as vice itself; and is chargeable with the reproach which Demodocus made to the Milesians, that though they were not a stupid people, yet they acted stupidly. In like manner, the weak man acts viciously; but does not, like the intemperate man, give a deliberate preference to vice. His mind, therefore, is still open to persuasion, and his life capable of reformation, since his character is not so totally depraved as to make vice his end and aim. In the affairs of life, this end and aim forms a practical principle, which cannot be taught any more than the axioms and postulates of geometry; and the perception of which results entirely from virtue, either natural or acquired. The temperate man pursues right ends, from which he feels no inclination to deviate; the character of the intemperate man is directly the reverse. Between these two, an intermediate place is held by him, who is hurried into bad actions by the impetuous strength of passion; but whose mind is not so totally vitiated as to make the gratification of sensual appetites the deliberate object of his pursuit. Persons of this description do bad actions; but as the principle of action itself, which is the main thing, still remains sound, their condition is not hopeless. They are indeed better than those who are intemperate on principle; but still they are the objects of great disapprobation; whereas those who, though liable

BOOK VII.

Chap. 9.

Difference between incontinency and intemperance is that between weakness and wickedness.

liable to be moved by corrupt desires, have yet sufficient strength of mind to restrain and curb them, are held praiseworthy; notwithstanding their characters fall far short of that perfect temperance, with which no improper desire is compatible.

That firmness of mind called continency, implies a resolute adherence to right opinions in opposition to the seductions of appetite: it is totally different from obstinacy, which often yields to passion, but perversely resists the dictates of reason. Obstinacy bears the same analogy to true firmness, that prodigality bears to liberality; and rashness to courage. It is inseparably connected with self-conceit, ignorance, and clownishness. An obstinate man takes pleasure in resisting conviction; victory, not truth, is his aim; and, as if his opinions were laws, he is mortified and provoked by their rejection or reversal. His character, therefore, so far from implying firmness and self-command, is rather a-kin to incontinency; since he is diverted from propriety of thought and action, by the allurements of false pleasure. A man may want stedfastness in his purposes, without being chargeable with incontinency or weakness. Of this we have an example in the character of Neoptolemus in Sophocles' Philoctetes. Pleasure made that young hero change his resolution; but an honourable pleasure, the love of truth, after he had been persuaded by Ulysses to consent to be made an accomplice in falsehood; for incontinency and intemperance do not originate in pleasure simply and absolutely, but in that kind of sensual pleasure which is blameable and base. Men, as we have said before, may be diverted from propriety of conduct by being too little, as well as by being too much affected by bodily pleasures. Both extremes are bad; but as the former is observed in few persons,

and

and on few occasions, it is not distinguished by a name; and the praiseworthy habit of continency is contrasted with that blameable disposition which consists in being too strongly affected with the desire of sensual gratifications. Temperance and self-command are in common discourse often confounded, from the resemblance which they bear to each other; but the man deserving the praise of true temperance is above self-command, because his character is such, that he could not derive any enjoyment from base or blameable pleasures. The man endowed with continency or self-command, resists, indeed, and overcomes such pleasures; but still to him they seem to be pleasures, and he occasionally feels an inclination to enjoy them. In like manner, intemperance and incontinency are often confounded, for both lead to the same voluptuous kind of life; but the former prefers pleasure on principle; the latter pursues it against principle.

BOOK VII.

Men deficient in self-command may have cleverness but cannot have prudence; which latter is a practical principle, implying not only that we know, but that we do, what is right. In reference to the understanding, wit or cleverness are nearly the same with prudence; but in reference to the will they are very different from it, because prudence always implies a rectitude of moral election; it is therefore absolutely incompatible with the dominion of vicious passions. How such passions should be indulged knowingly, has been explained by shewing that the knowledge of those who indulge in them, is confined to mere speculations which are not applied; that it is knowledge not roused to energy, but lying in a sluggish state of mere capacity, like the knowledge of persons asleep or intoxicated. The incontinent man is only wicked by halves,

Chap. 10.

Additional proofs thereof.

because

BOOK VII.

because he is not wicked on principle; as he acts without design, he is not chargeable with injustice. He either does not deliberate at all; or if he deliberates, is like a state which has good laws, but does not obey them; as Anaxandrides reproached the Athenians,

"The state consults how to make void the law."

The real profligate, on the other hand, obeys laws, and those bad ones. A man is praised for self-command, when he excels most others in that habit; he is blamed for incontinency, when he yields to temptations, to which most men are superior. The incontinency of those who deliberate rightly, but have not firmness to persist in their resolutions, is more curable than that originating in melancholy; which, through its quickness and vehemence, impels those affected by it to act without deliberation; and an incontinency depending on custom, is more curable than that which springs from nature. For custom is more moveable than nature, since the difficulty of changing the former, depends on its resemblance to the latter.—As the Poet Euenus says,

"Habits by long continued care imprest,
Are strong as nature in the human breast."

Let this much suffice for a description of the habits of continency and firmness on the one hand; of incontinency and softness on the other; and on the relations which those habits bear to each other[e].

[e] The four chapters which follow in the original of this work, are mere transcripts from the Sixth Book of the Ethics to Eudemus; they treat of pleasure; a subject more fully and more philosophically explained in the Tenth Book of the Ethics to Nicomachus; of which the reader will find the translation in its proper place.

ARISTOTLE's ETHICS.

BOOK VIII.

INTRODUCTION TO BOOKS VIII. AND IX.

IN these Books Aristotle treats of friendship, a subject, he observes, intimately connected with morals; "since friendship, if not a particular virtue, at least shines most conspicuously in the virtuous." He explains the nature of friendship, and resolves the doubts concerning it. He divides it into different kinds, according to the principles in which it originates, and shews how the best kind of friendship may be acquired, maintained, and uninterruptedly enjoyed. Friendships differ, not only according to the sources from which they spring, but according to the condition of the persons by whom they are cultivated. Our author examines the friendships between equals, and the friendships of inferiors with the great; he explains the relations which friendship bears to justice, and how both are modified by political institutions. The rules of friendship are far less precise than those of justice, because the subject to which they apply is far less definite; scarcely any two cases being exactly alike. The author explains what is meant by loving our friends as ourselves, and wherein true self-love consists, in opposition to blameable selfishness. He expatiates on the exquisite

quisite delight of virtuous friendship, like a man who (as appears from the history of his life) had warmly felt its charms. The whole treatise, indeed, comprised in the following two Books, is distinguished by just sentiment as much as by solid argument; it is equally full and perspicuous, rejecting paradox, disdaining declamation, and shewing, by an illustrious example, how an important moral subject may be unfolded with scientific accuracy, and impressed with practical energy.

BOOK VIII.

ARGUMENT.

Utility and beauty of friendship.—Qualities by which it is generated.—Three kinds of friendship.—These kinds compared.—Characters most susceptible of friendship.—Unequal friendships.—Their limits.—Friendships founded on propinquity.

WE proceed next to treat of friendship, which is either a particular virtue, or which at least shines most conspicuously in the virtuous. It is also most essential to the enjoyment of life, for without friends no one would choose to live, though possessed of all other advantages[a]. The rich and powerful stand most in need of friends, without whom their prosperity could neither be preserved nor enjoyed; for wherein consists the pre-eminence of power and wealth, but in the pleasures of beneficence, which is most laudably exercised towards friends? And how could this precarious pre-eminence be maintained without the steady assistance of friendly adherents? In poverty and other distresses, friendship seems our best, or rather our sole, refuge. It is necessary in youth as the preservative against irreparable

---

[a] Si quis in cœlum adscendisset, naturamque mundi, et pulchritudinem siderum perspexisset, insuavem illam admirationem, &c. "To ascend to heaven, and behold the nature of the universe, and the beauty of the stars, would afford an admiration barren of delight, unless we had some one with whom we might talk of those wonders." Cicero de Amicitia, c. 23. Cicero's Treatise on Friendship abounds with sparkling passages: he has often expanded and embellished Aristotle's remarks; but considered as a philosophical work, it neither shews that deep insight into human nature, nor takes that comprehensive view of the subject, which form the principal merit of the Greek original.

BOOK VIII.

reparable errors; it is necessary in old age, as the consolation amidst unavoidable infirmities; it is necessary in the vigour of manhood, as the best auxiliary in the execution of illustrious enterprises, both sharpening our thoughts and animating our exertions.

> " By mutual confidence and mutual aid,
> Great deeds are done and great discoveries made:
> The wise new prudence from the wise acquire,
> And one brave hero fans another's fire [b]."

Friendship is implanted by nature in parents towards their children, as appears manifestly, not only in the human race, but in the various tribes of birds, and in most animals; it prevails also among those of the same class or family, but chiefly among men; whence philanthropy is so often the just subject of praise. During long and dreary journeys, in every man the traveller meets, he beholds the face of a friend; such congenial sympathy subsists among the human race! Friendship holds mankind together in communities and cities; and lawgivers study more earnestly how to promote friendship than how to maintain even justice itself; for concord, which is a-kin to friendship, is the perpetual aim of all wise legislation, which unceasingly strives to extirpate the seeds of dissension and sedition, as of all things the most hostile to its views. When concord ripens into friendship, the rules of justice are superfluous, but justice without friendship is insufficient for happiness; and the most perfect and most comprehensive justice is that which most resembles friendship in its operations and effects. Friendship unites beauty with utility, it is not only necessary but ornamental; we praise it as a virtue; we desire it as adding lustre to our characters;

[b] Iliad, X. v. 265. & seq.

characters; and to be a good friend seems to many synonymous with being a good man. Yet various doubts may be started concerning the nature of friendship. Some think that it results from similarity of character and pursuits, and cite the vulgar proverb, "that fowls of a feather flock together." Others maintain that this similarity more naturally begets emulation and hatred; quoting from Hesiod,

BOOK VIII.

Doubts concerning the nature of friendship.

"Potters hate potters; bards quarrel with bards."

They seek the principles of friendship in the high philosophy of nature, saying either with Euripides,

"The parched earth longs for refreshing showers;
The skies, heavy with rain, seek to unload
Their weight of waters on the solid earth."

or with Heraclitus, "that each nature requires and seeks its counterpart:" thus the best harmony results from differences, and thus all things proceed from contrary elements. Other philosophers, particularly Empedocles, assert directly the reverse, "that like draws to like." The consideration of these physical difficulties we at present omit, because they are beside the purpose of this discourse, which is confined to the examination of such questions only as have a reference to life and manners; as whether friendship can subsist among all sorts of persons, or only among the virtuous; whether there are various kinds of friendship specifically different; for those who think there is but one kind, because friendship admits of different degrees of warmth and intensity, trust to a fallacious proof, since other general terms as well as friendship comprehend divisions of things specifically different from each other, and yet partaking more or less, in a stronger or weaker degree, of the characteristic quality

BOOK VIII.

Chap. 2.

The proper objects of friendship, or the qualities by which it is produced.

which the general term denotes. But of this subject we have formerly treated [e].

To illustrate the nature of friendship, we must examine what are the qualities by which it is excited or produced. Whatever is an object of our friendship, must promote either our good, our pleasure, or our utility; and as utility is desirable merely as the cause of what is either good or pleasant, the causes of friendship ultimately resolve themselves into goodness and pleasure; considered, not absolutely in themselves, but in reference to the person in whom the friendship is generated; whether that person has just notions of what is good and pleasant, or takesth ofe for *real* goods, which are only *apparent*. The qualities by which friendship is excited are not, when abstractedly considered, able to produce this amiable disposition; for that which is an object of friendship is loved on its own account; and it is necessary that between friends there should subsist a reciprocity of affection. Things inanimate therefore cannot be the object of friendship. A drunkard indeed loves wine; but it would be ridiculous to say that he desires its good, although he indeed wishes for its safety, that he himself may drink it. . Mere goodwill may subsist on one side, without meeting a return; and persons who have not any opportunity of being acquainted, may mutually bear to each other much good-will; but friendship not only implies a reciprocity of affection, but requires that this reciprocity should be known to both parties.

Chap. 3.

Three kinds of friendship.

Friendship may be distinguished into three kinds, according to the three qualities by which it is produced; and in each of the three there must be a known reciprocity of affection depending on the cause in which the friendship originates. When this cause is utility, men love each other as long as mutual advantage

[e] See Analysis, p. 65. & seq.

vantage results from their friendship: a similar observation is applicable when their affection is founded on pleasure. Neither the utility nor the pleasure which any man affords, constitute an essential and unalterable part of his character; and when on account of those circumstances he himself becomes an object of friendship, he is so, merely by way of accession or appendage to qualities not inseparably connected with him, and which being actually removed, he himself ceases to be an object of friendship. Friendships founded on utility prevail most among persons advanced in years; for interest, not pleasure, is their aim. Manhood, and even youth, often imitate too faithfully the selfish manners of age; choosing their friends according to views of interest. Persons of this character delight but little in each other's society. Even their convivial hospitality has personal advantage for its object. Youthful friendships however, for the most part, are founded on pleasure; for youth is the age of passion, which pursues and prefers present and immediate gratification. But as our pleasures change with our years, youthful friendships are as easily dissolved as they were speedily contracted. Besides, youth is much addicted to love, which is full of mutability, its principal ingredients being pleasure and passion, so that it varies many times in a day. Youthful attachments, while they last, produce close and habitual intimacy, because such friendships have no other foundation than the delight resulting from mutual intercourse. The only perfect friendship subsists among those who resemble each other in virtue, because those who love their friends for their virtue, love them for what is not a temporary appendage, but a permanent essential in their characters. The worth of a virtuous friend is not relative to circumstances, but universal and absolute, comprehend-

ing

ing both pleasure and utility, and uniting all those qualities which either produce friendship or render it unalterable; but his inestimable value cannot be fairly appreciated, except by those who are his rivals in moral or intellectual excellence; for men delight chiefly in those qualities which resemble their own. Such friendships are rare, because virtuous men are rare; and even *they* cannot perfectly know each other, until, according to the proverb, they have consumed many bushels of salt together. Time and familiarity are requisite for proving mutual affection, and for creating that steady confidence which cements friendship. Friendly acts produce rather an inclination to friendship than the thing itself, which must be the effect of time and habit operating on excellencies reciprocally exerted, and mutually experienced, in those who are respectively conscious of being the objects of love and affection the one to the other.

Chap. 4.

The different kinds of friendship compared with respect to their durability.

Friendships founded on utility and on pleasure bear a resemblance to that founded on virtue; for virtuous men afford both pleasure and utility to their friends. But friendships of the former kind are the more durable in proportion as they originate on both sides in nearly the same principle, that is in nearly the same kind of pleasure or utility. Thus, they naturally last long between men recommended to each other by their companionable qualities, their wit and pleasantry; they are less durable among lovers, when, as for the most part happens, the love on the one side arises from an admiration of beauty, and on the other from the attentions bestowed by the lover. When beauty is impaired by years, the admiration ceases, the attentions are withheld, and the friendship founded on this kind of love is sometimes at an end; but many times also it lasts, when cemented by congenial manners, strengthened and

and confirmed by long habits of familiar intercourse. Friendships founded on the love of gain are of all the most unstable; for persons governed by this principle are not friends to each other, but both to their respective interests. All persons promiscuously, the good, the bad, and those of an intermediate character, may feel towards each other that kind of friendship which originates in pleasure or utility; but good men only can be the objects of friendship properly so called, independent of circumstances and resulting from what is most essential and most unalterable in the character itself. The friendships of the virtuous are not to be destroyed by fortune, nor shaken by calumny. What accident or event can change or disturb confirmed habits of virtue? What calumny can prevail against known and approved worth? The friendship formed from interest therefore, like alliances between states, and those formed from pleasure, like the friendships of our boyish years, are called friendships only by way of similitude or metaphor; and those metaphorical friendships resemble other metaphors in this, that they do not naturally mingle, or easily blend and unite; for how seldom do we see the same persons friends to each other on the combined principles of profit and of pleasure? Such then are the different kinds of friendship. That formed by the virtuous alone deserves the name, the others are so called merely by a figure of speech.

BOOK VIII.

Men procure the denomination of friendly as they do that of virtuous, either from their actions or from their habits. Friendly actions can take place only among those who are members of the same society; but the habit of friendship may subsist among persons widely separated from each other, though, when their

Chap. 5.

The characters most susceptible of friendship.

their separation continues long, their friendship is apt to be forgotten; whence it is said,

"Long absence often is the bane of friendship."

Old persons, and those of austere characters, are, from this principle, but little disposed to friendship; because in them both the love of pleasure, and the power of communicating it, is commonly so much weakened, that they have not any great inducement to keep company with each other; for as pleasure is the great aim of nature, the society of those who are capable neither of affording nor relishing it, cannot possibly be desired; and if they occasion real and positive uneasiness, will not long be endured. Those who, without delighting in each other's society, are however respectively the objects of mutual approbation, may have great good-will towards each other with very little friendship; for nothing is so productive of friendship as the habitual intercourse of life. The wretched seek succour in society, but the happy seek society for itself, and can least of all men bear solitude; but the love of society itself is founded on the pleasure afforded by those with whom we live; which pleasure implies that their characters be agreeable, and much of the same stamp with our own. Friendship, therefore, as has been often said, prevails chiefly among the virtuous, to whom only that is good and pleasant, which is good and pleasant absolutely and essentially, independently of any circumstances that may concur, or of any consequences that may follow; and to whom the mutual enjoyment of their correspondent excellencies is of all things the most delightful.

Chap. 6.
———
Friendship cannot at

Aged persons and those of austere characters are unfit for friendship in proportion to their austerity, and to their aversion to society. Young people therefore sooner form friendships than the old and austere; who, though they may often bear great good-will to each other, and shew much readiness in mutually conferring the most essential services, are yet slow and cold in sentimental attachment, because they are averse to that social intercourse in which chiefly it originates. Friendship in its highest perfection cannot extend to many; and for a similar reason that it is impossible for us to feel the passion of love for many persons at once. There is an intensity in friendship as well as in love, which naturally confines it to one object. Men have different tastes, each of which has something in it too peculiar to be alike pleased with many; and it is right that it should be so. Friendship, besides, requires long and intimate knowledge, which is not easily obtained of many characters by one person, who cannot live in equal and close familiarity with them all. Friendships of interest or pleasure are indeed speedily contracted, because their offices may be speedily performed, and many are able to fulfil them. Of the two, those of pleasure most resemble true friendship, especially when the pleasure is mutual, and resulting from the same objects and pursuits. Such are the friendships of youth, which are of a warmer and more liberal kind than those formed among money-getting men on the cold principle of interest. Men prosperous in their circumstances prefer pleasure to utility; they choose the society of agreeable friends, since worth itself, joined with harshness and austerity, soon becomes offensive and irksome; but if they loved and preferred, as right reason would direct, agreeable qualities only when ennobled by virtue, they would find in their friends all advantages united. Men invested with power have two distinct classes of friends; the one chosen from taste, the other

BOOK VIII.
once comprehend many objects.

The great have two distinct classes of friends.

other from interest. The friends calculated to please are not qualified to benefit them; for as they seek pleasure distinct from virtue, and pursue interest distinct from honour, merry buffoons are best qualified for the first purpose, and dexterous knaves best adapted to the second; the man of virtue alone answering the double end of pleasure and utility. But a virtuous man cannot live in friendship with the great unless *they* be as much disposed to respect his superiority of virtue, as he is disposed to honour their superiority of fortune, because the law of equality, which is the soul of friendship, would otherwise be violated; and as men in power are generally too much intoxicated with their prosperity ᵉ to make this just sacrifice, they seldom enjoy the inestimable benefit of virtuous friendship. Such then are those kinds of friendship in which men interchange either pleasures or utilities on both sides, or exchange pleasure on the one side for utility on the other. They resemble true friendship in this, that they are productive of pleasure or profit; but they differ from it in many other respects, and particularly in being easily shaken by calumny, and easily subverted by a change in the external circumstances of those between whom they prevailed.

Chap. 7.
Unequal friendships: their limits.

Friendship, strictly so called, requires, as we observed, equality; but there is also a species of friendship which subsists between persons of extremely unequal conditions; namely, that between fathers (or those who hold the place of fathers) and children; husbands and wives; rulers and those subject to their authority. This species of friendship admits of many subdivisions: the friendship of a father towards his son, differs from that

---

ᵉ Non enim folum ipsa fortuna cæca est, sed eos etiam plerumque efficit cæcos, quos complexa est. "Fortune is not only herself blind, but she, for the most part, renders those also blind whom she embraces." Cicero de Amicitia, c. xv.

that of a hufband towards his wife, and that of a king towards his people; it differs alfo from that of a fon towards his father; for the parties ftanding in this and other relations, have each of them their refpective offices and their refpective duties; the habitual performance of which can alone give ftability to their friendfhip. When the pre-eminence is greatly on one fide, whether in the power of beftowing profit or pleafure, the friendfhip ought to be greater on the other, in nearly the fame proportion, that the rules of equal juftice may thus be maintained. But equality in point of juftice confifts primarily in this, that each man fhould have his due: tha the fhares fhould be nearly equal in quantity, is only a confequence that fometimes follows from this rule; for when the perfons are equal in worth, then only their fhares fhould be equal in value. But in point of friendfhip, equality in quantity or worth is a primary confideration; for between perfons extremely unequal as to virtue, power, wealth, and other caufes productive of diftinction, friendfhip cannot eafily fubfift. The gods are the great benefactors of mankind, but they are far too exalted for our friendfhip. Kings do not choofe their friends among the loweft claffes of their people: nor do men eminently diftinguifhed by virtue and wifdom, affociate with perfons of no confideration or merit. It is impoffible accurately to afcertain the precife limits beyond which the elevation of the one party becomes too great to admit of friendfhip with his inferior. The friendfhip may ftill fubfift, after many advantages are taken from the one and accumulated on the other. But with the exaltation of the latter to divinity, the relation of friendfhip would unqueftionably ceafe [d]; wherefore it is doubted, whether a man can wifh for the

[d] Does this bear any reference to the friendfhip between Ariftotle and his pupil Alexander?

BOOK VIII.

Chap. 8.

The ordinary foundations of unequal friendships.

the deification of his friend, since this would be to wish for the destruction of their friendship. Perhaps he does not even wish for him all human advantages; for a man desires that every good thing may happen to his friend, provided only what is a good to his friend be not an evil to himself; and it would be a great evil to himself to lose a good friend.

Most people, through vanity, wish rather to be beloved than to love. They are therefore fond of flatterers; who are, or rather pretend to be, a kind of unequal friends, that love more than they are loved. Love is near akin to honour, which most men desire, not indeed for its own sake, but for the advantages which accrue from it. They delight in marks of distinction from the great, which they regard as pledges of future and more solid bounties. Those who are ambitious of honour from persons well acquainted with them, and whose characters are esteemed for equity, wish thereby to confirm their good opinion of themselves. They delight in thinking favourably of their own characters, in consequence of this impartial verdict in their favour; and the pleasure which they take in being the objects of love and approbation, is the cause for which they desire external marks of honour and respect. To be loved, therefore, is better than to be honoured, and friendship is still more than honour ultimately desirable. The former however consists more in loving than in being loved; in proof of which we may allege the behaviour of mothers who give out their children to nurse, pleased with loving them and knowing that they are well, without expecting or desiring any return of affection. To love one's friends is a common topic of praise; and the *virtue* of friendship depends on the strength and propriety of our affection, which can alone render it permanent, levelling all those inequalities, and removing all those obstacles

which

which might interrupt its duration. Such is the friendship of virtuous men, who being stable in themselves, remain stable in their relations to each other; neither requiring nor admitting any association with the worthless. These last are inconstant in all their ways, and there can be no stability in their relations to each other, since none of them acts uniformly or consistently, nor remains long like unto himself. Their friendship is but a league in villainy, which, for the most part, ends when it ceases to be profitable: when pleasure conspires with profit it is naturally more durable. The friendships resulting from contraries resolve themselves into the principle of utility; as those between the poor and rich, the learned and ignorant; for a man is always ready to give something in exchange for that of which he stands in need. In the same class we may place, without much violence, the handsome and the ugly, the lover and the object of his affection. Wherefore some lovers justly incur ridicule when they expect to meet with a return of love similar to their own. Were their persons calculated to inspire a mutual passion, their expectation would be reasonable; but when they are the reverse, their pretensions are ridiculous. Perhaps contraries do not primarily affect each other, but both of them are fond of that intermediate condition which is preferable to either. Thus what is dry loves moisture, only that it may attain an intermediate state; and that which is warm affects cold, only that it may be reduced to a due temperature[e]. But such questions may be omitted, as beside the purpose of the present discourse.

Justice and friendship, as we already observed, seem to belong to the same persons, and to be conversant about the same objects. They are both found in every partnership or community,

BOOK VIII.

Chap. 9.

Of the relation which friendship bears to justice.

[e] See Analysis, p. 111, & seq.

BOOK VIII.

munity, even among those who sail in the same vessel, and those who fight under the same standard ; and in proportion to the closeness of the partnership or community, the more closely and intimately is the friendship cemented. The proverb says rightly, " that all things are common among friends ;" for friendship results from the community of goods, advantages, and pleasures ; it is most perfect among brothers and companions ; and in the same proportion as the ties of the partnership or connexion are loosened, and fewer things are common, the friendship becomes less intimate, and even the rules of justice seem less binding. It is a more heinous crime to rob our friends than our fellow-citizens, and our fellow-citizens than strangers. Not to succour a brother in distress is more odious than to refuse similar assistance to a stranger ; and to strike a father is the most atrocious of crimes. Friendship and justice thus march hand in hand, and the vigour of the one is followed by equal intensity in the other. But all other connexions and partnerships are but parts of the great partnership of political society, which utility first collected and still holds together. Public utility therefore is that chief and ultimate aim of which wise legislators never lose sight. To promote particular branches of this utility, all inferior associations are formed ; fleets sail, armies march ; their aim is wealth or victory ; to invade, conquer, and plunder ; to subdue provinces, and storm cities. Even the peaceful communities of tribes and wards, and those mirthful assemblies which meet to feast, to drink, and to dance, depend on the same principle ; for legislators have not merely present and temporary advantage in view, they look farther, to the permanent comfort and sure enjoyment of life, and therefore establish solemnities during which human industry may repose

repose from past labours, and prepare for future exertions, by which the gods are honoured, and the heart of man is gladdened. The ancient solemnities of this kind were held towards the end of autumn, the season of greatest leisure, when men having gathered in the earth's productions, might offer the first fruits to the gods. Political society, then, comprehends all other partnerships or associations; from the varieties of which the different kinds of friendship result.

BOOK VIII.

There are three just forms of government, each of which is liable to deviate into a corrupt form, which is a counterfeit resemblance of the former. The just forms are royalty, aristocracy, and what may be called timocracy, because all men enjoying a certain income are entitled to a share in the government. This last, most writers distinguish by the general name of polity, or a republic. It is the worst of all legal governments, as royalty is the best. Tyranny is the corrupt resemblance of royalty, for both forms are monarchical; but they differ most widely, a tyrant consulting only his own advantage, a king only that of his people; for the latter does not deserve the name, if he be not in all things pre-eminent, independent, and all-sufficient in himself; so that with him personal considerations being superfluous, he can have no other reasonable pursuit but that of the public good. If kings are not of this description, they might as well be chosen by lot. Tyrants, on the other hand, pursue only their own interest, and their government is the worst of all, since it stands in direct opposition to royalty, which is of all the best. As kings may be corrupted into tyrants, so aristocracies degenerate into oligarchies, through the corruption of the magistrates, who make an unjust distribution of honours and emoluments, of which they usurp and retain the greater

Chap. 10.

Of the different forms of government.

BOOK VIII.

greater part for themselves, accumulating enormous wealth as the instrument of exorbitant power, and continually narrowing, through selfishness, the basis of the government. Timocracy naturally degenerates into democracy, which is nearly akin to it; since whenever men of limited fortunes are entitled to share the government, power will have a natural tendency to fall into the hands of the people. Democracy therefore is a less deviation from what is called a republic, than tyranny is from royalty, or oligarchy from aristocracy; and in this particular circumstance, it is less depraved and odious than the other two vicious forms of government. Of political revolutions we find the resemblances, and, as it were, the patterns in what passes in families. The paternal authority is the model for that of kings, for children are their fathers' dearest concern. Whence Homer addresses Jupiter by the appellation of father, denoting the near affinity between royal and paternal power. But in Persia fathers are tyrants, treating their sons as slaves; and slaves are treated merely as best suits the interest of their masters. This may be agreeable to the nature and principles of servitude, but the Persian system, in extending these principles to children, is vitious in the extreme; for different descriptions of persons require different modes of governance. Domestic authority is the best model for aristocracy, for the authority of a husband is founded on the superiority of his abilities and his virtues. He exercises those functions which this superiority enables him best to perform, leaving to female care those offices which women are best qualified to fulfil; since if he usurped all management to himself, his equitable aristocracy would degenerate into an unlawful and rigid oligarchy. When women, being rich heiresses, acquire thereby more than their due share of of power, their authority alſo originates in an unjuſt oligarchical principle, ſince, in their prepoſterous pre-eminence, wealth is preferred to worth: the gifts of fortune, to the diſtinctions of nature. Timocracy reſembles the equal commonwealth of brothers, among whom there is no other diſtinction than that made by a ſlight difference of age; for when this difference is very great, brotherly friendſhip cannot eaſily ſubſiſt. Democracy reſembles thoſe families which are without a head; or in which all avail themſelves of the maſter's weakneſs, to aſſert equality, and to defy controul.

BOOK VIII.

Friendſhip, as well as juſtice, varies with the different forms of polity; ſince both ultimately depend on the different relations in which men ſtand to each other in ſociety. The relation of a king to his ſubjects, is that of a benefactor to thoſe benefited by his care. He provides for the welfare of his people, as a ſhepherd does for that of his flock: whence Homer calls Agamemnon the ſhepherd of the people. Of a ſimilar kind is the relation of a father to his children, but pre-eminent in the magnitude of benefits, ſince he is the cauſe of their exiſtence itſelf, which ſeems of the utmoſt moment, as well as of their education and nurture. A father is naturally a king in his own family; and the ſame holds with regard to more remote anceſtors and their deſcendants, the former of whom are entitled to honour from the latter, and therefore the friendſhip between them is not that of equals, but is modified by the natural and indelible ſuperiority of the one party to the other. The relation of huſband to wife is ſimilar to that which prevails in ariſtocracies between the magiſtrates and citizens. The honours and advantages belonging to the former, reſult from the ſuperiority of their abilities and virtues. The huſband's honour is

Chap. 11.

Of the variations thereby occaſioned in the nature and intenſity of friendſhip.

BOOK VIII.

pre-eminent not absolute, he has his duties as well as his rights; both parties have their allotted functions, namely, those which are best adapted to their respective characters. The relation of brothers is that of equal companions, resulting from the near similitude of their strength and stature, their common education, and similar manners. They resemble a republic, strictly so called, in which the citizens are treated justly, when they are all treated alike; and as they cannot all rule at once, the government is managed by rotation. Their justice consists in equality, and their friendship is that of equals. In corrupt governments there is little justice, and therefore but little friendship. Tyranny, which is the greatest corruption of all, scarcely admits of any friendship at all. Since there is nothing common between the sovereign and subject, there is not any room for justice, nor therefore for friendship. The relation of a tyrant to his subjects is that of an artist to an instrument, of the soul to the body, of a master to a slave. The interest and safety of all these subservient things are consulted by those who make use of them; but there cannot be any friendship nor any justice between living and inanimate objects, because they cannot enjoy any thing in common. Neither can men have friendships with horses, cattle, or slaves, considered merely as such; for a slave is a living instrument, and an instrument a lifeless slave. Yet considered as a man, a slave may be an object of friendship; for certain rights seem to belong to all those capable of participating in law and engagement. A slave then, considered as a man, may be treated justly or unjustly, and therefore may be a friend or an enemy. There is little friendship and little justice in tyrannies; but most of both in republics, because, among equals there are most common rights, and most common enjoyments.

Friendship,

Friendship, then, results from the community of rights and enjoyments among persons living in the same commonwealth, belonging to the same tribe or district, sailing in the same vessel; in which, and all similar cases, the parties seem mutually engaged to each other to maintain and uphold their reciprocal advantages. The friendship arising from hospitality is of the same nature; but that depending on propinquity in blood, or congeniality of character, may perhaps be referred to a different principle. Friendships between relations, though they branch out into many kinds, may be all traced to one source, namely, the affection between parents and children. Parents love their children as parts of themselves, and children love their parents as the source from which they spring. The love of the former is the strongest, because they better know their children for their own, than the children can know them for their parents; because the production more belongs to its author, than the author to his work; and because parents know and love their children for a longer time, that is, immediately from their birth, whereas children cannot begin to love their parents till they become capable of perception and intelligence. The love of parents for their children is merely an expansion of self-love, for they still regard their children as parts of themselves; but children have, in their own minds, a separate and independent personality, distinct from that of their parents, which they are inclined, however, to revere as the fountain of their blood. From the common relationship of brothers to the same father, they become mutually related to each other; wherefore they are said to come from the same blood, which flows in different streams, or from the same stock, which spreads into different branches. Their friendship is confirmed by nearness of age, sameness of education,

BOOK VIII.

Chap. 12.

Of friendships founded on propinquity of blood.

BOOK VIII.

education, and similarity of pursuits. They are companions as well as brothers, and therefore warmed with all that affection for each other, which confort and fociety is calculated to infpire. The connexion between other relations originates in the fame principle, and is more or lefs intimate in proportion to their proximity to the common fource. Children fhould love their parents as men do the gods, fince they are to them the authors of the greateft benefits; their life, nurture, and education; and the friendfhip between them, from their continual intercourfe of life, contains far more than any other, whatever is fweeteft and moft ufeful. Brothers, we have faid, are companions, whofe fellowfhip will be the more intimate, in proportion to the fimilarity of their virtuous characters and honourable purfuits, and to the confirmation which the affection of their early years derives from confidence approved by time and experience. The friendfhip between more diftant kinfmen depends on the fame circumftances, according to which it will either invigorate or decay. That between hufband and wife is moft ftrongly prompted and enforced by nature itfelf; for domeftic fociety is more natural than even the political; fince it is prior and more neceffary, being effential to the prefervation of the fpecies, and common to all kinds of animals. But with the inferior tribes, this fociety is limited by the fole end of reproduction; in man it extends to all the offices of life, which naturally divide themfelves between hufband and wife, each fupplying what their refpective qualities beft enable them to furnifh for the accommodation and comfort of the other. The induftry and excellencies of each are thus brought into the common ftock of domeftic happinefs, which their diftinctive virtues are calculated wonderfully to augment, fo that this kind of friendfhip

Between hufband and wife.

friendship is recommended and strengthened by every circumstance of pleasure as well as of utility. Their children too form a new and powerful tie, being a common good, in which they mutually share; and which has the strongest effect in binding them indissolubly together. The varieties of friendship thus depend on the various kinds of justice, which themselves result from the multiplied relations of men in civil society. For very different rights and very different duties have place between friends, strictly so called, and those who are partners in the same concern, companions in the same studies, or who are mere strangers the one to the other.

BOOK VIII.

There are then three kinds of friendship, each of which depends on a different principle, and in each of which the friendship may subsist either between equals, or between persons extremely unequal, not only as to their respective worth and dignity, but as to the relative importance of their friendship to each other. When the friendship subsists between equals, equal attentions and an equal degree of affection ought, as much as possible, to be aimed at; but when the pre-eminence is greatly on one side, the affection and attentions of the inferior ought to rise in the same proportion. The friendship founded on utility is that which is by far the most likely to produce between the parties mutual altercation, and often mutual reproach. When the connecting principle is virtue, friends are eager to benefit each other; the only rivalship between them is, who shall do to the other most good, and he who gains the victory in this amicable contest, is so far from creating ill-will in his friend, that he only provokes him to new works of kindness. Nor are mutual accusations frequent where the sole end of the friendship is pleasure. While this purpose is attained, the parties keep company

Chap. 13.

Disputes between friends, how they ought to be adjusted.

pany with each other; and when it is not, a mutual feparation is fo eafy, that complaint would be ridiculous. But when utility is the principle, refufals on one fide muft be as frequent as exactions on the other, and both parties will think they are ill treated, becaufe each expects more than his due. As law is either written or unwritten, fo friendfhip founded on utility is either legal or moral; the firft is where exact returns are fpecified, as if you give to me that, I will give to you this; or where the agreement is more liberal than merely from hand to hand, and allowing a fpace of time to be interpofed before the fervice performed on the one fide is requited by an equal fervice on the other. When friendly confidence is repofed by one party in the other, an action at law is not granted by fome nations, for the fulfilling even of conditions, the reality of which admits not of any uncertainty; for to them it feems equitable, that he who has imprudently trufted to the good faith of another, fhould not be entitled to correct by law the error of his own credulity. The moral friendfhip founded on utility takes place, where fomething is given, or fome fervice is rendered, without the fpecification of any thing, or any fervice to be given or done in return. Yet by the party who has conferred the benefit, an equal, or even more than equal return is on many occafions expected; and when this is not made, he complains of ill treatment. His complaint is occafioned by what occafions almoft all other complaints of breach of friendfhip, his unfteadinefs of principle, giving liberally, but craving like a niggard: affecting the praife of generofity in the firft part of the tranfaction, but fhewing in the laft that he is guided merely by intereft; for moft men, though they love what is honourable, prefer what is ufeful. It is honourable to do good without expecting a return; it is useful to have every good action requited with interest. Yet those who have received favours ought to requite them according to their ability, when such requital is desired by their benefactors, for no man's friendship can be obtained against his will; so that when we have met with an act of generous friendship, from one who afterwards appears not to entertain for us any friendly disposition, we ought doubtless, when able, to make a suitable return; when this return is not in our power, even the interested benefactor himself would not be so unreasonable as either to require or expect it. When favours are conferred, we must consider therefore, both the man and his motives, in order to determine whether they ought to be returned, and in what manner the return should be made. It is sometimes a matter of doubt by what standard this return should be measured, whether by the benefactor's good will, or by the advantage therefrom resulting to the person benefited. The latter is often inclined to extenuate his obligations, and to think the favours which he has received both slight in themselves, and such as many others would have been ready to bestow on him. The benefactor on the other hand, represents them as the greatest favours that he could possibly have done, such as none other would have conferred, and enhanced too by being bestowed in a moment of danger, or some other exigency. Since utility is the sole basis of such friendships, and of the actions proceeding from them, ought not the advantage accruing to the person obliged, to be regarded as the just standard of the obligation incurred, and of the return to be made? For *his* exigency required relief; a relief afforded to him in expectation of an equal return; and the assistance bestowed on the one hand is exactly measured by the

benefit

BOOK VIII.

benefit received on the other. His return therefore ought to be equal to this benefit, or greater, which will make his conduct laudable and honourable. In virtuous friendships there is not any room for such complaints. In them intentions, not consequences, form the standard of obligation; for, as we have often observed, the deliberate election of the will is the principle by which all questions concerning virtue and morals must be determined.

Chap. 14.

The same subject continued.

Unequal friendships are extremely productive of altercations and differences, each party desiring to have more than his due, which has a tendency to disturb, and finally dissolve concord. He who is pre-eminent in virtue and ability, claims a proportional share of regard and affection; thinking that men should always be considered suitably to their characters. In the same manner, he who is most useful, expects to be loved and regarded in proportion to his utility; saying, that friendship would be a burden if it were not returned on the one side proportionally to the benefits conferred on the other. They think that the same rule is applicable to friendship which holds in a partnership in trade, where he who employs most stock also receives most profit. The needy man holds a very different language, saying, that it is the duty of a friend to assist his friend in distress; and asking what benefit could otherwise result from the so much envied friendship of the good and great. Both parties are partly in the right, since both ought to have the advantage; the good and great in point of honour, the inferior and indigent in point of gain; for honour is the meed of beneficent virtue, and gain is the cure of distressing poverty. This rule obtains in states. Those who benefit the public, are honoured by the public, for honour is a public reward; but to

expect

expect from the public, both great honours and great gains is highly unreasonable; since the public would thereby submit to an inferiority of advantage in both points at once; a disgraceful inferiority which every individual would spurn. For reciprocal and proportional favours equalise and preserve friendship, the good and great benefiting their friends as to their characters or their fortunes, the needy inferior giving in return the only thing he can give, honour, and even of this not always a full proportion; since it is impossible sufficiently to honour the gods and our parents: but those are commended who do it to the best of their power; for the returns of friendship must be limited by possibility. Wherefore it is not allowable for a son to renounce his father, though the latter may renounce the former. For the son has to pay obligations, which are too great for him ever to discharge; he must always therefore remain a debtor. But the father, on the other hand, to whom the debt is due, may discard and abandon a worthless son, though he will seldom do it, but for excess of wickedness; since both paternal affection and natural humanity strongly oppose so cruel a measure [c].

[c] The subject of this and the following Book is less fully treated in the seven last chapters of the second book of the Magna Moralia; and in the thirteen first chapters of the seventh book of the Ethics to Eudemus.

ARISTOTLE's ETHICS.

BOOK IX.

ARGUMENT.

Friendship does not admit of precise rules.—Dissolution of friendship when justifiable.—Analogy between our duties to ourselves, and those to our friends.—Happiness of virtue.—Wretchedness of vice.—Good-will.—Concord.—Exquisite delight of virtuous friendship.

WHERE friends possess qualities totally dissimilar, and extremely different in value, their friendship, as we have said, must be equalised and maintained by a due observance of those rules of proportion which obtain in the commercial intercourse of society; where the shoemaker and weaver, and other artizans, exchange the productions of their several manufactures according to their respective values. That this might be done conveniently, the use of money was established, which served as a common measure, with which all other things were compared, and by which their relative worth was estimated. Lovers often accuse the objects of their affection, that they do not meet their warmth of love with equal ardour, when perhaps there is nothing in themselves that is at all lovely. The persons beloved, on the other hand, often accuse their admirers,

BOOK IX.
Chap. 1.

According to what rules the returns of friendship may be best estimated.

that they once made to them the most magnificent promises, but now totally deceive them. The origin of these complaints is, that the friendship of the one party is founded on pleasure; that of the other on utility: on delight which the one has no longer the power to excite, and benefit which the other has no longer the means to confer; so that as the causes of such friendships are variable and inconstant, the friendships themselves must be destitute of stability; which is the case with all others, except those subsisting between virtuous men in consequence of their congeniality of characters. Those who are friends through interest, not only are likely to disagree, when either of them ceases to meet with a return, but when the return is not such as he either wished or expected; for an improper return is considered as none at all. We have an example of this in him who promised a musician that he should be paid according to his performance, and being asked next day for the reward which he had promised, said that it had already been bestowed, since he had given one pleasure in return for another. But profit, not pleasure, was the return which the musician expected; for in order to obtain what they want, men willingly part with that which is either superfluous, or which they can most easily spare; which is the basis of all commercial intercourse. It is asked, who ought to ascertain the measure of the return, he who has performed the service, or he who has received it? The former seems to commit his interest to the discretion of the latter: as Protagoras is said to have done, for he desired his disciples to estimate the value of what they had learned, and to pay him accordingly. In such cases, some approve the rule, " clear bargains make sure friends." Those who receive payment in advance, and then perform nothing

worthy

worthy of the magnificence of their promises, are liable to the reproach of injustice; a reproach which perhaps the sophists necessarily incur, since unless they received their payment in advance, nobody would think their labours worthy of any pecuniary remuneration. In virtuous friendships, there is not any room for complaint, because each party desires only the heart and affections of his friend; and the only contention between them is, which shall be productive of most good to the other. Such is the friendship that ought to subsist between those who teach and those who study philosophy, the value of which cannot be appreciated in money; and to the teachers of which no adequate honours can be assigned. Their scholars must honour them as they do their parents and the gods; not sufficiently, for that is impossible; but in proportion to the extent of their ability; shewing to them all the respect they can, since they never can shew to them enough. In those friendships where certain and full returns are expected, it is desirable that they should prove satisfactory to both parties; but when this cannot take place, it seems just as well as necessary, that he who has received the favour should determine the return most proper to be made; because he is the best judge of the value of the advantage which he has received, and of the value of the pleasure which he has enjoyed. It is thus in those bargains where confidence is reposed by the one party in the other; for the fulfilment of which, the party disappointed is not entitled in some countries to any legal redress; his cause must stand or fall according to the good faith or dishonesty of him in whom he voluntarily confided. This rule is founded on the principle, that he who has received a favour is better qualified to ascertain its value, than he who conferred it: for men estimate too highly
the

BOOK IX.

the favours which they bestow, as they are apt to do all good things which proceed from themselves. The person first benefited decides therefore what return he should make, because he best knows the value of the benefit which he has received; but this benefit is perhaps more justly estimated by the value which he set on it, while it was still an object of his desire, than by that which he continues to set on it after it has been put into his possession.

Chap. 2.

That it is impossible to assign precise rules for the proper exercise of friendship.

A doubt may be started as to filial friendship, whether fathers ought in all things to be obeyed? In matters respecting health, ought a son to follow the advice of his father or his physician? In electing a general, ought he to prefer to him a person skilled in war? In the same manner it may be doubted, whether favours are best bestowed on friends, or on men of merit; and whether we ought to be grateful to our benefactors or liberal to our friends, when we have not the means of exercising both gratitude and liberality. All these questions are too indefinite to admit of such general solutions as may be practically useful; because there is not any one case exactly similar to another, but each is marked by circumstances peculiar to itself, and distinguishable in their degrees of magnitude, as well as of propriety or necessity. It is manifest in general, that all advantages ought not to be accumulated on any one individual, and that before we are liberal to our friends, our debts of gratitude ought to be discharged towards our benefactors. Yet this rule will not always hold, as in the case of a man ransomed from robbers, and whose ransomer, perhaps a person of no value, should afterwards stand in need of the same favour, or, at least, should demand back his money. In both cases, the man ransomed, if his own father happens also to be in captivity, will prefer ransoming foming his father, if his fortune does not enable him to acquit both obligations at once. Though it is said in general, therefore, that every kindness ought to meet with its due return, yet cases may be proposed in which generosity is, in point of propriety or necessity, a paramount duty even to gratitude itself. Sometimes the same favours, done by different persons, are of very different values; and the benefactor therefore has not always a right to expect a precisely similar return. When a bad man obliges a good one, or a knave lends money to a man of property and probity, the persons obliged may, with propriety, decline to return exactly similar favours; since those favours are, in different circumstances, of very different values. The knave by lending runs no risk of losing his money, but the honest man would run this risk by lending to a knave; nay, should he only suspect him of being either a knave or a spend-thrift, he will not act absurdly in refusing to return his favour in kind. It is evident therefore, as we have often observed, that all rules concerning the passions and actions of men are precise, only in proportion as the subjects to which they relate are definite. We ought not (to answer the question first started) to have deference, in all particulars, even to our fathers, since all kinds of sacrifices are not offered to Jupiter. Our parents, brethren, companions, and benefactors, are severally entitled to their respective marks of kindness and regard. This is sufficiently indicated by general practice; for relations, principally, are invited to assist at marriages and funerals, as things essentially interesting to the whole family, and all its branches. To provide for the subsistence of our parents, who are the causes of our being, is a duty as indispensable, and still more honourable, than even that of providing for our own. We ought to

honour

BOOK IX.

honour them too as we honour the gods; but each parent is entitled to diſtinctive marks of our reſpect, a reſpect different in kind from that beſtowed on perſons unrelated to us, but eminently conſpicuous for their abilities or virtues. Our ſeniors, in proportion to their years, ought to be treated with more or leſs deference. With companions, familiarity and full freedom of ſpeech is allowable; with kinſmen, neighbours, fellow-citizens, in a word, with every deſcription of perſons with whom we are connected, it is incumbent on us to behave ſuitably to the relations of affinity or utility in which thoſe perſons ſtand to ourſelves, as well as to their own perſonal merit and inherent virtues. When the relations between others and ourſelves are ſtrong and intimate, the rules of our behaviour towards them are more eaſily defined; the ſtrict limits of our duty are with more difficulty aſcertained towards perſons remotely and faintly connected with us. Yet we muſt not be deterred by this difficulty from inveſtigating thoſe rules of conduct which will enable us to behave towards all men with propriety.

Chap. 3.

Juſtifiable grounds for the diſſolution of friendſhips.

Doubts are ſtarted concerning the diſſolution of friendſhip between perſons whoſe characters no longer remain the ſame, or at leaſt no longer continue to bear the ſame relation to each other. Where friendſhips are contracted for the ſake of pleaſure or utility, it is not wonderful that when neither utility accrues to the one party, nor pleaſure to the other, ſuch friendſhips ſhould of courſe be ſubverted; for the foundations are deſtroyed on which only they ſtood. But a man may juſtly complain of bad faith in him who affected to cheriſh his character and his virtues, while intereſt or pleaſure were at bottom the ſole grounds of his regard; for differences between friends chiefly proceed from this, that they think their friendſhip

founded

founded on one principle, when it is really founded on another. When therefore a man is deceived, and thinks without reason that he is loved for his character and his virtues, he has himself only to complain of; but he may complain of the duplicity of his pretended friend, when the hypocrisy of the latter is the source of his own mistake; and he may complain of him more justly than men do of coiners and clippers, since he is defrauded by him in an object more valuable than money. But when our friend changes his manners, and contracts by evil communication a depravity of character, ought we still to regard him with affection? Or, is it impossible to love that which ceases to be amiable? "Like," we have said, "draws to like;" and a good man neither can nor ought to love a bad one. Are we then instantly to renounce and forsake him? Not unless he has unalterably renounced and forsaken his character; for while he is not totally incorrigible, it is our duty to endeavour to reform his morals, a thing incomparably more important than alleviating his pecuniary distress, and also more peculiarly the work of friendship. To detach ourselves entirely from a friend who becomes worthless, has nothing in it unreasonable; since he is not in fact the same man with whom we contracted the friendship; and when we find that there is not any hope of his ever again becoming such, we naturally wish to have done with him. But what shall we say when one of the friends remains what he was, and the other changes for the better. Can their friendship continue to subsist? Or is this also impossible? The question will be best answered by proposing a case where the difference is great in the extreme. Of two persons who are friends in their early years, the one may remain a child in understanding through life, and the other may become a man of the most distinguished abilities. What friendship can subsist between such different characters, who can neither take any pleasure in each other's society, nor have any occupations and pursuits in common? As all congeniality of mind is at end between them, their friendship, it should seem, must cease. Yet will the superior, if he is a man of humanity, treat the friend of his youth very differently from what he would do an absolute stranger. The remembrance of his early affection will still cling to his heart; and he will never entirely abandon an ancient attachment, unless on account of extreme worthlessness in him who was its object.

Chap. 4.

The analogy between the duties which we owe to ourselves, and those which we owe to our friends.

The duties which we owe to our friends, seem analogous to those which each individual willingly pays to himself. We ought, it is said, to wish their good, or what appears to us to be such, and to promote it to our best ability, merely on their own account. With this kind of disinterested affection, mothers are animated towards their children, and those friends towards each other, between whom some disgust has arisen which, though it interrupts their intercourse, does not destroy their mutual kindness. Others say that friends must spend much of their time together, have the same inclinations and pursuits, and sympathise with each other in their joy as well as in their sorrow. On whichever or how many soever of those conditions friendship principally depends, we shall find that all of them belong to the affections by which a good man is animated towards himself; and by which all men are animated in proportion as they either approximate, or only think they approximate, to an honourable and praiseworthy character; which, in questions concerning human nature, is justly considered as the sole unerring standard. The virtuous man only is at peace within himself,

The happiness of virtue.

himself, since all the powers of his mind are actuated by the same motives, and conspire to the same end: always aiming at good, real and intrinsic, the good of his intellectual part. To him existence is a benefit, which he earnestly wishes may be preserved, especially the existence of the thinking principle within him, which is peculiarly himself; for every individual strives after its own good, real or apparent; which in the virtuous man only coincide: but could an individual love its change into something quite different from itself, the good of the latter would be to the former a matter of slight concern. In Deity all goods are accumulated, because he is ever and invariably that which he is; and in man the thinking principle is the part that is properly and permanently himself. He who pursues the good of his mind, is pleased in his own company, being delighted with the recollection of the past, as well as animated with the prospect of the future; and having ever at command innumerable speculations, in which he exercises himself with the most exquisite pleasure. Both his joys and his sorrows are respectively consistent with themselves, since they invariably proceed from fixed and regular causes; for he does not delight at one time in what will excite his repentance at another; and thus harmonized within his own breast, he is similarly affected towards his friend, whom he considers as a second self; and his sympathy for whom, when it reaches the highest perfection, resembles that internal concord which is experienced in his own mind, when the various principles of his nature coalesce into one movement, and flow in the same homogeneous stream of virtuous energy. Yet many men of very irregular lives seem to be highly satisfied with themselves. Is this because they mistake their own characters? It should seem so, since the

BOOK IX.

The wretchedness of vice.

BOOK IX.

the complete villain is always visibly at variance with himself; and all others are similarly affected in proportion to their progress in wickedness; willing one thing, yet desiring and preferring another; as those who allow themselves to be subdued by vicious pleasure, and who may be said, with their eyes open, to rush into voluntary destruction. In the same manner others, through laziness or cowardice, avoid that conduct which they know most likely to promote their happiness. When men proceed to the last stage of depravity, they become as odious to themselves as they are detestable to others, and therefore often destroy their own lives; and even before they arrive at this deplorable condition, they fly from, and avoid themselves; preferring any kind of society to that of their own reflections; the past crimes which haunt their memory, and the meditated guilt which is continually occurring to their fancy. As they have nothing in them that is amiable, they cannot be the objects of their own love. Neither their joys nor their sorrows are consistent. Their whole soul is in sedition, distracted between contending principles, the pleasure of one giving pain to another; and when the worst principle prevails, a foundation is laid for the bitterest remorse. If such be the wretchedness of wickedness, how strenuously ought we to exert ourselves to become good men, that we may live in friendship with ourselves, and be worthy of the friendship of others.

Chap. 5.
Of good-will.

Good-will resembles friendship, but is not the same thing. Good-will we may entertain for those not personally known to us, and without being ourselves conscious of it. This cannot happen with regard to friendship, as we formerly observed. Besides every act of friendship implies an affection and expansion of the soul, it is also much connected with custom;

whereas mere good-will arises suddenly, as towards the combatants in the public games, to one or other of whom we immediately wish well, though we would not make any great exertion in order to promote his victory. Good-will, then, is but a sudden and superficial emotion; and at best but an element of friendship, as the first element or beginning of love is the pleasure received by the eye; without which, though the passion of love cannot commence, yet that pleasure does not by any means constitute this passion, to which it is necessary that we should not only delight in the object when present, but exceedingly long for it when absent. Speaking metaphorically, we may call good-will an incipient and indolent friendship; which, through time and custom, naturally improves into friendship strictly so called; not that founded on pleasure or utility, which have but little to do with good-will, since he who has received a favour ought in justice to return it; and he who does a kindness in expectation of meeting with a greater, has good-will only to himself. Good-will, in one word, is always excited by some laudable quality, such as generosity, or courage: witness the manner in which we are affected by the prize-fighters, abovementioned.

Friendship implies concord, which is not merely agreement in opinion. This latter may prevail among persons totally unknown to each other; and what connection has friendship with sameness of opinion concerning the heavenly motions, and other such subjects? Concord prevails among cities and commonwealths, when they conceive the same designs to be conducive to the common interest, and agree in the same measures for promoting them. It relates therefore to practical subjects only, and those of a certain magnitude in themselves, and bearing

BOOK IX.

Chap. 6.

Of that kind of concord which friendship implies.

BOOK IX.

ing an important relation to the parties concerned; for example, that the magistracies should be elective; that an alliance should be made with the Lacedæmonians; that Pittacus should be archon, when he himself is willing to discharge that honourable office [s]. When each party wishes the same thing for himself, then dissension ensues, because the factions in the state, though they agree in the object, yet differ as to the person. But genuine concord requires that each party and each individual should obtain his wish; as when both the people and the better sort agree in choosing virtuous men for their magistrates. This concord is, as we have said, the basis of political friendship. It is conversant about matters essentially useful to the comfortable subsistence of men in society; and can only be found among men of virtue, who being firm in their purposes, and not variable like the Euripus, are alone qualified to maintain the relations of concord and amity with themselves and others. As justice and utility have long regulated their private behaviour, they carry the same principles along with them into their public administration. But neither concord nor friendship can durably subsist among dishonest men, who will be continually striving to engross every advantage, and to shift off every burden; and who must soon fall into sedition by their endeavours to compel others to comply with those rules of justice which they themselves disdain to practice.

Chap. 7.
Why there is more love in those who confer bene-

How comes it that men love those to whom they have done good, better than these love their benefactors? Most are of opinion that this happens because debtors are more concerned about the safety of their creditors, than the creditors are about theirs,

---

[s] Diogenes Laertius, l. i. seq. 75. tells us, that Pittacus laid down the archonship after he had held it ten years; to which transaction Aristotle seems here to allude.

theirs, and that merely from motives of interest; which Epicharmus [b], perhaps, would say, is judging of mankind by the worst examples among them. The accusation, however, is certainly too just, for with regard to the services which they have received, the greater part are of weak memories, and more willing to receive benefits than inclined either to confer or to return them. Yet the question just started must be solved on deeper principles than those of debtor and creditor, which imply nothing of love or friendship, but depend entirely on dull considerations of interest. Those to whom we have done good, are objects of our love and affection, though they neither return, nor should ever be expected to return, the obligation: for we are naturally disposed towards them as artists are towards their works; and particularly poets towards their poems; which they love as parents do their children; that is, much more than their productions, were they endowed with life and perception, would love them. For each individual loves every excellence proceeding from himself in proportion as he desires and loves his own existence, the energies of which are concentrated and preserved in his works. Besides, our own good actions are more pleasing subjects of reflection, than any past benefits that we may have received: for the first are honourable, and the second only useful; and utility, however delightful in prospect, is often forgotten with the occasion which required it; whereas honour is permanent and unalterable; and every praise-worthy deed is not only pleasing in prospect, but delightful on remembrance, above all most transporting when actually exercised; giving

BOOK IX.

fits than in those who receive them.

---

[b] A disciple of Pythagoras, who seems to have had better principles of morality, than he is said to have entertained of religion. Vid. Cicer. de Natur. Deorum, l. i. and Menag. ad Diogen. Laert. l. iii. sect. 9. & seq.

giving to us a consciousness of that kind of existence which is most peculiarly agreeable to our nature, the happiness of which results not from passive sensations, but from active exertions. Besides, whatever is obtained with much labour, is naturally regarded with much affection. Those who have acquired their fortunes, delight in them far more than those who succeed to hereditary wealth; and for a similar reason, maternal tenderness often rises to the highest pitch. On such principles we may explain why the affection of those who confer benefits, which is commonly a work of some exertion, should be stronger than that of those who receive them, which requires no exertion at all.

Chap. 8.

Of the different senses in which a man is said to love himself.

It is doubted which we ought to love most, ourselves or our friends. Selfishness is branded as a vice of the blackest die, and thought to sink deeper into each individual, in exact proportion to the worthlessness of his character. A bad man has nothing but himself in view; while a good one loses sight of himself, and aims chiefly at friendly or honourable actions; and this the more in proportion to his progress in virtue. Yet these observations ill accord with what is commonly said, that a friend wishes to promote our good for our own sakes, and though we should ever remain ignorant of his good offices; which is surely the disposition of each individual towards himself, and comformable to this disposition are all the other circumstances, and all the proverbial expressions by which friendship is indicated and ascertained; as that friends have but one soul, that all things are common between them, that friendship is equality, and that the knee is nearer than the foot. But a man stands in all those relations to himself, and being most his own friend, ought most to love himself. These contradictions

cannot

cannot be reconciled but by distinguishing the different senses in which a man is said to love himself. Those who reproach self-love as a vice, consider it only as it appears in worldlings and voluptuaries, who arrogate to themselves more than their due share of wealth, power, or pleasure. Such things are to the multitude, the objects of earnest concern and eager contention, because the multitude regards them as prizes of the highest value; and in endeavouring to attain them, strives to gratify its passion at the expence of its reason. This kind of self-love, which belongs to the contemptible multitude, is doubtless obnoxious to blame; and in this acceptation, the word is usually taken. But should a man assume a pre-eminence in exercising justice, temperance, and other virtues, though such a man has really more true self-love than the multitude, yet nobody would impute this affection to him for a crime. Yet he takes to himself the fairest and greatest of all goods, and those the most acceptable to the ruling principle in his nature, which is properly himself, in the same manner as the sovereignty in every community is that which most properly constitutes the state. He is said, also, to have, or not to have, the command of himself, just as this principle bears sway, or as it is subject to control; and those acts are considered as most voluntary which proceed from this legislative and sovereign power. Whoever cherishes and gratifies this ruling part of his nature, is strictly and peculiarly a lover of himself, but in a quite different sense from that in which self-love is regarded as a matter of reproach; for all men approve and praise an affection calculated to produce the greatest private and the greatest public happiness; whereas they disapprove and blame the vulgar kind of self-love as often hurtful to others, and always ruinous to those who indulge it. A bad

Self-love, well understood, wherein it consists.

BOOK IX.

bad man, we have said, is really at variance with himself; pursuing a conduct directly opposite to what his own duty and his own interest most powerfully recommend. But the man of morals obeys and follows the dictates of his intellect; and every intellect, when free and uncircumscribed, necessarily prefers and pursues its own individual good. The virtuous man indeed strenuously exerts himself in the cause of his friends and his country; and readily lays down his life for their sake. He willingly resigns honours and emoluments; but firmly defends the first share of generosity and probity. The transports of one glorious day, he would not exchange for a whole life of listless insignificance; one year spent in honourable exertion, he prefers to ages vulgarly and casually consumed; nay, a single effort of splendid virtue is more valuable in his eyes than an indefinite series of small and ordinary actions; and, on such principles, he is ready to lay down his life in the cause of his friends or country. He is ready also to employ his fortune in their service; so that, while they are enriched at his expence, he may acquire an unrivalled share of well-merited applause. As to offices and honours he is similarly affected, easily relinquishing them all; nay, even the fame of illustrious actions, when it appears to him more praise-worthy, to give an opportunity to others of performing them, than to effect them by his own agency. Thus, amidst all his liberalities, he is still most selfish, since he still claims for himself what is incomparably most valuable, that internal delight arising from the consciousness of merit.

Chap. 9.

Whether friendship be the greatest good in prosperity or in adversity.

It is disputed whether or not happy men need friends. Happiness seems all-sufficient in itself without such auxiliaries; whence they say,

" When Fortune's goods abound, what boots a friend ?"

Yet

ARISTOTLE's ETHICS.

BOOK IX.

Yet on the other hand, it appears abfurd, if happinefs includes all good things, to deprive it of friendfhip, which of external goods is the greateft. Befides, if friendfhip, as we above proved, confifts rather in conferring favours, than in receiving them, and it is honourable to do good to thofe who are peculiarly recommended to our love in preference to all others, profperous and happy men muft ftand in need of fit objects, towards whom they may exercife their beneficence. It is difputed, therefore, in which of the two ftates men require friends the moft, the ftate of profperity, or that of adverfity; the former needing favourites as much as the latter does benefactors. It is alfo abfurd to think that happinefs can be enjoyed in folitude; man being a focial and political animal by the conftitution of his nature itfelf; without conforming to which, human happinefs cannot be attained; nor fo completely attained in cafual or indifferent fociety, as in that of amiable and virtuous friends. What is the meaning then of the obfervation firft made, or by what arguments can it be juftified? The people regard only thofe as their friends who promote their utility, and friends of this kind a profperous man does not need; nor does he feem greatly to need thofe who may adminifter to his pleafure, fince his life being delightful in itfelf, he has not much occafion for adventitious enjoyment. Thofe two claffes of friends being excluded as unneceffary, it is too haftily inferred that he needs not any friends at all. For we faid in the beginning, that happinefs is energy, that is, a thing confifting in our own exertions, not refulting from our acquirements or poffeffions; and the life of a good man confifts in a feries of virtuous and delightful energies, which will be far more unbroken and uninterrupted, if he contemplates them not only in himfelf,

The exquifite pleafure of virtuous friendfhip.

BOOK IX.

himself, but in those who are around him, whose behaviour he is able to view more attentively and more steadily than he can possibly do his own[i]. Friends of this description, therefore, he requires, that he may sympathize with their sentiments, and participate in their actions; for a good man is charmed with good actions more than a skilful musician with the finest melody; and as the latter is provoked by diffonance, so is the former grieved by depravity. Besides, as Theognis[k] says, virtuous friends exercise, improve, and perfect each other. But if we examine the matter more deeply, we shall find that one good man is naturally an object ultimately desirable to another; for a good man delights in what is naturally delightful, and values what is really and absolutely valuable; and as the life of animals consists barely in sensation, but that of man both in sensation and intellection, and that not merely in the capacities but principally in the exercise of those powers, for the sake of which the capacities are given to us, it is plain that the more widely we extend the sphere of our energies, our happiness will be the more complete; provided those energies be, like every thing that is good, definite in their nature, not variable and undetermined, like the lives of bad men, which appear under innumerable forms of wretchedness. But neither such lives, nor those overwhelmed by an accumulation of pains and sorrows, (of which we shall speak hereafter,) are calculated to make us rightly

---

[i] ωσπερ ει οταν βλεψαι και ι αυτον τοι προσωπον ιδειν, εις τοι κατοπτρου εμβλεψαντες ιδωμεν, ομοιως; και οταν αυτοι αυτους γνωθωμεν γινεται εις τον φιλον ιδοντες γνωρισαιμεν αι, &c. " As when we wish to see our own countenances, we must view it in a looking-glass; in the same manner when we wish to know our own characters and virtues, we must contemplate those of our friend; for a friend, as we say, is another self." Magn. Moral. l. ii. c. xv. p. 194.

[k] The gnomic poet of Megara, some of whose sententious verses are still preserved.

rightly appreciate the value of existence, which to wife and good men is an object so truly desirable. For when we see or hear, we are conscious of those perceptions; and when we think and theorize, we are conscious of those intellections; and the higher and nobler our thoughts are, the more pleasure we derive from the consciousness of entertaining them. This consciousness makes us feel the pleasure of existence; for the energy of life itself, which is of all things most delightful, consists in nothing else but perceiving and thinking. But a good man, being affected towards his friend nearly as towards himself, derives therefore the highest gratification from communicating his thoughts and reflections with others like himself, and living with them in a perpetual participation of intellectual and moral enjoyments; since he thereby attains nearly as clear a perception of their pleasurable existence as he has of his own. This indeed is human society properly so called, in contradistinction to that of cattle, which consists in feeding at the same stall. Since then his own life is, to a good man, a thing naturally sweet and ultimately desirable, for a similar reason is the life of his friend agreeable to him, and delightful merely on its own account, and without reference to any object beyond it; and to live without friends is to be destitute of a good, unconditional, absolute, and ultimately desirable; and therefore to be deprived of one of the most solid and most substantial of all human enjoyments.

Ought this reasoning to make us desirous of multiplying the number of our friends? Or ought we to adopt as to friendship what seems to be well said with regard to hospitality,

"For many guests are often worse than none."

BOOK IX.

Chap. 10.

Different kinds of friendship require different limitations as to number.

In

BOOK IX.

In the same manner ought the number of our friends to be limited? Of friends chosen from motives of utility or convenience, it undoubtedly ought; for more than serve our purpose, are only obstacles and hindrances; and it is impossible for us to return the services or civilities of too numerous a list. Neither need those chosen from motives of pleasure to be many; for too much seasoning is pernicious in diet. But as to friendships strictly so called, originating in sympathy of minds and congeniality of characters, ought there to be defined limits, beyond which that number ought not to extend; any more than the populousness of a city, which, for the supply of mutual wants, requires more than ten, but, for the sake of wise regulation and good morals, ought not perhaps to exceed ten myriads of inhabitants? The number of friends, even virtuous friends, must be limited by the extent of human activity, which is incapable of cultivating beyond a certain proportion, who must all likewise be friends to each other, on the supposition, which is necessary, that they should spend their time together in amicable concord. This cannot easily happen to a great multitude, especially since such is the instability of human affairs, that we cannot cordially sympathize with many persons at once, for if we ought to rejoice with one, it will too often happen that we ought to grieve with another. Many friends, therefore, are neither to be desired nor expected, and their number will be the smaller in proportion to the closeness of the intimacy; for intimate friendship is almost as exclusive as love, which admits but one only object. Experience justifies this observation, for the friendships most celebrated have subsisted between two only. In political life we see popular men, who seem to have

innu-

innumerable friends. They are often flatterers of the multitude. But a public character without flattery may, by his real worth, recommend himself to the gratitude of many who are his friends politically. But friends, strictly so called, cannot be numerous. Happy is the man who finds only a few such!

Whether are friends most desirable in prosperity or in adversity? Both conditions of life peculiarly require them; the prosperous, that they may have objects towards whom to exercise their beneficence; the unfortunate, that they may have sources from which they may derive relief. The necessity for friends is greatest in the latter, who therefore seek persons who may be useful to them; but the lustre of friendship shines most conspicuous in the former, who seek persons with whom they may spend their time agreeably, and whom it is a real pleasure to benefit. The company of friends is delightful both in prosperity and adversity. In the latter, our grief is alleviated by their sympathy; whether it be that they disburden us of part of our sufferings, or that their sympathy is itself delightful. Both causes seem to concur, for in misfortune the presence of a friend affords a mixed pleasure. The very sight of him cheers our minds; and if he has any dexterity, he knows how to administer to us that kind of comfort of which our tempers and characters are most susceptible. Besides, we ourselves, in his presence, endeavour to moderate our sorrow, that we may not be the cause of suffering to our friend; and persons of firm minds are careful how they impart their secret misfortunes, and reject all excess of commiseration as unsuitable to the dignity of their characters; whereas women, and womanish men, delight in echoing groans and sympathetic lamentations. In all things the best

BOOK IX. best characters are the fit models for imitation; and as amidst prosperity the best men delight in the presence and congratulation of their friends, which is agreeable to the benevolence of their nature, we ought therefore to be forward in calling those who love us to participate in our joy, but very backward in calling them to participate in our sorrow; remembering

" Their own misfortunes are enough to bear."

Above all, we must summon their presence when, without giving much trouble to ourselves, we may greatly benefit *them*. But, on the other hand, to act with laudable propriety, we must go readily and uninvited to the house of mourning; for it is as honourable as delightful to assist our friends in distress, especially without any solicitation on their part, which might lessen them in our esteem. It is our duty strenuously to co-operate with fortune in promoting the prosperity of our friend; but to be slow and modest in craving his assistance; yet without too fastidiously rejecting his beneficence; which has sometimes made a breach in very solid friendships.

Chap. 12.
Conclusion.

As love enters first by the eye, so friendship is produced by the habitual intercourse of life; and as the sense of sight is that which lovers would be most unwilling to lose, so habitual intercourse is the advantage which friends would be most unwilling to resign. Friendship is a community of enjoyments; and as a man delights in the energies of his own existence, so he also does in those of his friend; wherefore, in whatever those energies principally consist, their chief enjoyment results from exerting them in company; some drinking and playing dice together, while others make parties of hunting, practise their exercises, or cultivate philosophy. The friendship of bad men is as corrupt and unstable as themselves; and is so far from being advantageous to either party, that it tends only to plunge them both still deeper in depravity and wretchedness: whereas virtuous friendships grow continually more firm and more intimate, the example and admonitions of good men mutually improving and perfecting each other[1]. Thus much concerning friendship. It remains that we should next treat of pleasure.

BOOK IX.

[1] Aristotle quotes a few words from Theognis which have this meaning.

# ARISTOTLE's ETHICS.

BOOK X.

INTRODUCTION.

THIS Book treats of pleasure and happiness. It is too concise to admit of abridgment, and sufficiently perspicuous not to require elucidation. In the concluding chapter, Aristotle shews the inseparable connection between Ethics and Politics; and prepares the reader for an easy transition from the former to the latter. By way of conclusion to these short introductions, I shall observe, that Aristotle's Moral Philosophy is, perhaps, of all others the least liable to the following objection, which has been often made by thinking men to the too fashionable philosophy of the times: " A professed sceptic can be guided by nothing but his present passions; and to be masters of his philosophy, we need not his books or advice, for every child is capable of the same thing without any study at all."—GRAY.

BOOK X.

ARGUMENT.

Pleasure — Its ambiguous nature — Defined. — Happiness — Intellectual — Moral — Compared. — Education. — Laws. — Transition to the subject of Politics.

WE proceed to treat of pleasure, a thing most congenial to our nature; and by which, therefore, and its opposite, pain, the motions of the minds of children are guided as by a rudder. In morals the main point is attained, when our love and hatred, our grief and joy, are respectively excited by natural and worthy causes; since these affections are as extensive as the multiplied affairs of life itself, and their proper regulation is of the utmost importance to virtue and happiness. For we are all prompted by nature to pursue pleasure, and to avoid pain; the consideration of which ought not to be omitted in a treatise of this kind, especially as the opinions concerning them are perplexed by much contradiction; some regarding pleasure as the highest good, others calling it a thing contemptible in the extreme, whether from the real conviction of their minds, (which perhaps may be the case with some,) or because they think it best to speak of pleasure in terms of reproach, since most men are tempted to disgrace themselves by indulging in it immoderately. Severe moralists, therefore, think that they cannot too much stigmatise pleasure, that those whom they wish to benefit

BOOK X.
Chap. 1.
The love of pleasure.

ARISTOTLE's ETHICS.

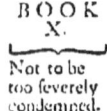

BOOK X.

Not to be too severely condemned.

benefit by their discourses may be deterred from excess, and confined within the bounds of propriety. They should take care however, lest this proceeding be not attended with effects contrary to their expectation; for in practical matters, men pay less attention to what is said than to what is done; and when opinions, just and reasonable within certain limits, are carried to a length manifestly inconsistent with experience, they are rejected disdainfully and completely; even the truth which they contain being overwhelmed and lost in the surrounding falsehood. Thus those detractors of pleasure, when they are observed on any occasion to pursue it with much eagerness, appear to the bulk of mankind no better than hypocritical voluptuaries; for the people at large are not capable of making distinctions; they consider things in the gross, and therefore continually confound them. The truth, therefore, best serves not only to enlighten our understandings, but to improve our morals. For when our doctrines are true, our lives will more naturally be conformable to them; and our precepts being confirmed by examples, will produce conviction, and excite emulation of our virtues, in those with whom we live. But enough on this subject: we proceed to enumerate the opinions held concerning pleasure.

Chap. 2.

Different opinions concerning it.

Eudoxus[a] thought pleasure the chief good, because he perceived it to be universally desired by all animals, rational and irrational; that every thing is good in the same proportion as it is desirable: that animals find out, each tribe, what is best for themselves, as they do their proper food; and that therefore the

---

[a] Eudoxus of Cnidus τυτον αιτι Ευδοξυ Ευδοξον ικαλυν δια την λαμπροτητα της φημης. See his life in Laertius, B. viii. sect. 86, &c. By a pun on his name, he was called "Illustrious."

the supreme good must consist in that which is universally and 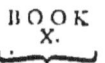 most eagerly desired by them all. The regularity of his life added great weight to his arguments, for he was a man of singular temperance; so that his commendation of pleasure did not appear to proceed from any prejudice in its favour, but rather to be extorted from him by the force of truth. His argument he confirmed by considering pain; which, being the contrary to pleasure, all animals endeavoured to shun and escape.. That is chiefly desirable, he remarked, which is desirable ultimately and on its own account. This description peculiarly applies to pleasure, which no one desires for the sake of any thing beyond itself, nor finds the necessity of assigning any reason why he should enjoy it; pleasure always carrying its own recommendation along with it, and rendering every object, however valuable, to which it is joined, still more desirable, not excepting virtue itself. As pleasure improves every other good with which it is combined, it is manifestly a good in itself; a good not inferior to that which it heightens. Yet Plato employed a similar argument to prove that pleasure was not the supreme good; since pleasure, joined with virtue, is better than alone and separate; which cannot happen to the supreme good, a thing incapable of augmentation, and disdaining admixture. But what is that good or happiness which mankind, by the constitution of their nature, are best qualified for enjoying? This only is the question with which we are concerned in the present treatise. Those who deny that which all desire, to be a part of this happiness, should take care lest they fall into an absurdity. For *that* we say is truth, which to all appears such; and he who is dissatisfied with this kind of proof will not easily meet with a better. If only creatures

void

BOOK X.

void of understanding pursued pleasure, much might be plausibly urged against it: but what shall we say, when we find it an object of desire with the best and wisest of the human race? Nay even irrational animals may afford perhaps a strong argument in favour of it, since in pursuit of what is best for their nature, they are actuated by a wisdom far superior to their own[b]. The argument drawn from pain, which is the opposite to pleasure, seems not liable to the objection made to it. The objectors say, that though pain be an evil, this is not any proof that pleasure, its contrary, is a good; because both contraries are often bad, and the good is often something intermediate between them. But this observation, though true in many cases, is not applicable to the present. For if both were evils, both would be objects of aversion; but the one, we see, is universally pursued as a good, and the other universally shunned as an evil.

Chap. 3.

The ambiguous nature of pleasure.

It forms not any objection to pleasure, that it is not one of those indelible qualities by which things are characterised and distinguished; for neither to the class of qualities can the energies and operations of virtue itself, which are so highly and so justly praised, in strict philosophical language, be ascribed: no, nor happiness itself, which is of all things most valuable. It is farther objected, that pleasure is of a vague indefinite nature, admitting of various degrees of intensity; whereas whatever is truly good, ought to be uniformly perceived, and accurately defined[c]. But justice, fortitude, and the other virtues admit of various degrees, when considered as attributes of the persons in whom those habits exist; the same is true of health; yet the health of the mind, as well as that of the body, considered abstractedly

[b] See Analysis, p. 114. and Conf. p. 134. & seq.   [c] See Analysis, p. 112.

abstractedly in themselves, are things sufficiently definite, though they do not, in each individual, reach that state of perfection which properly constitutes their nature [b]. The same thing may possibly hold with regard to pleasure. It is further objected, that pleasure is motion; and that all motions are imperfect, since they are only tendencies to certain ends [c]; whereas whatever is absolutely good, ought to be complete and perfect in itself, independently of any separate purpose for which it may serve. But, that pleasure is motion, is not likely to be true; for all motion admits of slowness and celerity; since the motion of the universe itself, though it cannot be called swift or slow, abstractedly considered, yet deserves the former of those epithets when compared with the peculiar motions which belong respectively to its parts [d]. But pleasure is not characterised by either of these qualities. We may indeed be speedily pleased, as we are speedily made angry; and as walking, growing, or any other motion, is performed with celerity, in the same manner, we may rapidly change from a state of indifference or pain, to a state of pleasure; but to the energy of pleasure itself, that is, to pleasure actually enjoyed, the epithets of swift or slow do not apply. This energy is complete in itself in every instant; and is not perfected by the accomplishment of any distinct and separate end, in which it terminates. It is therefore a thing totally different from generation or production, or motion of any kind; since all of these are mere changes of material substances, passing from one place, or one state, to another; not indeed at random, but according to certain and fixed laws of motion and rest, generation and corruption; so that from the

same

[b] See Analysis, p. 117.   [c] Ibid. p. 119.   [d] Ibid. p. 120. & seq.

BOOK X.

same materials out of which any compound is generated, into the same, that compound is, by corruption, dissolved [a]. If pleasure then be generation, pain must be corruption; and that which is generated by pleasure, must by pain be dissolved into the same materials from which it was produced. But to speak thus of pleasure and pain, is to talk unintelligibly; and to confound immaterial with material things. It is said also, that pain consists in natural deficiencies or wants, and that pleasure is nothing else but the supplying of these wants. But deficiency and fulness are plainly affections of body; and if pleasure is the supply of corporeal deficiencies, that which receives the supply ought to feel the pleasure, which therefore resides in the body; a conclusion resulting from the premises, but highly unreasonable. Pleasure, therefore, is not the supply of bodily wants, though it accompanies this supply; as pain, on the contrary, accompanies the laceration or maiming of the body. The opinion seems to have arisen from considering the pain of hunger, and the pleasure of feeding; the latter of which must always be preceded by the former. But all pleasures are not preceded by pain; those, for instance, of the intellectual kind; and even those of the senses of smelling, hearing, and seeing; besides innumerable enjoyments, resulting from pleasing recollections, as well as from agreeable and animating hopes. Of what deficiencies can such pleasures be the supply, since previously to their existence in us, there was not any thing defective? With regard to gross and reproachable pleasures, which our adversaries may cite in proof of their erroneous theory, the very name of pleasures may, with propriety, be denied to them; since they are acknowledged as such only by men of corrupt minds

---

[a] Analysis, p. 107. & seq.

minds and perverse sentiments. Persons diseased are not fit judges of the relish of wholesome food; nor is that white, which appears such to those afflicted with an ophthalmy. It may be observed also, that pleasure is not desirable, unless it proceed from an honourable, at least an innocent source; any more than wealth is a good, when too dearly purchased by dishonesty. Different pleasures are adapted to different characters. Just men only know the pleasure of justice; as those only who have an ear for music, enjoy the pleasure of melody; the same differences are observable in other particulars. The very dissimilar gratifications which we derive from friends and flatterers show, that either pleasure is not in itself desirable, or that there must be pleasures specifically different from each other. A friend aims at promoting our good, a flatterer aims only at giving us pleasure; and the behaviour of the one is as universally and as justly praised, as that of the other is universally and justly condemned. None worthy of the name of a man, would choose to have the understanding of a child, that he might spend his life happily in childish amusements; nor would he submit to do base actions, whatever pleasure he might derive from them, and though assured that they should never afterwards be followed by pain or punishment. But, on the other hand, he would desire most earnestly to have the use of his eye-sight, of his memory, and of his understanding, as well as to be endowed and adorned with virtuous habits, although no pleasure whatever resulted from the exercise of those capacities or powers. That this exercise is necessarily accompanied with pleasure makes not any difference, since it is an object of desire on its own account, and independently of the delight which necessarily attends it. It seems plain, therefore, that pleasure

BOOK X.

Chap. 4.

Pleasure consists in exercising the proper energies of our nature, which it improves and perfects.

pleasure is not the supreme good, nor that all kinds of pleasures are desirable; and that whether or no pleasures are desirable ultimately, and on their own account, depends on the source from whence they spring. Such are the opinions held concerning pleasure and pain.

But what pleasure is in reality, and under what class of things it ought to be arranged, will more fully appear from the following induction. The act of seeing is perfect in every instant of time, needing nothing to give to it the specific completion and fulness of which its nature is susceptible. Such also is pleasure, a whole, perfect in each instant, and not more perfect than at the first instant, how long soever it may be enjoyed. Pleasure therefore is not motion, because all motion co-exists with a certain portion of time; and tends to a certain end, in which it terminates, being, from its very nature, imperfect; because, as soon as the end is effected, the motion by which it was attained ceases to exist[1]. Thus of the art of building, the end is a house; and until the house is made, the building is imperfect; but when the house is built, the action or motion by which it was produced ceases to exist: and the parts of that action or motion are, until the whole is finished, each different from another, and each imperfect in itself; as rearing the walls, chamfering the pillars, building the dome; all of which, as well as laying the foundation and adding the ornaments, are but parts of one action, which, taken together, constitute a whole, when the work is completed. The same holds, with regard to that kind of motion which consists in change of place, and its various modes, namely, walking, jumping, flying, and others of that sort; each of which consists of imperfect parts, specifically

[1] Analysis, p. 117. & seq.

fically different from each other, and from the whole collectively. Thus, in the Olympic race, a different part of the stadium is run over in each particle of time, till the goal is attained; and as each part is different from another, so must the motions performed in them be all different; nay, though the same part be run over, yet if the racer proceed, in the one case, from the starting-post to the goal, and in the other, from the goal to the starting-post, a difference in the motions must arise from the difference in their directions. But concerning motion, we have treated accurately in another work[g]. Pleasure is manifestly a thing quite different; since it is complete in each *indivisible now*, that is, in each instant; not requiring for its perfection any the smallest portion of time: but motion, as we have elsewhere proved, cannot exist without time or succession. In the same manner, the act of vision, a point, and an unit, are things which have not any connection with generation, nor any kind of motion; every modification of which must belong to things not essentially wholes, but partible; and to them only. Of this kind is pleasure, essentially a whole, since essentially perfect; accompanying the operation of each percipient with regard to the perceptible object, when both the perceiving power is properly constituted, and the perceptible object the fairest and the best on which that specific act of perception can possibly be exercised[h]. To say that the perceiving power exercises its energies, or the substance in which that power resides, makes not any difference as to the present subject. Pleasure accompanies every act of perception by sense in a higher or lower degree, in proportion to the prevalence of the conditions above stated; and also every act of reasoning or intelligence.

But

[g] Analysis, p. 119 & seq. [h] Ibid. p. 51. & seq.

BOOK X.

But as the physician and the medicines which he prescribes, are in different senses the causes of health, so our percipient powers are enlivened and perfected in a different manner by the proper objects of those powers, and by the pleasure attending our perception of them. Each sense has its appropriate pleasure: the eye is delighted by sights; the ear by sounds; and in proportion to the soundness and vigour of the sense itself, as well as the beauty and excellence of the object on which it is exercised, the pleasure will be the greater; but pleasure there always must be, wherever the agent and the object are naturally adapted to each other. Pleasure does not perfect our energising powers as a pre-acquired habit, but rather as a supervenient end; in the same manner as beauty accompanies the flower of youth. The powers of man are not capable of unceasing activity, and therefore our pleasures cannot be continuous, for they are inseparably connected with our energies. Things which delight when new, often cease to give pleasure, and that because our attention is no longer roused by their presence, nor the energies of our mind called forth in contemplating them. They are disregarded as an old and familiar show; and in proportion to the weakness of our exertions, our pleasure is blunted. It may be suspected that all love pleasure, because all are fond of life, which consists in exercising the energies of our nature. Life then is energy, which each individual exercises on those subjects in which he most delights; the musician, on melodies; the mathematician, on theorems; and others, on other subjects. Pleasure therefore is naturally desirable, because it perfects our energies, that is our life, in the continuance of which all delight. But whether life is desired for the sake of pleasure, or pleasure for the sake of life, needs not at present be examined; since

since these two seem so intimately combined as not to admit of separation. Pleasure, then, cannot exist without energy; and our energies are strengthened and perfected by the pleasures accompanying them.

BOOK X.

It seems to follow from these observations, that as energies or actions widely differ from each other, so must also the pleasures by which they are perfected. This holds in the several operations both of nature and of art, the different kinds of which respectively terminate in different and appropriate ends; namely, animals, plants, pictures, statues, houses, and furniture. The action of the senses, or what is called perception by sense, manifestly differs from the action of the understanding; and the pleasures respectively accompanying those operations, bear a near affinity to the operations which they respectively accompany; for each operation or energy is encreased, improved, and perfected by a pleasure that is a-kin to it. Thus the exertions of the geometer, the musician, and the architect, are enlivened and invigorated by the delight which they take in their respective pursuits; and the cultivators of those sciences thereby improve themselves gradually, until they attain the most consummate skill, and most decided pre-eminence. But pleasures, on the other hand, which are not a-kin to the operations which they accompany, are so far from improving and perfecting them, that, on the contrary, they weaken and obstruct them. Thus, those who are agreeably employed in reading or study, cannot, if they are lovers of music, persevere in applying to their books and meditations, should they happen to hear at a distance an agreeable melody; for the two pleasures not being a-kin, the stronger overpowers the weaker. Wherefore, when we are much delighted with one thing, we cannot attend to any

Chap. 5.

BOOK X.

any other. At a well acted play the mind is fixed in delightful transport, but when the stage players are bad, many spectators amuse themselves with sweetmeats[1]. Pleasures not a-kin to the operations which they accompany, have the same effect (though they produce it differently) with congenial pains; for these also have a tendency to weaken and destroy our energies. Thus, those to whom it is painful to write or to reason, have little inclination to do either, and commonly do them incorrectly. Of operations and the pleasures accompanying them, some are laudable and respectable; others are blameable and contemptible. The former are to be pursued, and the latter to be avoided. Pleasures are more a-kin to energies, than even the desires which precede them; for these desires are easily distinguishable from the energies which they prompt, both in their own nature and in point of time; whereas pleasures and energies are so difficultly separated even in thought, that many suppose them to be one and the same thing. They are indeed intimately connected; but as energies both of sense and intellect are often not only unpleasant but painful, it is absurd to think that pleasure and energy are the same, though the former cannot subsist without the latter. But it is of more importance to observe that the nature and qualities of our pleasures depend entirely on the nature and qualities of our energies. In this manner the pleasures of the sight differ in purity from those of the touch; and the pleasures of the ear from those of the palate; while the intellect affords pleasures totally dissimilar to any resulting from the senses. As each animal is endowed with peculiar energies, each having his appropriate work to effect, and his assigned task to perform, so each species is destined for the enjoyment of congenial and kindred pleasures; those of a man

---

[1] Aristotle says, " they do so most when the players are bad."

man differing specifically from the pleasures of the horse or the dog, the animals with which he is most familiar. As Heraclitus says, an ass would prefer straw to gold, loving food more than money. But among individuals of the same species it might be expected that the same effects should follow from the same causes; and that there should be a complete community of pleasures as well as of pains. Yet in the human race we find the thing far otherwise; one loving what another most detests, and that giving pain to one, which affords the most exquisite pleasure to another. This however need not appear extraordinary, if we consider that the same food has a very different relish to a man in health, and to another in disease; and that the warmth agreeable to persons of weak constitutions, is unpleasant to those of a firmer temperament. Innumerable other examples to the same purpose will occur; with regard to all which, we affirm *that* only to be right, which appears so to persons rightly formed and properly constituted. Virtue therefore, and the man of virtue as such, is the only natural and correct standard; and those only are true enjoyments, with which he is delighted. That the pursuits which *he* rejects and spurns, should to others afford gratification, is not to be wondered at, since human nature is liable to corruptions and depravities of many kinds; and each corrupt individual will delight in pleasures akin to the specific depravity under which he labours[1]; which are pleasures indeed to him, but to none besides. But the question is, what are the pleasures of a man in his natural and most perfect state? That they are inseparably connected with his energies, we have above proved; so that if

[1] —— Mala mentis Gaudia. VIRG. vi. 73.

if there be peculiar works to be performed by a man, and peculiar tasks assigned to him, his proper and natural pleasures must consist in the operations by which his work is done, and his task accomplished. Other pleasures are only secondary, and separated by a wide interval.

Chap. 6.

Of happiness;

Having examined the nature of virtue, friendship, and pleasure, it remains to speak of happiness, the end, as we observed, of all human pursuits. Our discourse will be rendered more concise by resuming some conclusions already stated. Happiness, we said, consists, not in mere capacity unroused, or in mere habit unexercised; for were that the case, it might belong to a man who should remain for ever asleep, living the life of a plant, or involved in the greatest calamities; since a man thus circumstanced might be endowed with the noblest capacities, and most excellent and most honourable habits. Happiness, then, must be classed with operations or energies, some of which, as we already remarked, are necessary for the attainment of farther and distinct ends, and others are desirable merely on their own account; with which last, happiness is, manifestly, to be numbered. Energies terminating in themselves, and desirable merely on their own account, include all the amiable and laudable actions which proceed from confirmed habits of virtue; they appear also to include those innocent amusements which are sought so entirely for their own sake, that men often pursue them to the prejudice of their health or fortune. In such amusements it is common for the wealthy and powerful to place the principal enjoyment of life, and persons most dexterous in promoting them are not unfrequently the highest in esteem with princes; since they are the best qualified for supplying them with those gratifications, of which they have the strongest relish.

relish. In such amusements the vulgar, too, are apt to place happiness, because they see them pursued as such by those who, in the gifts of fortune, are greatly their superiors. But neither the vulgar nor the great ought to serve for models. Virtue, intellect, ardent feelings of the heart, and exalted energies of the mind, are not appendages of greatness; and though men invested with power, but incapable of tasting genuine and liberal pleasure, often seek delight in gross gratifications of sense, this affords not any proof that such delusive pursuits are entitled to a just preference. Children think all things inferior in value to their own childish amusements; and as different objects please men and children, so good and bad men might be expected to have very different delights; but, as we have often said, those things only are truly valuable and truly delightful, which are recognized as such by men of virtuous habits; for, as our habits are, such will be our pleasures and our pursuits. Happiness, then, cannot consist in mere recreative pastime; for it is absurd to think that all our serious exertions and strenuous labours should terminate in so frivolous an end [k]. We do not labour that we may be idle; but, as Anacharsis justly said, we are idle that we may labour with more effect; that is, we have recourse to sports and amusements as refreshing cordials after contentious exertions, that having reposed in such diversions for a while, we may recommence our labours with encreased vigour [l]. The weakness of human nature requires frequent remissions of energy; but these rests and pauses are only the better to prepare us for enjoying the pleasures of activity. The amusements of life

[k] Neque enim ita generati à natura sumus, ut ad ludum et jocum facti esse videamur. Cicero de Offic. l. i. c. 29.

[l] Ludo autem et joco, uti illo quidem licet; sed sicut somno et quietibus cæteris. Ibid.

life therefore are but preludes to its bufinefs, the place of which they cannot poffibly fupply; and its happinefs, becaufe its bufinefs, confifts in the exercife of thofe virtuous energies, which conftitute the worth and dignity of our nature. Inferior pleafures may be enjoyed by the fool and the flave, as completely as by the hero or the fage. But who will afcribe the happinefs of a man to him, who, by his character and condition, is difqualified for manly purfuits?

If happinefs confifts in virtuous energies, the greateft human happinefs muft confift in the exercife of the greateft virtue in man; which muft be the virtue or perfection of his beft part, whether this be intellect, or whatever principle it be, that is deftined to command and bear fway; having knowledge of things beautiful and divine, as being either divine itfelf, or at leaft that principle in us which moft approximates to divinity. The greateft human happinefs, then, is theoretic and intellectual; which well accords with the properties which we formerly found, by inveftigation, to be effentially inherent in that moft coveted object. The intellect is the beft principle in man; its energies are the ftrongeft, and the objects about which it is converfant are far the moft fublime. The energies of intellect are alfo the longeft and moft continuous, fince we can perfevere in theorifing and thinking much longer than in performing any action whatever. Pleafure, it was obferved, muft be an ingredient in happinefs; but contemplative wifdom offers pleafures the moft admirable in purity and ftability, and the pleafures of knowledge continually encreafe in proportion to our improvement in it; certainty concerning the fublimeft truths affording ftill higher delight in proportion to the intenfe efforts of intellect by which they were difcovered. That all-fufficiency, which we remarked as a property of happinefs, belongs to intellectual energies

energies more than to any other; for though the sage, as well as the moralist or the patriot, stands in need of bodily accommodations, yet in exerting his highest excellencies, he is not like them dependant on fortune, both for his objects and his instruments; for objects towards whom he may exercise his virtues, and instruments which may enable him to effectuate his ends. Even unassisted and alone, though perhaps better with assistants, he can still think and theorize; possessing in the energies of his own mind, the purest and most independant enjoyments. These enjoyments are valuable peculiarly on their own account, since they terminate completely in themselves; whereas all practical virtue has, beside the practice itself, some distinct and separate end in view. The tranquillity of leisure is naturally more agreeable than the bustle of business; we toil for the sake of quiet, and make war for the sake of peace. But the practical virtues are most conspicuously exercised in political and military functions, the latter of which none but the most savage and sanguinary minds would submit to from choice, converting friends into enemies for the mere pleasure of fighting with them. Politics, too, forms an operose and troublesome occupation, which would not be undertaken from the sole love of exercising political functions, independently of distinct and separate ends; power, wealth, and honour; in one word, prosperity to ourselves, friends, or fellow-citizens. But intellectual energies are complete and perfect in themselves, supplying an exhaustless stream of pure and perennial pleasure, which in its turn invigorates and enlivens the energies, and thus encreases and refines the source from which it unceasingly springs; all-sufficient, peaceful, and permanent, as far as is compatible with the condition of humanity. Were unalterable permanency

BOOK X.

added

added to such a life, its happiness would be more than human; but even within a limited term, its inestimable delights may be enjoyed by those who attain the perfection of their age and faculties; living not merely as partners with a frail and compound nature, but according to the simple and divine principle within them, whose energies and virtues as far transcend all others, as the intellectual substance in which they reside excels all other substances of which our frame is composed [m]. We ought not, therefore, according to the vulgar exhortation, though mortal, to regard only mortal things; but as far as possible, to put on immortality, exerting ourselves to taste the joys of the intellectual life. This is living according to the best part of what we call ourselves, which, though seemingly small in bulk, is incomparably greater in power and in value than all things besides [n]. The intellect indeed is the best and sovereign part of our constitution, and therefore strictly and properly ourselves. It is absurd therefore to prefer any other life to our own. What was above observed will apply here. The pleasure and good of each individual must consist in that which is most congenial to his nature [o]. The intellectual life, therefore, must be the best and happiest for man; since the intellect is that which is peculiarly himself.

Chap. 8. and moral.

The moral life follows next, both in fitness and in dignity; for the practice of justice, fortitude, and other virtues, are highly

---

[m] Analysis, p. 50. & seq. [n] Ibid.

[o] In the third chapter of the third book of the Topics, p. 209, there is an excellent practical rule for distinguishing real goods from those merely of opinion, και ιι το μεν δι' ἑαυτο, το δι, δια την δοξαν αιρετοι· οιον υγιεια καλλως, ὁρος δι τω, προς δοξαν, το, μηδενος συνειδοτος, μη αν σπουδασαι ὑπαρχιιν. Things desirable in themselves are to be preferred to those which are desired merely on account of the opinion entertained of them, as health to beauty; but we may know what those things are that are good merely in opinion, by the following test, "they are those about which we would not give ourselves much trouble, if no person were to know that we possessed them."

highly suitable to the nature of man, and essentially requisite in social intercourse, that mutual wants may be supplied, and mutual duties may be performed; that individual passions may be regulated with propriety, and rendered as ornamental to those affected by them, as beneficial to the public. Moral virtue, then, is intimately connected with the passions and affections, many of which have their origin in the body; and, on the other hand, it is equally connected with the intellectual virtue of prudence; since the first principles of this practical wisdom originate in good moral habits; and those habits only are good which prudence justifies and approves. The moral virtues, therefore, are essential to the well-being of our compound nature; but the virtues and happiness of the intellect are, like the intellect itself, separate and independent: thus much only I shall say concerning it, for to treat more accurately of our intellectual part, belongs not to the subject of the present discourse. The happiness resulting from its energies, requires but few external advantages; fewer by far than are requisite for the exercise of political or moral virtues. The sage indeed, as well as the patriot, must be furnished with the necessaries of life; and although the labours of the latter have more connection with the body and its wants, yet this circumstance need not make any great difference in their personal accommodations; but it will make a difference of the greatest magnitude as to the exercise of their respective energies. For the man of liberality must be furnished with the means of beneficence; and the man of probity or equity, with the means of making, for received favours, fair and reasonable returns; mere intentions are obscure and doubtful; and being often pretended, can only be clearly ascertained when carried into effect. In the same manner,

BOOK X.

Pre-eminence of the former proved.

manner, fortitude shines most conspicuously when armed with power to repel dangers; and temperance displays its brightest charms, amidst temptations to voluptuousness. The vulgar controversy, whether virtue consists principally in action or intention, proves that both are requisite to its completion. But actions are dependent on external circumstances; and the greater and more illustrious they are, they require, for their performance, the greater number of instruments and auxiliaries. Speculation, on the other hand, is far less operose; it would be rather obstructed than benefited by a cumbersome apparatus of externals; which, how useful soever they may be for the display of practical virtue, are not at all essential to the exercise of intellectual energy. That the latter composes the best and firmest portion of human felicity may appear also from this, that it is difficult to conceive in what operation or energy besides, the felicity of the gods, whom universal consent acknowledges most happy, can possibly consist. In the exercise of justice? It would be ridiculous to suppose those celestial beings employed in making bargains, restoring deposits, or in performing any other actions about which the virtue of justice is conversant. There is, if possible, still less room among them for courage. Can it redound to their glory, that they encounter dangers manfully? Liberality cannot be ascribed to them, unless we suppose, absurdly, that they make use of money, or something equivalent. The praise of temperance is beneath those who have not any unruly appetites to restrain. Were we to go through the whole catalogue of the moral virtues, we should find that they are conversant about actions totally unworthy of the grandeur and sublimity of the gods. Yet we all believe those glorious beings to live exercising the energies

The exercise of intellectual energy the best and firmest portion of human happiness.

energies of their nature, not sleeping like Endymion. After what manner, then, can they be employed? Not in practical virtue, far less in productive industry. It remains therefore that they live an intellectual life; which, as essentially belonging to the gods, must be pre-eminent in happiness; a happiness pure and permanent, to which the life of man, in proportion as it is intellectual, will more nearly approximate; and of which inferior animals, as they are destitute of the divine principle of intellect, can never in any degree partake. Happiness is not an accessory to the energy of thought. It is connected with it substantially and indivisibly; a rich stream, unalterably flowing from an inexhaustible spring. The sage indeed requires bodily health and bodily accommodations; but the measure of his external advantages needs not be large; for superfluity will neither assist his own exertions, nor sharpen his judgment concerning the performances of others. To display the beauty and gracefulness even of moral virtue, it is not necessary for him to be master of the sea and of the land. A mediocrity of circumstances is sufficient for the exhibition of moral excellencies; which is evident from this, that they appear more frequently in private persons than in those invested with power. This mediocrity, therefore, as it contributes most to virtue, is most conducive to happiness. Solon well delineated the condition of those whose happiness he admired, saying, " that they had enjoyed a moderate proportion of the goods of fortune, performed most illustrious actions, and lived correctly and soberly[o]." Anaxagoras seems not to have thought happiness an attribute of wealth or power, when he said[p], that it would not surprise him,

---

[o] See History of Ancient Greece, v. i. c. vii. p. 305 and 306.

[p] In the Ethics to Eudemus, l. i. c. iv. p. 197. the circumstance here alluded to is

BOOK X.

him, should he be deemed a very absurd personage by the multitude; who judge, and who are capable of judging, only by externals. The opinions of wise men are likely to be conformable to reason; but in practical matters, experience alone can afford conviction; and those opinions only are to be approved, which the lives of those who hold them, confirm. There is still a farther reason why those who most cultivate their intellectual powers should also be most happy; for such persons not only attain the best temper of mind, and the highest perfection of their own nature, but they are also the most pleasing in the sight of the Divinity. If the gods (as they appear to do) concern themselves about human affairs, it is reasonable to conclude that they should most delight in the energies of intellect, which are the best, and highest, and most congenial to their own; and that they should remunerate and reward those who love and honour those exercises and occupations which they themselves hold dear; and who, in preferring and adorning the intellectual part, act rightly and honourably [q].

Having

more fully explained. "Anaxagoras of Clazomené, being asked who most deserved the epithet of happy? answered, not such men as you would imagine, but, on the contrary, such persons as to you would appear egregious fools. He probably answered thus, because he perceived him with whom he was conversing incapable of appreciating happiness by any other standard than that of mere externals, power, wealth, beauty, &c. whereas he himself thought *that* man the happiest who lived exempt from pain or perturbation, practising justice, and cultivating his understanding."

[q] The highest energy of intellect consists in contemplating the Divinity; and when any inferior principle in man, through its rebellion and irregularity, restrains him from thus meditating on and worshipping God, that principle is destructive of human happiness. Eudem. l. vii. c. ult.

Having thus delineated virtue, friendship, and pleasure, ought we to consider our undertaking as now finished? Or ought we rather to consider, as has been already said, that in practical matters, practice, and not theory, is the main object; and that, independently of good actions, the mere speculative knowledge of virtue is not of any avail. The important question then is, how men may be rendered virtuous? If moral discourses sufficed for this purpose, they could not be purchased, as Theognis says, at too high a price. But the influence of such lessons extends only over the liberal minds of ingenuous and well-disciplined youths, who may thereby be retained within the paths of honour and duty: they are too feeble to controul the multitude, whose wickedness is to be restrained, not through the dread of shame, but through the fear of punishment; since the many, being enslaved by their appetites, make it the business of their lives to pursue sensual pleasures, and to avoid bodily pains; having no taste nor perception of refined and laudable enjoyments. What eloquence can persuade, what words can transform men thus brutified? It is impossible, at least hardly possible, for reasoning to extract the evils which custom has riveted; and when all favourable circumstances concur, the felicity of those is still worthy of envy, who, through the combined energy of conspiring causes, are retained and confirmed in the practice of virtue. This inestimable possession, some ascribe to the bounty of nature; others think that that they have acquired it by custom; and a third class acknowledge themselves indebted for it to instruction. The virtue bestowed by nature evidently depends not on our own exertions; it is given by a certain divine disposal, to those

BOOK X.

Of laws.

whose lot is surely beyond that of all other men most fortunate. Instruction and reasoning will not succeed, unless the mind is previously wrought on by custom, as a field is ploughed and prepared for receiving and nourishing the good seed: for those who are not habituated to love what is amiable, and to detest what is odious, would neither listen to, nor understand, exhortations to virtue; because their affections lead them not beyond the pursuit of course animal gratifications, the unrestrained appetite for which is of too stubborn a nature to yield to mere reason; and which, when no contrary passion intervenes, can be checked only by force. Before virtue therefore can be acquired, affections congenial to it must be implanted; the love of beauty and excellence, the hatred of baseness and deformity; which preparatory discipline cannot take place, except in those states which are governed by good laws; for a life of soberness and self-command is irksome to the multitude, and peculiarly unpleasing to the headstrong impetuosity of youthful passions, which must therefore be bridled by the authority of law; that what is painful by nature, may become pleasant through custom. The superintending aid of discipline ought not to be confined to children, but must extend to adolescence and manhood; the greater proportion of human kind remaining through life rather slaves to necessity, than subjects of reason; and more susceptible of the fear of punishment, than sensible to the charms of moral excellence. Legislators, therefore, it is said, ought to employ admonitions and chastisements, as well as punishments that are final; admonitions, for those whose character and morals render them open to conviction; chastisements, for those whose immoderate and beastly passion for

selfish

selfish pleasures must be subdued and corrected by coarse bodily pains; (the pains inflicted on them standing as nearly as possible in direct opposition to the pleasures which they unlawfully pursued;) and total extermination, or perpetual banishment, for the extreme evils of incurable profligacy and incorrigible villany. Since then the condition of the greater proportion of mankind is such, that to be kept within the bounds of propriety and virtue, they require not only the benefits of early institution, but the watchfulness of perpetual discipline through life, good laws become essentially necessary for upholding this discipline by their coercive authority. The influence of fathers over their children is too feeble for that purpose; or indeed the influence of any individuals not invested with public authority. Law has a compulsive and necessary force, since it is acknowledged as the commanding voice of prudence and reason; and its power is not invidious, like that of men, who are apt to offend us, when they oppose, even most justly, our favourite propensities. In Lacedæmon, the legislator, with the assistance of a few friends, established a regular plan of public education and moral discipline; things neglected in the greater part of states, where men, in these particulars, live like the Cyclops:

> By whom no statutes and no rights are known,
> No council held, no monarch fills the throne;
> Each rules his race, his neighbour not his care,
> Heedless of others, to his own severe.
>
> Iliad ix. v. 127, & seq.

A public education, when good, is doubtless preferable to a private one; but what is omitted by the public, individuals ought, as far as possible, to supply; instructing and benefiting their

BOOK X.

their children and friends; which task they will be the better qualified to perform, if they are acquainted with those principles of legislation from which public happiness flows; for the same principles that operate conspicuously on nations, will also have their due weight within a narrow domestic sphere, especially since the ties of blood, and the remembrance of benefits, will recommend paternal examples, and enforce paternal admonitions. Private education enjoys this peculiar advantage, that it may be adapted to the disposition and character of each individual. Besides this, physicians who have few patients, and masters of exercises who have few scholars, are most likely to be attentive to those intrusted to their care. But their power of being useful to them depends on their skill in their respective professions; and although some, from experience merely, without science, may learn to be good physicians to themselves, while they are incapable of curing any besides, yet it is always most desirable, whether it be our business to benefit one or many, to instruct one or many, that we should understand those general theorems from which the particular rules of practice flow. A teacher of morality therefore ought to be acquainted with the science of legislation, that he may apply to the improvement of individuals the same maxims which have been found beneficial to communities. But how is this science to be acquired? It seems to be a branch of politics, and ought therefore to be learned from statesmen. Yet do not statesmen differ from physicians, painters, and all those employed in other liberal arts, or other learned professions, in this important particular, that all the rest not only exercise but teach their respective vocations? whereas statesmen are

The science of legislation, how to be acquired.

never

never the teachers of politics, nor are the teachers of politics often employed in affairs of state. The sophists who profess politics, take not any share in the public administration; and the statesmen, who administer public affairs, do not profess politics; they neither give lectures on the subject, nor write treatises concerning it; although this employment would be more useful and more dignified than that of polishing their pleadings and embellishing their speeches. Neither do they transmit their political knowledge to their children and friends, which they certainly would, if they were able, since they could not bequeath to them a nobler present, nor one more beneficial to their country. It is plain, therefore, that the knowledge of statesmen is a matter, not of science, (which always may be taught,) but of experience merely; and this experience, which is sufficient to form politicians, must be essentially necessary to those who would understand politics as a science. The sophists who pretend to teach this science, deviate widely from the mark. They neither know what is the nature of politics, nor what are its objects; otherwise they could not regard it as a subordinate branch of rhetoric, nor think it an easy matter to copy good laws from one state, that may be safely adopted by another[r]; as if it were not a work of the utmost delicacy, and requiring much reach of thought, and much experience, to adapt laws and institutions to occasions and exigencies, and to change and vary them according to each variation of circumstance. In music and painting, the vulgar of mankind are contented with perceiving the effect, which is the only thing of which

---

[r] How strongly applicable is this remark to the sophists of the present day!

BOOK X.

Transition to the treatise on "Politics."

they are judges; but persons skilled in those elegant arts must understand how this effect is produced, what colours kindly blend, and what sounds sweetly harmonize. Laws are productions or works of political art; an art which, being practical, cannot, any more than the art of physic, be learned merely from books; for though medical books not only contain recipes or prescriptions, but accurately distinguishing different habits and different maladies, distinctly point out how each separately is to be treated and cured, yet all these observations cannot be of the smallest use to men totally destitute of experience in the healing art. The same holds with regard to treatises on the subject of politics, which cannot be of much value to those who have not learned by their own observation to appreciate and apply them. An aptitude and readiness for acquiring knowledge, books, doubtless, may communicate and augment; but real practical knowledge cannot possibly be acquired without the aid of experience. As our predecessors, therefore, have left the science of legislation unfinished, it may be proper here to examine it, as well as to treat the subject of politics in general, that the philosophy which bears a reference to the affairs of human life may be perfected to the best of our ability. We shall first collect what appears to us judiciously written by others on particular branches of the subject. We shall, then, from a wide survey of commonwealths and governments, endeavour to explain the means through which those political edifices in general, and the different kinds of them in particular, are preserved or subverted; as well as to unfold the causes which render some constitutions worthy of applause, and others liable to censure. The result of our speculations will enable us to determine which is the best form of government; and what are the different regulations respectively best adapted to each particular constitution [a].

[a] The method here laid down by Aristotle agrees not precisely, either with that followed by the editors of his Politics in Greek, or with the arrangement which, for the sake of perspicuity, I thought fit to give to my translation.

In the act of finishing this first volume, I was much pleased to read the following passage in an excellent discourse lately delivered before the University of Cambridge: " Aristotle's Nicomachean Ethics afford not only the most perfect specimen of scientific morality, but exhibit also the powers of the most compact and best constructed system which the human intellect ever produced upon any subject; enlivening occasionally great severity of method, and strict precision of terms, by the sublimest, though soberest, splendour of diction. If moral philosophy, I mean specifically and properly so called, is to be studied as a science, in such sources it is to be sought. Thence will be formed a manly intellectual vigour, an ingenuous modesty and dignity of habit, an energy of thought and diction, and a reach of comprehensive knowledge, which distinguishes the true English scholar. On the contrary, it is to be feared that the feeble speculation which almost all modern systems of morality encourage, and the superficial information they afford, superseding the necessity of all active and real employment of the faculties, have operated more fatally upon the mental habits of the rising generation than total ignorance could possibly have done." See " Benevolence exclusively an Evangelical Virtue," p. 19, & seq. by Thomas Rennell, D. D. late Fellow of King's College, Cambridge.

INDEX.

A

Abstraction defined, page 57.
Accident improperly substituted for adjunct or appendage, 65.
Acroatic philosophy, 19. Highly prized by Alexander, 20. Lectures, 25.
Actions different from motions, 133. Human, consist in operation or production, 149. Voluntary, involuntary, and mixed, 196, & seqq.
Air, analysis thereof, 103.
Alexander, his munificence to Aristotle, 13. His character, 17. His love of learning, 23. His saying of the Celts, 212.
Analytics, First, design thereof, 77. Second, design thereof, *ibid.*
Anaxagoras, his doctrine of the omœomeria, 100. Of mind, 101. His opinion of happiness, 402.
Anaximenes maintained air to be the first principle, 99. Grounds of his opinion, *ibid.*
Andronicus of Rhodes, arranges and corrects Aristotle's writings, 36.
Anger, its connection with courage, 215.
Animals, history of them, 125, & seq.
Apellicon of Athens, purchases Aristotle's writings, 35.
Apprehension, quickness of, 298.
Archytas the Peripatetic, 59. Confounded by Mr. Harris with Archytas the Pythagorean, *ibid.*
Aristotle, when born, 4. His birth-place, *ibid.* His parentage, 6. Education at Atarneus, 7. At Athens, *ibid.* Literary industry, *ibid.* Want of ambition, 8. Person and supposed foibles, 8. Gratitude to Plato, 9, & seqq. Leaves Athens in consequence of Plato's death, 10. His residence with Hermeias, *ibid.* Revisits Atarneus, 11. His escape from thence, and flight to Lesbos, 14. Marries Pythias, *ibid.* Invited by Philip to Macedon, 15. Undertakes the office of Alexander's preceptor, *ibid.* Honors bestowed on him by Philip, 16. Held in admiration by Alexander, *ibid.* His success in the education of Alexander, *ibid.* His dignified behaviour at the court of Pella, *ibid.* His taste for poetry, 22. His plan of life in Athens, 25. Calumnies against him refuted, 27. Their origin, 28. His accusation, 29. Retreat to Chalcis, 31. His testament, 32. His death, 33. His sayings, *ibid.* His character as a man, *ibid.* His writings, 31. Their extraordinary fate, *ibid.* Their number and magnitude, 37, 38. His method defended, 144. His style, 145, & seqq.
Art, what, 97. Its nature and object, 291.
Arts, their variety and gradation, 149.
Association of perceptions defined, 57.
Astronomy, Aristotle's account thereof, 123, & seqq.
Atoms, doctrine thereof refuted, 105.
Axioms, mathematical, improperly applied to logic, 75.

B

Babylon, the astronomical tables preserved there, 130.

Benefactors, why less beloved than those who have received benefits, 366, & seqq.
Buffon, criticised, 126.

C

Callisthenes, his character, 23.
Capacity, state of, what, 117.
Caracalla destroys the schools in Alexandria, 25. The pretended motive thereto, *ibid.*
Categories, their nature and number, 59.
Causes, their nature and division, 88. Infinite progression thereof impossible, 91.
Cercinus, his play of Alope, 321.
Change, its different kinds, 107.
Cicero misrepresents Aristotle's theology, 137, 138. His treatise on friendship compared with Aristotle's, 329.
Classification, its rules, 63.
Commentators, Aristotle's, their classes, numbers, and errors, 2, 3.
Concord, its nature and definition, 365.
Continence and temperance, their nature and differences, 324, & seqq.
Contraries, selection of, 89. What, 111.
Conversion of propositions, rules thereof, 74.
Courage, its definition and nature, 200. Five kinds thereof explained, 213, & seqq.
Courtesy, and its contraries, 245.
Cowardice compared with intemperance, 222.
Crimes distinguished from errors and misfortunes, 275, & seqq.
Cudworth cited, 50.

D

Definition, its nature, 66.
Deity, doctrine thereof, 134. His attributes, 135. The source of being, 136.
Delos, its inscription, 163.
Demodocus, his saying of the Milesians, 323.
Democritus refuted, 105.
Demonstrations, universal and particular, 84. The former more satisfactory, and why, 85.
Depravities, unnatural, 316, & seqq.
Desires, natural and adventitious, 220.
Difference, specific, 65.

Diogenes maintained air to be the first principle, 99. Grounds of his opinion, *ibid.*
Division, its nature, 63.
Doctrine, double, not found in Aristotle, 138.
Duty, analogy between that to ourselves, and that to our friends, 362.

E

Earth, analysis thereof, 103. Aristotle's doctrine concerning it, 124.
Education, its efficacy, 403.
Election, moral, its nature explained, 195, & seqq.
Elements, analysis thereof, 102. Their continual transmutations, 103.
Empedocles, his four elements, 100.
Encyclopedie, its strange account of Aristotle's works, 38, *note*.
Energy, state of, what, 118. Doctrine concerning it, 133. First energy, 134. His attributes, 135.
Equity, nature of it explained, 281.
Ethics, foundation thereof, 194.
Eudoxus, his ingenious argument in favour of pleasure, 168. Advocate for pleasure, 382. His temperance and regularity, 383.
Exoteric and acroatic writings, their nature and differences, 19, & seqq. Discourses, 25.
Experience, what, 97.
Experiments, Aristotle's philosophy built thereon, 139.

F

Facetiousness, and its contraries, 250.
Faults, distinguished from misfortunes and crimes, 277.
Feeling, ethics not solely founded thereon, 194.
Ferocity, and its opposites, 307.
Fire, nature thereof, 103.
Fishes, Aristotle's wonderful knowledge concerning them, 129.
Fontenelle criticised, 121.
Form, what, p. 112. Species or sight, what, 115. Its different significations, 132.
Friendship, what, 33. Its beauty and utility, 329, & seqq. Doubts concerning it, 331.
Divided

INDEX.

Divided into three kinds, 333. Qualities by which excited, ibid. & seqq. Different kinds of it compared, 335. Persons most susceptible of it, 336. Its relation to justice, 341, & seqq. Both relative to the different forms of government, 343. Unequal friendships, their limits, 339. Their foundation, 340. Variations in the nature and intensity of friendship, how occasioned, 345, & seqq. That founded on propinquity, 347. Between husband and wife, 348. Disputes between friends, how to be adjusted, 349, & seqq. How its returns are best estimated, 355, & seqq. Its exercise does not admit of precise rules, 358, & seqq. Justifiable grounds for its dissolution, 360, & seqq. Rules concerning its dissolution, 361. Whether most desirable in prosperity or in adversity, 370. The exquisite delight of virtuous friendship, 371.

G

Genus, what, 63.
God, his goodness, 137.
Gods, wherein their happiness consists, 401. Concern themselves about human affairs, 402. Those whom they love and reward, *ibid*.
Good, Plato's notion thereof refuted, 156. The Supreme, delineation thereof, 158.
Good-will, its nature and definition, 365.
Gray, his character of Aristotle's writings, 143.
Greek, difficulty of translating it, 147.
Grotius, his character of Aristotle, 173. His objections to Aristotle's Ethics answered, 174.

H

Habits, moral, 206. Are voluntary, 207. Objections thereto, 208. Answered, *ibid*. & seqq. Intellectual and moral, their difference, 257.
Happiness, different opinions concerning it, 152. Properties ascribed to it, 161. Whether the gift of heaven or our own work, 164. Above praise, 168. Its nature, 394. Intellectual 396. Moral, 398. Pre-eminence of the former, 399.
Harris, his erroneous account of Aristotle's doctrine of ideas, 60. Mistakes Aristotle's philosophy, 85.
Hearing, sense of, 43, & seqq.
Heraclitus maintained fire to be the first principle of things, 99. Grounds of that opinion, *ibid*.
Hermeias, tyrant of Atarneus, his character, 10. His singular history, 11, & seqq. His connection with Aristotle, 11. Provokes the resentment of Artaxerxes, *ibid*. Is destroyed by Mentor the Rhodian, 12.
Hermotimus first introduced the doctrine of mind, 101.
Herpylis, Aristotle's wife, 32.
Hesiod quoted, 153.
Hippasus maintained fire to be the first principle, 99. Grounds of his opinion, *ibid*.
Hobbes mistakes Aristotle, 115, 116.
Homer quoted, 189, 190.
Honour, anonymous virtue respecting it, 250.
Hume, his principles of association erroneous, 45.

I

Ichthyology, Aristotle's, 129.
Ideas, or perceptions, their association, 45. General, refutation thereof, 57—60.
Imagination, its nature, 44, & seqq.
Incontinency, in contradistinction to intemperance, 312. Its nature explained, 313, & seqq.
Infinity, what, 121.
Intellect, the source of first principles, 263.
Intellectual principle, its power and dignity, 29, & seqq. In man, proof thereof, 48.
Intemperance compared with cowardice, 222, & seqq.
Ionian school, 99.
Justice, in how many acceptations taken, 259. Justice strictly so called, what, 212, & seqq. Distributive, 263. Corrective and commutative, 265, & seqq. Consists in mediocrity, 271. Strict and metaphorical, 273. Natural and legal, 274. Solution of doubts concerning it,

INDEX.

K

Kaimes, Lord, mistakes and misrepresents Aristotle's logic, 76.
Knowledge, human, its sources, 42.

L

Language, analysis thereof, 56. Philosophical 141. Aristotle's perverted, ibid.
Laws, their efficacy, whence derived, 405.
Legislation, source thereof, and errors concerning it, 407. How the science of it is to be acquired, 408.
Letters, men of, evils to which they are peculiarly exposed, 9.
Liberality, and the vices contrary to it, 226, & seq.
Locke mistakes and misrepresents Aristotle, 119.
Logic, Aristotle's, its real uses, 70, & seq.
Lyceum, 26.

M

Magnanimity, and its contraries, 235, & seqq.
Magnificence, and its contraries, 232, & seqq.
Malbranche mistakes Aristotle, 115.
Matter, the first, what, 108.
Mayow, account of his discoveries, 105.
Mechanism, of sensation, fancy, &c. 45, & seqq.
Mediocrity, the essence of virtue, 177 & 184. Of all conditions, most favourable to happiness, 401.
Meekness, and its contraries, 242, & seqq.
Memory, its nature, 44, & seq.
Men of letters, the misfortunes attending their celebrity, 9.
Mentor the Rhodian, his dexterity and treachery, 11, & seq.
Metaphysics, Aristotle's, their subject, 86. & seqq.
Mind, the parts or faculties thereof, 169, & seq.
Misfortunes distinguished from errors and crimes, 275, & seqq.
Mixture, what, according to Leucippus and Democritus, 113. According to Aristotle, ibid.
Monboddo, Lord, his account of Aristotle's philosophy examined, 60. Mistakes Aristotle's doctrine of ideas, 85. Cited and criticised, 52.
Money, its nature and use, 269.
Moral powers, analysis thereof, 170, & seq. Election, objects about which it is conversant, 202, & seqq. Faculty, analysis thereof, 204.
Morton, Dr. 87.
Motion, defined, 119.
Motions different from actions, 133.
Mundo, Aristotle's treatise de, 38, note.

N

Names, rules by which they ought to be assigned, 67.
Natural history, Aristotle's philosophy thereof, 127. Its merits, 128.
Nature, her works, 109.
Neleus carried Aristotle's writings to Scepsis, 34. His heirs bury them under ground, ibid.
Nicanor, gratefully treated by Aristotle, 9. Dedications offered for his safety, 33.
Nicomachus, Aristotle's father, 6.
Number, notion of, how obtained, 66.

O

Olympias, her respect for Aristotle, 15.
Operation distinguished from production, 149.
Opposition of propositions, rules thereof, 76.
Organum, its proper subject, 54. Aristotle's, generally mistaken, 75.

P

Pearson, Dr. 114.
Peripaton, 26.
Persia, the hereditary effeminacy of its kings, 321.
Petit, Samuel, 87.
Phænomena, natural, their causes, 105.
Phestis, Aristotle's mother, 6.
Philip of Macedon, his letter to Aristotle, 15. Honours bestowed by him on Aristotle, 16.
Philosophers, ancient, disdained operose and painful experiments, and why, 140.

Philosophy

INDEX.

Philosophy of Aristotle, 40. Its division, 53. The first, why so called, 96. Its nature and dignity, 98. Its history, 99. Natural, Aristotle's account thereof, 102.
Pittacus resigned the archonship, 366.
Plain-dealing, and its contraries, 247.
Plantis, Aristotle's treatise de, 38, *note*.
Plato, his observations concerning Aristotle, 7. His ideas, 101. Æra of his death, 9. Is succeeded by Speusippus, *ibid*.
Pleasure, the test of virtue, 178. The love of it not to be too severely censured, 381, & seqq. Different opinions concerning it, 182, & seq. Its ambiguous nature, 384. What it is not, 385, & seqq. What it is, 388. Inseparably connected with energy, yet different from it, 390, & seqq.
Pliny grossly mistakes Aristotle, 137.
Policy, general and particular, 296.
Politics, science thereof, its object, 150. Proper method of treating it, 151.
Polybius, his account of the origin of morals, 204.
Powers, rational, irrational, and moral, 170, & seq.
Principles, general, how formed, 57. Definition thereof, 88.
Privation, what, 112.
Property, what, 64.
Propositions, their nature, 64. Their conversion and opposition, 74, & seqq.
Protagoras, his liberal bargain with his disciples, 356.
Proxenus, Aristotle's early protector, 7.
Prudence, its nature and object, 292.
Pythagoras, his numbers, 101.
Pythias, Aristotle's first wife, 14. Her death and last request, *ibid*. Her affectionate request gratified, 32.

Q

Quality, the characterising, 120.
Quantity, what, 59.

R

Reid, Dr. mistakes Aristotle's Organum, 77.

Reminiscence, its nature explained, 47, & seq.
Rennel, Dr. 409.
Retaliation does not apply to justice, 268.

S

Sceptics refuted, 94, & seqq.
Scherer, his Antiphlogistische Chemie, 105.
Science, treatise thereon, 90, & seqq. Its nature and object, 290.
Self-command, and its contraries, 309, & seqq.
Self-love different from selfishness, 368, & seq.
Senses, their nature and objects, 41. Their exercise ultimately agreeable, 96.
Sentiment, justness of, 299.
Shame, nature thereof, 252.
Sight, sense of, 43, & seq.
Simonides, his proverbial avarice, 229.
Smith, Dr. *Adam*, his mistaken account of ancient physics, 104. He expanded Polybius's moral reflections into a theory, 204, & seqq.
Solon, his saying concerning the dead examined, 166. His opinion of happiness, 401.
Soul, doctrine concerning it, 131.
Space, what, 120.
Species, what, 63.
Speusippus, 9. His character, 10. Commended, 156.
Stagira, its history, 4, 5, 6.
Strabo, his account of the restoration of the peripatetic philosophy, 37, *note*.
Sylla seizes Apellicon's library, 35. Transports Aristotle's writings to Rome, *ibid*.
Syllogism, its nature and use, 70. All syllogisms reduced to those of the first figure, 73. Rule by which the justness of all syllogisms may be tried, *ibid*.

T

Taste, sense of, 42.
Temperance, its definition and nature, 218, & seqq.; distinguished from continence, 324, & seqq.
Terms, general, how formed, 56.

Thales

Thales maintained water to be the first principle, 99. Grounds of his opinion, *ibid.*
Theodectes, his tragedy of Philoctetes, 321.
Theology, what, 96.
Theophrastus, 26. Bequeathed Aristotle's writings to Neleus, 34.
Time, what, 120.
Topics, design thereof, 78.
Touch, sense of, 42. Qualities discovered thereby, *ibid.*
Triad, definition thereof, 66.
Truth, demonstrative, 82. Wherein it consists, 83. Universal and particular, 84. Its existence and nature, 92. & seqq.
Tyrannion procures a copy of Aristotle's writings, 36.

U

Unity, not number, 66.
Understanding, powers thereof, differ as widely as those of sensation, 285, & seqq.
Vice, its wretchedness, 364.
Vices mistaken for virtues, 188. Why, 189.
Virtue consists in mediocrity, 185. Proved by induction, *ibid.* & seq. Mistaken for vices, why, 188, & seq. Practical rules for its attainment, 189, & seq. Intellectual virtues, 287. Their utility in practice, 301. Happiness attending virtue, 363.

Virtues, moral, not implanted by nature, 175. Acquired by action and custom, *ibid.* Rules for attaining them, 176. Wherein they consist, 177. The surest test of virtue, 178. Four requisites to form a virtuous character, 188. That the virtues are not capacities nor passions, but habits, 181. The nature and essence of virtue, 182, & seqq.
Velition distinguished from election, 205.
Voluptuousness compared with irascibility, 318. The former more odious than the latter, and why, 319.

W

Warburton refuted, 50.
Water, analysis thereof, 103.
Will, all-will, free-will, 193.
Wisdom, its nature and object, 293, & seqq.

X

Xenocrates, 26.

Y

Youth, all depends on its management, 176.

Z

Zoology, Aristotle's, 125, & seqq.

END OF THE FIRST VOLUME.

www.ingramcontent.com/pod-product-compliance
Lightning Source LLC
Chambersburg PA
CBHW051732300426
44115CB00007B/531